The
Shattered
Cross

The Shattered Cross

FRENCH CATHOLIC MISSIONARIES
ON THE MISSISSIPPI RIVER, 1698–1725

Linda Carol Jones

LOUISIANA STATE UNIVERSITY PRESS
BATON ROUGE

Published by Louisiana State University Press
www.lsupress.org

DESIGNER: Michelle A. Neustrom
TYPEFACE: Adobe Garamond Pro

The cover map is used courtesy of the Library of Congress.

LIBRARY OF CONGRESS CATALOGING-IN-PUBLICATION DATA

Names: Jones, Linda Carol, author.
Title: The shattered cross : French Catholic missionaries on the Mississippi River, 1698–
1725 / Linda Carol Jones.
Other titles: French Catholic missionaries on the Mississippi River, 1698–1725
Description: Baton Rouge : Louisiana State University Press, [2020] | Includes bibli-
ographical references and index.
Identifiers: LCCN 2020018582 (print) | LCCN 2020018583 (ebook) | ISBN 978-0-8071-
7356-5 (cloth) | ISBN 978-0-8071-7443-2 (pdf) | ISBN 978-0-8071-7444-9 (epub)
Subjects: LCSH: Jesuits—Missions—New France—History—18th century. | Canada—
History—To 1763 (New France) | Mississippi River—Discovery and exploration. |
Indians of North America—Missions—History—18th century. | Indians of North
America—Mississippi River Valley—History—18th century. | Jesuits—Biography. |
Missionaries—Mississippi River Valley—Biography. | Séminaire de
Québec—Biography.
Classification: LCC F1030.7.J66 2020 (print) | LCC F1030.7 (ebook) | DDC
971.01—dc23
LC record available at https://lccn.loc.gov/2020018582
LC ebook record available at https://lccn.loc.gov/2020018583

To the best scholarly surfers and treasure finders in the world,
Robin, Lisa, and the Interlibrary Loan staff at the University of Arkansas.

And in fond remembrance of JT.

Contents

ILLUSTRATIONS

Maps

Figures

Acknowledgments

It has been a long journey writing this book, and there are many people for whom I am grateful in helping me see this publication come to fruition. I offer these points of gratitude in no particular order and beg forgiveness to those I may have forgotten. I am grateful to you as well!

First and foremost, many thanks go to George Sabo, who started me on this path of French Colonial Mississippi history when I entered his office in early 1992, heard the strange words "French Colonial Arkansas," and began my pursuit of these first French missionaries on the Mississippi. His encouragement and wisdom have remained steadfast all these many years. Many thanks also to Morris "Buzz" Arnold, whose expertise in the topic of French Arkansas history has served as an inspiration toward learning more about this relatively unknown period of time in our great state of Arkansas and beyond.

I am also grateful to individuals within the University of Arkansas's Department of History who helped me with my various questions relevant to book writing, vocabulary selection, and the like. Jeannie Whayne, Laurence Hare, and Jim Gigantino, thank you for your varied points of reference in this research endeavor. In particular, I extend much gratitude to Bob McMath and Elliott West, who took the time to join me for a cup of coffee or a lunch and allowed me to ask questions no matter how large or small to help me through this process.

Gratitude also to Todd Shields and Calvin White, who provided funds to help me finish up important research in archives in Montréal. Many thanks to Josh Smith, John Duval, and Daniel Levine, who helped me translate the trickier Latin passages within the missionaries' letters.

My special thanks to Suzanne Stoner and Elliott West for their friendship and for graciously permitting me time in their beautiful cabin, a place that often helped me find focus and inspiration in writing this book throughout these many years.

Special thanks also to the many friends, colleagues, and students who read portions of this research, offered helpful suggestions, and pushed for clarification throughout—Mary Ellen Hartford, Doug Cummins, Kathleen Lehman, Myria Allen, Kay Duval, Sonia Toudji, Jacqui Brandli, JT Shrigley, Charlie Rigsby, and Kim Penhallegon.

Particular appreciation to my gracious colleague Kathleen Condray, whose support for me as a teacher and whose passion for German Arkansas History provided me with a sister soul-mate for exploring early European cultures in Arkansas and Mississippi.

Gratitude as well to my beloved research colleagues, friends, and roomies— Judi Neal and Rhonda Bell-Ellis—for their support of my attempts to connect these eighteenth-century missionaries to modern-day spirituality in the workplace.

Thanks also to Evan Garner and his sermon on crumbs and dogs, a poignant homily that clarified Father Bergier's own compassion in his work.

Thank you to Maggie Bridges and her expertise in designing maps. Thank you as well to Martha Anderson and Dexter Merrick Fairweather for their extraordinary skill at turning nineteenth-century colorized book prints into exquisite images.

And finally, much love and appreciation to all my family and friends who patiently supported me as I engaged in this long project. Most especially, I give thanks for Rudy and Cuthbert, my best friends who were by my side every step of the way and whose unconditional love never wavered.

The
Shattered
Cross

Introduction

On a hot, steamy July day in 1702, Father Antoine Davion neared the end of his journey from the Tunica village on the Yazoo River to the Quapaw village near the intersection of the Arkansas and the Mississippi. As one of several missionaries from the Séminaire de Québec called to serve in the Lower Mississippi Valley in the late seventeenth century, Davion was no more than a day away from seeing his colleague Father Nicolas Foucault, and certainly in hopes to commiserate with him about their ongoing efforts to Christianize regional Native communities. But on this fateful summer day, as Davion traveled up river to the Quapaw village, he came across a hat, a few papers, and a dressed altar for the Holy Eucharist and knew immediately that his journey was over. Soon enough, Davion discovered that Foucault had been murdered.[1]

Father Foucault's brief time among the Quapaws had been difficult. According to Marc Bergier, a fellow Seminary missionary who served among the Tamarois Indians, Foucault had been "forced to leave this barbarous nation by which he had been abused several times."[2] While these "abuses" remain unknown, the assertion raises far more questions than answers. Why did the relationship between the Quapaws and Foucault appear so troubled when Seminary missionary François de Montigny and Récollet missionary Zénobe Membré described the Quapaws as mild, warm, cheerful, and generous? Even Seminary missionary Father Jean-François Buisson de Saint-Cosme wrote of their extraordinary honesty and fidelity, that the Quapaws "had a good nature about them and were extraordinarily loyal." What, then, caused such curious discord between Foucault and the Quapaws?[3]

As a parish priest, Foucault was a man strongly devoted to high moral standards, quite meticulous, and often at odds with officers and colonists along the St. Lawrence River for their lack of piety and adherence to the Catholic tradition. Antoine de la Mothe, Sieur de Cadillac, commander of the fort at Michilimackinac, went so far as to describe Foucault as an "odd man if ever there was one."[4] With very little written on or by him during his days among the Quapaws, it is difficult to determine what exactly transpired between Foucault and this Native community. But understanding Foucault's previous activities as a parish priest and exploring Quapaw societal systems and spirituality can shed some light on possible interactions and the resulting relationship.

Foucault was one of five missionaries from the Séminaire de Québec who were sent with the blessing of Bishop Jean-Baptiste de la Croix de Chevrières de Saint-Vallier to serve in Native communities along the Mississippi River. In late July 1698, Fathers de Montigny, Saint-Cosme, and Davion first departed for the Mississippi from the small town of Lachine, Canada, in four birch bark canoes. Variously between 1698 and 1725, these three pioneer priests, along with Fathers Foucault and Bergier, worked among the Tamarois, the Tunicas, the Taensas, the Natchez, and the Quapaws. These Native peoples offered the Seminary priests access to their communities and variously embraced elements of Christianity that fit into their spiritual world view. At times, interactions between these missionaries and the Native peoples led to new understandings and interpretations that transformed members of one if not both cultures. At others, misunderstandings shattered hopes for alliance and kept strengthened relationships at a distance.

Roaming Frenchmen, referred to as *coureurs de bois,* also resided sporadically along the Mississippi River, but often proved disruptive for the Seminary missionaries and the communities in which they served. Nonetheless, new ways of proceeding developed when interactions between these loosely affiliated Frenchmen and the Seminary missionaries transformed their understanding of the other in times of need. Even Jesuit missionaries brought forward unanticipated trials for the Seminary priests, leading to strife that disrupted Christianization efforts for both groups. And yet, amid that friction emerged a compromise, a congruence of spiritual and sometimes regional goals that led to deep brotherhood between members of the two Catholic groups when least expected.

The diverse religious bodies and cultures, as well as environmental, personal, economic, and leadership challenges, heavily influenced the Seminary missionaries' work and, at times, led to new ways of functioning along the Mississippi River. In this zone of intercultural interaction, actions, reactions, and activities of the Native peoples and the various French individuals led some toward new, unanticipated patches of middle ground, small but significant places where individuals of different cultures came together to forge new meanings and understandings.[5]

The lack of comprehensive information published on the Seminary missionaries both prior to and during their time along the Mississippi, the dearth of knowledge in print regarding Seminary leadership in Québec and Paris and its perspectives on the missionaries' work, and the absence of thorough analyses of the missionaries' interactions with regional Native cultures and peoples have led me to tell the story of these men and the Native communities within which they served. While many are familiar with the history of the Jesuits in New France, these missionaries from the Séminaire de Québec have remained far less known, perhaps because their writings, typically in the form of letters written between themselves and their leadership, provide little information regarding interactions with Native peoples, yet are quite eye-opening in terms of the hardships and challenges they faced. Indeed, far from writing in order to gain donor funds, prestige, or recruits, they described the plight of their missions, their efforts to survive, and the desires, frustrations, and feelings of hopelessness they felt on the Mississippi. Unlike the Jesuits, who between 1632 and 1673 published much of their writings in the *Jesuit Relations* as a way of promoting their work, the Seminary priests' letters remained private, focused on administrative and liturgical issues, at times deeply personal and anguished, but always meant just for the eyes of the Seminary leadership in Québec and Paris.

Historic French documents from archival sources in Canada, France, and Italy, but most importantly from the Archives du Séminaire de Québec, provide support for this holistic examination of the five missionaries and their interactions with the Native communities and other Frenchmen along the Mississippi. These documents—letters, lists of requested goods and supplies, formal decrees including *lettres patentes*—provide unique insight into what may have influenced their Christianization efforts and ultimately transformed some personally and spiritually. Because the priests wrote so little about the people with whom they worked, deeper analysis of their words in conjunction with knowledge of Native cultures helps to more closely determine what occurred between the missionaries and the Native communities and subsequently led to cultural transformations and new meanings on the Mississippi.

Unique to this book is its investigation into these missionaries' lives before they set foot on the banks of the Mississippi River. Documents found in judicial, notarial, municipal, diocesan, and military archives throughout Québec and France provide insight into the varied personalities of the men. Many of these documents shed light on the strength of each man's work ethic in his pre-Mississippian activities and further highlight personal characteristics that eventually interacted in noticeable fashion with certain Native cultural traditions. Indeed, the selection of some missionaries raised questions concerning their suitability for the region and their capacity to adhere to the expectations of their superiors. For some, their lives were fragmentary, uneasy, seemingly uncommitted, and fearful. For others, they completely and willingly entrusted themselves to God. Even those charged with the missionaries' oversight—Bishop François de Laval, Bishop Saint-Vallier, and their *Procureur* (Procurator), Henri-Jean Tremblay—curiously acted and reacted to the missionary efforts, and even wavered in their desire or lack thereof for the Mississippi venture.

Each Native community interacted with these men through cultural politics, economic ventures, and unfamiliar linguistic forays. Typical of many Native groups, the Quapaws, for example, engaged in a system of reciprocity. Their sharing of goods and the *calumet,* a ceremonial pipe that served to instill relationship and peace, was meant to bring the stranger into their community so as to establish kinship with the other. Understanding Father Foucault's strict life as a parish priest sheds some light into how he may have responded to these and other traditions among the Quapaws. The Tunicas found spirit in all that surrounded them—sun, fire, thunder, sky, and the four directions (north, south, east and west). When Father Davion aggressively challenged elements of the Tunica world view that helped to maintain balance in their community, instability and anger ensued, but violence was avoided. Other Native communities also embraced sacrificial ceremonies, polygamy, the exchange of goods, and reciprocal relationships. Each Native group adhered to particular societal norms that proved curious at best for the Seminary missionaries. And yet, some stepped into individually and holistically experienced middle grounds that led those involved toward new understandings and interpretations.

This book helps readers better understand who these missionaries were, what motivated them to work in little-known lands, what made them suffer such hardship for the risky venture of Christianization, and how their experiences and personalities, at times, transformed them spiritually and personally. This book further shows alternative perspectives: who the Native men,

women, and children were, what they experienced at the arrival and installation of the missionaries, and the extent to which they evolved in terms of
their own spirituality and that of the Christian tradition. It also highlights the
Jesuits and their own missionization strategies, as well as some of the unsavory
antics of roaming Frenchmen throughout the region. Thus, this holistic view
of these missionaries' lives before and during their time on the Mississippi, the
Seminary leaders' expectations of these missionaries, the Native communities
and cultures with which they interacted, not to mention the Jesuits and other
Frenchmen, provides greater insight into this historic period on the Mississippi. Such an analysis proposes to tell this story as richly as possible.

Too often these missionaries have been ignored. Too often they have been
labeled as Jesuits or Récollets rather than who they truly were, missionaries of
the Séminaire de Québec. As these priests entered the region, they believed
they had strong potential to gain many Native converts for the white man's
Catholic Kingdom. However, as they worked within their distinctly varied
cultures and geographical boundaries, the resulting interactions, linguistic
challenges, and creative misunderstandings, not to mention poor planning
and lack of funds, all subsequently led some to develop unanticipated new
meanings and practices within a middle ground, but eventually shattered their
hopes for establishing Christianity on the Mississippi. Ultimately, two of the
five missionaries were murdered in the field, one missionary died due to his extreme devotion to his flock, one fled to East Asia, and the final one reluctantly
remained in the region for over twenty-five years only to be sent home due to
poor health and die one year later. This is their story . . .

CHAPTER I

Prelude to the Mississippi

A ndré was nineteen years old, a Vietnamese convert to Christianity who faithfully served the Jesuit missionary Alexandre de Rhodes in his small village in East Asia. Steadfast in his beliefs and a stalwart in his work, André helped de Rhodes teach fellow villagers of the Christian faith. One July day in 1644, soldiers entered André's village in search of a man named Ignace, a minister of de Rhodes's who was greatly despised by the regional queen. Not finding Ignace, nor wanting to return to "her majesty" empty-handed, the soldiers imprisoned André. As they began their parade to the local jail, André spoke favorably of Christ, preaching and telling his captors of his love and faith in Him, much to the chagrin of the irritated guards, who found André's proselytizing more of an annoyance than a path to conversion. Once in jail, de Rhodes and numerous Portuguese clergy sought André's release, but to no avail. The young convert was sentenced to death. Knowing his execution was imminent, André embraced his imposed path to heaven. At the moment of his execution, André sank to his knees, lifted his eyes, and pronounced Christ's name as a lance was thrust three times through his torso. Ultimately, his captors decapitated him. As his head fell away from his body, the name *Jesus* emitted from André's severed throat. In that brief moment, André became the region's first Christian martyr. In that split second, de Rhodes committed himself to enhancing the training and oversight of East Asian missionaries. In that single encounter, and unbeknownst to him, de Rhodes established the foundation for missionary work in the Mississippi Valley.[1]

Perhaps it seems far-fetched to link early seventeenth-century East Asia to the Mississippi River, but stranger connections have existed. Indeed, when Father Alexandre de Rhodes made the conscious decision to leave his mission and to seek support to install *Vicaires Apostoliques* (Apostolic Vicars) in East Asia, the Mississippi River was unheard of except among those familiar with Hernando de Soto's sixteenth-century wanderings in southeastern North America. For that matter, when Seminary missionaries François de Montigny, Antoine Davion, and Jean-François Buisson de Saint-Cosme left Lachine, Canada, for the Mississippi River in July 1698, it is doubtful that East Asian missionary history was at the forefront of their thoughts. And yet, years before their departure, de Rhodes's global activity set the stage for their late seventeenth-century venture. Through his own firsthand insight into the challenges missionaries faced in East Asia, de Rhodes informed church officials in Italy and France that more men and episcopal leaders were needed in eastern regions. As an unexpected outcome, his efforts led to the elevation of the first bishop of Québec, François de Laval, and the establishment of the Séminaire des Missions Étrangères in Paris. In time, Laval founded the Séminaire de Québec that ultimately supported and influenced the work of the Mississippi missionaries during the late seventeenth and early eighteenth centuries.

A global vision for missioning to Native peoples began as a result of the 1494 Treaty of Tordesillas. As Portuguese and Spanish missionaries and explorers came upon astounding individuals, "wild men" never before encountered by Europeans, they felt compelled to plant seeds of Christian conversion into the minds of courts and clergy back home. It was, after all, their Christian calling to "save" those who had no knowledge of Christ's goodness and love. It was their charge to keep the "unsaved" from "burning eternally in hell."[2]

Although they held the monopoly in East Asia, Portugal often recruited clergy from other countries, including France. De Rhodes, a French priest, worked with them. But de Rhodes's focus on strengthening Christianization efforts in East Asia led him to return to Europe to find better ways not only to Christianize the East Asian peoples but to provide leadership for the region. At first, no one embraced his designs. Portuguese Jesuits were not in favor of Frenchmen serving as leaders in East Asia. Nor did the Congregation de la Propagande Fide, an organization under the purview of the pope and overseer of missions worldwide, wish to see Jesuits monopolize overseas regions. As a Jesuit, de Rhodes did not interest them. But a nudge away from Rome and toward Paris changed things.

During the first part of the seventeenth century, France was caught up in the Counter-Reformation movement, with intensified concern for institutional reform and increased support for missions both at home and abroad. So determined were the French Catholics to lead missioning efforts that by the early seventeenth century France was a religious stronghold with some sixty-five different religious orders established in Paris alone. Although lack of funding led many of these religious houses to disband, the strength of several seminaries, colleges, and organizations provided seminarians with a strong educational foundation to spread the Catholic faith.[3]

Smaller organizations also emerged, including the Société des Bons Amis (Good Friends Society), an assembly of clergymen on the famous Rue St. Jacques in Paris who pledged to live a fervent Christian life under the protection of the Holy Virgin. Encouraged to meet the Société de Bons Amis, de Rhodes dined with them one evening in 1653. He described his work in East Asia and his desires for the region and its people, all of which received the *Bons Amis'* enthusiastic praise and moral support. Consequently, de Rhodes felt heard. His designs for East Asia could proceed with enhanced interest, but in a manner not even he could have imagined. For at the same time that de Rhodes asked for and received support for East Asia, the Canadian government sought a leader to oversee religious activities within its fledgling colony.[4]

French Jesuit missionaries had worked among Native peoples in Québec since the early seventeenth century. Although no one had official oversight of such religious efforts in the colony, by 1646 the archbishop of Rouen, Harlay de Champvallon, presumed such authority, particularly over those who left from the port of Rouen to serve in Québec. Alternatively, the Jesuits had a relationship with the pope, mostly "to invoke the authority of the papacy for their own protection." It was a relationship that existed "for sheer survival, as well as for the freedom they wanted to perform their ministries according to their own 'way of proceeding.'"[5]

The Jesuits were not interested in anyone who threatened their independence in New France. Thus, when the search for a religious leader of Québec began, the Jesuits voiced their preference for the *Bon Ami* and Jesuit-trained François de Laval so as to ensure the support of a brother of their order. After some discussion and debate, on June 8, 1658, and in accordance with de Rhodes's wishes, Pope Alexandre VII assigned not just three *Vicaires Apostoliques* for East Asia, he also assigned Laval to oversee religious activities in Canada and eventually become its first bishop. Many, including King Louis XIV and Anne d'Autriche, strongly supported Laval's nomination. The Jesuits were content as well, seeing in Laval "an Angel of consolation sent from Heaven; and as a good Shepherd coming to gather up the remnant of the

Blood of Jesus Christ—with a generous purpose not to spare his own, and to try all possible ways for the conversion of the poor Native peoples."[6]

Born April 30, 1623, in Montigny-sur-Avre, France, François de Laval had an extensive religious education that prepared him for his future as the first bishop of Québec. At the age of eight, he began his Jesuit education in La Flèche, France, at the Collège Royal Henri IV. There, Laval studied letters and philosophy and interacted with future Canadian missionaries, including Claude Dablon, who later recorded segments of Louis Jolliet's trip down the Mississippi after Jolliet lost his journal in a canoe accident near Montréal. At this school and later in his studies at the Collège de Clermont in Paris, Laval, Dablon, and their classmates had direct access to the popular *Relations des Jésuites*, a publication begun in 1632 that provided news about the spread of Christianity among Native communities in New France. These Jesuit writings often described the languages and cultures they encountered, their successes and failures, life and death, all material eagerly read by individuals in Old and New France. But while writing was a standard practice for Jesuits, useful for recruitment and fundraising, personal contact was influential as well. In January of 1644, Laval and his classmates met Isaac Jogues, a Jesuit missionary who provided the young students with visual and verbal evidence of the difficult life of a Canadian missionary. Father Jogues's hands had been mutilated by the Iroquois, and upon his return to Canada he was ultimately killed.[7] While Father Jogues's tortuous death and André's execution were horrific, they nonetheless were examples of seventeenth-century martyrdom and the desire of many to suffer accordingly to do God's will. Called to similarly serve God, Laval let go of any sense of possessions and entitlement and chose to fully pursue his ministry as a priest and as a missionary.

Laval was ordained on May 1, 1647. Seven months later he was appointed as archdeacon to the bishop of Evreux in France. This position gave the young priest oversight of some 155 churches and the charge to "clean up" a lax monastery in the region. In little time, Laval developed a reputation as a strong leader, enthusiastic and pastoral in all manners of his work, a man "of great piety, prudent, and of unusually great competence." When offered an opportunity to serve as a missionary in East Asia, Laval resigned his position and entered the Hermitage de Caen. There, he sought to spiritually and pastorally prepare himself for the charitable life of a missionary and to better determine "the designs which God might have for him."[8]

Although East Asia was a strong center for French missioning work, it was not to be Laval's final destination. Instead, as Louis XIV sought to establish a Canadian bishopric in 1658, Laval's name quickly surfaced. Court and Jesuits alike supported this young clergyman, while Laval's deep affinity for the Jesuits shown through: "God alone . . . knows how much I am indebted to your society [the Society of Jesuits], which warmed me in its breast when I was a child, nourished me with its salutary doctrine in my youth, and has not ceased since then to encourage and guide me."[9] But the last thing Rome wanted was a continuous Jesuit monopoly in New France. Laval, as a Jesuit, had the potential to give his religious order even greater power. Nonetheless, after much discussion, the pope agreed to install Laval as bishop of Petraea *in partibus infidelium* (in the land of the unbelievers) and as *Vicaire Apostolique* of New France with the power to build the church in Québec. Neutrality and fairness toward all religious bodies were expected of him, while Laval, the missions of Canada, as well as the Jesuits were to remain answerable to the Propagande Fide and the pope. Finally, on December 8, 1658, the feast day of the Immaculate Conception, Laval was consecrated as *Vicaire Apostolique* in the Gothic Chapel of the Holy Virgin at the Benedictine Abbey, St.-Germain-des-Près, in Paris. Easter Sunday, April 13, 1659, the thirty-six-year-old Laval left from La Rochelle, the principal port of call for Québec, ready to do God's work in the new, unfamiliar land.[10]

In the months prior to his departure for Canada, Laval and fellow priests François Pallu and Pierre Lambert de la Motte established the Société des Missions Étrangères, a Parisian organization focused on sending secular priests to work in missions in East Asia. More importantly, the latter two founded the Séminaire des Missions Étrangères de Paris, an institution designed to instruct and to prepare clergy to serve in missions and to help bishops in foreign lands.[11] As the first "secular" seminary established in Europe, its mission included a vow of obedience, a spirit of poverty, devotion to an ordinary ecclesiastical discipline, and an apostolic spirit to serve God until death. Thus, secular meant "of the world" and not bound by strict rules that guided clergy of religious orders such as the Jesuits. Overall, their strategy was simple—perfect one's love for the other; love as much as possible.[12]

Although he likely was involved in the initial steps taken to establish the Séminaire des Missions Étrangères, Laval did not actually witness its creation since he was already engaged in his own work. Laval had much to learn about

Québec. The climate, the terrain, perilous Indian attacks, the dispersal of *eau de vie* (brandy) among the Native peoples, skirmishes with the English, all remained foremost in his thoughts. But more importantly, Laval needed clergy to help expand Christianity throughout the region. While some priests came willingly and zealously worked in Québec, their numbers did not meet the colony's actual demand. For these priests, leaving a country they did know for an unknown colony demanded certain personal assurances. Was a central location available to oversee the distribution of men and goods throughout the region? Was there a religious center for fellowship and community? Laval's founding of the Séminaire de Québec in 1663 was meant to address such needs. As Laval intended it, "the Seminary was principally created to advance the Kingdom of God in the establishment and progress of religion, be it among the French in the colony or among the Native peoples." This focus required the directors of the Séminaire "to form within young clerics who will be under their care so that one can pull from them missionaries for the infidels as well as for the French." The Séminaire also served as a common house for all clergy, a place of support and spirituality. Laval organized it in line with the ancient institution of *Presbyterium,* such that his Apostolic domain was governed in community, with *Vicaire Apostolique*/bishop and Seminary leadership working side by side. Always, Laval sought the opinions of the Seminary priests.[13]

Laval also reached out to the Séminaire des Missions Étrangères in Paris to support his efforts in New France. With little delay, an important union between the Séminaire de Québec and the Séminaire des Missions Étrangères established a permanent bond that permitted the Séminaire in Paris to send their seminarians and clergy to Canada so as to expand Christianity throughout the region. This union further gave the Séminaire de Québec a complimentary name—the Séminaire des Missions Érangères de Québec—often used in documents to confirm and reconfirm their union and to establish various missionary activities throughout the region. To avoid financial confusion, the two institutions maintained separate accounts, although the Paris leadership oversaw funds and the shipment of goods from France to the Séminaire de Québec and later to the Mississippi missions. This union further charged that neither seminary could engage in any activity that involved both institutions without permission of the directors of the Séminaire in Paris. Finally, with his Seminary established, Laval's deepest desires for New France could more richly advance: to spread Christianity throughout the region, to carry out all possible functions in service to the church, and to develop missionaries to serve among Native peoples.[14]

Although Laval was installed as *Vicaire Apostolique* in 1658, fifteen years passed before Pope Clement X established the Diocese of Québec and named Laval as its first bishop on October 1, 1674. Despite the delay, life in Québec was in constant motion. The colony developed a clearer understanding of the region's health challenges, knew better how to survive the harsh winters, and had a growing record of establishing churches and hamlets throughout the St. Lawrence River Valley. As the population expanded, more and more Jesuits, Sulpicians, Récollets, and Ursulines arrived in the colony. And with tremendous pride, Laval's greatest desire was fulfilled when the Séminaire de Québec sent out its first missionary, Louis-Pierre Thury, to establish a mission in Acadie among the Crucientaux people. By 1684, Laval had attained his deepest yearnings—his seminary, diocese, and missionary efforts were well underway.[15]

Laval worked arduously to develop the Catholic Church throughout his diocese. He supported his Jesuit brothers who, during his tenure, expanded their missioning efforts among many Native communities of New France. Further, under Laval's watchful eye Father Jacques Marquette and his companion, Louis Jolliet, traveled down the Mississippi and wrote of their first encounters with the Illinois and the Quapaws in 1673. Nine years later, René-Robert Cavelier, Sieur de la La Salle and Henri de Tonti ventured below the Arkansas River to the mouth of the Mississippi, claimed the territory in the name of God and Louis XIV, and created posts among the Kaskaskias, the Peorias, and the Quapaws. Thus, by 1682 Laval's diocese was immense. He held spiritual jurisdiction over the French colony, from Cape Breton to Lake Superior and down the Mississippi to the Gulf of Mexico.[16] Although another sixteen years passed before Seminary missionaries served along the Mississippi, the tide had turned—de Rhodes's vision for East Asia, Laval's interests and calling, the Jesuits' zeal for missionary work, the establishment of seminaries in Paris and Québec, and exploration by Marquette, Jolliet, La Salle, and de Tonti all served as a foundation for future Mississippi missionary efforts from the Séminaire de Québec.

Many lessons had been learned, adjustments made, and goals accomplished. However, the arduous task of overseeing such a vast diocese and the conditions in which Laval and all others lived took a toll on his physical health. Needing to remove himself from his labors of the past twenty-six years, Laval traveled to France in 1685 to submit his resignation to Louis XIV. Although it would not become official until January 1688, a search for Laval's successor began immediately. Within a matter of months, Jean-Baptiste de la Croix de Chevrières de Saint-Vallier rose to the forefront of the selection process and seemed the perfect match.[17]

Saint-Vallier was a king's chaplain, educated by both the Sulpician and Jesuit orders. He was considered of high birth, well educated, extremely pious, and zealous. A perfect example at court, Saint-Vallier took his role quite seriously. He always dressed in his cassock and regularly participated in pastoral duties. But negative opinions persisted as well. Saint-Vallier was not just zealous but prone to perfection with regard to his own demeanor and that of others. Some felt him rigid and unbending. He had only four years' experience as a priest, was just thirty-one years of age, and only wanted to serve in Québec so as "to avoid working as a bishop in France." Despite such negative evidence, Laval trusted that Saint-Vallier was the best man to replace him and supported his selection in good faith.[18]

It was a risk assigning such a young and inexperienced man to serve as bishop of a wild and fledgling colony of some eleven thousand French souls, but Saint-Vallier took the assignment head-on and immediately spent time at the Séminaire des Missions Étrangères in Paris to familiarize himself with the organization and its relationship with Laval's seminary in Québec. In preparation for the move, he gave the Séminaire in Paris his entire library and proposed to sell his worldly goods so as to live at the Séminaire de Québec like Laval.[19] Shortly thereafter, the bishop-elect traveled to the young colony to explore his future diocese firsthand.

Saint-Vallier found favor in many of the things he saw, including the Jesuits and their devotion to converting the "infidels" to Christianity. "No other Jesuits in the world were as established as those in Canada," he remarked. But after having promised to make no significant changes during his visit, his memory proved short, and Saint-Vallier made several modifications that concerned many important constituents well before his consecration as Québec's second bishop. One change, in particular, doubled the number of students at Laval's beloved trade school at Cap Tourmente from thirty to sixty. This vocational school, located on the Seminary farm thirty miles to the east of the village of Québec, was established by Laval in 1668 to help boys learn a trade such as woodcarving, masonry, or shoemaking. More precisely, Laval intended the school "to prepare expert hands to build and decorate churches in what was still an infant colony, and to provide an educational alternative for boys who were unsuccessful in their academic and sacerdotal studies [at the Seminary's Petit Séminaire de Québec], to give them the opportunity to learn a skill so they would not be a burden to themselves or others." But Saint-Vallier's proposed upturn in enrollments increased monetary demands on the Séminaire de Québec and bound its leaders to construct additional residences for the boys. The directors of the Séminaire agreed to this request in obedience to Saint-Vallier's rank, but sensed a disconcerting air of change, particularly when the bishop-elect showed no interest in providing funds to pay for the construction costs. Further, Saint-Vallier renounced intentions of living at the Séminaire de Québec, proposed instead to build his own *Maison Episcopale* (bishop's house), and, once back in France, demanded "that the library of the bishop be returned, not seeing why the Seminary is keeping it." The Seminary had kept the library because everyone assumed that Saint-Vallier had donated his books; the bishop-elect had asked that they be marked with the Seminary's inscription.[20]

By the time Saint-Vallier returned to Paris in 1687, efforts were underway to stop his consecration as the next bishop of Québec. Many were concerned by Saint-Vallier's unwillingness to take advice, his inflexibility, and his desire to spend money, most especially at the expense of the Séminaire de Québec. Saint-Vallier's failure to consult with the Seminary leadership—Henri de Bernières, Louis Ango de Maizerets, and Charles Glandelet—about any intended changes deeply troubled these men, who consequently expressed grave concerns at his selection as bishop. Friends in Paris tried to convince Saint-Vallier to "moderate himself so as to not be off-putting," to "curb the vivacious nature of his character," to "lessen his own confidence in his *lumières*," and "to try to not carry everything to excessive perfection." No less than three times, Saint-Vallier was asked to step away from the nomination but refused. Louis XIV continued to fully support the bishop-elect and on January 25, 1688, Laval's retirement became official and Saint-Vallier was consecrated as the second bishop of Québec.[21]

To avoid conflict between the two bishops, Louis XIV initially refused to allow the now retired Laval to return to New France. For Laval, this was "the rudest cross he had ever had to bear," one that so devastated him that he felt it "a bitter wound that would not only be difficult to cure but would last until death." Saint-Vallier denied having anything to do with Laval's banishment from the colony and intervened on the now Monseigneur (Mgr) l'Ancien's (former Bishop Laval's) behalf to help gain his return. Upon his majesty's change of heart, Laval wasted no time in returning to his beloved Québec. Although sixty-five years old and somewhat infirm, Laval traveled on horseback from Paris to La Rochelle to catch a ship back to his beloved diocese.[22]

In April of 1688, Laval, along with Nicolas Foucault, the future Quapaw missionary, left La Rochelle for Québec on board the *Soleil d'Afrique,* a ship granted to Pierre le Moyne, Sieur d'Iberville, to help the Compagnie du Nord better compete with the Hudson Bay Company in the fur trade. Iberville, who eventually established the Louisiana colony at the mouth of the Mississippi and played an inadvertent role in Foucault's death, sailed across the Atlantic with Laval and the young seminarian. Two months later, they arrived in Québec City to "universal joy," a celebration of Laval's return after a three-year absence.[23] A few weeks later, Saint-Vallier arrived on board the *Diligente.* As he disembarked, Saint-Vallier received welcoming words from city officials and then, "between two columns of musketeers who saluted him all along his path," made his way from the lower to the upper city and on into the stone cathedral, established as the first parish church in the colony in 1664. Ceremonies continued, and the new bishop blessed those there gathered. Although fatigued, Saint-Vallier visited the Ursulines later that day. "It was close to seven in the evening when he came to our home, accompanied by Father Dablon, Supérieur Général of the Jesuit missions. We all gathered in our small chapel and sang the *Te Deum* with unprecedented joy and affection. Since it was late, and he could not share all of his compassion with us, he came back on the 5th of August to say the Holy Mass and to offer communion from his hand."[24]

Initial celebrations completed, Saint-Vallier began making decisions that impacted many individuals and institutions for years to come, Mississippi missionaries included. The new bishop demanded a dismissal of Laval's beloved *Presbyterium,* whereby Laval openly shared his authority with the leadership of the Séminaire de Québec. Saint-Vallier refused to relinquish any power to such collaboration. The new bishop further sought to reduce their funds and to limit public access to the Seminary chapel. Anguished at the resulting changes he witnessed, Laval was certain that "everything the bishop did was destined to ruin the Séminaire."[25]

As anger and frustration toward Saint-Vallier increased, the responsibility fell to Jacques-Charles de Brisacier, superior of the Séminaire in Paris, to try and curb the ever-growing fire. De Brisacier provided the Québec Seminary leadership with guidelines on how to work with Saint-Vallier. He encouraged them to "always act civilly and honestly toward him so that he would not be suspicious . . . that they have true confidence in him and when an opinion opposite of his arose, or if there was a delicate proposition to present to him, to ask his forgiveness three or four times before offering him their thoughts or opinions." De Brisacier even suggested that they "let any of his enraged fires cool before they returned 'gently and respectfully' to the topic at hand."[26] Québec's Seminary leadership worked hard to accept the advice given and to adjust to Saint-Vallier's personality and administrative style, unpopular as they were, for the good of the Séminaire and the diocese. Such advice was no doubt hard for Laval, who was deeply concerned by the changes underway. But he was even more personally offended by Saint-Vallier's behavior. De Brisacier had given the new bishop a packet of letters specifically addressed to Laval. Ultimately, these letters "quickly burned the fingers of the suspicious Saint-Vallier," who wanted nothing to pass by him as the new bishop of Québec.[27]

As frustrations mounted, Saint-Vallier lashed out at the Seminary and his diocese, accused them of "acting against him," and demanded all "to repent and to pray to ease God's anger." He insisted that the priests double their zeal as they served in the afflicted church that "was on the verge of ruin." From afar, de Brisacier held his breath: "I tell you with confidence that it is danger-ous to want the best with so much ardor." Consequently, by early 1691, the relationship between Saint-Vallier, Laval, and the Séminaire de Québec was so strained that no communication was addressed directly to a recipient but in-stead through *personnes interposées* (intermediaries). Saint-Vallier subsequently left for France to seek royal approval of his unpopular changes "without even naming someone to administer the diocese." Court and king agreed with Saint-Vallier's efforts. With that, the embattled bishop returned to Québec in 1692, triumphant. The Séminaire de Québec became an institution solely committed to clergy formation, removed from its role as collaborator with the bishop.[28]

Amid all of the diocesan turmoil, Governor Jacques-René de Brisay de Denonville initially praised Saint-Vallier, "whose heart was so penetrated by the love of God that he would no doubt bring all the gentleness needed into their work in Québec." Denonville's replacement, Louis de Buade de Frontenac, also initially embraced the new bishop, and together the two worked on a variety of mandates to address immoral behavior in New France. However, Saint-Vallier's sternness and rigidity pitted religious order against the public, government, and military, and led to numerous conflicts brought forward to judicial council. Some colonists enjoyed breaking the bishop's ordinances, thumbing their noses in the face of the religious establishment, leading Saint-Vallier to describe his flock, its drunkenness, impurity, and luxuries, as "an enemy, much like the English and the Iroquois."[29]

Saint-Vallier strove for high moral standards. Any challenges to religious authority and to the Catholic faith were met with reprimands, fiery sermons, or even excommunication. Even a simple church service could be met with severe disdain. During the Affaire du Prie-Dieu, or the "War of the Kneeler," Saint-Vallier engaged in a tit-for-tat with Louis-Hector de Callière, governor of Montréal, regarding the placement of a kneeler at the altar. Because Saint-Vallier's kneeler was placed in a less prominent position compared to that of the Montréal governor, he refused to participate in the service, left abruptly without reverencing the altar, and thus failed to offer his blessing for the installation of two new members of the Récollets' order.[30] Although such strife over a kneeler may seem trifling today, at the time a sense of honor and decorum was expected. There was a right and a wrong place to kneel. There were "precise roles to play to which were attached certain allotted honours that had been minutely evaluated and rigidly fixed." As such, "anyone who felt that he was being wronged in a question of position defended himself bitterly." Nonetheless, Saint-Vallier's response disturbed many of the congregants there present. With this and other unfortunate events early in his tenure, many were certain that Saint-Vallier was bent on destroying the church, the Séminaire, and the colony.[31]

Not one person could influence Saint-Vallier toward a more temperate light. Military officers, government officials, colonials, and religious groups turned against him. Governor Frontenac soured in his views of the bishop. Louis XIV himself received numerous inflammatory reports regarding Saint-Vallier and subsequently summoned the embattled bishop to Paris to speak to the accusations. No Seminary representatives were invited to court since the king was "well instructed of their interests."[32] Saint-Vallier honored Louis XIV's summons, but before leaving Québec he made one last controversial decision, assigning oversight of the Montréal region of his diocese to a

Sulpician superior from Montréal, François Dollier de Casson, and oversight of the Québec City region not to Laval but instead to a twenty-five-year-old, quite inexperienced priest—François de Montigny, a future Mississippi missionary. King and clergy expressed displeasure with the latter choice, but Saint-Vallier's motivation was clear: He had no interest in sharing his power with Mgr l'Ancien. By the winter of 1694, Québec was once again holding its breath, longing for an answer to its cacophonic leadership.[33]

In Paris, king and court coldly received Saint-Vallier and refused to support his return to Québec. Despite seemingly humble pleas to go back to his diocese, Saint-Vallier made harsh threats to those in Canada who otherwise "retained him" in France, Jesuit and Seminary leadership included. Laval confronted Saint-Vallier: "[You] ordered Dollier and de Montigny to do all they could on your behalf to make those who have caused your retention in France to feel the force and the weight of Episcopal authority if they did not effectively secure your return . . . it would be much more effective to imitate the spirit of Christ, to have them feel the force of his [a bishop's] kindness and humility, more capable, incomparably, of winning hearts than your menacing ways." The *Procureur,* Henri-Jean Tremblay, provided an alternate yet equally damaging first-hand reflection: Saint-Vallier, he wrote, "sought every manner possible to win over the Jesuits, suggesting that if they procured his return, he would be fully devoted to their order, would ensure that they alone served in Indian missions, and would act according to their counsel. But if he did not return, then he would send Récollets into their missions."[34] Although frustrated with Saint-Vallier's constant presence at the Séminaire in Paris, Tremblay nonetheless felt a "secret joy" that the bishop had been recalled from Québec.[35]

Despite repeated requests to step down, Saint-Vallier continued to plead his case, called himself a friend of the Séminaire de Québec, admitted his faults, and offered to fix them to the advantage of all. Not one to mince words, Tremblay wrote to Saint-Vallier: "There is no evidence to hope for or find peace under your leadership. Those who know you do not believe you can ever do any good there." Laval read a copy of Tremblay's letter to Saint-Vallier and wrote his own thoughts in the margin of the letter: "He cannot change without a miracle and the grace of conversion. His return would be the greatest blow to this church. . . . It is assured that one must consider Saint-Vallier as the greatest and most certain scourge and punishment on this church in Canada."[36] But Saint-Vallier persisted and ill-advisedly sought Laval's opinion on how to interact with those he "unintentionally" offended in Québec so as to secure his return.[37] Laval's follow-up response could not have been any more disappointing for the embattled Saint-Vallier:

> Let us seriously reflect on all that has happened since the day I retired from my charge over this church and the leadership passed to you. Think of the state in which you found it, the peace and the union that the church enjoyed . . . that your greatest distress was to find a church where you could find nothing to do to exercise your zeal. . . . Reflect similarly upon the great changes that one now sees . . . your principal design was to destroy all that you found so well established and your entire focus was to find all the means possible to entirely ruin the Seminary which you recognized as the soul of this church. . . . What did you not do to distance the superiors and directors of the Seminary from you? You took away their spiritual leadership and, in its place, gave it to clergy whose inappropriate behavior you cannot ignore . . . or gave it to young men whose age cannot begin to represent the experience necessary for the church. . . . I genuinely avow to you, I must not and can not in good conscience ask for and secure your return to Québec.[38]

Even before Saint-Vallier received Laval's piercing response, many had already read it. Tremblay himself had grave concerns as to how Saint-Vallier might react and did not feel comfortable handing him Laval's letter outright. Instead, he concealed it within a packet of other correspondence addressed to the bishop. Immediately Saint-Vallier "looked among all of them for the one from Mgr l'Ancien," wrote Tremblay. "I indicated to him the one that spoke of various matters and then I left him. He told me he would come to say Mass and to dine at the Séminaire des Missions Étrangères." A few hours later, he arrived, "and it was obvious to us that he had read the letter and that he was quite dismayed."[39]

Despite deep displeasure at how things had turned on him, and despite knowing that the letter in question had passed under the eyes of many at court, Saint-Vallier continued to plead his case and to promise reform. Finally, in 1697, when Saint-Vallier again pledged to be more moderate with his flock and clergy, and most precisely agreed to fully support the Séminaire de Québec in such areas as education and missioning, he was allowed to return to New

France. For his part, the king insisted that Saint-Vallier "take care to fully establish peace because if any further conflict reached him in Paris, his removal would be permanent." With great reluctance, Tremblay wrote to the Seminary leadership in Québec: "Here is some news that will surprise you; *Mgr de Québec* will return."[40]

When Saint-Vallier resumed his work in 1697, a distinct calm reigned in the diocese and everyone praised the peace and charity that subsisted between Saint-Vallier, the Séminaire de Québec, and Mgr l'Ancien. Even Governor Frontenac felt the refreshing harmony and welcomed opportunities to support the continuance of this good will that all enjoyed.[41] Pleased with de Montigny's work during his absence, and recognizing the king's command to work with and support the Séminaire de Québec and its leadership, on May 1, 1698, Saint-Vallier granted the institution permission to establish missions along the Mississippi among the Native peoples they deemed most appropriate.[42] Prepared by both Saint-Vallier and Laval, the *lettre patente* described the presence of many Native nations along the Mississippi and its tributaries whose "thousands of souls would be lost if they were not converted and saved before they perished."[43] Saint-Vallier approved the Séminaire de Québec's request to serve on the Mississippi "out of affection," and declared that any others previously assigned in the region "could be revoked of their power" if the superior of the missions felt it of benefit to the Seminary missionaries. Indeed, one of the Seminary's co-directors, Father Glandelet, pushed to strengthen the *lettre patente* so as to "avoid any contestation," presumably on the part of the Jesuits. It was a clear sign of anticipated trouble. Glandelet's fears, as we will later see, proved accurate.[44]

Saint-Vallier seemed to keep his promise to get along with his diocesan clergy. An ever-optimistic Marc Bergier, a future Mississippi missionary newly arrived in Québec in late summer of 1698, painted a positive, supportive portrait of Saint-Vallier's reception of him just days after the first missionaries from the Séminaire de Québec left for the Mississippi River. In a letter to his father, Jean-Jacques Bergier, the young Marc could not praise Saint-Vallier enough:

> I will not tell you a thing about the merits of Saint-Vallier, our bishop,
> because if I take on the task of telling you about his virtues, his piety, his
> gentleness, his goodness, his simplicity, his familiarity, his cordiality to all,
> particularly toward the curates and the missionaries that he regards and

treats as brothers and that he calls his colleagues, his generosity toward the poor, his care of his staff, the good order of his house, his work in his visits, his cares and concerns for the missions, his vigilance on all matters spiritual and temporal and on all affairs of his church and his diocese which extends more than 2,000 leagues, in a word of his work and his life, without speaking of his secret burdens, it would take me too long.[45]

Bergier described a calm, caring, and giving bishop at a time when little friction or resistance existed in his diocese. Indeed, Bergier never wavered in his support of this fellow clergyman from the Rhône Valley. Some six years later he exclaimed from the Mississippi: *"pontifici nostro multos annos* [may you be our bishop for many years!]." Such comments led some to fear that Bergier was too enamored with Saint-Vallier and that he might turn on the Séminaire itself. In the end, their fears never materialized.[46]

Laval helped to establish the Séminaire des Missions Étrangères in Paris, founded the Séminaire de Québec, and ultimately became the first bishop of Québec. Saint-Vallier replaced Laval and made changes, disrupted Laval's good order, and raised the ire of military officers, government officials, clergymen, and colonists alike. A recall to Paris and reprimands soon followed. Ultimately, the embattled bishop had to find a way to satisfy all concerned. Granting permission to the Séminaire de Québec to send five diocesan priests to serve in missions along the Mississippi proved to be his most consequential offer.

CHAPTER 2

The Seminary, the Church, and Its Priests

L aval founded the Séminaire de Québec in 1663 with a simple focus—develop clergy for the colony and missionaries for the Native peoples. But immediately, the demands of the growing diocese put clerical needs well ahead of any missionary assignments. After completing studies either at the Séminaire de Québec, the Séminaire des Missions Étrangères in Paris, or both, many, including the five future Mississippi missionaries, helped alleviate this clerical shortfall by serving as priests in rural churches or in other church-related positions throughout Québec. But even as these priests helped expand the Catholic faith, Laval "always had in mind that after he had provided all the churches of the French colony with good priests, one would develop missionaries within the Seminary to serve the Native peoples."[1]

The church in Québec began slowly. When Laval arrived in New France in 1659, there were only three established churches within the region, served by Jesuit missionaries. Beyond these religious structures, Mass might be held in a family's home, supported by the use of a portable altar, though hardly on a regular basis. A missionary might journey dozens of miles to the next community to serve *habitants* within the region, provided he or these early settlers of Québec could reach the makeshift chapel during the harsh winter months. It was extremely difficult serving the St. Lawrence region alone, with hamlets scattered across its entire length, from Montréal to Tadoussac, a stretch of some three hundred miles. But lest one forget, Acadie, today known as Nova Scotia, had settlers and clergy to support as well.[2]

As settlement populations increased and gained importance, communities variously requested a permanent church and a resident priest from the bishop. During his tenure alone, Laval sanctioned several such churches, and by 1683 some two dozen Seminary-trained priests provided Mass, baptisms, weddings, and funerals to communities throughout New France. But the availability of priests remained insufficient for the number of settlements in place. Even with Saint-Vallier's efforts during his own reign, by 1721 the lack of priests lingered—only twenty had titular curates while many rural *habitants* still heard Mass just once a month, served by itinerant priests.[3] Despite the continued lack of clergy, the Séminaire de Québec remained the colony's best hope for educating and increasing the number of priests to serve throughout New France.

The spiritual focus of the Séminaire was intimately influenced by Laval's education as a Jesuit and his active participation in various groups in and around Paris. While with the Société des Bons Amis, Laval and five others lived in community to support one another, to develop their spirituality and a fervent Christian life, all under the protection of the Holy Virgin. These *Bons Amis* focused on "personal sanctification through the diligent practice of prayer and penance," and maintenance of an "intimate bond between members . . . to facilitate the exercise of humility." Their regular spiritual regimen included daily prayers and weekly spiritual discussions, with honor given to the Holy Family. Their mantra was always *Cor unum et anima una*—"One Heart and One Soul."[4]

Laval's interactions with his mentor Henri de Bernières at the Hermitage de Caen further guided the Seminary's approach to Christian formation. Within this hermitage, a life of prayer and service included "surrendering to the will of God, self-forgetfulness, and worldly separation." In de Bernières's words, "those who expose themselves to work for the next, without being dead to themselves . . . make little fruit, and risk to lose themselves. . . . We don't have a better friend than Jesus Christ. Follow all of his council . . . humility and the emptying of the heart." To aspire to this, de Bernières' hermitage had regular daily activities that included spiritual discussions, acts of penitence, pilgrimages, and visits to the sick and the poor.[5]

As the leaders of the Séminaire de Québec embraced philosophies of the *Bons Amis* and the Hermitage de Caen, they strove "to promote a spirituality solidly anchored in the respectful veneration of the mystery of God, in a life united to the Incarnate Son, and in a devotion to Mary—all this in the conviction that every Christian is called to holiness."[6] Thus, seminary life was contemplative and missionary in spirit and included the communal sharing of goods and self, all for the development of one's spirituality, servanthood, and love of Christ. To Laval, "the Séminaire and the colony were one and the same; it formed a family with the bishop as father, and the Holy Family of Jesus, Mary, and Joseph as the models."[7] To visually express this devotion, Laval "had printed in France an image of the Holy Family that he circulated . . . in great number in his diocese."[8]

Candidates who entered seminary in either Paris or Québec had to have the right motivation for pursuing the priesthood. They had to demonstrate piety, good health, relevant talents, education, and sentiments toward being men of the cloth. Each had to guarantee a minimum "decency" threshold to ensure their ability to avoid activities or behaviors that could otherwise bring the church into disrepute. As such, "one could not be allowed into the Seminary without this spirit of Jesus Christ; or without evidence that they could attain this spirit and the disposition to receive it. One could dismiss an individual if he displayed outrageous mistakes or stubbornness . . . or did not want to better himself despite several warnings." Once admitted to seminary, a candidate recited a profession of faith in Latin—*Formula Propositi Sociorum*—and declared "that his only motivation is the desire to procure the glory of God and the salvation of souls, especially among the Infidels."[9]

Seminary life established spiritual and personal discipline. Each day, one participated in morning, noon, and evening prayer, recitations of the rosary, Mass, an *examen de conscience,* as well as studies in theology, liturgy, chanting, and administration of the sacraments. Each also participated in confession twice a week and visited prisons or hospitals monthly. Additional activities, assigned on a rotating basis, included washing sacramental vessels, praying with servants, teaching catechism, and serving as cantor. If one owned property or had funds, they were utilized in community, under the advisement of the superiors. One was also expected to participate in a spiritual retreat each year, to follow a rule of celibacy, to serve without any blemishes, all while maintaining a reasonable spirit, a good nature, and integrity.[10]

Once ordained, each Seminarian became a secular priest, that is, a priest "of the world" and not bound by a rule that guided those of religious orders. They represented the church and followed an ordinary ecclesiastical discipline and an Apostolic spirit to serve God until death. As secular clergy, they could continue to acquire, own, or inherit property or goods. They were, however, encouraged to practice charity, gentleness, simplicity, detachment, and obedience to the point of perfection so as to further develop their Apostolic nature.

A Seminarian vowed to maintain these essential rules, along with prayer and great devotion to the Holy Family, for the rest of his life.[11]

Each priest typically began his ministry within a hamlet either along the St. Lawrence River or in Acadie. But many, including the future Mississippi missionaries, often traveled to and served in multiple churches until more priests could either be trained or recruited from France. Antoine Davion and Nicolas Foucault traveled such a circuit. Davion, who hailed from Saint-Omer in Artois, France, arrived in Québec sometime before 1692 after attending the Séminaire des Missions Étrangères in Paris. Soon after, he was assigned to the Ile d'Orléans, where he ministered to the colonists for some six years and served variously at five churches in the region.[12]

For a priest like Davion, traveling from point to point in New France could be quite difficult—"entire days without encountering a soul, so happy to finally arrive to spend the night in whatever barn or cabin . . . the priest who had the courage to cross this vast countryside carried his altar and said Mass where he was found."[13] But the climate provided challenges as well: "One saw it a hundred times—go and administer the sacraments to the sick in town or in the country, rowing a canoe in summer, walking in snow shoes in winter, carrying one's altar and a morsel of bread on his back, traveling one or two leagues to say Mass in a cabin . . . to give last rights; returning, running, even while eating a morsel of bread, often while fasting."[14]

Father Foucault, at times, also ministered in multiple churches. Born in 1664, Foucault grew up within a publishing family located on the Rue St. Jacques in Paris. This birthright provided for a comfortable young life complete with access to learned materials such as books and pamphlets, some of which potentially enlightened Foucault to any number of subjects pertaining to the world and its peoples. Foucault studied at the Séminaire des Missions Étrangères in Paris during the mid 1680s, but "full of good will to suffer for God," he left for New France in late April 1688 to finish his studies at the Séminaire de Québec.[15] Ordained on December 3, 1689, Foucault soon after began to serve in several churches near his primary charge, the parish of Saint François Xavier at Batiscan, a small hamlet located on the north bank of the St. Lawrence River, to the southwest of Québec. Unlike some priests who were land-bound in terms of accessing different churches, Foucault best served the various regional hamlets by traveling the St. Lawrence and its tributaries utilizing his own rudder-driven boat.[16] While his strategy worked well during the late spring, summer, and fall, he had to make other arrangements during the winter, when the St. Lawrence "freezes over entirely, to a depth of some ten feet, and one travels with horse and cart across it just as if it were dry land."[17]

Like Foucault, Davion also had an assigned church within which to work. His primary charge, St. Jean on the Ile d'Orléans, was elevated to a parish on September 26, 1694. During the elevation ceremony, Davion "touched the doors as he entered the church, touched the holy water, rang the bell, knelt and prayed before the altar, touched it and kissed it; he opened the Missal . . . took his seat at the assigned place for a curate." By elevating the small church to a parish, its members were expected to tithe so as to maintain and orna-ment it with furnishings, books, sacramental and liturgical items, and any other goods needed to worship God in this sacred space. Parishioners' tithes also ensured that their priest was properly vested and fed so as to support his ministry within their community.[18]

Throughout the colony, tithing was established to support the needs of the church and clergy. Initially, many *habitants* were upset by this system since the they were often poor themselves. To accommodate the economics of rural life, Laval included the option of tithing at one-twenty-sixth of the harvest to allow grains to serve as a tithe beyond the usual fees for weddings, funerals, and pew rentals. Some of Foucault's church members provided offerings of wheat, oats, or maize to serve as their tithe. No matter the form of payment, many churches otherwise were quite poor, particularly during the seventeenth century, with many chapels "covered with straw, extremely dilapidated, with-out vessels and vestments." Once Bishop Saint-Vallier came into power, more stone chapels were built to replace the suffering wooden structures.[19]

Father Jean-François Buisson de Saint-Cosme, the only one of the five eventual Mississippi missionaries who was native to Québec, also served in an established church.[20] Born on January 30, 1667, Saint-Cosme spent his earliest years in rural Canada, where he likely interacted with individuals of all walks of life, Native peoples and *coureurs de bois* included, and also had ample oppor-tunity to experience the climate, terrain, travel, and sustenance strategies of the North American wilderness. Little else is known about Saint-Cosme's early life until his ordination to the priesthood on February 2, 1690. Shortly thereafter, Saint-Cosme began his ministry at Les Mines, Acadie. Unlike many of his col-leagues, Saint-Cosme maintained a very comfortable sum of money for a rural priest. He received a salary of 500 livres a year as well as "presents [of food and cloth] which, according to custom, they receive from their people." Goods and salary combined, Saint-Cosme maintained an income of some 800 livres per year. In comparison, Québecois carpenters of Saint-Cosme's era received an annual salary of 100 livres; more specialized vocations received 300 livres.[21]

While personal tithing demonstrated support and devotion to one's established church and priest, religious symbolism across the Canadian landscape displayed the colony's devotion to Christianity. Along the rural roads of New France, one often found large, wooden crosses ornamented with the symbols of Christ's crucifixion: hammer, tongs, nails, a ladder, and a cock at the top of the central post, recalling St. Peter's false denial to the Romans that he knew Jesus. Everyone who passed by these Christian landmarks crossed him- or herself or did some other type of reverence.[22] But though the cross served as a visible reminder of the Catholic faith throughout the colony, reverence to the sacred symbol did not always mean adherence to Catholic worship. Troubles abounded for many a priest. Father Davion, for one, suffered unknown hardships during his service on the Ile d'Orléans.[23] Although no known records exist to decipher what this trouble was, once on the Mississippi, Davion became frustrated that he was asked to carry out "church duties" with Frenchmen at the new parish in Mobile. The disgruntled priest wrote to Saint-Vallier, reminding him of why he had left Ile d'Orléans in the first place, "that I left Canada since I had no interest in being a curate, and because of the rotten sorts of souls" there present.[24]

More than likely, Davion's frustrations stemmed from church members whose carriage was less than ideal for the sanctity of Mass. While many *habitants* throughout Québec devoutly participated in Sunday worship, others used it as a time for socializing and "followed their own inclinations in church rather than the clerically sanctioned proprieties and formalities." Some came to church drunk, talked loudly during Mass, and/or smoked at the entrance of the chapel. Many took snuff and sang to entertain themselves rather than to demonstrate devotion. Gossiping, coughing, shuffling feet, staring—all "were commonly employed methods of passing time or expressing annoyance at an overly long sermon."[25] Any such disruptions to an ongoing Catholic church service likely angered Davion and led to his distaste for serving as a curate.

Non-Catholic bystanders certainly mocked the Catholic faith, particularly given its adherence to the Latin language. One Swedish Protestant named Peter Kalm wrote of the Catholic Canadians: "It was both strange and amusing . . .

A cross alongside a road in rural Québec. *On the Lachine Road,* by Frances Ann Hopkins, 1836–1919. Courtesy Library and Archives of Canada, Acc. No. 1936-67-8, Reproduction copy number C-002737K.

to see and hear how eagerly the women and soldiers said their prayers in Latin and did not themselves understand a word of what they said." As he witnessed it, "the people are very faithful in these observances, because everyone tries by these means to put God under some obligation and intends by it to make himself more deserving of some reward."[26] Ultimately, if the colonists did not understand Latin, they certainly understood French well enough to judge when to listen and when to leave the service. "Supernatural forces were active during the Mass, and its mysterious language [Latin] commanded awe and respect," while "popular resistance to the clergy's material and moral demands occurred." It is likely that some colonists developed a distinct value toward their faith, but a distinct defiance to "the church's human representatives."[27]

As leaders in their communities, priests had responsibilities to attend to, including church attendance, payment of tithes, and moral order. At Batiscan, Foucault was particularly keen in addressing immoral behavior, a stance likely reinforced not only by his seminary training but also by his early experiences in Québec. When Foucault began his seminary work, he also served as Saint-Vallier's clerk. This vocation provided Foucault with opportunities to assist in the development of various ordinances and to gain firsthand knowledge of the troubles experienced within colonial churches. Debauchery, *eau de vie,* lewd songs, adultery, dancing, improperly covered female necks and elbows— all led to ordinances that were meant to curb colonists' unsavory ways.

In Batiscan, Foucault found himself surrounded by soldiers and officers who established themselves in and around the hamlet because of Iroquois attacks throughout the region. As these new men arrived, some subsequently created problems for rural clergy.[28] One day, Jacques-Théodore Cosineau de Mareuil, a local officer, had too much to drink and performed a bawdy song before several individuals from Foucault's hamlet. The enraged priest quickly denounced this behavior to Frontenac, who in turn reprimanded the young officer. De Mareuil's antics led Saint-Vallier to develop a mandate that forbade clergy from granting absolution to any persons who composed such vulgar lyrics. For his part, Foucault denounced such behavior from the pulpit.[29] But due to the inability of the government to pay all of its troops, soldiers often stayed with area families and helped with farming and other chores. This led "several young people, in particular soldiers, under pretext of seeking girls to marry, to carry on in a licentious manner with these girls." Some suggested that these young ladies "allow[ed] themselves to be abused, under hope of marriage, persuaded that 'accidents' can arise, making this a motivation for their parents to pursue these marriages."[30] In response, Saint-Vallier and Foucault mandated that clergy were "forbidden from marrying persons who have not received signed permission from us by which we declare that [those permitted to marry] have not caused any disorder, nor scandal, in pursuing their marriage." But despite their efforts to improve the colony, licentiousness, drunkenness, crookedness, and debauchery seasoned the Québec landscape for further run-ins between soldiers, colonists, and clergymen.[31]

In 1694, Foucault publicly fought with Marguerite Dizy and Captain François Dejordy Moreau de Cabanac, who were having an affair in Batiscan. Marguerite, born sometime in February of 1663, was fourteen when she married her then twenty-seven-year-old husband, Jean Debroyeux, in 1677. Debroyeux, a *coureur de bois,* was often absent from Batiscan, trading goods in Native villages along the St. Lawrence River and down toward the Mississippi.

During his absence, Dejordy and Dizy began their relationship, which they refused to terminate despite warnings from the clergy.

Foucault and Father Claude Bouquin of nearby Champlain informed Saint-Vallier of the adulterous scandal. Together, they prepared a mandate that was read from the pulpit on February 9, 1694, banning Dejordy and Dizy from attending church in either Batiscan or Champlain. Almost immediately, Dejordy failed to comply when, in early March of 1694, he walked through the church doors at Batiscan to attend a funeral Mass. Accompanying the excommunicated officer was his friend, Jacques-François Chevalier Du Bourchemin, a rascal in his own right who was later accused of having poisoned his wife, Elizabeth Dizy, sister of Marguerite Dizy, so as to marry another young lady of Trois-Rivières.[32] Sieur de Cadillac described Foucault's reaction to Dejordy's appearance:

> The funeral was already underway. . . . Noting the presence of Dejordy, Foucault stopped the Mass, retired to the sacristy to remove his vestments, and returned to announce to the congregation that he would not continue the service as long as Dejordy was present. This surprised everyone. In that moment, Foucault's face, normally tan under benign situations, became as pale as the body in the coffin. For those in the church, the anger and the passion imprinted on the curate's face confused them greatly. Dejordy and the parishioners departed, Foucault locked himself and his clerk inside, and finished the Mass where neither Dejordy nor the soul of the deceased lad had good reason to hope for any blessing from God based on the obvious devices of Foucault and his noble sacrifice.[33]

Because of Foucault's strict scruples and the canons of the church, he could not continue the funeral with an excommunicant present.[34]

Funeral aside, Foucault's troubles continued, as this "odd man if ever there was one" delivered particularly daunting sermons from the pulpit. In one sermon alone, he exclaimed:

> Only the wretched and damned could declare that Madame Dizy was an honest woman, that if someone were bold enough to do so, he would have him beaten with a stick, placed in shackles for six months, and only pro-

vided bread and water; that Frontenac would not be alive much longer, and that Bishop Saint-Vallier was young and would lead them along a beautiful path; further, that Foucault himself would mock any complaints made against him to the *Conseil Souverain,* that he was only doing what his bishop, above all others, ordered him to do, that only the pope was the judge of his actions and would fully see his efforts as an expression of truth, just as there is a sun in the sky.[35]

Although not typical of all priests, some did single out and rebuke individuals by name, excommunicate the fallen, or even scold individuals for the books they read, for the clothes they wore, or simply for behaving in some unfavorable manner. Clearly, Foucault showed no reluctance in chiding brazen sinners such as Dizy and Dejordy from the pulpit.[36]

While Foucault's stance stemmed from his staunch adherence to the Catholic tradition and moral order, Father Saint-Cosme's run-ins with the government, the military, and parishioners were not just moral but also political, and culminated in actions taken against him, including a passive attempt to have him removed from the church. But Saint-Cosme's situation differed significantly from Foucault's, for he was in Les Mines, a hamlet in Acadie that was home to dozens of French men, women, and children whose ancestors had established villages and farmsteads several decades earlier. Those individuals had migrated mostly from southwestern France, where knowledge of a similar landscape helped them to develop dikes and sluice gates so as to foster rich agricultural fields on the island. Although under Louis XIV's rule, *Les Acadiens* became quite accustomed to governing themselves since France poorly supported them. Indeed, early in his work, Saint-Cosme wrote to the governor of Acadie, Joseph Robineau de Villebon, "to approve a choice which these settlers had made of three of their number to settle the differences which arise daily among them concerning their lands, and other disputes."[37]

Governor Villebon personally offered to give the Acadian priests all the assistance he could to help them keep faith and service to God active among the Acadians.[38] But many a priest proved difficult for the governor, Saint-Cosme included, particularly when he and others "openly declared that all authority was in their hands," meddled in local affairs, and subsequently behaved arrogantly toward government and military officials.[39] Several missionaries, including Saint-Cosme, even "exclaimed before the *habitants* that they had little obedience that they owed their bishop, being masters of themselves, and able, without permission, to leave the places where they are located."[40]

Politically charged events ensued. On April 24, 1693, René LeBlanc reported the arrival of two small English vessels at Les Mines with designs on engaging in trade. While there, the commander of the vessels invited the local French priest, presumably Saint-Cosme, to go aboard, where "he had dined very well."[41] Not one year later, Villebon sent Mathieu Degoutin to Les Mines to obtain provisions for his men. Degoutin did as commanded, and once in the village, the *habitants* "promised me flour and peas . . . three or four offered to help me out . . . they would quickly bring me what I requested." At the same time, however, Saint-Cosme sent out two *habitants* from his church to join up with those who had already promised to help Degoutin. In so doing, Saint-Cosme's men told those who offered assistance to Villebon's agent that they were wrong to have promised him food, "that this would cause problems with the English." Nonetheless, those who pledged to help Degoutin fulfilled their promise.[42] To bypass Saint-Cosme and obtain future supplies, the governor developed more deceptive strategies. With letters meant only for trusted *habitants,* Villebon asked them to "make it appear that provisions were only given . . . under duress so as to relieve them of responsibility should the English learn about it."[43]

Although Saint-Cosme's actions appeared disruptive and unpatriotic, he was attempting to protect his flock from potential English retaliation. Acadie was a troubled region, caught between the French and English, neglected by its own compatriots, yet scolded at times as it sought to survive. Saint-Cosme and his *habitants* often came into contact with the English out of necessity, for it was no secret that some *Bostonnais* often travelled to Acadie to trade brandy, sugar, utensils, and cloth for Acadian grains and pelts. French counterparts simultaneously traveled to Boston to sell their own grains, such as wheat and flour, for funds and similar goods. Englishmen and Acadians alike tolerated such activities since the *habitants,* without help from France, needed the *Bostonnais* to survive. But despite such helpful exchanges, religious figures in any region of Québec were expected to ensure that the *habitants* not only maintained their faith but also maintained their devotion and loyalty to King Louis XIV. Consequently, letters to the bishop followed citing "complaints regarding Saint-Cosme's interference with *habitants* of Les Mines . . . that Saint-Cosme disrupted the help that the *habitants* could give to officers in service to his Majesty."[44]

Letters of complaint also reported on an abusive scandal that broke out in the Seminary priest's church.[45] According to Degoutin, Saint-Cosme "chased the wife of Pierre Theriot from the church," stating that she was engaged in an affair with Jean Theriot, the nephew of Pierre, who also lived in her house. It was one of her servants, La Bauve, who accused the wife of "having *commerce* with her nephew." As a judicial official in the region, Pierre Theriot demanded La Bauve go before judges at Port Royal to speak to these accusations. On April 1, 1694, La Bauve was found guilty of creating the scandal and was ordered to publicly repair the honor of Theriot's wife and nephew.[46] Although both aunt and nephew were deemed innocent of the allegations, Saint-Cosme ignored the ruling and imposed his own excommunication for three consecutive Sundays. The fourth Sunday, when normalcy should have prevailed, Jean Theriot was again chased from the church. "I [Degoutin] was present . . . and I can verify that the clamor in the church led most attending to begin to cry, and once done with Mass, to remark that they feared for their honor as long as Saint-Cosme could do whatever he wanted, whenever he wanted."[47]

Saint-Cosme's seeming abhorrence of adulterous behavior, his lashing out at the otherwise innocent aunt and nephew, eventually served as a thin veil to his own actions within Acadie that challenged his adherence to his Seminary vows. Saint-Cosme was characterized as *mal de son esprit* (poor in spirit), quite arrogant, and under consideration by the Seminary leadership to be removed from Acadie if not from the church altogether. Curious discontent with Saint-Cosme's demeanor led to proposals "to not do him any harm, but to [have him] live in a family where there were three or four older, marriageable girls." For this to occur, Tremblay asked the Seminary leader, Charles Glandelet, "to counsel Saint-Cosme in such a way as to not discourage him but to encourage him" to live in the home.[48]

Tremblay's concerns stemmed from his and others' observations of the Acadian priest. "I am very afflicted by the dispositions that you [Glandelet] noted in Saint-Cosme," wrote Tremblay. "I saw them in him when I visited him in Acadie when returning from Canada, or at least I saw the seeds in a full and sufficient enough manner like I had seen in him the time we went together to teach the catechism along the Petite Rivière." What specifically these men referred to remains unclear, but placing him among marriageable women suggests that they wanted to test him, that quite possibly Saint-Cosme was attracted to women and was in danger of bringing scandal to the church since "such mannerisms did not at all fit a missionary."[49]

In hopes of resolving Saint-Cosme's situation, "one thought of sending him coded letters" to recall him from Acadie, but Tremblay hesitated. He hoped that Saint-Cosme, as well as another problematic priest, Father Louis Petit, might recognize "that it was God's will that they no longer live there, that it would suffice for them to manifest this will of God without being sent coded letters."[50] But Saint-Cosme did not manifest such an understanding of God's will. He did not resign, and consequently, by the mid 1690s, the dubious priest had clearly developed a reputation for being quite difficult and overly interested in political intrigue, disruption, and women.[51]

When each Seminarian became a secular priest, he vowed to follow an ordinary ecclesiastical discipline and an Apostolic spirit to serve God until death. Each was to practice charity, gentleness, simplicity, detachment, celibacy, and obedience to the point of perfection so as to further develop an Apostolic nature. These essential rules had to be followed for the remainder of one's life. But Saint-Cosme's work as a priest in New France was filled with strife in relation to government and military authority as well as local churchgoers. While distinct vows were made in seminary, witnesses seemed to concur that Saint-Cosme challenged adherence to these lifelong commitments, most especially obedience, charity, and celibacy.[52]

With Saint-Vallier back in Paris to address his own woes, Governor Frontenac took charge and recalled Saint-Cosme to Québec to discuss his poor attitude and demeanor. Satisfied that Saint-Cosme intended to improve his composure, Frontenac allowed him to return to Les Mines in August 1695 accompanied by a letter indicative of a change in conduct and attitude, and some 100 ecus (300–500 livres) to entice him to maintain good behavior. Fathers Petit and Abel Maudoux, two other troublesome contemporaries, received the same reprimand and reward.[53] On some level, Saint-Cosme and the others did change. In a brief accounting, Villebon remarked: "the missionary priests of Acadie have witnessed that they want to satisfy me . . . the letters they received this year have produced this change."[54] Nonetheless, after a stint serving as chaplain to the Mi'kmaqs, and under the leadership of Governor Villebon, Saint-Cosme's term in Acadie ended in 1697 with lingering legacies, both good and bad. Saint-Vallier elevated Saint-Cosme's church at Les Mines into a parish due to the large number of French in the area "that had been spiritually cultivated by the priests who had served there over the years"—in part, a favorable view of Saint-Cosme's work. And yet, Villebon could only remark on Saint-Cosme's departure: "As there have been changes this year among the missionaries of Acadie, I believe, Monseigneur, that things will run more smoothly."[55]

Unlike Saint-Cosme, Marc Bergier had a reputation for being a devout priest who had an internal confidence and commitment to God that never wavered. Born November 8, 1667, in the rustic Rhône Valley of France, in a tiny town called Tain (Tain l'Hermitage, today), this future Mississippi missionary lived a quiet, comfortable life while exposed to well-educated and respected family members. His father, Jean-Jacques, served as a registrar in the judicial system of Tain, but became a priest after the death of Marc's mother, Magdeleine Barbier. Marc's uncle, Jean-Aymard, served as a curate himself in the local church, while Marc's godfather, Louis Bergier, was a *Procureur Jurisdictionnel* and *Notaire Royale* in Tain. Marc's cousin, François Bergier, also served as a lawyer in the region.

Bergier began his education at the Collège de Tournon near Tain. He went on to complete his classical studies, eventually obtained a doctorate in law, and served as a lawyer for the Grenoble Parliament. But with a family heavily engaged in the Catholic Church, not to mention his own devotion to his Christian faith, Bergier pursued seminary training in the Grand Séminaire de Vienne and soon after at the Séminaire des Missions Étrangères in Paris. By the spring of 1697, Bergier completed his studies and was ordained to the priesthood.[56]

Described as a wise man of great virtue and undeniable talent, Bergier could have had a brilliant career as a lawyer, a professor, or even a theologian in France. Nevertheless, the call to serve God captured his heart and soul, and Bergier chose to seek his calling in Québec.[57] The timing could not have been any better. The young, eager priest arrived in New France at a point when the Séminaire and Saint-Vallier were on their strongest, most cordial terms ever. With his boat anchored off the coast of the village of Québec, Saint-Vallier "sent out a canoe to bring me ashore, a canoe of bark so light that a single man can easily carry it everywhere," wrote Bergier.[58] Once on dry land, Saint-Vallier "witnessed the joy he felt" at Bergier's arrival and invited him to stay at his house until a decision was made concerning his role in the church.

As a part of his bargain to return to his diocese in 1697, Saint-Vallier had vowed "to exercise hospitality toward the clergy when they come to Québec, by offering them rooms in his abode."[59] In a letter to his father who was in retirement in Vienne, France, Bergier described Saint-Vallier's hospitality and welcoming home that fully provided for all who stayed there: "Each entered, left, drank, and ate as boldly as if they were boarding in an inn . . . it is rare that we are without strangers, if one can call them strangers, since one does not make a difference between them and the occupants."[60] Within the bishop's home, "they shared meals together, a seminarian read several verses of holy scripture before they began to eat, and after the meal, *le Martyrologe.* During the meal, a domestique read the *Life of the Saints.* Each day, morning, and evening, Saint-Vallier himself lead prayers, the *examen de conscience,* and the meditation for the following day."[61] Thus, spiritual activities and hospitality immediately and richly inspired Bergier's life in New France.

Bergier's fresh pair of eyes and open heart for the colony led him to enthusiastically describe all he saw in late seventeenth-century Québec—the many similarities compared to his birthplace in Haut Dauphiné, as well as the differences: "This place is colder because of the large number of waterways and forests," wrote Bergier. It has "beautiful wheat fields that one sows in April and May and then harvests toward the middle of September. Toward Montréal, one has beautiful apples, good plums, melons, and other fruits; even grape vines are coming along. Peas and vegetables are plentiful, especially cabbage, lettuce, and herbs . . . cheese is abundant, one eats beef and mutton, good pork, numerous wild birds—chickens, hens, goose, duck; lots of game, fur, and feathers."[62]

Bergier certainly showed interest in and compassion for all things and peoples around him. His "new eyes" allowed him to see and experience things that many had likely come to take for granted. But two things in particular moved Bergier greatly. The first was "the honor, several days after I arrived, to canoe with Laval together to St. Michel, one league away." This location served as "the recreation house of the Seminary leadership," a place to which Québec clergy retreated "once a week," wrote Bergier. While there, "we dined together, and I was moved by the prayers, the devotional practice, and the carriage of all these men there gathered."[63] But even more moving for Bergier was his interaction with the region's Native peoples: "I almost never encounter the Indians in the churches that my heart does not blossom and give thanks; and who would not be charmed to see these poor souls, after having remained so many centuries in darkness and shadows of death, sing . . . *le Sacris Solemnis* [a hymn written by St. Thomas Aquinas for the Feast of Corpus Christi] in their language along with other hymns and canticles to praise the true God."[64]

Although Bergier arrived in Québec just days after the departure of the first Seminary missionaries for the Mississippi, he actually learned of their venture south while still on board his own ship from France. A separate vessel, out from Québec, passed by his ship and several Canadians on board told him of the missionaries' departure. Unfamiliar with the waterways of North America, Bergier "hoped with all my heart that *Le Pontchartrain* could go straight to the Arkansas. I felt courageous and strong enough to take on a second trip of a thousand leagues." Although highly motivated, he maintained his innate sense of patience nonetheless: "I hope this will come with time, because I have great desire and believe that the Good Lord will give this to me."[65]

While he awaited his official assignment, Bergier settled into life in the growing city of Québec. He celebrated Mass within the Ursuline community and assisted with daily offices at the cathedral. With a forgiving and unhurried nature, Bergier calmly dismissed delays in deciding his future, citing Saint-Vallier's "large numbers of letters and other concerns that overwhelm him to meet the departure date for the ships." Patience, acceptance, and humbleness were key to Bergier's ultimate assignment: "God, grant me the grace to carry out and to be faithful in all the duties it pleases him to give me, large or small, near or far. They matter not to me as long as they are in his hand. I am content because I desire nothing other than God's will in everything and that this be accomplished perfectly by me."[66]

Unlike Bergier, François de Montigny was somewhat less patient in his duties. Born in Angers, France, in 1669, de Montigny entered the Séminaire de St. Sulpice in Paris to pursue the priesthood. In 1692, while in France to plead his case before king and court, the embattled Saint-Vallier met the young seminarian and invited him to complete his studies in Québec. Once in New France, de Montigny entered the Séminaire, quickly followed his path toward ordination, and completed his vows as a priest on March 8, 1693. Shortly thereafter, Saint-Vallier appointed him to l'Ange-Gardien on the Ile d'Orléans.[67]

De Montigny hardly served for one year but "so succeeded in attracting the good graces of Saint-Vallier" that the latter called upon him, as well as the Sulpician superior from Montréal, François Dollier de Casson, to help oversee the diocese during his recall to Paris in 1694.[68] Court and king were not pleased with de Montigny's assignment, while others were certain that Saint-Vallier had chosen him so as to avoid sharing any power with Laval. Mgr l'Ancien, himself, was astonished that the embattled bishop had so brazenly "entrusted the governing of the church to two young men whose ages could not yet give them the experience needed to fulfill their duties." Many could only hope that "the Seminary put its interests in the hands of God, and [that] the superiors of the Séminaire de Québec interact only moderately with de Montigny" so as to avoid additional strife and hardship. Regardless, once Saint-Vallier surprisingly returned to Québec in 1697, so content was he with de Montigny's work that he made him *Co-Vicaire Général* of the entire diocese along with Charles Glandelet.[69]

What stands out most during de Montigny's oversight of the diocese was his developing vision of serving as a missionary, a deeply personal interest that emerged well before Saint-Vallier returned to Québec. De Montigny began hinting at placing a missionary within the Tamarois village quite near the Jesuits' own Illinois mission at Lake Peoria. Laval's "indignation with de Montigny's proposal" quickly emerged. Laval intended to hold de Montigny "within the bounds of charity by showing him God's spirit—one of gentleness and peace, and that one must not enter into a career [like the one proposed by de Montigny] through the door of division." Nevertheless, when the decision was made in 1698 to send Seminary missionaries to the Mississippi River, Saint-Vallier again relied on de Montigny, this time assigning him as the *Grand Vicaire,* sometimes referred to as the *Vicaire Général,* of the Mississippi missions. Perhaps rewarding the young priest further, Saint-Vallier provided de Montigny with *lettres patentes* not only for the Mississippi venture but also to establish a mission among the Tamarois.[70]

The summer of 1698 was certainly a time of excitement for all. Saint-Vallier, the clergy, the diocese, and the Seminary were all on good terms. Many believed that the Mississippi region was fertile, abundant in wildlife and game, with large herds of buffalo, extensive prairie land, and even "horses in abundance." Many were certain that the region was beautiful, quite sustainable in terms of agriculture and fruits. Unlike Québec, the southern wintertime was perceived to be less harsh and the climate "so beautiful that one compares it to Italy." But what was best of all was the presumed presence of "millions of souls to convert."[71] It all sounded like a missionary's paradise, far more hospitable than serving as a priest in the wintry north. Perhaps most intriguing was Bergier's description of the first three missionaries sent to the Mississippi. As he put it: "The priests that they have sent are recognized as saints; you must believe that they were well chosen."[72]

As Bergier and others later learned, these descriptions proved inaccurate. The terrain, the environment, and the number of Native peoples present fell far short of expectations. How the first priests were chosen was a mystery as well. Davion seemed more bent on fleeing what troubled him in Québec, telling Saint-Vallier that he no longer desired to be a curate because of difficulties that remain unknown. Saint-Cosme may have been sent to the region to rid Canada of his arrogant and difficult nature. De Montigny had proven his worth with Saint-Vallier but had an impatient, zealous drive that threatened the work of others. And while Foucault was not selected to serve until later, even his entry into the Mississippi venture seemed curious. Sometime in 1699, Foucault wrote to Tremblay and expressed the desire to serve as a missionary on the Mississippi. Tremblay left his response to Foucault's request in his drawer for a year, unwilling to support a man he saw as too poor in health to work as a missionary.[73] Nonetheless, the Séminaire de Québec assigned Foucault to the Mississippi in 1700.

Quite different from his colleagues, Bergier's deep faith upheld his spirits. Saint-Vallier patiently kept Bergier in Québec, as he wanted "to receive news in a year" to determine Iberville's success in establishing a colony at the mouth of the Mississippi River.[74] Within the year, the news arrived and a decision was made—Bergier was received into the Séminaire de Québec on July 30, 1699. The next day he was appointed as missionary among the Tamarois and *Grand Vicaire* of the Mississippi Valley, to serve as de Montigny's co-leader in the northern region of the missionary domain.[75] As soon as he was assigned to the Mississippi, Bergier wrote a letter to Father Louis Tiberge, the superior of the Séminaire des Missions Étrangères de Paris, in which he pledged his commitment to his work along the Mississippi.

> My name is Marc Bergier, priest, around thirty-two years of age, native of the Thain Parish, diocese of Vienne in Dauphiné, with a doctorate in law. My father's name is Jean-Jacques Bergier, also a priest for around twenty-eight years, a vocation taken on shortly after the death of my mother. . . . Coming to Canada, not knowing a soul, I arrived here with a

spirit of renouncing all of my goods and all of my pretentions, abandoning
myself entirely to Providence, very persuaded, as I still am, that the more
I worked or desired to work for God, the less I would need. Therefore, I
came here completely raw, not counting on paying with my goods but only
with my person, believing that this is similar to Jesus Christ.

Plain, simple, powerful—every word penned in this letter on the eve of his
departure for the Mississippi was true to who Father Marc Bergier was.[76] The
young priest chose to maintain a life of poverty and to live with deep spiritual
devotion in the region, much like he had displayed throughout his lifetime.
Bergier pledged his efforts to the Seminary and to the Native peoples and
vowed to carry out his work with respect and obedience. Shortly after writing
this letter, Bergier left for the Mississippi Valley and the Tamarois mission,
never to return to Québec.[77]

Like many priests in New France, Davion, de Montigny, Saint-Cosme,
Foucault, and Bergier pursued seminary studies in Paris, in Québec, or at
both institutions. Thus, each had a similar education and went on to serve
as priests and as witnesses to the life one lived in the French colony during
the late seventeenth century. For each man, his seminary education helped to
develop his spirituality and his liturgical skills so as to serve at the altar. But
once the decision was made to send Seminary priests to the Mississippi, guidance on how to maintain one's spirituality and piety while on the Mississippi
had to be addressed since serving a mission was quite different from serving a
church. *Lettres patentes* and a governmental passport also had to be prepared
by Saint-Vallier, Laval, and Governor Frontenac. Further, the terrain had to be
researched to ensure that no other religious group's efforts might be compromised. The first three missionaries themselves (Saint-Cosme, Davion, and de
Montigny) had to obtain supplies and hire workers to assist them along their
journey south. Once they completed these necessary measures, the transformation of these men from priests to missionaries could begin.

CHAPTER 3

Preparation for the Mississippi

The Seminary priests had to transform from serving as curates in Québec to serving as missionaries on the Mississippi. As a part of this change, permission had to be granted, passports and the like secured, workers hired, and an understanding of how to care for oneself on the Mississippi purposefully designed so as to help these men carry out their work. Up until the day of their departure, their concepts for missioning stemmed from the Jesuits, who had long pursued their vocational focus with the Montagnais and the Hurons, among others, during the first half of the seventeenth century. While the Jesuits were hopeful to Christianize these various nations, they struggled nonetheless. Disease, warfare, starvation, and slavery left the Hurons hopelessly scattered, their confederacy collapsed. The infliction of torture and death at the hands of the Iroquois on such missionaries as Jean de Brébeuf, Gabriel Lalemant, and Isaac Jogues only strengthened the Jesuits' resolve to Christianize Native peoples. But hunting and migration patterns had proven frustrating, incompatible with the "settled life" of Christianity, leading the Jesuits to create Sillery, a reserve to provide Native peoples with settled living, agriculture, and regular Catholic practices.[1] Sillery proved only mildly successful, with few converts and little year-round stability. Native peoples were not willing to give up their seasonal movement toward hunting and fishing grounds. They knew best how to sustain themselves, and by the 1680s Sillery was all but abandoned.

During the colony's early years, Frenchification was the desired course of action: pull the Native peoples into the French way of life by having them learn the French language, focus on Christianity, and embrace French culture so as to form a single people, a united Canada. But the Jesuits ignored Frenchification. To them, it made much more sense to assimilate into Native cultures, learn their languages, and interject Christianity into their way of life

rather than to force them to become French. It was "a more flexible model
. . . significantly more tolerant of Indigenous traditions."[2] But placing missions far from the colony's center was not what the king desired. Adapting
to the Native peoples' lifestyles and learning their languages was not what
governmental officials ordered. Nonetheless, the Jesuits resisted. They wanted
to develop missions and to work with Native groups far from *eau de vie* and
from those that distributed it among the region's communities and consequently disrupted progress toward Christianization. They wanted to work on
their own terms, through assimilation, a very "conscious, strategic decision" on
their part.[3]

In the Pays d'en Haut, which encompassed the western end of the St. Law-
rence River Valley, the Great Lakes, and on into the Illinois country, Father
Claude Allouez founded the mission of Saint François Xavier near modern-day
Green Bay, while Father Jacques Marquette established missions at Sault Sainte
Marie and Michilimackinac. By 1673, Louis Jolliet and Father Marquette, "the
one pursuing pelts and the other in search of souls," traveled from the Pays
d'en Haut to the Arkansas River and in between encountered the Illinois, the
Tamarois, and the Quapaw Native communities.[4] Marquette worked variously
among the Illinois and other neighboring groups to convert them to Christianity. He claimed early success, particularly certain that the Illinois' presumed
worship of one god and their "gentle and tractable disposition" supported
easy Christianization.[5] But Marquette never saw his desires for the Illinois
achieved, as he spent little time among them and succumbed to the region's
health hazards.

Despite Marquette's premature death, a seed was planted: the Illinois remained a focal point for the Jesuits, and on December 15, 1690, Saint-Vallier
granted this Catholic order a *lettre patente* to serve among the Illinois and their
circonvoisines (neighboring groups). Soon, Jesuits, including Fathers Jacques
Gravier, Julien Binneteau, Joseph de Limoges, Gabriel Marest, and Pierre-
François Pinet, variously lived among Illinois-related communities, including
the Kaskaskias and the Miamis. Although seasonal migration and hunting
continued, the Jesuits adapted to the "times, circumstances, and persons . . .
a hallmark of 'our way of proceeding.'" The Jesuits applied themselves to be
"flexible, not rigid," since they encountered a diversity of individuals, cultures,
and languages everywhere they went.[6]

The Jesuits relied on the teachings of Saint Ignatius of Loyola and Saint
François Xavier, the two founding fathers of the Jesuit tradition, to guide them

in "the way of proceeding."[7] Modeled on the early description of the Apostles in the church, and in obedience to the pope, the heart of their order was "to devote itself with God's grace not only to the salvation and perfection of the members' own souls, but also with that same grace to labor strenuously in giving aid toward the salvation and perfection of the souls of their neighbors."[8] It was a call to accept the danger of their work, but also to strengthen and complete their own conversion "by dying each day, by going against our own will in seeking not what is our own but what is of Jesus Christ."[9] As the Jesuit Father Jérôme Lalemant described it, "rich harvest is only secured by watering those lands with sweat and blood . . . a Missionary destined for this great work must make up his mind to lead a very strange kind of life, and endure unimaginable destitution of all things."[10]

Jesuit spirituality stemmed from how Loyola and Xavier lived their lives—through poverty, chastity, and the desire for its members to "spend their lives for the good of souls."[11] Theirs was an active ministry, out in the world, focused on the salvation of others, always emulating Christ's Apostles—teaching and missioning to those they believed needed salvation. The Jesuits gave of themselves in ardent ways so as to demonstrate total service to God, most assuredly by working "against their human sensitivities . . . against their carnal and worldly love." This "abnegation of self" called on each missionary to embrace the life of a martyr, to suffer accordingly to do God's will, and thus to develop the deepest union possible with God.

During the seventeenth and eighteenth centuries in particular, "showy suffering" gave precedence to a "martyrdom of the interior" such that "the faithful, especially those in holy orders, were to submit to misfortune without complaint."[12] Stemming from a Protestant tradition of *martyrology*, such torment was "accompanied by a Pauline insistence that the sufferings of life itself (rather than death alone) constitute[d] martyrdom." Marquette's and Allouez's own distresses aligned with this description. Marquette found himself "in the blessed necessity of exposing my life for the salvation of all these peoples." Physical sufferings and death in God's service brought Marquette great joy. Allouez also happily separated his soul from his body as he exhausted his physical being in pursuit of teaching the Native people. In this enthusiasm to suffer for change, he demonstrated his deep devotion to God, his own spiritual growth in God's hands.[13] As Allouez remarked: "I am where God wants me . . . the more I suffer, the more I will be consoled . . . one never finds a cross, nails, and thorns where one does not also find Jesus."[14]

The *Spiritual Exercises* were the corpus by which the Jesuits prepared themselves for their vocation. Through meditations, visions, and readings they placed themselves within the biblical events in question so as to interpret their lives and apply their understanding to their work. These *Exercises* gave them the foundation needed to support everything they undertook and to develop and maintain union with God in all they did. A triad of meaning existed in their approach—"in the spirit, from the heart, practically." "In the spirit" meant that a direct and ongoing sense of God's presence remained at the forefront of all they did. "From the heart" signaled how Jesuits interacted with others and how they hoped others responded to them, "not simply conforming to the received wisdom of the day but a pursuit that correlated with their deepest pastoral impulses." "Practically" equated with "pastoral," the ultimate model being the disciples of Christ who journeyed to preach and heal others in body and soul without recompense.[15]

Embraced by their order was Thomas Aquinas's belief that "God's grace was available to all people and that because human will had not been entirely obliterated by original sin, it could cooperate with grace and so be active in salvation; in this view, grace perfected nature."[16] To manifest this grace, the Jesuits learned the Native languages and, in so doing, translated Christian prayers, sacred creeds, and biblical passages using Native words. As language comprehension evolved, adjustments helped Native peoples come closer to understanding Christian terms. Jean de Brébeuf adapted his teaching of the Lord's Prayer and the Holy Trinity to help the Hurons better understand the Christian prayers and concepts. "They cannot say simply, Father . . . but are obliged to say one of the three, my father, thy father, his father." With regards to the phrase, "In the name of the Father and of the son, and of the Holy ghost," Brébeuf was challenged by Huron words that reflected all three versions of father if used alone. With permission from his superior, he taught instead: "In the name of our Father, and of His Son, and of Their Holy Ghost." But one also had to be careful with the words "Our Father" in the Lord's Prayer. In Huron tradition, if one's father were not alive, he or she could not make such an utterance without insulting "the dead whom they have loved."[17]

Father Lalemant believed that "all men are created in order to know, to love, and to enjoy their God; all have the means to do this, but very diversely."[18] Thus, flexible and creative strategies were used to impress Christianity upon young and old alike. The Jesuits provided children with gifts meant to encourage them to learn the Christian faith. Gravier, for one, found that "the fathers and mothers are delighted when I question their children. They themselves encourage them and beg me, when I go into their cabins, to question them. . . . It is true that the hope of getting a red bead . . . or a needle, a medal, a cross or a rosary (especially if it be red), a small knife, or other curious object, given as a reward, incites the children to answer well."[19] The sung word further added a sweet, auditory element to Christian words. Allouez had "certain spiritual songs that he was wont to have the children sing to French airs . . . so that our mysteries were published in the streets and cabins, and were received with applause, impressing themselves insensibly on people's minds." Some songs were composed to combat superstitions or other vices that went against Christianity. "After teaching the children to sing them to the accompaniment of a sweet-toned flute, he went everywhere with these little Indian musicians, to declare war on jugglers [shamans], dreamers, and those who had several wives."[20]

Although the Jesuits worked among Native communities for many years, they were not always the lone missioning group in New France. René-Robert Cavelier, Sieur de la La Salle, Henri de Tonti, and several Récollets from the Order of Friars Minor traveled to the mouth of the Mississippi, erected a cross, and claimed the region in the name of God and king. La Salle had chosen the Récollets for personal reasons. He was not fond of the Jesuits, who, he believed, "sought both religious domination in the colony and monopoly of the fur trade." As a youth, and under the authority of his father, La Salle had studied in a Jesuit school. Ever rebellious, he withdrew from it "with the blessing of his superiors, who at last saw that he was too headstrong and self-willed for such a calling." Thus, "at odds with the Jesuits, who regarded his defection in much the same way the military regarded desertion," La Salle chose the Récollets to accompany him down the Mississippi.[21]

Just which religious groups gained access to the Mississippi River or traveled with explorers in the region was a frustrating issue for both Laval and Saint-Vallier. Movement of the various missionary groups throughout New France was meant to be under the jurisdiction of the bishop of Québec. When Allouez moved west in 1663 to establish missions, Laval appointed him as the region's *Grand Vicaire*. As Marquette and Jolliet prepared to descend the Mississippi, they did so with the approval of the Jesuit superior Claude Dablon and Laval. But oversight was difficult such that "the farther one recedes from the centre of authority the less one feels its controlling hand."[22] Some might secure permission from the bishop of Québec, others from Rome, still others from the king, who, as "defender of the church [and] holder of ecclesial prerogatives," held jurisdiction over all lands in his name.[23] In the case of the Récollets, they "had obtained the power of *Missionaries Apostoliques* [from Rome] to work in the places where the missionaries from Canada were not yet located." The Holy See even granted them a *Récollet Préfecture* in the Mississippi Valley without Bishop Laval's knowledge or consent. A Seminary official, Father Jean Dudouyt, expressed concern that "this will be a source of division." He, like Laval, believed it much better "if this was dependent upon the bishop of Québec, who would maintain peace and union and could watch over them [the missionaries] more strongly than would Rome."[24] In the end, the Récollets never established themselves on the Mississippi River, and the *Récollet Préfecture* granted to them by the Holy See was removed.[25]

Competition for terrain also brought out harsh, critical opinions of the various orders' strategies for missioning. One Récollet, Father Louis Hennepin, viewed Jesuit tactics among the Illinois as abhorrent. Accommodating Christianity to these "brutish, wild and stupid" Illinois, with "manners being so opposite to the morals of the Gospel," or even striving to teach Christianity through Native languages left him fully confident that the Jesuits would fail.[26] As for his own approach to Christianization, Hennepin did not attempt to share the Gospel through a Native community language. Instead, he utilized Frenchification strategies and expected Indians to learn prayers from rote memory, reciting them in a language for which they had no direct equivalent to certain sounds. Hennepin assumed that this would instill Christianity within them, certain that the removal of anything "Indian" from a Native group was the path to conversion. But time was needed: "there is in these Indians such an alienation from the faith, so brutal and narrow a mind, such corrupt and un-Christian morals," wrote Hennepin's Récollet colleague Membré, "that great time would be needed to hope for any fruit."[27] While the Jesuits saw them as filled with "good sense, a tenacious memory, and a quick apprehension season'd with a solid judgment," the Récollets considered the Native peoples "stupid, gross, and rustic persons, incapable of thought or reflection."[28]

Disdain for each other's tactics began in the early years of the fledgling colony. Jesuits first arrived in Acadie in 1611 to work among the Mi'kmaqs and Maliseets. The Récollets also came to Québec at the invitation of Samuel de Champlain, who found favor in their vow of poverty and their work as missioners in East Asia. But the Récollets failed to Christianize many since they preferred to convert and colonize simultaneously and thus Europeanize the Native peoples. Dissatisfied with the Récollets' efforts and assured by their own strategies of adaptation, the Jesuits determined themselves to secure exclusive rights as missioners to the colony. By 1632, monopoly in hand, the Jesuits served alone around the St. Lawrence Valley for the next several decades.[29] But by the late seventeenth and early eighteenth centuries, jockeying for position among the variously related Illinois villages, or even within the fledgling forts at the mouth of the Mississippi, led many religious groups to once again vie against each other so as to carry out God's work. Favoritism by La Salle for the Récollets and later Iberville for the Jesuits disillusioned many trying to heed God's call in the region.

In 1689, Henri de Tonti himself jumped into the religious fray when he wrote to Father Claude Dablon, superior of the Jesuits in Québec, and specifically asked him to assign a Jesuit missionary to serve the French and to Christianize the Quapaws along the Arkansas River. De Tonti's motives stemmed from his strong relationship with the Quapaws and his desire to further attract their loyalty and trade.[30] For their part, the Quapaws wanted a missionary among them so as to strengthen ties with the French and increase protection and access to French goods. A missionary, they believed, had special powers and could provide a strong new *manitou* (spirit) to compliment those they already called upon as a part of their own spiritual tradition.[31] As a manner of enticement, de Tonti highlighted the presence of Arkansas Post, its small fort, and ten Frenchmen present. To attract a Jesuit to this post, de Tonti offered to "build him a chapel and a house with the condition that he will lend us his man to help us [and] he will raise a cross of fifteen feet in height." The chosen missionary was also expected to "grow grain and vegetables," and to "reside here throughout the year if he is not obliged to go away because of illness or recalled for a period of time by his superiors or for any other unforeseen reason." Otherwise, de Tonti hoped that an assigned Jesuit could "help with the spirituality of all of the French . . . to come say Mass in the French quarter near our fort . . . so that he pleases God and leads us to the door of salvation."[32] Although a passionate plea, no Jesuits established themselves among the Quapaws, nor any other Indian nation south of the Illinois at that time. The Jesuits instead enjoyed the permission granted to them by Saint-Vallier in 1690 to work among the Illinois and their *circonvoisines*.

The Québec government had its own opinion of missionary service throughout New France, but more particularly toward the Jesuits' efforts in the Pays d'en Haut. While considered a formidable missionary, the Perigueux native Pierre-François Pinet "fell under the displeasure of the irascible Cadillac by denouncing roundly from the pulpit the prevalent traffic in strong drink and the resulting ruin to his Indian flock." Although Pinet had just established his mission of L'Ange-Gardien among the Miamis at Chicago in 1696, hardly one year later Governor Frontenac ordered it closed because of Pinet's fiery sermon and the Jesuits' strict adherence to assimilation rather than Frenchification.[33] In an impassioned letter to Laval during Saint-Vallier's absence, Father Gravier, *Grand Vicaire* of the Illinois missions, asked Mgr l'Ancien for his help with this matter. Within the year, Pinet was reinstalled in his Chicago mission.[34] More importantly, Laval demonstrated that when he could help his Jesuit brothers, he was quite willing to do so. Gravier's letter, written from his Illinois mission, passionately spoke of the Jesuits' fondness for Laval.

This is your mission, Monseigneur, since she is under the protection of the Immaculate Conception of our Holy Mother. You chose her feast day for your ordination, and you chose her as the patron of our diocese. Father Marquette could do nothing more fitting for you than to place the Illinois mission under the protection of the Immaculate Conception of our Holy Mother. And because you have always been the father of all of our missions, Monseigneur, you are particularly attached to this one because . . . of the beautiful gift you gave to it . . . the *Ciborium*. . . . It is a great treasure since you had to melt down all of your silver vessels to make it. It will remain an infinite treasure, and nothing will ever be as highly esteemed in our mission . . . within it are all of your silver vessels including a small cup, only used at the holy altar, and one should not use it in any other way lest one profane it. As the number of communicants increases in this mission, the number who pray to God before this beautiful *Ciborium* that holds the Savior of the world will increase as well. . . . I can say nothing more consoling to our Fathers among the Ottawas, amid the persecutions that we suffer, than to assure them that you are doing well, that your prayers remain with us, and that we live with the gentlemen of your Seminary in perfect union, and that you consider us always, Monseigneur, as your children.[35]

When Saint-Vallier returned to Québec in 1697, everyone praised the peace and charity that existed within the religious community. Glandelet was certainly pleased with the rejuvenated and conciliatory Saint-Vallier: "I tasted what you told me; that God, all good, takes pleasure in establishing his work by paths that seem to lead toward its destruction. We see some proof of this in what has happened here, where one thought that the return of the person you know about [Saint-Vallier] would continue with trouble and division more than ever. However, what has arrived is a pain-free, perfect reunion with those whom he seemed to have divided. Only God could have done this."[36] Tremblay was hopeful to see the newfound collegiality continue as well and offered to do all he could to ensure that this charity and peace did not fail. Otherwise, if it did, he "would be the most miserable of all men."[37] Indeed, Saint-Vallier "wanted absolutely to end all division and wanted to interact with the Séminaire de Québec and above all Mgr l'Ancien in ways he never had."[38]

Aside from promising to improve relationships, Saint-Vallier had other requests to honor, notably the Seminary's desires to "allow it the freedom to carry out its essential functions, such as the education of children, the formation of young seminarians, and missions," and specifically to "go toward people that no missionary had yet to evangelize."[39] Saint-Vallier's diocesan overseer, François de Montigny, played a distinct role in the latter. Likely he had read writings by such Jesuits as Marquette, Gravier, and even Allouez, whose tantalizing comment that "all the nations of the South have this same wish to see God" caught the young priest's fervent attention. Even Father Paul Le Jeune's cry—"the harvest is abundant, but the laborers are few . . . the cry is raised on every hand, send aid; save bodies and souls"—must have influenced de Montigny, not to mention the Séminaire.[40]

Convinced of the need to Christianize Native communities, come May 1, 1698, Saint-Vallier granted the Séminaire a *lettre patente* that gave them exclusive permission to establish missions along the Mississippi. The *lettre patente* permitted the missionaries to move southward and "to establish themselves in the areas they judge the most proper, exhorting them with all our power to make solid establishments and missions where they can send, over the following years, missionaries of their body without permitting other bodies to make establishments in the same area without their consent." The *Grand Vicaire* of these missionaries would have "power to revoke and restrain powers and privileges [of other missioning groups] as they deem appropriate for the good of our work in this region."[41]

The goal of the Seminary missionaries was to work where the Jesuits did not reside, where "the Jesuits could not complain."[42] But choosing to go to nations the "furthest away and abandoned to work toward the salvation and conversion of these poor people" still necessitated working in a community closer to Québec so as to ease communication between the Séminaire and the more southern villages. De Montigny suggested establishing a mission among the Tamarois, the first community on the Mississippi and just to the south of the Jesuits' Illinois efforts.[43] Consequently, the Seminary leadership, along with Laval and Saint-Vallier, poured over regional maps. They consulted people knowledgeable of the region in question, including the Jesuit Father Joseph Germain. In the absence of the Jesuit superior, Father Jacques Bruyas, Germain remarked that "no Jesuit had to this point ever written to him about this location" and subsequently "that the Tamarois were not a part of their missions; there was no establishment there."[44] With that, Saint-Vallier prepared a second *lettre patente* and designated the Tamarois as the Seminary's focal point for a coordinating mission on the east bank of the Mississippi.[45]

With the *lettres patentes* completed, Saint-Vallier appointed de Montigny as the *Grand Vicaire* (or *Vicaire Général*) of the Mississippi missions.[46] De Montigny quickly gathered together twelve men—various blacksmiths, hunters, paddlers, carpenters, and trained brethren—to help the missionaries finalize preparations for their journey and to subsequently travel with them into the vast wilderness. Some were to be paid with goods, others with money, still others, nothing beyond sustenance, a form of "*donné*" similar to indentured servitude whereby the men provided upright and steadfast services as craftsmen or laborers in exchange for food, clothing, and care. Expectations were interwoven into their work. All had to follow particular spiritual practices while employed by the Séminaire. There was "no toleration for anyone who is scandalous, quarrelsome, a drunkard, a curser, or free with words." For any *engagés,* taverns were "forbidden to them as well as excursions at night." Even when dining at the Séminaire, the directors assigned an individual to watch over them as they ate to ensure that no food was wasted.[47]

Of the twelve men hired, the first two resided in Batiscan, where Father Nicolas Foucault served as the curate for some ten years. Although Foucault was not a part of the first wave of Seminary priests to descend the Mississippi,

Claude Rivard *dit* Lorenger (age thirty-five) and Jacques Rouillard (age twenty-six) certainly knew him, having either attended or participated in Mass, baptisms, weddings, or funerals officiated by Foucault. Indeed, François Lorenger, the first child of Claude Rivard and his wife, Catherine Roy, was baptized by Foucault on June 5, 1697. Both Rivard and Rouillard were charged to help transport the missionary entourage from Montréal to Michilimackinac, whereupon they were to leave the expedition. Although their contract did not mention a salary, they were promised "sustenance in the form of biscuits, salt pork, peas, and six pots of *eau de vie* each for their own use."[48]

Fezeret and Guibault were next on the list of workers. René Fezeret, the father, was fifty-six years old. His son, Jean-Claude Fezeret *dit* Guibault, a twenty-five-year-old blacksmith in Montréal, promised "to go with de Montigny to the missions and to bring his forge." He further promised "to serve for free for two years," after which de Montigny "would do his best to grant him land" along the Mississippi. However, neither continued the journey beyond Michilimackinac. René returned to Québec to his wife, Marie Carlie, and to numerous children born before his departure. Guibault never returned to Québec but died in the Louisiana territory, "killed and maimed in the king's service."[49]

Luckily for the missionaries, de Montigny hired two men who knew the Mississippi well and could help the missionaries obtain sustenance along the journey. André Hunault was forty-one years of age when hired. He served at Fort Frontenac in 1677, among the Illinois in 1680, and then two years later accompanied La Salle to the mouth of the Mississippi River. Joseph Charbonneau, thirty-eight years of age, was also an experienced traveler who served with a group led by de Tonti that went in search of La Salle after his ill-fated attempt to find the mouth of the Mississippi from the Gulf of Mexico. Both Charbonneau and Hunault received the same contract: they were to "faithfully serve de Montigny and the priests for two years beginning the day of departure." In addition, each received 500 livres per year for their work.[50]

A more curious name on the list was Perrot. Saint-Cosme identified him as "the son of Nicolas Perrot," presumably the famous interpreter and adventurer. This lad was to receive 500 livres per year. Of all of his sons, the most likely "Perrot" was young Claude, who was fourteen years old at the start of the missionaries' journey. Unlike his older brother Michel, Claude's absence from church registries and judicial proceedings provides some evidence that he was not in the Québec region between July 1698 and May 1704.[51] Whichever Perrot this was, his contract was prepared on June 2, 1698, by the notary Antoine Adhémar, but without specific terms other than his salary.[52]

Charles Rochon (Rocheron) also accompanied the men. He was the son of Simon Rochon and Mathurine Buisson de Saint-Cosme, aunt of Father Saint-Cosme. Thus, the missionary and Rochon were first cousins. At the age of twenty-five, Rochon was considered an honest, solid young man. As soon as he was hired, he placed his affairs in order and shared his possessions with his father, his parish church, and his young goddaughter. For his work, Rochon received 200 livres the first year and then 300 livres for each of the following years.[53]

The remaining four men included Father Davion's domestique, St. Martin, as well as a man by the name of de la Source. Both received 150 livres in advance, while de la Source was later given ten pounds of vermillion, twenty-one pounds of powder, five pounds of beads, and two dozen pocketknives. Another gentleman by the name of Charles Dumont served de Montigny and then later Father Davion.[54] Finally, Frère (Brother) Alexandre Romain Turpin, twenty-eight years of age and a devout member of the Institut des Frères Hospitaliers de Saint-Joseph-de-la-Croix, otherwise known as the Frères Charron, participated as well. While Alexandre received no payment, his devotion and service fully supported all others on the journey, particularly when they were ill. After the missions were chosen, Alexandre returned to Montréal, professed his *voeu de stabilité* (his vows) on July 27, 1704, and served among the Hospitaliers de Saint-Joseph until his death on August 9, 1747.[55]

Prior to his departure for the Mississippi, Frère Alexandre, like Rochon, set up his will and testament. He requested that he be buried at the chapel of the Frères Hospitaliers, that 1,000 livres be given to his sister, Marie, and that his furnishings be given to the poor.[56] Leaving a will was not unusual. Whenever an expedition was planned, explorers and *coureurs de bois* were never certain of their return. Oftentimes they placed their secular and spiritual affairs in order with the assistance of a notary. Typically, they offered a sum of money for Masses to be said for the repose of one's soul, and designated their property to family, friends, and/or organizations.[57]

Before the journey could begin, the missionaries also had to obtain a passport from the Governor of Québec to descend the Mississippi. Frontenac was particularly pleased that both Saint-Vallier and Laval were working together, and that peace held in the diocese for the first time since Saint-Vallier's elevation to the bishopric. To support this newfound energy of good will and solidarity, Frontenac gave the Séminaire de Québec an official passport that "permitted these missionaries to leave from Montréal [and] to go to Michilimackinac whenever ready in four canoes which will be led by twelve men whose names were given to us. From said place, to continue their route to the Mississippi River, allowing these missionaries to embark with food and other items they need to sustain themselves and to establish themselves." Because clergy working outside of Québec could not engage in economic ventures, such as the fur trade, the passport included a clause that "there are no other human interests or intentions among these gentlemen missionaries. They are only filled with the pure glory of God and the desire to spread the faith to all who are under our domain." All those whom the missionaries encountered along the journey were thus asked "to let them surely and freely pass and repass, these missionaries, their crew, and their four loaded canoes, without barriers."[58]

Lettres patentes, men, and passport in place, the Seminary missionaries had to prepare themselves for a difficult life that was never limited to what a priest might do under "normal" circumstances. Each man faced working hundreds of miles away from European civilization, "with no conveniences, no provisions, and most frequently with no resources but the liberality of the people who know not God, compelled to live like them, to pass whole years without receiving any tidings of his country."[59] The missionaries were soon to enter a region with no knowledge of the Native peoples' languages and cultures, not even sure among which Native communities they intended to serve. They only knew the life of a parish priest in Québec. And yet, those most deeply committed believed they were a part of a "glorious enterprise," with promises of abundant returns, provided they themselves offered up sweat and blood, day in and day out.[60] To support themselves spiritually and emotionally, each missionary had to be active, humble, faith-filled, detached, prayerful, reflective, charitable, and patient, yet zealous in his service to those without knowledge of Christ. They had to attract the Native peoples to Christianity and somehow demonstrate to them that they already had a "hint of God" within their own spirituality.[61] In short, these men had to prepare for "a life filled with thorns and roses," for "if one wished to make missionaries, you literally had to make them saints, otherwise they would do very little or nothing at all."[62]

Like the Jesuits, the Seminary missionaries committed themselves to a spiritual life and regimen to support their ministry. Elements of many Catholic organizations, including the Jesuits, played a part in their regular, contemplative spirituality that was enriched by prayer and devotion, piety, obedience, poverty, chastity, and charity. However, unlike the Jesuits, missionary work was new for these chosen men. None had any previous exposure to the wilds of the Mississippi terrain, nor to a rustic life far from their more modern comforts. Other than Saint-Cosme, who escorted a group of Mi'kmaqs to Fort Nashwaak on Acadie, and had resources provided so as to sustain himself on the journey, the remaining missionaries had no known instruction or experience in camping, food preparation, agriculture, or construction. Consequently, they would have to rely on the talents of Rivard *dit* Lorenger and Rouillard for transportation, Hunault and Charbonneau for hunting, and all others for protection and additional daily concerns. As for their spiritual and vocational sustenance, the Québec seminary leadership developed its own Mississippi advisory document that professed to assist these men with the enormous task before them, with conformity crucial to helping them in their work.[63] This was to be their "way of proceeding."

New directives in hand, the Seminary missionaries were advised to be faithful to their spiritual practices, meditation, short and ardent prayers, a spiritual reading, and the *examen de conscience,* "things that they must never omit and that will internally support them in their work." Part of this included never omitting the rosary, "the most beautiful and most useful of all the devotions when well said," and remaining devoted to the holy scriptures, ensuring that they helped the internal while working on the external. With God's presence within one's heart and soul, a deep sense of faith and trust was the anticipated result, leading one to feel that nothing was impossible.[64]

Each missionary also had to be mindful of his demeanor and had to "lead by good example and words . . . so as to preserve others from the corruption of sin." They had to support each other and maintain "vigilance over their actions, and words, which must be pleasant and modest in order to not scandalize the weak but lift up all." This included "being charitable . . . toward missionaries of other bodies." Chastity had to be maintained as well, so as "to give not a single shadow of suspicion or scandal to anyone." A strong sense of decorum was a must since individuals from all walks of life—French soldiers, Jesuits, *coureurs de bois,* and Native peoples—often deeply challenged missionaries and their efforts within their missions. Adjustment was encouraged, in fact, the "most important advice of all . . . to know how to adapt based on the example of Jesus Christ." Being able to rework one's strategies to new situations and new individuals was their best hope in maintaining charity on the Mississippi. After all, they, like the Jesuits, were there "to advance His glory and to save souls, a task that cannot succeed if missionaries do not maintain perfect intelligence between themselves."[65]

The missionaries were also "obligated to take reasonable care of their health and to conserve it for the glory of God . . . to avoid a bad spirit that can ruin a missionary and make him useless, to prefer the light of others to one's own [since] obeying is more agreeable to God than sacrifices." While expected to take care of themselves so as to maintain their strength, the juxtaposition of a sense of health care with the harshness of their surroundings was all the more magnified by the life of poverty expected of them on the Mississippi. Each missionary was to use his items according to the intention of the superiors of the Seminary and was to "share possessions according to their needs and the proportions of items owned in order to guard a spirit of poverty . . . [to] only ask for necessary items so as to not wrong others." Since funds were short, the expectation was that each missionary would possess only what was of absolute necessity.[66]

Finally, each missionary had to obey his leader along the Mississippi. "They were not to choose the place of their missions," but instead could "only go where sent by their superior." Commitment to one's mission was crucial so that each man could adequately learn his community's Native language, come to understand some elements of their culture, maintain consistency in teaching Christianity, and develop a trusting relationship with those with whom he lived. If such a commitment was not adhered to, any possibility of advancing Christianity within a given village was heavily compromised.[67]

While their rule of life required daily religious and spiritual practices, their spirituality also had to reflect qualities of the human spirit, including compassion, patience, tolerance, forgiveness, love, and responsibility. And as the document itself suggested, they had to adjust "based on the example of Jesus Christ." This, in fact, gave them the capacity to transform, to potentially step into a middle ground with their respective flock, to find new meanings and new ways of proceeding if they opened themselves to such possibilities.[68] Most certainly, with the enormous challenge before them, the Mississippi missionaries had to realize that they were powerless without God. Each had to be motivated by their profound faith, not by adventure or discovery, and had to find their source of strength and sustenance in God with the conviction that "the Christian faith is a precious gift that they have a duty to spread among populations which, up to that time, have been deprived of access to the 'true religion.'" In short, the missionary had to be prepared spiritually, mentally, physically, and emotionally while understanding that "the Mission is clearly not an ordinary human undertaking, but the work of God with its own element of mystery."[69]

The rhetoric here seems little different from that of the Jesuits, but the largest variance boils down to a question of education and preparation. While the Jesuits often spent years preparing to work within a particular region—learning the language and culture of select Native peoples—the Séminaire's advisory document offered no such advice or encouragement. For that matter, the whole venture was pulled together in less than three months. None of these Seminary missionaries had ever served in a Native village. All they understood was the life of a parish priest and the strict moral standards expected of their parishioners. None, perhaps with the exception of Saint-Cosme, had any previous direct interaction with a Native community, or had ever attempted to learn elements of a Native language. Somehow these Seminary missionaries had to transform from understanding life based on daily functions surrounded by French men, women, and children, and with immediate access to supportive authority and personal goods, to understanding life within a Native community hundreds of miles from Québec.

Although the bishop supported the Séminaire in its quest to work among the Mississippi's Native peoples, he, along with the Seminary leadership failed to fully comprehend the needs and costs for such an undertaking. Two months after the missionaries departed for the Mississippi, Saint-Vallier and Laval wrote letters to Jérôme Phélypeaux, Comte de Pontchartrain, Madame de Maintenon, and the bishop of Paris seeking their help in securing funds from the king. In particular, they cited their "perfect knowledge that there are several million souls who unfortunately perish without salvation and knowledge of Christ." In writing these letters, Saint-Vallier and Laval hoped that "a court as full of piety and religion" as the king's would "want to embrace the interests of so many poor souls." But within the letter the two *prélats* also voiced concerns for the entire enterprise: "Unless the king can give us an annual fund to sustain this work, it will be impossible for the Séminaire des Missions Étrangères de Québec to continue what it has begun."[70]

Curiously absent from this list of recipients were Tremblay and the Séminaire in Paris. The two bishops seemed to have bypassed their Paris colleagues, perhaps fearful of Tremblay's hard stance on spending, or even that the Paris leadership might put a stop to their proposed venture altogether. In 1695 alone, the ever responsible Tremblay was so driven to ensure the Séminaire's survival in Québec that he implored its leadership to vigilantly watch over their funds: "We must work to maintain stability as much as we can; five or six years of savings will help."[71] Tremblay, who often wore his anxieties on his sleeve, pleaded with the Séminaire de Québec to be mindful of their spending: "Perhaps you may complain about the decrease in paying your bills and the decisions that I made, but put yourself in my place and consider the difficulties that arise when one must always use credit, purchase more expensive things, and eat more than one's revenue and in advance. I believe I will be worse off next year."[72] Such a request was well founded given that France itself was suffering from its own miseries while at war: "Money is rare, bread, and other foodstuffs. One says the enemy is suffering less than we are."[73]

The Séminaire in Paris certainly had its own struggles. In 1696 alone it funded missionary work in many regions of East Asia and thus had to sacrifice its own spending to survive: "Our Seminary [in Paris] is currently so reduced that we hardly have eleven people present, all so busy that there are no longer any great Masses except for the four Holy Masses of the year; no more conferences, no more recitations of the Breviary. It is a pity."[74] But Laval seemed to have forgotten that any major decisions that jointly involved the Seminaries in Paris and Québec had to be approved by the Séminaire in Paris. For it is true that after all was said and done, finding funds for the Mississippi missions proved difficult. The Séminaire de Québec itself scolded Laval regarding the financial situation at hand, remarking that one seeks "on all sides to ask for money that one does not have." The Séminaire was stretched thin, "involved in so many extraordinary expenses" that it was already "indebted to those from whom one might otherwise borrow money." They had done all they could to stay afloat; they "turned in all directions to find some door to leave from, but one has not been found."[75]

Requesting funds from the king after the venture had begun was risky. Even more remarkable was the fact that the Paris Seminary only "learned of this adventure at the end of 1698." The Paris leadership was stunned at the haste with which the Québec missionaries departed for the Mississippi, "astounded" that they "began this enterprise before seeing if those who were

charged by the king to find the mouth of the Mississippi River succeeded."
They had great "difficulty understanding how, as prudent as you [the Séminaire de Québec] otherwise are, you became involved in such an expensive
undertaking the success of which remains uncertain."[76] Tremblay certainly believed that their hasty advancement was ill-advised, "to trust that the court
would fund this undertaking without assurances of possessing the land."[77]
Not to mince words, Tremblay exclaimed: "You took this on, you take care of
it."[78] But it was too late to wallow in the past, for there were men and missions
to care for. Even as late as 1712, some fourteen years after the departure of the
missionaries for the Mississippi, Tremblay's anger toward the hasty decision
lingered: "I assure you, sirs, that you threw me into great troubles when you
took on these missions and when you threw them on my back without you
yourselves wanting to be a part. Thus, it is you that this reflects and not me."[79]

The king initially refused to fund the venture altogether, as he was "charged
with other expenses for Canada and could not increase his offerings."[80] No
doubt grappling with what lay before him, Tremblay himself went before the
king on behalf of the Séminaire de Québec and, beginning in 1700, gained
a royal pledge of 3,000 livres a year for the missions, two years after the first
missionaries left for the Mississippi. And yet, over the course of the next three
years, efforts to sustain and send additional missionaries down the Mississippi
required some 20,000 to 25,000 livres "to equip them, feed their canoers, and
give them what they needed to subsist for several years in the region," all without accurate accountings of the money spent. The king supported the Mississippi effort throughout the first fifteen years of the eighteenth century, but
his allotment never increased, nor was it consistently received. Tremblay had
to reach out to Iberville early on to provide the missionaries with "1,000 or
1,200 livres of clothing, vestments, and other provisions to help them."[81] Even
some twenty years later, he had to find resources to support Davion once the
king's support ceased altogether. The ever responsible *Procureur* felt the heat
from all sides, as the lack of funds affected every missionary on the Mississippi
for years to come. Unfortunately, monetary requests and refusals, appeals for
patience, and knowledge of Iberville's own venture all took place after the
missionaries had left Québec. De Montigny, Saint-Cosme, and Davion were
already headed for the Mississippi at an initial cost of some 10,832 livres, 4,030
of which were covered by the personal funds of Saint-Vallier, Davion, and de
Montigny. There was no turning back.[82]

By the end of the seventeenth century, the Jesuits had long paved the way for missioning activities throughout New France, with decades of missionary work completed. For the Séminaire de Québec and its missionaries, 1698 began and ended with great, yet uncertain promise for their own efforts to Christianize Native communities along the Mississippi. Davion, de Montigny, and Saint-Cosme had their *lettres patentes,* their passport, as well as their twelve men and supplies. They were provided with spiritual norms and obligations, and on some level had their own internal and external motivations that brought them to this tremendous undertaking. Meager funds helped them begin their trek to the Mississippi with sincere hope that additional monies would later trickle in. On July 16, 1698, these ecclesiastical pioneers left Québec to firm up their preparation for their descent of the Mississippi. Passport in hand, preparations finalized, the party of men began their transformation from priests to missionaries as they left from Lachine, Canada, on July 26, 1698, in four birch bark canoes.[83]

CHAPTER 4

First Encounters and
Final Choices

On July 26, 1698, Fathers de Montigny, Davion, Saint-Cosme, and the twelve men who took on roles as *engagés, domestiques,* or *canotiers* left from Lachine, Canada, to travel to the Mississippi River. This extraordinary opportunity to explore realms of the Québecois diocese seen by very few seemed perfect for quenching the Frenchmen's thirst for adventure. For the priests, their desire to spread Christianity among those who did not yet know Christ was finally underway. But little did they realize that they were about to experience an "exploration of accommodation and social change." They were headed toward a region of uncertainty whereby villages combined with villages, nations with nations, and cultures with cultures to overcome loss due to warfare, illness, and starvation. Soon enough, first observations, encounters, and interactions between the Seminary missionaries and various Native communities would lead to the creation of new missions as well as unanticipated ways of seeing or interacting with the world.[1]

Enthusiasm is perhaps an understatement. These priests were literally leaving for the rest of their lives to serve among Native communities they did not yet know, intending to utilize strategies they did not fully have in mind. But not one day into the journey, the Frenchmen realized that their ambitiously filled canoes were far too heavy to continue. Rivard *dit* Lorenger and Rouillard themselves transported "1,000 pounds of goods . . . 400 pounds of lead, 100 pounds of powder, three chests weighing 200 pounds," as well as other bundles and goods weighing almost 300 pounds. De Montigny additionally transported 288 pounds of peas, salt pork, and flour obtained from the Seminary farm on Ile Jésus. Conscious of difficult terrain on the horizon, not to mention dozens of portages along the way that demanded each to carry hundreds of pounds of supplies over rocks, through forests, and eventually across treach-

Image of a portage, the carrying of goods and canoes across land to avoid rapids, ice, and shallow river sources. *Portage de la Rivière Cachée, St. Maurice, Canada, 1837,* by Phillip John Bainbrigge, 1817–1881. Courtesy Library and Archives of Canada, Acc. No. 1983-47-107, Reproduction copy number C-011892.

erous ice, the Frenchmen abandoned some of their precious cargo and on this "26th of July, the feast day of Sainte Anne, we placed our journey under her protection, and we continued."[2]

As they began their voyage on the Ottawa River, the missionaries passed through the Chaudière Rapids, some forty leagues to the west of Montréal, and continued on toward Mattawan, the halfway point of the journey from Montréal to Michilimackinac. After conquering "a very dangerous small river . . . full of rapids with very difficult portages," they passed through Lake Nipissing, continued down French River, and finally "arrived on August 27 at Lake Huron, in perfect health, thanks be to God." In this first part of their journey they had passed through some thirty portages between Chaudière and the Great Lake, with many more on the horizon.[3]

After several days' travel across Lake Huron, the missionaries arrived at Michilimackinac on September 8, 1698.[4] There they met Jesuit Fathers Etienne de Carheil and Jacques Gravier, who warmly welcomed the Seminary priests to the Mission de St. Ignace. "They received us with all the charity and cordiality possible," wrote Saint-Cosme, "and helped us with all they could. Their good advice for the success of our voyage, the food they gave us—we owe them everything." Gravier was equally impressed with the Seminary trio. In a letter to Laval, he described how both he and Carheil "received these missionary servants with sincere and cordial joy." The Jesuits were charmed by "the good judgement, zeal, and modesty that Messieurs de Montigny, Saint-Cosme, and Davion have displayed in the discussions that we had together during the seven days they were here."[5]

It was during one of these conversations that the Jesuits told the Seminary priests that they were already established among the Tamarois, assuredly a disappointment to de Montigny, who subsequently promised to "not establish a mission among them." Alternatively, Gravier suggested that de Montigny serve among the Arkansas Indians, as "their work with this nation and other peoples who did not yet know God would benefit the Jesuits as well." Calling the Seminary priests "our true brothers," Gravier hoped his offer might encourage de Montigny "to convert the poor Quapaws and the other nations who do not yet know the true God," and otherwise keep his distance from the Tamarois.[6] Although de Montigny later offered to build a mission among the Quapaws, the Tamarois remained ever present in his thoughts.

Time spent at Michilimackinac proved helpful for the missionaries. Strong collegiality developed between themselves and the Jesuits, so much so that no hint of future strife between the two groups seemed possible. The missionaries also met Henri de Tonti, the experienced Mississippi explorer who had journeyed with La Salle to its mouth almost twenty years prior. De Tonti offered to accompany Saint-Cosme and his men to the Arkansas River so as to help them "pass through upcoming regions where the nations there present sometimes pilfer canoes that they encounter."[7] But de Tonti's offer "gave me some fear," wrote Saint-Cosme, for he was well aware that several years earlier "Gravier had reproached de Tonti for disrupting their work among the Illinois and for not reprimanding the bad behavior of his cousin, Deliette." Nonetheless, the Jesuits assured Saint-Cosme that "de Tonti had changed his conduct and that for several years he had served well [in the region]." Regardless of the Jesuits' favorable view of the Italian explorer, Saint-Cosme remained skeptical and would "see [if de Tonti continues with us to the Arkansas] once we get to the Illinois."[8]

De Tonti was not the only personnel concern for Saint-Cosme and his colleagues. Although pleased with Charbonneau and Hunault, who "were very good men who help us out a great deal," or Rochon, "who has always steered a canoe straighter than other men," some of their entourage proved intolerable, most especially those from Montréal, "who we may have to leave behind, but who boast themselves that they will leave us when they want." Particular problems arose from Guibault, the son of Fezeret: "When we hired him on at Montréal, several people reassured us that he was wise, although he did love to play tricks," wrote Saint-Cosme. But the priest and his colleagues soon learned from the Jesuits that Guibault "is one of the most famous *débauché* who has ever come here and that he had given them plenty of trouble."[9]

Although the Jesuits had moved west in part to distance themselves from such debauched souls, nothing could prevent roaming Frenchmen from infiltrating their missions. Even the military proved problematic for the Jesuits. Father Carheil described how the soldiers' various occupations included "gaming," "keeping a public tavern for the sale of brandy, wherein they trade it continually to the Indians, who do not fail to become intoxicated," moving from post to post "in order to carry their goods and liquors there," and finally turning the fort into a place "where the [Native] women have learned that their bodies might take the place of merchandise and be even better received than Beaver-skins." Carheil was quite aware of the Canadian soldiers' expertise and was certain that "if these sorts of occupations can be called the king's service, I confess that they have always rendered him one of those four services, but I have never seen any other than those four."[10]

Based on the fourth occupation alone, Carheil and the Jesuits viewed the open relationships between Native women and Frenchmen "as simple prostitution." But these men did not understand that in some Native communities, women, particularly those enslaved by a nation, had greater "freedom in engaging in sexual relations with Frenchmen." These young women were not prostitutes—they did not sell their bodies, nor did they solicit customers. Instead, as single women, they had the power to negotiate interactions with men on their own. Consequently, French/Indian sexual relationships went on to serve as a bridge to a middle ground, "an adjustment to interracial sex in the fur trade where the initial conceptions of sexual conduct held by each side were reconciled in a new customary relation." As we will see momentarily, sexual relationships and subsequent marriages between Frenchmen and

Illinois women strengthened ties between the two cultures. Such liaisons led to a middle ground of accommodation that enhanced security, economics, relationships, and spirituality.[11]

Knowing the disruptive nature of his countrymen, Saint-Cosme could only hope that "French vagabonds who fled into the woods against the order given not to come down from Québec do not come into our region and destroy everything."[12] Consequently, as witnesses to the poor influence of Frenchmen at Michilimackinac, whereby "hardly any Ottawa people prayed, this because of the poor example of the Frenchmen who are always here, who are almost all bad," the Seminary missionaries did rid themselves of Guibault. "It was better to pass up the convenience of a forge/blacksmith than to have a *débauché* with us. If a blacksmith is needed later on, we can get one."[13]

On September 14 the missionaries journeyed on foot from Michilimackinac to a nearby Ottawa village so as to access their canoes, which had been carried there, and continue their journey. Prior to their departure, the missionaries hired on a man named Nirgue for 135 livres and bid farewell to Rouillard and Rivard *dit* Lorenger, who had only contracted to paddle to Michilimackinac.[14] Once the missionaries reached their canoes, they entered Lake Michigan, skirted its northern side to avoid Iroquois threats to the south, and then stopped at the Ile de Detour (Summer Island), where they remained for six days, "tending nets, catching a great quantity of very good white fish, welcome manna, unlike game, which was lacking all along the coast." Departing on September 28, they moved into the Baye des Puants (Green Bay) and passed by Des Noquest (Bay de Noc) on their right. They planned to continue to the Jesuit mission of Saint François Xavier, located at the base of the bay at modern-day de Père, Wisconsin. Although the Wisconsin River was the fastest route to the Mississippi, the Fox Indians were not letting anyone pass toward the Wisconsin out of fear that they were headed to the Sioux, with whom they were at war. Consequently, the missionaries headed toward the Jesuits' Miami mission at Chicago.[15]

As they made their way southward, they paused at a Potawatomi village near modern-day Kewaunee, Wisconsin, to trade for needed supplies. On October 4 they passed another small Potawatomi village near present-day Manitowoc, Wisconsin, and journeyed on to Milouakik (Milwaukee), where they remained for a couple of days to rest and to take advantage of the abundance of duck and teal. October 11, they reached Kipikawi (modern-day Racine,

Wisconsin), just twenty leagues from Chicago. But as they made their final push toward the Miami village, near disaster struck: "All of a sudden, the wind arose on the lake and we had to go ashore just a half league from Chicago. We had a hard time landing and saving our canoes. We all had to jump into the water." Saint-Cosme and the others learned firsthand that "care must be taken along the lakes, especially Lake Michigan. With its low shores, one must land quickly when the waves arise. They become so high in such a short amount of time that one risks losing his canoe and all of his belongings."[16]

Since they were just a half league from Chicago, the missionaries went on foot to the Miami mission and soon met Jesuit Fathers Pierre-François Pinet and Julien Binneteau. As experienced at Michilimackinac, the missionaries were warmly welcomed by their Jesuit colleagues: "I cannot tell you Monseigneur the extent of cordiality and marks of friendship these Jesuit priests showered us with during the time that we had the great fortune to stay with them." Saint-Cosme was impressed with Pinet's Miami mission and "the labors and zeal of this holy missionary." Their house was set "on the banks of a small river with the lake on one side and a beautiful large prairie on the other." Within the village itself Saint-Cosme saw more than 150 huts, with an equally large village just a league away.[17] All he observed assured him that "a great number of good, fervent Christians will be the result." The shamans, "even the most opposed to Christianity, allow their children to be baptized," he remarked. But the Seminary missionaries' time within the Miami mission proved brief and somewhat disappointing. While de Montigny placed the population of the village as high as six hundred men, the missionaries "saw no Indians there."[18] Being mid-autumn, many were off hunting, a sure sign that those villages they visited along the next leg of their journey could be mostly empty as well. Aware of portages on the horizon, the missionaries left a cache of goods at Chicago under the watchful eye of Frère Alexandre and continued their journey toward the Mississippi.[19]

To this point, Saint-Cosme had spent most of his time writing of their laborious movements along the various waterways and likely had had little time to absorb what he saw. But once past Chicago, he began to describe the environment through which they traveled. Saint-Cosme and the others saw "prairies bordered by hills and beautiful woods full of deer." They encountered great quantities of all sorts of game, "so much so that one of our men, while taking a walk, amassed enough to provide us with an abundant supper and breakfast the next morning." Over the course of two days, Charbonneau killed several turkeys, geese, and a deer, which made them all "very glad to rest for a day and enjoy a good meal."[20]

A respite was well needed since the next several days proved hard and treacherous, with numerous portages, until they reached the Kankakee River on November 11. Once there, "we put all our baggage in the canoe, with two men paddling, while the rest of us went on foot." Again, Saint-Cosme described the ever-changing environment: "We slept next to the little Massane River [Mazon Creek] which flows into the Illinois. Here, we began to see bison" with fur so thick "that a lead ball cannot penetrate it." The next day, "two of our men killed four but they were so thin during this season that they only took the tongues." The emaciated bison likely forced the Miamis and other Native communities to travel farther away to hunt for healthier animals that could sustain them throughout the winter. Nonetheless, from this point to the Arkansas River, they saw bison nearly every day.[21]

In due course, the Séminarians made their way to Gravier's Mission de l'Immaculée Conception, which he had established among the Kaskaskias after 1690. At this mission along Lake Peoria, near de Tonti's Fort Pimitéoui, "there are now Indians," joyfully exclaimed Saint-Cosme. But so too was Father Gabriel Marest, along with Fathers Pinet and Binneteau, who, "not at all burdened with goods," had moved more quickly from the Miami mission westward. As before, the Jesuits received the Seminary missionaries well, "only saddened," remarked Saint-Cosme, "that we had to leave so soon due to freezing weather."[22] As a part of their hospitality, the Jesuits provided them with food and a collection of translated prayers and the catechism in the Illinois language to help them interact with those who spoke Illinois. With this gesture, "we showed them every possible attention and kindness," wrote Marest.[23]

Gravier's Illinois mission at Lake Peoria was comprised of Kaskaskias and Peorias, two groups of the greater Illinois nation that also included the Tamarois and the Cahokias. It was, Saint-Cosme believed, "the finest [mission] the Jesuits have from here up." Within the village, the Seminary missionary saw "many adults who have abandoned their superstitions and live as perfect Christians, who attend Mass and have married in the church." Although the village was said to contain at least eight hundred men, many were still absent, "dispersed, hunting down the banks of the River." Alternatively, the missionar-

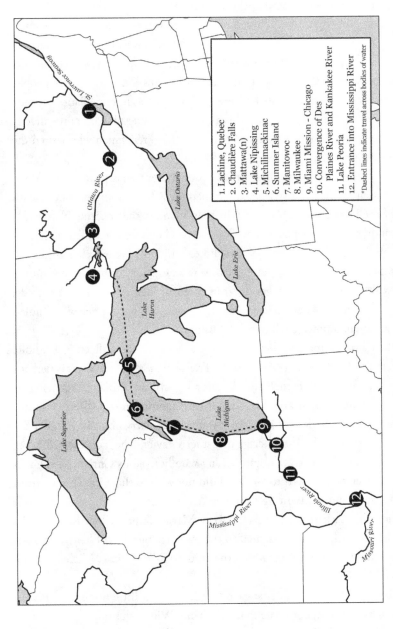

Initial descent of Davion, Saint-Cosme, and de Montigny toward the Mississippi, beginning late July 1698 at Lachine, Québec, and reaching the Mississippi on December 5, 1698. (Map developed by Maggie Bridges, Department of Geosciences, University of Arkansas)

1. Lachine, Quebec
2. Chaudière Falls
3. Mattawa(n)
4. Lake Nipissing
5. Michillimackinac
6. Summer Island
7. Manitowoc
8. Milwaukee
9. Miami Mission – Chicago
10. Convergence of Des
    Plaines River and Kankakee River
11. Lake Peoria
12. Entrance into Mississippi River

*Dashed lines indicate travel across bodies of water

ies saw "several women, married to Frenchmen, whose modesty and diligence at attending prayers in the chapel several times a day pleased us."[24]

Marriage between Frenchmen and Native women was not uncommon among the Illinois, as "alliances with Indian women were the central social aspect of the fur traders' progress across the country." Since French traders' success depended on their ability to interact proficiently with the Native people, oftentimes they married Native women, who served as intermediaries between the Frenchmen and the Illinois. This allowed the trader to work more directly with the village and assist as translators for other Frenchmen who visited the Native community.[25]

Marriage provided security, trade, nourishment, and protection. When Frenchmen married Native women, no matter if *à la façon du pays* (in the manner of the Native people) or in a Christian manner, they became Native kin, husbands, brothers, nephews, and fathers. This better secured alliance, friendship, and hospitality. Otherwise, Frenchmen without a Native relationship had no status within the village, and thus "were strangers without social standing . . . wealthy strangers, with goods far in excess of their own immediate needs, who stood virtually defenseless." In other words, "failure to marry an Indian woman often doomed a white man's business."[26]

The Christian marriage between Marie Rouensa, a very influential Catholic convert among the Kaskaskias, and the Frenchman Michel Accault is perhaps the best known of all French and Illinois relationships. Initially, this marriage was unwelcomed by Marie, for Accault was "famous in this Illinois country for all his debaucheries." When Marie was told to marry him, she refused. Being a Christian under the tutelage of Father Gravier, "she had resolved never to marry in order that she might belong wholly to Jesus Christ . . . she had already given all her heart to God and did not wish to share it." Thrown from her home for not consenting to marry Accault, deep strife ensued between Gravier, the Kaskaskias, and particularly Marie's father, Chief Rouensa. To end this discord, Marie consented to the marriage but only if her parents became Christians themselves, which they did do.[27] With time, Michel became a model Christian as well.[28]

Marriage *à la façon du pays* gave Illinois women little power and placed them in a position subordinate to the husband. Within this marriage tradition, adulterous women in particular potentially suffered severe abuse while adulterous men experienced few if any consequences. During the seven years he lived among the Illinois, the French officer Deliette witnessed "that more than a hundred women had been executed for adultery." Aside from death, adulterous women could have a nose or an ear cut off, or could even suffer gang rapes at the request of their husbands. At best, a wife's response to a husband's abuse or adultery was to call on male relatives to avenge any mistreatment endured. But a wife could also leave her husband and consequently divorce him whenever she chose to do so.[29]

Native women who married in the Catholic tradition, however, found a new alternative, a stronger voice that helped to promote monogamous relationships. Catholicism even offered the option of celibacy in "the narrow range of acceptable female behaviors among the Illini." The Jesuits taught the Illinois women about the Virgin Mary and emphasized chastity and virginity within their teaching. Consequently, some young women chose to embrace a celibate life and thereby empowered Christian doctrine within their society and otherwise diminished the powers of their elders or shaman. They controlled their own bodies and, as a result, "outraged both the young men, who found their own sexual opportunities diminished, and the elders and shamans who were directly challenged."[30]

Although Marie Rouensa initially fought to remain unmarried and to give her life to Christ, she used her Christian conversion "to assert control over her life." Conversion transformed Marie "into a public figure, and allowed her to challenge the authority of both her father and her French fur trader husband." Their marriage, in fact, created a middle ground that strengthened their relationship as well as that of the Illinois and the French. Through her Christian marriage, Marie "echo[ed] the Algonquian tenet that unmarried women were 'masters' of their own bodies." She gained control over her life and brought her family into the Catholic tradition. Gravier gained what he longed for as well—a monogamous Christian relationship, diminished promiscuity, and additional followers of the Catholic faith. Michel gained entrance into the Illinois society and increased his standing and access to trade, while the Illinois, as a whole, benefited from trade and greater security. The French and Illinois attained these goals without force, but with their own understandings that they put "to their own purposes."[31]

Father Allouez first reported on the Illinois Indians in 1666 when they arrived at his mission of Saint Esprit in the Pays d'en Haut. He described them as "the fairest field for the Gospel." Most encouraging to Allouez was their spirituality, that they "worship one who is preeminent above the others . . . because he is the maker of all things." As Allouez taught them of Christ, he found that "they honor our Lord among themselves in their own way, putting his Image, which I have given them, in the most honored place on the occasion of any important feast, while the Master of the banquet addresses it as follows: 'In thy honor, O Man-God, do we hold this feast; to thee do we offer these viands.'"[32] The Illinois treated the image of Christ as a *manitou,* the Illinois' spiritual connection with the environment that surrounded them. A *manitou* or spirit resided in anything and potentially everything—an animal, a rock, a plant, a bird, a fish, even a river. Each Illinois had a personal relationship with his or her *manitou* that they invoked in war, when hunting, journeying, sowing, or harvesting so as to protect or benefit the owner and promote success. The Illinois relied on these spirits to understand and interact with their world. Thus, the Illinois knew to handle all *manitous* with extreme care, respect, and awe. They knew the importance of giving to their sacred spirits.[33]

A great *manitou* for the Illinois was the sun. The Jesuits believed that "when they are instructed in the truths of our Religion, they will speedily change this worship and render it to the Creator of the Sun." But the Jesuits did not understand that such reverence did not transform laterally to reverence of the Christian God. The Jesuits did not see that balance and order were important to Illinois spirituality and were best maintained through reciprocity, a fundamental orientation of their world view that spoke to the interconnectedness of themselves with all that surrounded them and spoke to the mutual obligation of one for the other. As an Illinois invoked his or her *manitou* through some form of sacrifice, the expectation was a generous return of what was requested—bounty in hunting and/or harvest, success in warfare. Even within the sacred calumet ceremony, whereby a pipe of peace and other items were given to welcome the other into one's community and society, there was always hope for reciprocal benefit: a stronger alliance, peace, profitable trade. Alliance and balance were reinforced by passing the calumet from person to person: "it creates social communion; it joins all into a sacred circle."[34]

The Jesuits were certainly struck by some of the ways that the Illinois interpreted reciprocity in relation to Christianity. Marquette noted the Miami's homage to the cross: "I was extremely consoled to see a beautiful cross planted in the midst of the town, adorned with several white skins, red belts, bows and arrows, which these good people had offered to the Great Manitou (such is the name they give to God) to thank him for having had pity on them during the winter, giving them plenty of game when they were in greatest dread of famine." One woman prayed to God upon learning that her slave was killed by her brother. Rather than seeking forgiveness for him, the woman prayed to the Christian *manitou*: "Let [God] make my brother die . . . and I will be a good Christian." For the woman, this was an equal, "proper material exchange in an Illinois society that placed such importance on reciprocity."[35]

With these and other views of Christianity came "a vitality in their traditional culture that they effectively used to interpret Christianity." To be clear, the Illinois did not fully abandon their traditional way of life. Although Marie Rouensa had come to embrace Christianity, she still maintained Kaskaskian traditions of clothing, language, agriculture, and kinship, among others. Even upon her death in 1725, she asked that her will be translated from French to Illinois, likely evidence "that she continued to balance a variety of influences in the self-identity she constructed."[36] And yet, she transformed. Marie became a stronger woman, a power force in a culture more often ruled by men. Marie herself served as a translator and teacher. She entered huts, taught the women gathered, and empowered them to fight the institution of polygamy.[37] Those Illinois who were open to Christianity utilized select elements that fit best within their world view while they maintained their traditions and their spirituality. The priests welcomed these attempts to assimilate Christianity into the culture but always hoped that its acceptance might increase.

Saint-Cosme and his colleagues spent just three days in the Illinois mission. After chanting high Mass in honor of the feast of the Presentation of the Blessed Virgin, they commended their journey to her and then left the mission the following day. Several eager Frenchmen "who really wanted to go with us, partly because of de Tonti who is well liked, and partly because of adventure," also joined them. One Frenchman, Charles Delaunay, was very familiar with the Arkansas River. He had helped de Tonti build a house at Arkansas Post when established in 1686 and had already spent several years with the Quapaws. With knowledge of their language, he could help the missionaries interact with the Arkansas nation. Another Frenchman, Michel Bizaillon, joined them as well. He came to the region years earlier with Delaunay and Father Gravier and lived primarily among the Kaskaskias with his wife, Maria Thérèse, and their son, Pierre. Even Michel Accault chose to accompany the group south. Being married to the daughter of Chief Rouensa, he was considered an influential Frenchman along the Mississippi.[38]

The departure from the Kaskaskia village on November 22 coincided with the arrival of harsher conditions. Just to get out of Lake Peoria they had to "break the ice for two or three *arpents*." Once their travel eased, they reached the hut of Rouensa, "the most considerable of Illinois chiefs and a very good Christian," wrote Saint-Cosme. "He received us with honesty, not as an Indian but as an honest Frenchman. He took us into his cabin, asked us to sit, and gave us presents."[39] During their encounter, Rouensa cautioned the missionaries of violent warfare to the south, whereby the "Chaouanons, Chickasaws, and Kickapoos had attacked the Cahokias . . . they had killed ten men and took more than 100 slaves, women and children." His concerns were not just idle commentary but were clear warning of the warfare that existed throughout the region. Nonetheless, the missionaries understood that Native peoples could voice trepidations for other nations simply to keep Frenchmen from continuing beyond their villages.[40] Should Frenchmen move on to another village, they might find greater favor within the new community, while those left behind might lose an opportunity to make a deeper relationship with the foreign men, their goods, and their mysterious power. In a somewhat scolding tone, Saint-Cosme told Rouensa that he "should have no greater pleasure than to see other Native communities participate in the happiness he has enjoyed [as a Christian]. Thus, he is obligated to facilitate, as much as he can, the missionaries' designs [to go south]."[41] Saint-Cosme's "language of Christian judgement" showed the extent of his feelings for those who might try to stop their progress toward the south. He had a willingness to exchange in a reciprocal manner but was unwilling to be denied access to other Native communities.[42]

On November 23, after celebrating Mass with Rouensa and his family, the missionaries continued toward the Mississippi River. For several days the missionaries traveled across rivers of ice. Sometimes they walked, other times they jumped into the frigid waters to pull the canoes along. At one point, blocked from continuing, Saint-Cosme expressed no concerns: "We did not have to fast during our time on that river. All types of game were in great quantity: swans, geese, duck. The river is bordered by a line of very fine timber. It is not too thick, and one can quickly reach beautiful prairie land full of deer." Finally, on the Feast Day of Saint François Xavier, a "heavy wind broke up a section of the ice" and the missionaries continued on for another league. The following day they obtained "wooden canoes," and after having used them "to break up three or four acres of ice, up to four fingers thick," their route opened up considerably. On December 5 they reached the Mississippi River.[43]

Travel eased from their point of entry southward. The landscape provided new pleasurable scenery, such as high cliffs and riverbanks, islands, woods, hills, and bountiful provisions of bear, deer, and turkey—so many creatures in fact that they could pass by herds of bison without any need to kill one for food. When desired, with "bear and deer so numerous, we easily killed several with swords." The missionaries spent one night in a Cahokia village whose people "were still devastated by the attack made on them by the Chickasaws and Chaouanons." As the missionaries entered their village, "they all cried at our arrival," wrote Saint-Cosme. He and the others found them "to not be as mal-intent, nor as mean as the Illinois persuaded us that they were. We had more pity for them than fear."[44]

The next day, the missionaries arrived at the neighboring Tamarois village that "had received news of our arrival from some of the Cahokias." Not one year had passed since they "had had a run-in with de Tonti's men." Afraid, "all of the children and women fled . . . [while] the chief and several men came and met us along the river and invited us to their village." The missionaries initially declined the invitation so as to celebrate the Feast of the Concep-tion on the west bank of the Mississippi. But the next day, the group entered the village with de Tonti "and seven of his well-armed men." The missionar-ies "accepted the chief's invitation to his hut, where all of the children and women were present. We were hardly inside when the young men and women broke in a segment of the chief's hut so as to see us. For many, this was their first opportunity to see any Robes Noires [Black Robes] except for those who vaguely recalled Father Gravier's visit for a few days" several years earlier. Out of hospitality, the Tamarois gave the Frenchmen food to eat. Saint-Cosme and the others in turn reciprocated with "a little present as we had done with the Cahokias." The missionaries hoped to show them that they were sincere, that they "wanted to make an alliance with them." They needed their friendship so that their men "might be well received as they passed through; that they [the Tamarois] might provide them with food."[45]

In this first encounter with the Tamarois, the missionaries saw some six hundred warriors, all "camped on an island below their village to obtain wood . . . and out of fear of their enemies." As with other villages, many were off on the hunt, and the missionaries could not otherwise get an accurate accounting of their numbers. However, four months later, as the missionaries returned north to Chicago, they found the village to have "a population as large as that of Québec," wrote de la Source. By that point, the Michigamias and the Missouris had joined the Tamarois village, increasing its population to some eight thousand souls.[46]

Although nothing further was written on this first encounter between the Seminary priests and the Tamarois, a seed was planted. In sharp contrast to what Gravier had told them, there was no Jesuit establishment to be found. Without a visible Jesuit presence, Saint-Cosme felt certain that the Seminary missionaries could "establish a very fine mission" among the Tamarois. Nonetheless, despite promises made that they would have a missionary by springtime, no final decision to work among the Tamarois occurred during this first encounter.[47]

The missionaries' journey continued, and by December 12, just below Cap St. Antoine, they came upon a well-known bluff on the right bank "that projects out into the river . . . narrows the channel, makes the river turn very short, and creates a whirlpool that takes out canoes during high water." In recent years, some fourteen Miamis had lost their lives there. Consequently, those who passed through this Mississippi gauntlet "offered sacrifices to the rock to ensure safe passage." To provide their own symbol of protection, the Frenchmen climbed to its summit, planted a cross, chanted the *Vexilla Regis,* fired off three shots, and prayed: "May it please God that the Cross that has never been known in these lands triumph here, and that our Lord and Savior may abundantly spread the merits of His Holy Passion so that all the Indians may come to know Him and serve Him."[48]

As Richard White has stated, "any congruence, no matter how tenuous, can be put to work and can take on a life of its own if it is accepted by both sides."[49] Understanding the danger of this bluff line, both Native peoples and missionaries sought safety through some form of spiritual means. But the missionaries hoped that the congruent need for spiritual power could lead to prayer for safety through the Christian God and cross that towered above them and not simply through sacrifices to the spirit of the rock. Thus, they "acted for interests derived from their own culture" but also for interests of Native communities. The hope was that the presence of the cross would pull Native peoples toward faith in its Christian power and belief in the protection it could offer.

As they continued on toward the Arkansas River, the environment proved far different from what they had ever experienced in the north. The Frenchmen encountered new plants—fruit trees, cane, sweet-scented gum trees—and a distinctly different climate as well: "Once we were on the Mississippi, we no longer even thought of ourselves in winter. The further we descended, the more heat we found, although the nights were cool." Even the animals differed in this new region. Saint-Cosme caught sight of a pelican that was "almost as large as swan, with a beak as much as a foot in length, and an extraordinarily large throat that could hold as much as an entire bushel of corn." With much curiosity, the missionaries watched the pelican catch fish. It "places itself in a current and opens its mouth to gather in the fish and then stuffs them into its throat."[50]

On December 24 the men paused for two days to celebrate Christmas Eve and Christmas Day. At a place near modern-day Helena, Arkansas, the men built a small chapel and chanted high Mass at midnight. "All of our French participated," proudly exclaimed Saint-Cosme. The next day they celebrated Christmas Mass, followed later in the afternoon by vespers. But much to their surprise, an earthquake struck at one o'clock in the afternoon. Although it did not last long, all felt it. As they were within the region of the New Madrid Fault, such a geophysical event was not uncommon.[51]

After spending the night of December 26 at a former Quapaw village that was recognizable "only by its old outworks, for not a cabin remains," the missionaries encountered the Quapaws for the first time: "Seeing several wooden canoes along the riverbank, and a Quapaw standing next to them, one of the Frenchmen quickly grabbed a calumet and began to sing out of fear he would flee once he saw us. Hearing his loud voice in the nearby village, some fled, while several Quapaws came to the water's edge, calumet in hand. They approached us and rubbed our bodies and then themselves, a mark of esteem among their culture," wrote Saint-Cosme. "They then lifted us onto their shoulders and carried us to the chief's cabin. I sensed that the one carrying me would fall due to the muddy bank. I jumped off of his back and walked up the hill. But once at the summit, the Quapaw insisted I continue my hospitable ride to the cabin."[52]

The men had brought the calumet with them on their journey, for French and Native people alike understood that this powerful symbol served to display peaceful intent to those they encountered. Understanding full well its significance, the Quapaws hospitably welcomed Saint-Cosme and his men. While the missionaries were paraded into the village, "the Quapaws brought all of our goods to the chief's cabin and soon after came to sing the calumet for us. The next day, the Quapaws took us to a different cabin, where the three of

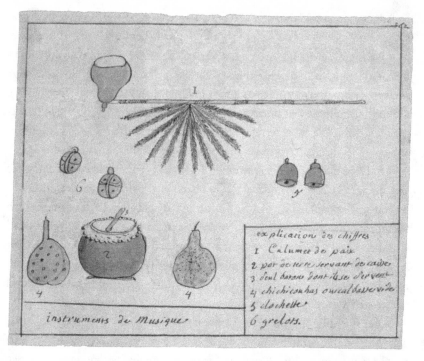

Instruments de Musique, by Jean-François-Benjamin Dumont de Montigny. Courtesy of the Newberry Library, Edward E. Ayer Digital Collection, Ayer MS 257, no. 16.

us and de Tonti sat on bearskins. Four chiefs each placed a calumet before us while others sang in rhythm to seed-filled gourds and skin-covered earthen-pot drums. This music was not the most agreeable. During this harmonizing, an Indian rocked us. We were soon put off by this ceremony, which they offer to all visitors they encounter." Although somewhat uncomfortable during this ceremony, Saint-Cosme nonetheless understood its importance: "It is necessary [to participate] if one does not want to come across as having a bad heart or bad designs. We put our men in our place after a while and they had the pleasure of being rocked all night. The next day, they gave us a little slave and some skins; we reciprocated with knives and other things which they highly prize."[53]

When Saint-Cosme and his colleagues stepped away from the ceremony, "someone had to participate or the alliance would not stand."[54] Thus, the placement of others in the missionaries' stead ensured that their developing alliance continued without disruption. More significantly, transformation was underway. By participating in the calumet ceremony, a middle ground was formed. The missionaries accepted the Quapaw tradition of welcome. In turn, the Quapaws brought these strangers into their society. The Frenchmen became fictive kin, fathers who entered "a superintending familial and fiduciary environment, where the duties of kinship, and the wants, needs, and deserts of the parties measured the obligations that each party owed."[55] The all-important balance needed in this first encounter became part of a social tie that strengthened the relationship of both cultures.

Balance, order, and unity were vital to Quapaw culture. Each person in their community participated in the life of their nation through membership in one of the two great moieties (tribal groups) that made up Quapaw society—the Sky People and the Earth People. The Sky People took care of the spiritual aspects of their traditions, while the Earth People took care of agriculture, fishing, hunting, and war. Shamans, religious figures who had undergone a long period of apprenticeship so as to be capable of transferring their souls into the spirit world, oversaw rites of passage, cures for illness, children's naming ceremonies, marriage and funeral rituals. In all instances, the shamans ensured that the power of Wah-Kon-Dah, the Quapaws' primary spiritual force, was immersed into the lives of the men, women, and children of their nation. Wah-Kon-Dah, a joining of male and female life forces, held everything in balance. All that surrounded them—the stars, the moon, the sun, animals, plants—possessed a spiritual quality, and provided guardianship, particularly when adopted as one's *manitou.* Even though one had a spiritual connection to a single *manitou,* this multi-faceted spirituality meant that not one power served as their guide, but a multitude to which they turned for hunting, fertility, agriculture, and the like.[56]

Regular ceremonies took place throughout the year in celebration of Wah-Kon-Dah's powers and gifts—the Green Corn Ceremony to give thanks for a good harvest; a planting ceremony to celebrate the beginning of growth anew; the calumet ceremony to welcome strangers and to establish relationship. Marriage also projected balance. A Sky person had to marry an Earth person so as to strengthen the presence of Wah-Kon-Dah within the heart of the community. This harmonized relationship between the two divisions "symbolized the productive power of male and female life forces and the continuity of the tribe through successive generations." Balance in the village was further maintained by a group of elders whose leadership abided by a system of equality without coercion. Warriors of the nation could listen to the chief but could also do as they pleased and not embrace his requests. As the Jesuit Father Pierre Vitry later wrote: "The Indian is independent and likes his freedom. If you press him for one thing, he will choose the other."[57]

Within the Quapaw village, the missionaries "planted a cross that we told them signified a union between us," wrote Saint-Cosme.[58] For the missionaries, the cross reconstituted the landscape to symbolize God's land, God's people. But the Quapaws saw it differently. Weeks later, when the missionaries returned north after having visited nations below the Arkansas River, they found the Quapaws utilizing the cross for their own purposes: "When they go to hunt, they do the same thing [plant a cross] . . . we found one that they had planted on the banks of the Mississippi." The Quapaws accepted the cross as a source of power, as another *manitou* to which they could turn for protection or gain, even as a show of alliance with the French. They did not look upon the cross as a purely Christian symbol or as a mark of European geographical usurpation. It was adoption for power, not Christian conversion or European possession.[59]

As Saint-Cosme continued to write of their encounter, his narrative turned somber as he and others felt a "deep affliction, finding these people, once so numerous, now entirely decimated by war and disease. Hardly a month had passed," wrote Saint-Cosme, "since they had rid themselves of smallpox which killed most of them. In the village, one saw all around graves where they were buried two together. We estimated that only 100 men remained, all the children were dead, and a large number of women as well." It was pure devastation since some ten years earlier "there were 1,200 warriors present," wrote de Montigny.[60] Even eight years earlier, when de Tonti visited the four villages of the Quapaws (Tourima, Kappa, Osotouy, Tongigua), he likely provided the "last picture we have of what might be called the unacculturated phase of Quapaw occupation."[61]

Despite his sympathetic words, Saint-Cosme at times judged the affability of the Quapaws as off-putting. He was particularly repulsed by the presence of a *berdache,* one of those "wretched souls," as he described him, "who from a young age dresses as a woman and serves for the most shameful of all vices." While Saint-Cosme did not understand the significance of this individual in the balance and integrity of a village, the region's Native communities certainly did, especially the Illinois, among whom such individuals held a fairly high position.[62] Marquette himself wrote of the mysterious nature of such individuals, that they never marry but "glory in demeaning themselves to do everything that the women do." These men could go to war but were only allowed to use clubs, not bows and arrows, "which are the weapons proper to men." The individual, more appropriately referred to as "Two Spirit" today, also participated prominently in ceremonies and dances, including the calumet ceremony. In any of these occasions, they could "sing, but must not dance," wrote Marquette. Whatever community they lived in, the Two Spirit was held in high esteem. As Marquette witnessed: "They are summoned to the councils, and nothing can be decided without their advice." These individuals were considered *manitous*, "spirits, or persons of consequence."[63]

Prior to European contact, a Two Spirit's position within his society demonstrated that all individuals of a community helped to maintain the balance so important to Native peoples. A Two Spirit was an individual who "was able to see the world through the eyes of both genders at the same time." For a Native community, such an individual was "a gift from the Creator."[64] Among the Winnebago tradition, the Two Spirit "was a man who had taken on this role because he had been directed to do so by the moon, a female spirit, at the time of his vision quest." As with the Illinois, a Two Spirit among the Winnebago "dressed as a woman, performed women's tasks better than any normal woman could perform them, and had the ability to foretell future events." Thus, the Two Spirit was "a highly honored and respected person." But European contact changed their status. By 1752, the French explorer Jean Bernard Bossu described these individuals as a disgrace, that some ran away while others, through success in battle, were given "a wife, that he might beget warriors."[65] The Winnebago "had become ashamed of the custom because the white people thought it was amusing or evil." Once the last known Two Spirit attempted to fulfill his role, his own brothers "threatened to kill him if he put on the skirt." To overcome their threat, the young man chose to wear a combination of male and female clothing so that he would not die if he "at least attempt[ed] to follow the directions given him in his vision of the moon." For many Native peoples, the Two Spirit became "something we want to forget and not talk about."[66]

Despite his criticisms, Saint-Cosme believed the Quapaws had a kind disposition and were extraordinarily honest. "They carried everything we had into a cabin where it remained for two days without anything taken or lost," he wrote. Even when a knife was left in a cabin, "a Quapaw at once brought it." To Saint-Cosme, the Quapaws were "the best formed I have seen, quite naked except in the cold when they wear a buffalo robe or some other animal skin. The women are partly naked, like the Illinois, and wear a deer skin over their shoulder."[67] Saint-Cosme's companion, de la Source, was equally impressed: "They are the best made, frankest, and best tempered men that we have seen. . . . They await a missionary in great impatience."[68]

Before continuing south from the Kappa village of the Quapaws, de Tonti and Bizaillon returned to the Illinois country, much to the chagrin of everyone. Saint-Cosme admitted that his initial fears of de Tonti never materialized, that all benefited from the Italian's ability to "secure friendship with some nations, intimidate others," and ensure safe passage as they descended the Mississippi. In a letter to Laval, Saint-Cosme described de Tonti as a brave man who "carried out the functions of a zealous missionary, accepting all of our views, and encouraging the Indians everywhere to pray and to listen to the missionaries. He soothed our servants and their petty issues, and by example backed up our devotional exercises when we could carry them out, and rather frequently attended the sacraments."[69] Laval and Saint-Vallier showed their indebtedness to de Tonti on behalf of the missionaries. They gave him letters of "compliment" and offered their support for him at court. De Tonti, in turn, praised the selection of the missionaries, ensured safe delivery of their letters and *mémoires* to Paris, and spoke highly of them at court.[70]

The relationship between de Tonti and Saint-Cosme began with suspicion and skepticism, particularly since de Tonti had been known as a man who failed to curb disruptive behavior between Frenchmen and Native peoples in some missions. Saint-Cosme, who was well aware of the problems associated with de Tonti and others, hesitated in accepting de Tonti's help. But with time and successful encounters and interactions throughout their journey, their openness to one another created a middle ground that united two vocational cultures that at first were like polar opposites. Saint-Cosme let go of his predisposed attitude toward de Tonti and found him to be a practicing Christian, a helpful explorer who safely navigated them through the Mississippi's waters and cultures. De Tonti, in turn, found these Seminary missionaries to be legitimate allies for befriending the Quapaws and other nations along the Mississippi. Both came to recognize the value of the other on the Mississippi.

After a night at the confluence of the Mississippi and Arkansas Rivers, the missionaries continued toward the Tourima village of the Quapaws at the mouth of the White River, some nine leagues to the south of the first Quapaw village encountered. As they approached Tourima, "six Indians met us with the calumet. They led us to the village, where we experienced the same ceremonies as we had during the last two days at the other village." Encouraged by the increase in numbers among adults and children alike, de Montigny and Saint-Cosme asked the Quapaws "to combine themselves into one village to better combat their enemies" and "to have a missionary." The Quapaws in turn "promised to work toward bringing the Osages to live among them." They further offered to build a house for the missionary visitors since "they will see us often."[71]

While the very hospitable Quapaws longed for a missionary, de Montigny felt it best to examine other villages and peoples further south before settling on the Arkansas nation. Quickly, he assigned Hunault, Charbonneau, and Perrot to remain among the Quapaws, while the missionaries hired on Pierre le Boeuf and Bourbonnais, otherwise known as Jean Brunet, son of François Brunet *dit* Bourbonnais, to journey south with them. Both men were paid some 200 livres. Before their departure, the Quapaws provided the group with a few provisions—a small quantity of smoked pumpkin and some dried squash—since the French otherwise counted on gaining sustenance via the hunt. But luck would not be on their side. As the men descended the Mississippi River, they encountered heavy rainfall. Despite "expecting to find game as usual," they found none. The rations provided by the Quapaws "did not provide us half a meal." By the time the missionaries arrived among the Tunicas, they were famished.[72]

The Tunica village lay some four leagues inland from the Mississippi, along the banks of the Yazoo, scattered into smaller communities. Altogether, there were some 260 huts throughout the region.[73] Although the Tunicas received them with an "indescribable joy," the missionaries saw nothing but desperation, as men, women, and children were suffering terribly from disease that had struck the village. Seeing such devastation, the missionaries immediately baptized several infants who were in danger of dying. They also baptized one of the chiefs after they taught him some of the mysteries of their faith through an interpreter. Given the Christian name Paul, the missionaries were certain that "during the little time we saw him, he spoke to us with a judgement and

the mannerisms of a very good Christian. We were amazed to see such sentiments in an Indian who had never been introduced to the light of faith. He
died not long after he was baptized."[74]

Sometimes, even after only one day of exposure to the Christian faith,
missionaries referred to select Native peoples they encountered as "very good
Christians." Shortly before arriving at Gravier's Illinois mission earlier in their
journey, they came upon two Native huts and were "consoled to see a perfectly good Christian woman" within one. Encountering Chief Rouensa after
visiting the Illinois mission, they too declared him a "good Christian."[75] But
while the Jesuits had worked within the Illinois region for some time, no missionaries had ever worked among the Tunicas. This Native community had no
experience with Christianity other than the teachings and baptisms quickly
introduced to them by de Montigny. A newly baptized Tunica man suffering
from illness—how did he so quickly earn the label "Good Christian"?

Among those Native communities they had already encountered, hospitality was a very real and important aspect of their culture. Actions and ceremonies that entailed welcoming the stranger, offering him food to eat, a soft fur
to sit upon, a calumet of peace to share, assistance up a muddy bank, caresses,
politeness, and affection were each deeply rooted within these communities
and represented their manner of proceeding with others. While one might describe such hospitality as Christian, one did not have to be Christian to utilize
these welcoming strategies with strangers. Engrained qualities of goodness and
hospitality among Native peoples were not what missionaries relied on to de-
fine these people as "perfect Christians." Instead, it was physical evidence that
similarly aligned with Christian gestures and verbalizations that likely caught
their attention.

Within the Catholic tradition, a priest would look for particular gestures,
movements, and various actions to outwardly demonstrate one's Christian
faith. But within Native spirituality, interactions with *manitous* and sacred
ceremonies also stressed performance—exterior physical expression, vital actions "that released the transformative power contained in ritual knowledge
and in relationships with *manitous*. Ritual action helped maintain balance
and order in the world."[76] Consequently, in those brief instances when missionaries saw physical evidence—holding the crucifix or bowing to the cross,
closing eyes as one heard prayer, even reciting words in a prayerful manner, or
lifting one's hands skyward—they could presume that Native individuals were

praying to the Christian God and thus were very good Christians. In truth, actions of bowing, closing eyes, praying, or holding a venerable object were just as equally Native as they were Christian.

Something attracted de Montigny to the Tunicas. Perhaps it was their outward display of devotion for his European faith, or their great need for help during a time of physical devastation. Whatever the influence, de Montigny immediately assigned Davion to live among them, thus making him the first Seminary missionary designated to serve in a Native community on the Mississippi River. Shortly after his assignment, the missionaries left Davion to his work and moved on to the Taensas village located near modern-day Lake St. Joseph, Louisiana, eighty leagues from the Arkansas, some one thousand leagues from Québec. De la Source described the Taensas as "humane and docile," while de Montigny remarked that the seven hundred souls present were "very gentle, quite welcoming, and with great esteem for the French."[77] Like other Native communities, reciprocity held great importance among the Taensas, as shown by the respect they had for gifts given to them. Upon accepting the Frenchmen's presents, they reverently carried them to their temple, "raised their hands to the sky, then placed them on their heads as they turned to the four directions," all in thanks to the spirits for these offerings. After this ceremony of thanksgiving, gifts were shared with the villagers.[78]

The Taensas' temple contained the eternal flame, grossly sculpted statues of men and animals, and several cases full of bones in honor of the most considered chiefs who had died. Death to the Taensas meant that the individual simply traveled to a far-away land. "This is why," de Montigny wrote, "they often cry when strangers enter their midst. They think of their deceased loved one [upon seeing a stranger]." When one dies, all relatives and friends bring precious items "to place in the grave," wrote de la Source. "One also places at the graveside flour and other foodstuffs in small baskets, gifts useful for them in the foreign country to which they go."[79]

The tradition of placing food at the graveside caught the attention of de la Source. In Christian culture, the dying gave goods to the living. Even de la Source's fellow travelers, Frère Alexandre and Rochon, willed their belongings to others in case of death along their journey. In contrast, the living among the Taensas gave gifts to the dead. Gifts of food at the graveside served to preserve their loved one in the beyond. And yet, a subtle congruence existed between the Taensas culture and Christianity. Catholics saw God's gift of eternal life as the only necessary offering to the deceased. God offered salvation, entrance into heaven to those who died. For both cultures, spiritually powerful gifts given at the time of death supported a joyful, filled afterlife.[80]

Missionaries often watched for similarities between Native peoples' spiritual practices and those of Christianity to strengthen attempts at conversion. Among the Taensas, potential congruences between Christianity and their spirituality included the Taensas' acceptance and thankfulness for gifts at the temple that echoed Christian peoples' thanksgivings and offerings in the church for the good of the community. The presence of an afterlife among the Taensas echoed the Christian heaven. For that matter, the worship of a personal *manitou* was not unlike the Catholic tradition of calling on one's patron saint to serve as "an intermediary for obtaining Heaven's favor." Within Christianity, this was the preferred route for prayer, for "a direct appeal to almighty God might be too audacious." An individual's particular saint "acted as their mediator with God."[81]

If the missionaries embraced such congruences, they could serve as "the basis for the creative re-expression of spiritual experiences."[82] But de Montigny and his men focused more on the dissimilar, particularly Taensas superstitions as they deemed them. Their large temple was covered "with snakes and other similar superstitious symbols," as well as with "a mural wall completely covered with skulls," wrote de la Source. "They did not want us to enter it, saying that those who did enter died." Nonetheless, de la Source and others "entered partway by force, partway by consent."[83] But more disturbing to the missionaries was the practice of sacrificing oneself upon the death of a chief. Taensas leaders were to be honored, to be treated with great veneration and respect. Just prior to the missionaries' arrival in the village, a chief had died, and numerous individuals, including some who "offered themselves as an honor to die with him," were sacrificed to accompany the chief into his afterlife. When the individual to be sacrificed was ready, "a certain root was lit and, once consumed, the assigned 'executioner' held the individual's head, which was then struck with several blows of a hatchet. One could also be strangled with a cord," wrote de Montigny.[84]

Missionaries questioned everything they saw that did not fit into their Christian world view. Long accustomed to combating the Huguenots and other presumed heretics in France, they often "cast a very negative eye on non-Christian religions" and were taught "to go in and 'save souls,' to deliver them from the darkness of error, to struggle against idolatry and paganism . . . to be on guard against heresies." The more superstitious the Native people appeared, the more the Seminary missionaries desired to transform them spiritually.[85] Consequently, viewing the Taensas as highly superstitious, de Montigny assigned himself to work within this community as well as with the Natchez, who were just twelve leagues to the south and spoke the same language as the Taensas. In his first encounter with the more southern nation, their chief "came to the water's edge . . . accompanied by some 200 men armed with bows and arrows. No women or children were with them because he [the chief] did not know if we came in peace or in war." De Montigny told them *"Robes Noires* [Black Robes] like us were not men of war, that we had not come to see them with such a mind-set. Instead, we exhorted all to live peacefully, something they would understand one day once I learned their language." Seeing that de Montigny and his fellow travelers were not a threat, the Natchez welcomed them to their village "with joy . . . and even though they made war with the Taensas, they provided us with a very good reception."[86]

The Natchez were the largest of the communities bordering the Mississippi. Their nation contained some ten to twelve villages that were widely dispersed within the modern-day state of Mississippi. Natchez spirituality was quite similar to that of the Taensas. They too had a great temple with a perpetual flame that was maintained by elders of their community. They also had hierarchical leaders who were honored, in death, by the sacrifice of individuals within their community. Just before the Seminary missionaries encountered the Natchez, the nation lost a chief for whom thirty individuals were sacrificed— a "foolish reaction," de la Source wrote. A Natchez chief later asked one of the missionaries' men: "If I were to die, wouldn't you like to die with me, giving you a great honor?" The unknown Canadian, with little hesitation, remarked, "I will die when I'm ready, but it is not in my design to follow the chief."[87]

By the end of January 1699, three southern nations—the Tunicas, the Taensas, and the Natchez—had been chosen to receive a missionary from the Séminaire de Québec. Within these three communities alone, the missionaries recognized significant cultural differences. But between the Tamarois region to the north and the more southern terrain, the men saw variation within the environment as well. In the deep south, temperatures and humidity soared: "There is never any snow among the Tunicas or Taensas or to the south . . . although being here from January 15 to February 15, the heat has been, and

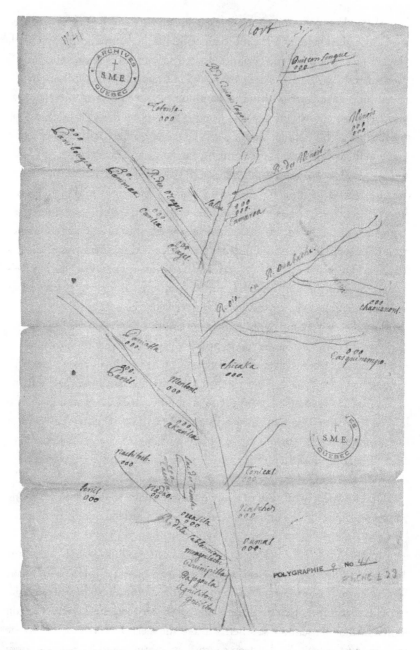

Map of the Mississippi River Valley marking the placement of Native communities along the river and its tributaries around 1700. Courtesy of the Musée de la Civilisation, fonds d'Archives du Séminaire de Québec, Polygraphie 9, no. 41.

I'm not exaggerating, as high as in Paris in the middle of summer," wrote de Montigny. "The grass is tall here, violets, peaches, and plums are in bloom." So plentiful were the peach trees that the Tunicas "cut some down." But creatures varied dramatically from those of the north as well: "There are a great number of crocodiles [alligators] in the Mississippi from the Arkansas down to the sea, and just as many along the rivers of the Arkansas, Tunicas, and Taensas. These rivers are full of fish which makes the alligators prefer to reside there." De la Source added: "The alligator is so great in number that you will see thirty together. He is the master fish, so frightening, made like a frog. I saw one that was as big around as half a barrel. Some, they say, are as big around as a barrel and twelve to fifteen feet long. I have no doubt they would swallow a man whole if they caught him." The *serpent à sonnettes* also caught de Montigny's fascination: "There are also a large number of rattlesnakes whose poison is subtly strong. They don't attack anyone unless you don't take care when walking through tall grass or cane and step on one. If you don't have any type of remedy, it kills you." On their journey back to Chicago, "a rattlesnake bit one of our men." De Montigny quickly administered an antidote that relieved the Frenchman's reaction to the poisonous venom.[88]

Serpent à Sonnettes, by Jean-François-Benjamin Dumont de Montigny. Courtesy of the Newberry Library, Edward E. Ayer Digital Collection, Ayer MS 257, no. 23.

On January 27, de Montigny, Saint-Cosme, and several of their men began the arduous trip up the Mississippi to Chicago, where Frère Alexandre had patiently remained with their extra supplies. Father Davion stayed with the Tunicas while the Frenchman, Nirgue, remained among the Taensas to build a hut for de Montigny. As they returned north, the missionaries stopped at the Tamarois village. Realizing the distance between Québec and the missions to the south and recognizing that the Jesuits were not missioning in the Tamarois village, de Montigny made his official decision—the Seminary missionaries would establish a Tamarois mission after all. With that, de Montigny assigned Rochon and Le Boeuf to remain with Saint-Cosme to build a house and a chapel.[89]

De Montigny and his companions continued up-river and arrived at Chicago on Maundy Thursday, April 16, 1699. Unbeknownst to them, King Louis XIV had sent Iberville to the lower regions of the Mississippi River to establish a colony: "I had not learned of this news when so close to the sea," exclaimed de Montigny.[90] It was a question of timing. De Montigny left the lower Mississippi in late January to return to Chicago. Iberville did not enter the mouth of the Mississippi River until early March of 1699. Thus, after just four days' rest, de Montigny, de la Source, Frère Alexandre, and others began a new descent of the Mississippi River the Monday after Easter. De Montigny had to inform Iberville and his men of the missionaries' presence on the Mississippi, but he also had to reassure himself that the missions would have a strong colonial center to their south. His enthusiasm was without question. Iberville, "who has always succeeded in all of his enterprises," was certain to strengthen their resolve, ensure their safety, and solidify the groundwork needed for "the establishment of faith in this country."[91]

As they returned south, the Jesuit Father Binneteau joined de Montigny and his men some fifteen to twenty leagues into their journey. Within a matter of days they reached the Tamarois village, where they found Saint-Cosme and his helpers hard at work: "house built, and the wood for my church ready, we finished it," exclaimed Saint-Cosme, and named it "La Chapelle de la Mission de la Sainte Famille des Tamarois." A great ceremony took place: "We planted a cross with the greatest *solemnité* possible, and all of the Indians helped us. They told us they had a great desire to be taught and to be made Christians. They brought their children to be baptized and to receive their names." Almost immediately, some thirty children were baptized by Saint-Cosme.[92]

On May 22 de Montigny and his men continued their journey south to the Arkansas River. They arrived "in very few days because of the high waters that render the river very fast." But the Quapaws were mostly absent from the village, frightened as they faced violent harassment from the Chickasaws to their east. "In previous years," wrote de Montigny, "the Quapaws could defend themselves." But more recently, the Chickasaws regularly used English firearms against the Quapaws, who were virtually defenseless with just bows and arrows.[93] Only by February 1700 did the Quapaws obtain some rifles when "several English went to trade at the Arkansas village and gave them thirty guns, powder, balls, and other merchandise as presents." But sustained access to arms waned. When Gravier passed through in late October 1700, the Quapaws still remained vulnerable. While some had swords, and most had bows and arrows, only "two or three [had] English guns, given to them last year by the man who brought them a lot of merchandise to alienate them from the French, and especially from the missionaries," against whom "he had an aversion."[94] Only

Sauvage avec ses Anciennes Armes, by Jean-François-Benjamin Dumont de Montigny. Courtesy of the Newberry Library, Edward E. Ayer Digital Collection, Ayer MS 257, no. 15.

by 1714 were the Quapaws almost completely armed with guns that they used "very skillfully."[95]

Father Davion experienced his own strife with the English just days before de Montigny and the others arrived in the Tunica village during their return south to find Iberville. At the invitation of what proved to be a conniving English scoundrel, Davion visited the Chickasaws and, through an interpreter, asked for "peace between this nation and all others from this point south." He particularly "asked them to not make war with those nations where the missionaries are established." Shortly after he returned to the Tunica village, a Tamarois slave informed the French that the Englishman had actually encouraged the Chickasaws to kill Davion.[96]

The English had been a regional threat before the French arrived. These unwelcome Europeans to the east claimed the lands from the eastern seaboard to the Mississippi River and disrupted nations within the region.[97] Two from Carolina constantly urged the Chickasaws "to make war on other nations so as to obtain as many slaves as possible and sell them to the English, who then sent them to Barbados and other places."[98] The Englishman who threatened Davion was named Ajean, a man whom de Tonti described as having "a very dirty blue shirt, no pants or stockings or shoes, a red blanket, and necklaces around his throat like an Indian." De Tonti "knew him as a wretch," solely desirous to destroy nations so as to acquire slaves. De Tonti himself confronted the unsavory Englishman for wanting to kill Father Davion, while the chief of the Chickasaws later caught him attempting to leave his village with one of de Tonti's Choctaw allies in shackles. The surly Englishman made threats to which the chief responded: "Take your leave and go. The French have only one mouth, but you have two . . . the French only long for furs and peace with all nations, but you have your head between your legs."[99]

De Montigny and his men continued toward the Gulf Coast. As they passed through the Taensas village, two Taensas and one Chaouanon joined their group. Twenty leagues further on, they arrived among the Houmas, where they were handed a letter written by Iberville, who had documented his arrival at this village but had "returned to their ships at the coast to establish a fort along the sea." The Houmas had nothing but praise for Iberville and his men, who had given them various gifts, including a cannonball that weighed some fourteen pounds. "They clearly understood that it had a different effect from their arrows," wrote de Montigny.[100]

Depiction of people protecting themselves from mosquitoes and other pests, much as experienced by the Mississippi missionaries. *Explorations in the Interior of the Labrador Peninsula: The Country of the Montagnais and Nasquapee Indians,* by Henry Youle Hind, 1863. Courtesy of the Musée de la Civilisation, don du Ministère de l'Environnement et de la Faune, MCQoo8190.

Iberville's letter confirmed that contact had been made by the French at the mouth of the Mississippi. A large cross planted by Iberville's chaplain, the Récollet Father Anastase Douay, as well as the presence of two French cabin boys further confirmed their arrival. The two boys, about fourteen or fifteen years old, had been placed among the Houmas and the Kinipissas so as to learn their languages. As spirited novices, they believed that they could easily lead de Montigny and the others to Iberville's Fort Maurepas. Taking advantage of this offer, the Frenchmen took one of the boys to serve as a guide to the fort.[101] But youthful enthusiasm soon turned into desperation to survive. The Frenchmen believed that "all we had to do was follow the banks of the sea to arrive at the fort . . . that we would continue to see beautiful country with streams of fresh water from point to point." But for the next ten days, such was not the case. "The heat was very oppressive. We lacked fresh water and only had corn meal to live on. We did not dare eat it without water out of fear of parching ourselves further. We suffered horseflies by day, mosquitoes by night." When they could take rest, the men placed leaves on the ground to clean a spot for a mat. They next gathered willow or another type of wood so as to build a frame over which they placed a veil or netting. Only by doing so could they gain any sleep without being overly harassed by mosquitoes. But so bad was their thirst "that even though the water was wretched, some drank it and consequently became sick with the bloody flux. The least sick nursed others as best they could although, under normal circumstances, their own weakness was proof enough of their need for care."[102]

Finally, on July 2, "the day of the Visitation of the Holy Virgin, and after having prayed to her for help, she led us to the fort where we happily arrived," wrote de Montigny. Those entrenched within Fort Maurepas were unaware of any Frenchmen in the region and were convinced that the two canoes coming toward them were Spanish. As they prepared to fire on the strangers, Iberville's brother, Jean-Baptiste le Moyne, Sieur de Bienville, clearly saw that those approaching were French and "in no condition to do them harm."[103] Once inside the fort, the soldiers quickly worked to address the needs of their distressed guests, who "would have all died if it had not been for some rain in the region," remarked Commander Antoine de Sauvolle. They "gave them all the pleasures that one could offer in such a place and replenished them with deer bouillon." During their time together, Sauvolle confirmed that colonization of the Lower Mississippi Valley had begun, no doubt good news that strengthened de Montigny's belief that they could convert the Native peoples.[104]

Unfortunately for de Montigny and his men, conversation proved short. There simply was not enough food for all to share. At Fort Maurepas alone, and not counting the officers, there were about fifty men present. Thus, de Montigny's entourage had to leave after only nine days of rest. Although guided by a Bayougoula man who "led us along a shorter and easier route," the men were not physically ready to leave and the number of those who were sick increased each day. Soon, both Taensas were dead. Having gone ahead of the others to try and retrieve food for those who were sick, de Montigny was unable to baptize the first Taensas that died. But "the second died more happily," wrote de Montigny, "having been instructed of our mysteries, he died after being baptized."[105]

Once de Montigny finished ministering to the ill, he returned to the Natchez for a brief visit. Unlike the first encounter, in which the Natchez met de Montigny with armed warriors and concerns of war, this time "they did not spare their joy in my arrival." Taking advantage of their "good disposition," de

Montigny asked them to make peace with the Taensas and with the Tunicas, particularly since he intended to spend "part of the year with them, and the other part with the Taensas." Despite the recent death of a Natchez warrior at the hands of the Taensas, they declared "that they no longer wanted to have war with them and before eight days had passed they would have peace with the Taensas and other nations."[106] The missionaries' motivation was simple. To Christianize Native communities, peace had to reign. To better ensure the missionaries' personal safety, the Native peoples had to cease fighting.

After walking north for three days, de Montigny and his men encountered "the most elite of the [Taensas] nation, who brought them the calumet of peace." Realizing that the Taensas were looking for their two men, and fearing that they might suspect something sinister, de Montigny quickly told them of their deaths. "They took the news well. They understood the health dangers of harmful water, and that those who had died were wrong to have not better managed their thirst during their illness." Mistakes aside, "the relatives mourned their loss nonetheless; cries of grief could be heard throughout the village, a witness to the extreme love they felt."[107]

While in the village, de Montigny learned that the chief of the Chickasaws had recently visited the Taensas and told them "they no longer wanted war against them, nor against the Tunicas." An *esprit blanc* (a white spirit) had convinced the Chickasaws that "it was not good to kill each other, that peace was more valuable." Likely, this *esprit blanc* was Davion, who had visited them several weeks earlier. Just three days later, the Natchez came to offer peace to the Taensas as well. After "a reception like anyone would desire," the Taensas "took them to the door of the temple," where the chief and members of the community were assembled. Several ceremonies took place "that would take too long to describe," wrote de Montigny. Presents were given, including "six robes of muskrat, well worked." An elder keeper of the temple addressed the spirits and those there gathered, "exhorting both nations to forget the past and to live in unalterable peace." Soon after, all writings of the missionaries' first encounters along the Mississippi ended.[108]

Many Native peoples resided in the Lower Mississippi Valley and its confluents when the Seminary missionaries arrived. The communities they chose to work with each had their own particular language, spirituality, and world view. None had avoided some form of societal change. Nations that owned arms provided by the English had devastated some communities by killing villagers and taking women and children as slaves. Illness struck many villages and took away dozens if not hundreds of warriors, parents, and children by the time the missionaries arrived. Access to European goods led to increased contact with French and English traders, whose own personalities impacted communities and increased access to *eau de vie*. For all of these trials, a response was needed. Each nation sought a way to increase their advantage, their strength, their protection and power. Access to the Frenchmen's spiritual *manitou* appeared timely. If they assimilated the Christian God into their culture, this additional spiritual power might give them greater prowess in war, greater strength over illness, more productive hunting and agriculture, and a more secure community.[109] Conversely, the Seminary priests encountered new cultural, social, and spiritual traditions. New languages made communication difficult, social roles proved foreign and easily misunderstood. Reciprocity proved a threat to them and their desire to have Christianity learned for its own sake rather than through the exchange of goods. None of the Seminary missionaries knew what lay ahead in terms of survival, much less sustainability. But with the Native communities chosen, it was time for each man to evolve, vocationally, from a Québec priest who served a French flock to a Mississippi missionary who served Native peoples. At this point, the missionaries could only suggest salvation if the Native peoples became devout Christians.[110]

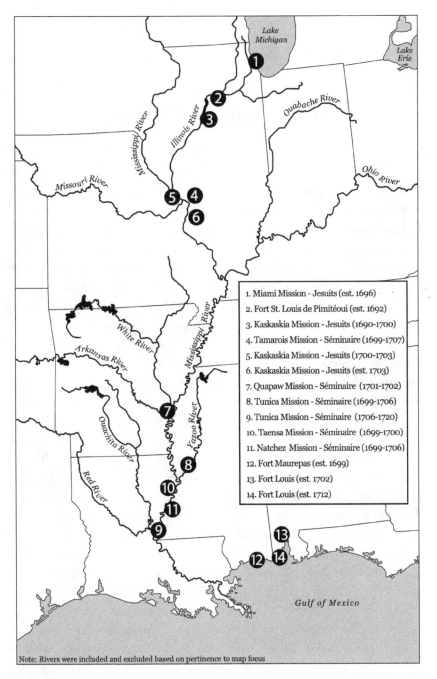

1. Miami Mission - Jesuits (est. 1696)
2. Fort St. Louis de Pimitéoui (est. 1692)
3. Kaskaskia Mission - Jesuits (1690-1700)
4. Tamarois Mission - Séminaire (1699-1707)
5. Kaskaskia Mission - Jesuits (1700-1703)
6. Kaskaskia Mission - Jesuits (est. 1703)
7. Quapaw Mission - Séminaire (1701-1702)
8. Tunica Mission - Séminaire (1699-1706)
9. Tunica Mission - Séminaire (1706-1720)
10. Taensa Mission - Séminaire (1699-1700)
11. Natchez Mission - Séminaire (1699-1706)
12. Fort Maurepas (est. 1699)
13. Fort Louis (est. 1702)
14. Fort Louis (est. 1712)

Note: Rivers were included and excluded based on pertinence to map focus

Location of various Jesuit and Seminary missions and French forts from Chicago to the mouth of the Mississippi River between 1699 and 1725. (Map developed by Maggie Bridges, Department of Geosciences, University of Arkansas)

CHAPTER 5

Les Vignes Contestés

y the time the Seminary missionaries arrived on the Mississippi, there was already a global issue at hand. For many years, the Chinese Rites controversy in East Asia pitted Jesuits and the Séminaire des Missions Étrangères in Paris against each other. The core strife begged such questions as: "Does the honor paid by the Chinese to their ancestors and to Confucius imply divine worship, or was it merely an expression of patriotism such as is the honor paid the great men of every country; and secondly, by what name should 'Almighty God' be designated in Chinese?"[1] Such questions came about because of a strategy of Christian accommodation that the Jesuits had utilized since the end of the sixteenth century whereby they embraced Chinese culture, language, clothing, and architecture and gave room for its continuance in their teaching rather than total imposition of Christianity on East Asian peoples.

The Séminaire in Paris became particularly involved in this dispute in 1687 when one of its priests, Father Charles Maigrot de Crissey, became the region's *Vicaire Apostolique*. Maigrot spent much time in study to understand the culture and challenges therein that heightened accusations of idolatrous acceptance among the Jesuits. By 1693, Maigrot declared ceremonies in honor of Confucius as superstitious and idolatrous. They had to end. But the accused Jesuits refused to accept Maigrot's views. They believed that the ceremonies and artifacts in question were social, not religious, and that those converted to Christianity should be allowed to continue their participation in these cultural activities.[2] Consequently, the Jesuits labeled Maigrot a Jansenist, an accusation they often levied at others who took a severe stance against their practices.[3]

In Paris, the Jesuits "tore into the Seminary" and composed inflammatory letters against the Séminaire and its missionaries in East Asia. Such attacks greatly distressed the Seminary directors, who did not want to see the Jesuits removed from East Asia but instead "wanted the dispute to terminate in one way or another."[4] With Pope Innocent XII involved, the Jesuits preferred that he delay his decision on East Asia since they still had permission to proceed almost as they wished. But on the eve of his decision, Innocent XII died and was replaced by Clement XI, "a good friend of the Jesuits," wrote Tremblay. The new pope initially "did not understand how such an important issue could not be resolved promptly." Nevertheless, "the affair was difficult, very troubling, and needed a lot of clarification," the pope believed. "Thus, it was better to wait another ten years before making a decision too hastily." Throughout this delay, discontent spilled into the Mississippi River Valley.[5]

When de Montigny, Davion, and Saint-Cosme descended the Mississippi River in 1698, they passed through a small Cahokia village whose people had recently suffered a devastating attack by Chaouanons, Chickasaws, and Kickapoos. Ten men had been killed and over one hundred women and children enslaved. "Still devastated by the attack," the Cahokias asked the missionaries "to live with them, that they wanted to pray and to be instructed." In this one encounter, "we had more pity than fear for them," wrote Saint-Cosme, who subsequently "promised them that they would have a missionary in the springtime."[6]

As the missionaries continued south, they visited the Tamarois village where no Jesuit mission was found despite being told otherwise. Like the Cahokias, they too were fearful of enemy attack and felt a sense of urgency and crisis that made establishing an alliance with the missionaries all the more appealing. Saint-Cosme was certain that he and his colleagues "could establish a very fine mission" among the Tamarois and the Cahokias, an opinion expressed well before the final decision was made to work among them. Consequently, as he had done with the Cahokias, Saint-Cosme "made the same promise," that they would have a missionary among them, although he did not exactly say who nor when.[7]

In the spring of 1699, as the missionaries returned north from their initial visit to the Taensas, the chief of the Cahokias, who lived alongside the Tamarois, gave the missionaries gifts in hopes that they would reciprocate and establish a mission. "It was into the Cahokia chief's cabin that I entered," wrote Saint-Cosme. "He gave me two slaves to obligate me to stay and to remind us of the promise we made that they would have a missionary. The chief himself gave me a place to build [a chapel and house] near his cabin."[8] Recognizing that over one thousand leagues separated the Taensas from Québec, that no Jesuits were established in the Tamarois village, and in response to the Tamarois and the Cahokias who "asked one or the other [Saint-Cosme or de Montigny] to stay with them and teach them," only then did de Montigny announce his decision to have Saint-Cosme establish a Tamarois mission.[9]

The forty-seven-year-old Jesuit Father Julien Binneteau witnessed the blessing of Saint-Cosme's chapel and home within the Tamarois village in May 1699. Soon after, Father Pinet left his Miami mission, despite the fact that "two missionaries had plenty of work" within, and joined Binneteau among the Tamarois.[10] Gravier, the region's Jesuit leader, quickly made his way to the village as well to confront the Seminary priests. Once there, he assigned Binneteau to build his own house and chapel and otherwise "treated de Montigny's initiative to establish Saint-Cosme [among the Tamarois] as an unjust usurpation."[11] Angered by the situation, Gravier wrote to Saint-Vallier: "It is true Monseigneur that your holiness does not mention in particular the Tamarois in the *lettres patentes* that you gave me nine years ago. But as your holiness gave us the Illinois, it also contains the Tamarois."[12]

No one denied that the Tamarois, Cahokias, Kaskaskias, and Peorias all spoke the Illinois language, for clearly "their words, accents, and economy of language were all the same without difference in a single word or syllable."[13] But the Jesuits insisted that this linguistic connection made them all a part of their regional missionary efforts. To strengthen their claim, the Jesuits began to "no longer call the Tamarois, Tamarois; nor the Illinois, Illinois," wrote Bergier, "but when they want to signify the village or nation of the Tamarois, they say and write . . . Illinois of the Great River. When they speak or write about the Illinois or those of Lake Peoria [also known as Pimitéoui], they say Illinois of Detroit or Little River." The Seminary missionaries simply called them Tamarois, as did everyone else in the region.[14] But if such pseudonyms were not enough, the Jesuits soon "no longer called the village Tamarois but Cahokia" in a ruse to win oversight of the "Cahokia" mission as opposed to the "Tamarois" mission clearly spelled out in Saint-Vallier's *lettre patente*.[15] The village itself carried the Tamarois name since this Native community was "the first to light the village fire," but even the members of the village were "unattached," having coalesced due to illness and warfare, not due to cultural or linguistic needs. Settling together simply "served to reconstitute Native concepts of order, geography, and human relations."[16]

The Seminary missionaries recognized a cultural issue that, in this situation, the Jesuits seemed to ignore—that Native nations sometimes declared villages as minimally associated, even when linguistically, culturally, and ethnically related.[17] While the Tamarois, the Kaskaskias, the Peorias, and the Cahokias fell under the umbrella "Illinois," they were not one and the same. Each named group was its own permanent political unit and acted as a single political entity that made its own decisions and allies.[18] This freeness of the Illinois nation made political and social loyalties extremely complicated, so much so that the Tamarois and the Kaskaskias were willing to war against each other when the former gave safe haven to the Missouris, who at the time were at war with Chief Rouensa and the Kaskaskias. To avoid bloodshed, "the chiefs of the Tamarois village told the [Kaskaskias] to promptly pull back if they did not want them to attack."[19]

In addition to the linguistic connection, the Jesuits believed that their Illinois mission "was not a fixed point on a map," but was made of a central post among the Kaskaskias that served the Illinois throughout the region. Although not fond of Native wanderings, oftentimes a Jesuit moved with his people during winter hunts and remained within their mission no matter where they went in an "attempt to graft Christianity onto Native cultural forms."[20] Although Gravier never installed a cross, chapel, or house in the Tamarois village as he "did not think it so prudent to do," the village, he argued, was a part of his mission. It contained "cabins of prayer," with devout individuals and "almost 300 baptized persons" recorded in his baptismal registry.[21] Whenever the Tamarois or Cahokias visited the Jesuits' Illinois (Kaskaskia) mission, Gravier "instructed them during their residence [at his missionary post]." Even when Kaskaskian catechists and Christians visited the Tamarois, Gravier encouraged them to teach the community "what they had learned from me, and I always asked the most learned to have no shame in leading prayer and in teaching their Tamarois and Cahokia kin all that I taught them."[22]

Despite Gravier's arguments, the Seminary missionaries saw no Jesuit presence, nor knew of any significant Jesuit experiences within the Tamarois village. The Jesuit Father Allouez, Saint-Cosme remarked, "had never been to the village, and had never seen these Indians except for a few who went one time to the Old Fort [Starved Rock] to trade while de Tonti had a house there."[23] For that matter, Gravier visited the Tamarois for a day or two but had to flee for his life and did not return for six years.[24] And as for the Jesuit Binneteau, although said to have established a Tamarois mission while the Seminary priests continued their initial exploration of the Mississippi, regional French-

men witnessed that "he never came to the village of the Tamarois before we established ourselves here. He had never even seen the Mississippi below the Illinois River . . . he was never within thirty leagues of the village." The Seminary
priests held firm: The Jesuits had done nothing among the Tamarois. "There
was no house, no chapel, no cross. To speak precisely, and with the strength
of words, one can better call it neglected." In short, "this was their attempt
to *cultiver une mission*," and therein began the strife and the first major challenge to the advice given to the missionaries—to "get along" with the Jesuits.[25]

Rather quickly, harsh personal attacks ensued. The Jesuits seemed
"strangely against de Montigny" and accused him of lying when he broke his
earlier promise at Michilimackinac to forego a mission among the Tamarois.[26]
They believed it was a ruse that he went down river to the Taensas, and then
returned to the Tamarois to install Saint-Cosme as their missionary.[27] Un-
questionably, the Jesuits were very suspicious of de Montigny and likely quite
aware of his mid-nineties aspirations to work in the Tamarois village, not to
mention to send Récollets into Jesuit missions in support of Saint-Vallier's own
desire for the latter "if the Jesuits failed to support his return from exile."[28] De
Montigny, after all, was a young, inexperienced, yet trusted servant of Saint-
Vallier who was willing to do anything to support his embattled bishop against
those who threatened his authority, Jesuits included. But Laval knew the im-
plications of such brash ideas and counseled de Montigny to engage in peaceful and charitable efforts rather than in potentially divisive activities.[29] Tremblay was equally disturbed. Fully aware that the Jesuits viewed de Montigny's
long-held spirit as "just as sordid as Saint-Vallier's," Tremblay made his own
stance clear: "I always declared myself strongly against this bad faith of M. de
Montigny . . . in every measure."[30]

The presumed usurpation of Jesuit regional coverage by the Seminary
priests led the former to threaten to disrupt delivery of any of their goods or
letters that passed through Michilimackinac, even to have the court "cut off
their 3,000 livres of support."[31] Consequently, Tremblay counseled his missionaries to avoid the Jesuits in all manners and, above all, to not go to their missions since "nothing was lower than the reproaches of the Jesuits who talked of
receiving the Seminary missionaries well only to receive 'ingratitude' from the
latter as a result." Tremblay's colleague Louis Ango de Maizerets alternatively
exhorted the Seminary missionaries to work charitably with the Jesuits. "Sensi-
bly mortified because of all of the differences present," de Maizerets knew that

a giving and congenial spirit between the two bodies had long existed. Since both groups sought the glory of God and the saving of souls, and since both preached the same Gospel and believed in Christ, he encouraged the missionaries "to not break the relationship [with the Jesuits] . . . that it was not impossible that subjects of different bodies can work to harvest the people."[32] Likely de Maizerets was hoping for a middle ground, a place where both Catholic institutions could find commonality in their work rather than anger and jealousy. While both groups had a mutual goal, the conversion of Native peoples, they nonetheless had differing strategies and opinions. The Jesuits' regional superior, Father Joseph Marest, encouraged Pinet to stay put, keep working, and prevent Bergier from serving the Tamarois. In contrast, the Seminary leadership strongly urged its missionaries to suffer without complaint so that by "gentleness and patience" they would show themselves as "Disciples of *Notre Seigneur*."[33]

Not knowing when a decision would be forthcoming, the Jesuits and Saint-Cosme both began their work in May of 1699. But the Seminary priest needed the prayers and liturgy in translation to interact with the Tamarois. Consequently, Saint-Cosme strove to remain cordial with the Jesuits. He offered Binneteau the use of his house and "prayed that we live in union and as if we were of the same body until you [Laval and Saint-Vallier] decide this affair." But Saint-Cosme's best laid plans fell short—Binneteau continued to disallow Saint-Cosme from "helping with prayers and instructions." Regardless of the Seminary priest's efforts "to do everything I could to avoid scandal," a tenseness filled the air.[34]

The Jesuits viewed the Seminary missionaries as "traitors and ingrates" and did all they could to sway Iberville and even de Tonti against them. Saint-Cosme, in turn, criticized the regional decisions of the Jesuits, who compromised their more northern missions so as to establish themselves among the Tamarois.[35] While on a trip to Pimitéoui (Lake Peoria), Saint-Cosme saw a great number of *priants* but only Father Gabriel Marest, brother of the Jesuits' regional superior, Joseph Marest, to instruct them. The Seminary priest could not understand in what conscience the Jesuits had left Marest alone in the Kaskaskia mission "with enough work for three missionaries." Although he did not know the language, Saint-Cosme believed himself "just as capable of instructing them" as Marest, "who could hardly put two Illinois words together."[36] Such criticism of the Kaskaskia missionary was rather harsh given that the Jesuit was considered quite linguistically talented and authored a French/Illinois dictionary in due time. Jesuit colleagues, in fact, spoke of Gabriel Marest's strong work ethic: "Dear Father Marest is somewhat too zealous; he works excessively during the day, and sits up at night to improve himself in the language; he would like to learn the whole vocabulary in five or six months. May God preserve so worthy a missionary to us."[37]

Saint-Vallier had to quickly find an answer, for as long as it lingered, Christianization efforts remained stalled. In July of 1699 he asked the Jesuits to refrain from any functions in the Tamarois mission without his consent. They did not obey.[38] Not long after, he assigned the thirty-two-year-old lawyer turned priest Marc Bergier to live among the Tamarois in hopes that his negotiation skills and calm demeanor might help all concerned to find common ground and move forward. With Bergier, Saint-Vallier sent Michel Buisson de Saint-Cosme, the seventeen-year-old brother of Saint-Cosme, to help in the mission and to learn the language alongside the others.

When Bergier arrived among the Tamarois in February 1700, he and the elder Saint-Cosme attempted to affably interact with Pinet and the thirty-two-year-old Joseph de Limoges. The latter had replaced Father Binneteau, who, while on a winter hunt with the Illinois, "died in the arms" of Father Marest, this due to "excessive labor and excessive abstinence."[39] The Seminary priests "received them with all the honesty and cordiality possible," wrote Saint-Cosme. "I showed them Saint-Vallier's letter" and reminded them of the Seminary missionaries' jurisdiction over the Mississippi. Regardless, the Jesuits were certain that Saint-Vallier "did not have the right to order them to leave an Illinois mission." The bishop, after all, had given them a *lettre patente* in 1690 that gave them oversight of the Illinois nation as a whole. This was, they believed, their authorization to stay put.[40]

Quite aware of his own limitations and out of his own charity and patience, Bergier "wanted to be honest, believing he could win over the Jesuits," wrote Saint-Cosme. He strove for a peaceful solution, a middle ground where, "just until the affairs were entirely resolved, he was content that they carry out their functions as missionaries."[41] With Bergier's softer, gentler strategy, not to mention various shared compliments between himself and Pinet, neither Bergier nor Saint-Cosme "could truly ascertain what the Jesuits were thinking," nor whether they would obey the bishop.[42] Nonetheless, Bergier's presence and approach brought calm and some sensibility to the mission. As he ministered in the village, Bergier did nothing without a Jesuit present. He preferred to include them rather than to jeopardize their relationship, whether "advantageous or disadvantageous to the mission." On some level, his strategy worked. Bergier wrote:

> A man, about fifty-five to sixty-years-of-age named La Tortue, chief of the Hableur clan, fell dangerously ill. No longer wanting to listen to Pinet, who never failed to visit him each day . . . we were alerted one morning that this man asked to see us so that we might teach and baptize him. I rushed there with [Father] Saint-Cosme and we found that what was said was true. We prepared him to receive the sacrament. However, out of all possible precaution, I went to confer with Father Pinet. He came with me to see the ill man and, finding him well prepared, he counseled me to baptize him and went to fetch some water. I baptized him on May the 16th in the presence of Pinet and several Frenchmen. I gave him the name Paul, intending at the same time to place this mission under the special protection of this great Apostle of the Gentiles, and to honor him as the first of my children.

La Tortue "lived twelve more days under the burden of his illness with great patience and resignation." He was "preserved in his faith as much as one can judge among these men, and died with the same disposition." Bergier added: "One can truthfully say . . . that I carried out the functions of a missionary."[43]

The Jesuits and the Seminary priests had to find some suitable way of functioning that would not disrupt their own attempts to work with the Tamarois. In this particular event, Bergier and the Jesuits reached a middle ground of mutual action between the two that "was fair and legitimate." They had a spiritual and spirited congruence—the desire to prepare La Tortue for baptism, to prepare him as a Christian for his death. But they also acted out of their own interests. Pinet, self-declared as the Tamarois missionary and certain of the Jesuits' claim of authority within the region, likely welcomed the opportunity to counsel Bergier's interaction with the Cahokia leader. Thus, Pinet retained his presumption of authority and power over the Seminary missionary. Alternatively, Bergier finally felt as if he had done something as a missionary within the village. Both sides embraced the task before them and willingly allowed the other to participate in La Tortue's baptism and Christian fate.[44]

At the start of this story, La Tortue asked for Saint-Cosme and Bergier. Initially, the Cahokias had made their accord with the Seminary missionaries and had invited them to establish a mission among them, not the Jesuits. But Pinet's assertiveness within the village, not to mention his language skills, allowed him to more quickly connect with villagers in comparison to the Seminary men. Father Pinet performed "all the duties of a missionary," and made it a point "to visit La Tortue each day," and probably others as well. Alternatively, Bergier worked only with the French, "a great relief for Father Pinet," wrote Gravier.[45] But the Cahokia chief preferred otherwise. He and his people had given gifts to the Seminary priests so that they might in turn teach them of Christianity. They gave the Seminary missionaries land on which to build a home and a chapel. They gave these men Native slaves to serve them. Such gifts were the first steps in a relationship that required reciprocal actions to maintain this union of trust and friendship. The chief wished to bring the Seminary priests more deeply into their social and cultural structures, to bring their Christian *manitou* into their spirituality. Relationship demanded response. Without it, relationship was compromised.

La Tortue may have had other reasons for preferring Saint-Cosme and Bergier. The chief may have found the Seminary priests less forceful than the Jesuits, who "went into the huts to scold women who brought their babies to Saint-Cosme to be baptized." The chief may have felt the Séminarians were more attuned to the Cahokias' demeanor of speaking and listening carefully, and thus were more reflective of their own views of the spiritual realm.[46] Indeed, a middle ground emerged when people gained cooperation or consent in unforced ways. To enter this middle ground, one had to find a way to "understand the world and the reasoning of others and assimilate enough of that reasoning to put it to their own purposes."[47] True to his nature, Bergier did not use force. Instead, he proceeded carefully, he justified his own actions, he called on those of importance to the situation, he strove to be generous to all involved. Consequently, when the Jesuits used force, the Tamarois and Cahokias turned toward Bergier and Saint-Cosme and welcomed their gentler methods.

More intriguing—La Tortue and his people may have believed that the Jesuits and the Seminary missionaries had access to different *manitous*. Not satisfied by Pinet's Christian spirit, La Tortue may well have sought the power of the *manitou* utilized by Bergier and Saint-Cosme. After all, these missionaries were "strange and powerful men" who lived separately, dressed differently (the Jesuits wore black robes; the Seminary priests, black robes and white collars or *blancs collets*), and approached the Tamarois differently as well. Bergier certainly believed that the Tamarois sensed a difference: "The French and the Indians perceive quite well that despite what one says, that we and the Jesuits are the same thing, we are two nonetheless."[48]

The first and perhaps most significant difference between the Jesuits and the Seminary missionaries was the latter's inability to speak the Illinois language. Many knew that the Jesuits "were more experienced in languages . . . and knew far better the manner of the Indians." The Jesuits had recognized years earlier that in order to work with Native peoples, it was far more efficient for them to learn a Native language than it was to teach the Native people French. Consequently, the Jesuits studied select languages and cultures oftentimes years before they served within a mission. Once within a village, they developed prayer books and dictionaries in the Native language to help themselves and others that followed. As the Jesuits developed their linguistic skills, it meant that they could teach about Christianity using Native peoples' words rather than unfamiliar French terms.[49]

The Jesuits initially provided Saint-Cosme with certain prayers—the Our Father, Hail Mary, and Apostles' Creed—in Illinois to "show" that they were truly "Disciples of Christ," that they could return a "good deed for the wrong done to them."[50] But nothing further was offered, for "under no circumstances would [they] . . . assist the seminary priest."[51] Alternatively, Saint-Cosme took the sympathetic offer of a Frenchman and his wife, a woman from Pimitéoui, to come and live near him so that the wife could teach him the prayers and catechism in the Illinois language. To retain the couple's services, Saint-Cosme compensated them with a house, some powder, and lead. Saint-Cosme's tutor arrived around June 15, 1699, and taught him "with great affection" until Gravier berated Saint-Cosme in front of four Frenchmen and forbade him from ministering in the village, citing that he, as *Grand Vicaire* since 1690, had authority to make such demands. The Jesuits also reproached the husband for his wrongs and demanded he repent, while Gravier did all he could to take away Saint-Cosme's linguistic *institutrice*. Quite confused, the young woman no longer taught Saint-Cosme "with the same affection as before."[52]

Bergier was quite willing to work with Pinet, who vowed to help the Seminary priest with the Illinois language "once the affair was resolved."[53] But Saint-Cosme remained suspicious: "Why not help him now? If the mission remains theirs, Bergier will do them no wrong. If it remains with us, Bergier will be better prepared to do good." Saint-Cosme was certain that the fact that he was writing letters to Québec influenced the Jesuits' actions toward them. "Pinet's promise was 'nice'; they said nice things during the time I had to write [letters to Québec]. Afterward, they treated him [Bergier] just as they treated me."[54] Although the Jesuits more stringently delayed providing any language assistance to Bergier, "despite their strong self-lauding, that they act with honor and virtue," Bergier did obtain some prayers and the catechism in Illinois directly from Saint-Cosme.[55] Otherwise, he relied on the more linguistically talented Michel Saint-Cosme to teach him the language. In so doing, Bergier began to develop his own dictionary that was still under development some six years later.[56]

Lack of adequate engagement with the language impacted the Seminary missionaries' work. After all, language was not just a code for expressing oneself or sharing information, it was a "conduit and catalyst for social relationships."[57] Even before they could teach about Christianity, the missionaries had to learn some elements of the language so as to avoid potential misunderstandings and cultural faux pas. Without sufficient access to the language, one could not easily negotiate his entrance into the culture of a Native community. As Bergier put it, not being as skilled with the language, "the Indians were right to follow the Jesuits and to make fun of me."[58] But no matter how hard anyone tried to learn the language, there still remained "limits of translation and the effects of intercultural mediation on the creation of indigenous forms of Christianity." Communication remained a constant challenge no matter how many words or phrases one learned.[59]

In the midst of this linguistic strife, the Tamarois were very astute in their observations, quite quick to notice the uneasiness and the profound discord present between the Jesuits and the Seminary priests. Early on, Saint-Cosme's language tutor lost interest in helping him due to Gravier's harsh reprimands. Saint-Cosme himself conducted prayers cautiously, uncertain of his language abilities, "not yet ready to stand against the Jesuits, who know the language perfectly, and not wanting to put out a public call since I wasn't assured of the bishop's decision."[60] But some Tamarois took sides. As Saint-Cosme learned, "the chief doesn't go to prayers out of fear that he will promote jealousy among the missionaries." Saint-Cosme encouraged him "to go and listen to the father," but the chief answered "that he was waiting until I did the prayer so as to instruct him."[61]

Bergier's own experiences proved further distressing. "If the Indians talked to me, if they entered our house, if they taught me, if they gave me some prayers, if I gave them food to eat, all of this was the subject of complaints, coldness, mutterings. That I was destroying their mission, that I was making the Indians lose the confidence they needed to have in their true missionaries [the Jesuits]."[62] Bergier even found that Tamarois women did not dare teach him any prayers or enter into his house out of fear of displeasing the Jesuits.[63] Indeed, once Pinet and de Limoges discovered that Bergier had obtained several hymns from the chief's daughter, "they saw this as bad, troublesome, pretending it was against the interest of God's glory for me to have asked them, and for the young women to have given them to me." As Bergier found, "most believe it bad if they instruct me. The chief's daughter and others refused to help me several times, at least up until they became discontent with Pinet this winter and then she taught me more or less what she knew."[64] But most disturbing to Bergier was the salacious accusation made by the Jesuits toward a young Cahokia woman. One evening, Bergier sang a hymn that he had translated— *Iam lucis orto sidere* ("Star of Light Now Having Risen")—to several Cahokia women. In so doing, he hoped that they might correct his language and pronunciation. But to the Jesuits, Bergier "turned one young woman named Anne into a whore" since "young men went into her cabin . . . to learn this hymn."[65] We do not know what Anne was doing when others came to learn the song. We only know that she had learned it, helped Bergier to perfect it, and was making an effort to teach it to others. But we also know that the Jesuits were likely looking for any opportunity to place the Seminary missionaries in a bad light. By seeing young men enter Anne's cabin, the Jesuits could make the accusation that Bergier promoted the young woman's sexual promiscuity.

A workable relationship between Native communities and a missionary "demanded a father who mediated more often than he commanded, who forgave more often than he punished, who gave more often than he received."[66] Thus, when Tamarois women brought their infants to Saint-Cosme to receive baptism, they likely did so because he, or perhaps the manner in which he performed his ceremonies, had some sort of beneficial power on their own spiritual realm. When Jesuits barged into their homes to complain, the women likely perceived this as violating their sanctity of decision making, thus making anything else the Jesuits did similarly displeasing.[67] Tamarois women, after all, "wielded considerable economic and political power." They tended to fields that provided sustenance for the community, they shared their bounty, they participated in village councils, and occasionally they served as a chief within the nation.[68] Ignoring the sanctity of a woman's home and her social power lessened her willingness to incorporate a scolding missionary or any other disruptive Frenchmen into Tamarois social structures. Ultimately, just because any of these missionaries were in the village did not mean that they were fully allowed to do as they pleased. No one could easily gain access to Tamarois women without acknowledging societal and cultural norms as well as the women's own level of persuasion and strength within their community.

By July 1700, Saint-Cosme was transferred to the Taensas and the Natchez missions, leaving Bergier alone with the Jesuits and the *vigne contesté*. In his first fifteen months among the Tamarois, Bergier "hardly learned any words." Nonetheless, devoted to his charge, he prayed "that God might abundantly communicate His spirit to me so as to maintain the discretion and character with which God has honored me and uphold the authority that Saint-Vallier has given me."[69] Bergier did all he could to live by the expectations set forth by the Seminary leadership, the hardest expectation at this stage being to remain charitable to the Jesuits and to do all in God's name: "I would be absolutely furious if I were to give the least subject for complaint on my part," wrote Bergier. "It would not be done with God's help."[70] Consequently, Bergier supported his Jesuit neighbors, particularly when their own superiors threatened them with disobedience if they did not follow their Lenten discipline as did others in Québec. Bergier knew firsthand that regional foods were insufficient. One literally risked his health if he bypassed any opportunity to eat meat, especially in areas where *sagamité* was the main staple. Lent, he believed, had to follow a more tolerable schedule so as to maintain the sacred discipline but also to maintain one's health. Nonetheless, risks remained: Pinet, for one, was "*incommodé* when he ingested the regional red meat. . . . Another missionary, and equally some Frenchmen, found that beans bloated them and sagamité *cause des vapors*."[71] But Bergier longed to do what he could to help his Jesuit colleagues. Even years later, when Father Gravier was nearly killed by a Peoria, Bergier offered assistance to help protect Gravier from further injury. He sent fourteen men from his village, but only one stayed with Gravier, the chief among them who "remained some time, watching over him."[72]

The Jesuits suffered in many respects. Writing to the superior general of the Jesuit missions, Martin Bouvart, Bergier described Father Jean Mermet's bitter distress at Chicago during the winter of 1701 into 1702, and wrote that Fathers Pinet and Marest, "despite their work and their illness, lack necessities and have been reduced to living a life of borrowing." Bergier certainly understood "that poverty is very agreeable to God, principally in his ministers, and that in your *Compagnie* you make an exacting profession, but this must have its limits." Quoting from I Corinthians 9:9, Bergier wrote: "Non Alligabis Os Bovis [you shalt not muzzle an ox while it is treading out the grain]."[73] The Jesuits were there, working hard, trying to reap a harvest among the Native peoples. Bergier plainly asked Bouvart "that one fulfill the requests of your missionaries. These are neither children nor squanderers. They ask for things that they judge necessary for their subsistence and to maintain the missions."[74]

The Jesuits had no reason to accuse the Seminary missionaries of being enemies or persecutors, Bergier believed. As he put it, "we have only sought to defend the purity of our religion, to destroy superstitions and idolatry, and not to persecute the Jesuits, for whom we are not lacking in esteem nor veneration."[75] But despite his support, and his own willingness to step into a middle ground, no amount of prayer or kindness could relieve Bergier from the feeling that the Jesuits "had the same attitude as was felt in East Asia," where Seminary missionaries and Jesuits fought ardently with each other regarding the Jesuits' approach to Christianization. Such a squabble over a relatively unknown Native community—so much interest in "*une pouce de terre* [an inch of land]" or "*une bagatelle* [trifle]"—troubled many. "It is shameful to make such noise over a little piece of land where they [the Jesuits] have no rights . . . they have no direct *lettre patente* for the Tamarois," wrote Tremblay. Searching for an end to the conflict, the *Procureur* and the Seminary leadership in Paris voiced their opinion to Laval: "If you believe this mission is absolutely necessary, then you must keep it and immediately inform our leaders. But if it can be bypassed, I believe this would be best."[76] Writing to Saint-Vallier, Bergier could only exclaim: "Note the authority that you gave me and under what conditions I will have to maintain it." As he put it, he lived in the midst of a "*vigne contesté.*"[77]

Despite the ongoing conflict, a middle ground arose, at times, within various activities and interactions of the missionaries, the Tamarois, and the Jesuits. Prior to Saint-Cosme's departure south, the three parties collectively responded to an attack by the Sioux on the village:

> The Sunday of Pentecost . . . four Sioux in the edge of the woods and within sight of the village slashed the neck of a Frenchman's slave and stabbed to death two women and scalped them, wounding further a girl,

and tying up another by her feet in the woods. We had just finished Compline when the chief came to our door to tell us the Sioux were killing them. Saint-Cosme jumped into his canoe with the chief, along with several Indians and French, to go and find the Sioux. Others went on foot. Finally, the Sioux were found. Three were taken, killed, burned, and eaten. This is something quite horrible to describe. They care less for men than for a wolf, a tiger, or a demon. The last of the three Sioux, who was not burned until the next day, was the nephew of 8akanasapé, chief of the Sioux. [The symbol "8" was often used by French writers to indicate a "hui" sound within a name.] Pinet baptized him prior to his execution, using Lorrain as his interpreter. Consequently, one fears greatly that the Sioux will avenge this death on their village. . . . One can say that we are: *inter lupos, in medio nationis praux et perversax* [in the midst of wolves, in the midst of a crooked and perverse generation]. Their greatest and most universal passion is to destroy one another, to take scalps, to kill men, to eat men; this is all their ambition, all of their glory, an essential impediment, as long as it lasts, to Christianization. But, the grace of Jesus Christ is all powerful. . . . Pray that He makes them peaceful as doves. Amen.[78]

Neither the Jesuits nor the Seminary missionaries could stop the executions. The Tamarois had to avenge the deaths of their deceased kin so as to allow their souls to enter the spirit world.[79] By executing 8akanasapé's nephew, his death "released a relative's wandering soul into the afterlife where he or she could rest peacefully."[80] Consequently, the missionaries could only "content themselves with imposing a thin Christian overlay upon what remained an entirely traditionalist ceremony." Baptism reassured them that the spirit of the soon to be killed Sioux was granted entrance into heaven. Since Native peoples believed that priests performed what one might call "death-bed baptism . . . with its watery cross, [that] actively marked an individual for death," there was no harm in allowing Pinet to baptize him. The Sioux's death was imminent.[81]

Even the condemned man had a say in his afterlife. A Native person was trained from a young age to courageously endure pain by listening to oral traditions focused on acts of bravery and by experiencing unpleasant things, such as ice baths, ceremonial scratching with gar teeth, and floggings.[82] The world could be both violent and deadly. A nation's people needed thorough mental, physical, and spiritual training to maintain courage under the direst of circumstances. Thus, in torture, "chosen victims . . . were seen as sources of might and strength for each person present. . . . The braver an enemy the more power his torturers could gain."[83] Once the victim was dead, "the clan gained access to the spiritual power he had managed to accumulate" through his unwavering bravery and courage.[84]

In this juxtaposition of two dramatically different cultural institutions, the participants entered a spiritual middle ground of mutual understanding. While the missionaries associated baptism with salvation and the granting of entrance into heaven, the Tamarois associated the tortured man's strength and courage as a source of power that allowed the souls of their deceased kin entrance into the afterlife. For that matter, the Jesuits and the Seminary missionaries found a space where they could work together for a mutual outcome, the salvation of the condemned Sioux.

The Seminary missionaries needed the Tamarois mission to communicate with Québec, to compensate for the extreme distances from one missionary to another. Conversely, the Jesuits' claim to the Tamarois remained influenced by a long-held belief that the Illinois and its family of related tribes could be easily Christianized given that they worshiped one god, the sun, "have hardly any superstitions, and are not wont to offer Sacrifices to various spirits." Marquette and his contemporary Allouez believed that the Illinois were perfect for accommodating Ignatius of Loyola's call—"to accommodate Christianity to Native life."[85] These early Jesuits believed it "impossible to find [a people] better fitted for receiving Christian influences."[86] But without the ability to verbally communicate fully with the Illinois, and without deep knowledge of Illinois spirituality, Allouez and Marquette did not recognize that the Illinois belief system went well beyond the realm of simplicity and assumptions of easy horizontal shifting from their one Great Manitou to the Jesuits' one God. Consequently, as Gravier and his Jesuit contemporaries more fully developed their language abilities, and subsequently spent more time with the Illinois, they better understood their culture and the "differences that divided them, differences they had ignored—or simply missed."[87]

Mastery of any language depends on linguistic talent as well as extensive, authentic spoken interaction with others.[88] Thus, Jesuit assumptions about the Illinois and the Tamarois culture evolved as they lived longer among them and developed their linguistic capabilities with the Illinois language. While they may have thought the Illinois came to hear explanations, teachings, and the like, the mere presentation of a picture at the chapel and the Native peoples' curiosity about it were sometimes more the attraction than the Word.[89] While *Kiche Manitou* may have meant great spirit, it could also mean demon, or even great serpent.[90]

Early on, the Seminary priests themselves showed signs of what White describes as "creative misunderstanding," self-confident as they spoke highly of the conversions quickly made, the baptisms performed, and the professions of faith of those with whom they interacted even after only one day.[91] They were certain that Christianity was understood by the Tamarois and was taking hold. Nonetheless, the Jesuits were determined to maintain their power in the region and to push back on any exterior interference from the bishop and the Seminary priests. If they lost the Tamarois, a village linguistically related to the Illinois (and in their eyes, a part of their Illinois flock), the Jesuits also lost an opportunity to Christianize additional peoples in the region. Conversely, the Seminary missionaries simply believed that they could make a difference and were called to do so. Not one to normally spout arrogance, Bergier was quite certain that the Seminary's presence had improved efforts along the Mississippi. "While the arrival of the Seminary missionaries into this region seems to have brought some trouble," Bergier wrote, "instead of having damaged the Jesuits' missions, the [Seminary missionaries'] publicly renowned ecclesiastical discipline has, by contrast, procured much good, *ecce coram deo, quia non mentitur* [before God, I do not lie]."[92] But the Jesuits believed otherwise. The Seminary missionaries had little prior understanding of the region and its people, nor did they have any missioning experience. Having these unproven priests in the region—their white collars, their fresh vestments, but also their initial inability to understand Native cultures—was a threat to the Jesuits' missioning efforts.

Work at a standstill, the Seminary missionaries labeled the Jesuits as "grumblers" and "carpers" who did nothing but "cry out before all of usurpation and bad faith. They complain that your holiness [Saint-Vallier] wants to destroy them, that they have always been persecuted by bishops, above all Jansenists," the Jesuits' "battle horse with which they dare to bring down on all of their enemies," wrote Saint-Cosme.[93] Although the Seminary priests were convinced that justice was on their side, the Jesuits subsumed the victim's role: Division and strife were their destiny, only now fueled by "shameful traitors and ingrates" who "have taken away their Tamarois children." From Paris, the Jesuit leader de la Chaise, a king's confessor, informed Louis XIV that the Jesuits "are accustomed to being chased from our missions by the Missions Étrangères . . . from Tonquin, Cochinchine, and now from this place [the Mississippi]."[94] Former Québec governor Jacques-René de Brisay de Denonville, "more Jesuit than the Jesuits," quipped Tremblay, questioned Laval's sincerity toward the Jesuits, only now "abandoning them in favor of the Seminary." Loosely citing Matthew 5:47, he remarked: "If you only greet your brothers, what do you do for the others? The heathens, are they not yours as well?"[95]

By the early eighteenth century, it was "altar against altar, even a war" that was disadvantageous to both sides.[96] Under the strain of the ongoing strife, Laval had to take a stand. In a letter to the Jesuit de la Chaise, he wrote: "I can sincerely say that we did not propose to place the Seminary priests among the Tamarois until after having fully informed ourselves, even with the help of the Québec Jesuits, that the Tamarois village did not have a mission in place nor were the Jesuits established there. . . . It is rude of your Fathers to suggest that they had spent money there and were being chased from the Tamarois. I tell you, I cannot understand how they could have written such things so far from the truth."[97]

Despite efforts to remain just and fair, all sides came down hard on Mgr l'Ancien. The Jesuit de la Chaise, who had "nothing but respect for Laval and would continue to have this sincerely for the rest of his life," found it most rude that the Jesuits were being usurped of their power after having learned the language, spent money, and taken great care to establish themselves among the Tamarois.[98] Others were less kind, suspicious that Saint-Vallier and Laval had "more friendship than they had ever had after ten years of strife." It was as if the Jesuits had become "the anvil; Laval, the hammer; Saint-Vallier, the hand," remarked the Jesuits.[99] Others in Paris were even less kind and called Laval "an ungrateful soul" who failed to recognize all that the Jesuits had done for him, including "having helped him become a bishop." These same men even insinuated that their "Compagnie" had been completely against establishing the Séminaire des Missions Étrangères in 1663. Such intimations astonished Saint-Vallier and Tremblay, who accused the Parisian Jesuits of being filled with ingratitude themselves. How could they forget that it was Fathers Bagot and de Rhodes, two prominent Jesuits of the early seventeenth century, who played a direct part in the elevation of bishops for East Asia and Canada, and in the establishment of the Séminaire des Missions Étrangères de Paris?[100] But even Tremblay came down hard on Laval and criticized his long-held "hands-off" attitude toward the Jesuits: "You did not dare touch them during your reign as bishop. At present, 'touch the mountains and they smoke.' It isn't that you haven't known that they [the Jesuits] can be difficult, but that you believed that for the good of peace, you needed to not ask too much of them, and to allow them to do as they wished. This is what makes them so frustrating at present, what with the establishments on the Mississippi."[101]

Tremblay was alluding to that period of time when the king insisted that Frenchification of the Native peoples take place within the bounds of Québec. Going far afield was not what the king desired. Adapting to the Native lifestyle and learning their language was not what governmental officials ordered. But the Jesuits resisted. They wanted to develop missions and work within communities that were far from *eau de vie* and from those who distributed it among the villages and disrupted their progress toward Christianity. They wanted to work with Native peoples on their own terms, through assimilation of Christianity into the Native culture—a very "conscious, strategic decision" on their part.[102] Thus, the Jesuits continued their missioning ways, certain that penetration into the Native culture and society provided far better results. Laval, as the leader of the Québec church, turned a blind eye to their Frenchification efforts. He was unwilling to disrupt their work.

While Laval attempted to maintain charity and brotherhood with both sides, Saint-Vallier otherwise scolded the Jesuits for their lack of respect toward him, that they "ought to better treat he who makes decisions regarding the missions."[103] It angered Saint-Vallier that they went "against the episcopal authority" and suggested that "the Mississippi was not under the jurisdiction of the bishop of Québec." For the latter, he asked Bergier to share with the Jesuits the *Bulle* of his bishopric that stated: "All lands of this continent that are under the jurisdiction of the king, or that will be, are deemed to be under the jurisdiction of the bishop of Québec until such time as the king judges it appropriate to ask the Holy Father to establish a new diocese and the pope approves it." Known to be "extremely jealous of his authority," Saint-Vallier fully intended to be obeyed. True to his personality, he would not change his mind.[104]

On October 10, 1700, Saint-Vallier left for Paris to address the Tamarois squabble. While in Paris he met with the king, who was quite disturbed by the brouhaha engulfing such a small village on the Mississippi. "The king was troubled by the divisions; the public scandalized . . . the difficulty [from afar] was not knowing if we caused the scandal or the Jesuits," wrote Tremblay.[105] To address the situation once and for all, King Louis XIV selected the archbishops of Chartres and Marseilles, both "friends of the Jesuits but more importantly friends of the truth," to examine and resolve the Tamarois dispute.[106] Finally, on June 7, 1701, the decision was made: "The Priests of the Foreign Missions are to remain alone in the place called Tamarois and are to receive fraternally the Reverend Jesuit Fathers when they pass through to go to assist the Illinois and the Tamarois in their fishing and hunting quarters, in which quarters the Reverend Jesuit Fathers will be authorized to settle, if they deem it proper."[107]

Although decided in June of 1701, the decision did not reach the Tamarois village for another twelve months. Once it did, Father Pinet closed his chapel and left the Tamarois so as to join his colleague, Father Gabriel Marest, at his Kaskaskia mission, two leagues away. But the decision itself did not bar the Jesuits from contact with the Tamarois. They could continue to serve among them during winter and summer hunts. Such an opening essentially led to "bouncing the Tamarois several times a year between missionaries of different bodies who did not have the same style of instruction," wrote Bergier. "I was unable to get from the Jesuits a copy of their catechism, and I must do it in the manner I can."[108]

While the Jesuits and the Seminary priests wrangled over the Tamarois mission, a smaller yet still bothersome dispute, most especially for Saint-Vallier, simmered in the Lower Mississippi Valley. When Iberville and Bienville first voyaged to the mouth of the Mississippi as official representatives of the king, they believed that they had their own say as to which missionaries served with them. Consequently, Iberville brought along Father Anastasius (Anastase) Douay, whom the Récollets hoped would play a prominent role in the establishment of the Louisiana colony. However, exposure to the region led Douay to return to his Récollet monastery, "never to leave it again."[109]

Just prior to Iberville's second departure from France for the Mississippi, Tremblay wrote him "the kindest letter I could to ask him if he would take one of our priests to serve as his chaplain." Tremblay hoped that this priest could correspond with the Seminary missionaries on the Mississippi and help to more firmly establish missions in the lower region of the river. Although Iberville responded that such a decision "was not up to him," Tremblay soon learned that "the Jesuits had secretly led this affair," and had obtained a chaplaincy appointment exclusive to the Jesuits. Rumor had it that the Jesuits, who had "a horrible itching to set up missions everywhere," had actually "obtained the entire mission from the king," wrote Tremblay, and thus "did not recognize the powers of the bishop of Québec." Tremblay knew better than to complain since it would be viewed as "bullying" at best. The Tamarois decision had not yet been made at this point, and further aggression toward the Jesuits could impact the outcome.[110] But Tremblay understood the region's status nonetheless—the bishop of Québec held jurisdiction over all lands that fell under the auspices of the king of France, the mouth of the Mississippi included. Saint-Vallier was the rightful decision maker when it came to assigning missionaries within the king's domain, and had already declared the Seminary priests as his representatives in that region. Although the *bulle* cited earlier was proof of his oversight, communication, distance, and personal preference made Saint-Vallier's authority easy to ignore.

Early in their colonization efforts, Bienville and Iberville preferred to work with the Jesuits, whose vast experience with colonization and missioning in New France, not to mention their talents for Native languages, seemed the most promising for success along the Gulf. A young, inexperienced Jesuit named Father Paul du Ru served as their first missionary in the southern field. Ordained in 1698, du Ru left from La Rochelle on board the *Renommé* on September 17, 1699, and arrived at Biloxi on January 8, 1700. Described as physically well built, du Ru could "hold his own with hardened Canadians . . . and wield an ax or hammer when the occasion required."[111]

Du Ru was bright and intelligent but had no previous experiences with Native peoples or foreign lands. Once in this unchartered territory, he was immediately challenged to learn multiple languages that no Europeans had ever heard, much less mastered. The Bayougoula language, in particular, proved difficult for him. "I have been the pupil of the old Bayagoula in order to learn his language," wrote du Ru. "I know already fifty of the most necessary words. I think this language is rather poor. . . . There are no R's, and I think the D's are not common either, for the Bayagoula cannot pronounce these letters in our words." The Jesuit historian, Delanglez quipped: "These Indians must have massacred Father du Ru's own name."[112]

Quickly, du Ru built a church among the Houmas and the Bayougoulas. "For an ax and a knife," he acquired the field behind the church "to make a beautiful garden and a fine orchard."[113] But despite his efforts to establish a mission, du Ru did not remain long among them. While he found the Bayougoulas hospitable, he also believed they were "indolent [and] superstitious," and thus difficult to convert. "Their whole desire is to get from everyone what they want," wrote du Ru, "though without violence and without treachery. They are superstitious, but not particularly attached to their superstitions, believing, or at least pretending to believe and to admire whatever is told them about religion. They are zealous observers of the laws of hospitality . . . great gamblers . . . [with] a dominant preference of these tribes for indolence." Sensing little hope for Christianization, du Ru returned to the fort to serve as its priest and chaplain. Once there, he built his own hut, erected a cross, and then thought last to build a chapel. Although du Ru longed to convert the Native people in the region, he did not commit to his missionary charge.[114]

De Montigny and du Ru had opportunities to interact with each other, the former by this time working among the Taensas and the Natchez. Never did du Ru give any indication that he held animosity toward de Montigny or any other Seminary missionary. Instead, du Ru felt de Montigny was a "saintly man," and it was du Ru's sincere desire that "we shall cooperate to promote religion and show by our actions that, though wearing different habits, we have the same purpose."[115] De Montigny, however, was far from impressed with the young Jesuit who, he complained, "makes little chapels in each mission," chapels "that count for little and will not stand long." De Montigny believed du Ru aspired to "take possession" of these villages and compelled one "to not dare go near them" unless one wanted to create another Tamarois debacle.[116]

Despite de Montigny's criticism, in May 1700 du Ru welcomed both de Montigny and Davion, these "excellent men who have tried missionary work with more zeal than precaution," to the fort. De Montigny announced his plan to return to Paris to seek aid for the missions, while Davion intended to return to the Tunicas to continue his work and to develop his own language skills. Du Ru's interactions with de Montigny seemed sincere and harmonious, so much so that "if later on M. de Montigny chose to accuse his fellow missionaries, and to give as an excuse for his refusal to return to Louisiana the difficulties he had with the Jesuits—it would seem that it was nothing but an excuse."[117]

Unlike the bickering missionaries among the Tamarois, these more southern missionaries were far more collegial and hospitable toward each other. When the thirty-year-old Father de Limoges eventually made his way to the lower end of the Mississippi to serve among the Houmas, the Seminary priests provided him with needed supplies after he nearly lost his life in a canoe accident and only managed to save his chalice and crucifix.[118] And when the Jesuit Father Pierre Dongé arrived in the region in early February 1702, he, along with Davion, de Limoges, and Balthazar de Boutteville, the Seminary's regional *procureur,* hunkered down for safety at Mobile after Father Foucault's murder later that July. Even Gravier spoke of the zeal with which the Seminary missionaries worked in the region. Davion made his appreciation clear: "I can truly say that it would be desirable that everywhere such perfect harmony be kept between the Jesuits and us as is kept here. We have been in Mobile for almost a year, four in all, and we are cooperating as if we were all members of one community."[119]

Although the two groups charitably worked together near the Gulf, Bergier still had concerns: "Ever since I have been in this country, I have always wanted to know one thing: if the Jesuits, by their privilege, have the right to establish missions wherever they want without consent of the bishop? If they have this right, then I don't oppose them and don't think badly of them for doing so. But if they don't have this right . . . from where does it come that they want to go against the order of the church and make themselves independent of the clergy and the bishop? I don't understand how they can dare make such demands."[120] Bergier's point was clear. No matter where du Ru or other Jesuits went, "each community had to be overseen by the bishop [of Québec] or by his *Grands Vicaires.*"[121] Saint-Vallier did not want the Jesuits near the mouth of the Mississippi, nor did he want them to have any authority in the region. Du Ru, the bishop exclaimed, "installed himself at Mobile without having been commissioned either by myself or by my vicar-general. Without order from me, [he] visited all the Indian nations on the sea shore, as if to take possession of the territory . . . the assertion made by the Jesuits that they are the first Mississippi missionaries is not true." From a canonical point of view, Saint-Vallier was correct: "Only those sent by the Bishop were to be considered as having been sent and could be said to be missionaries."[122]

By 1703, an unexpected boost to Saint-Vallier's authority arose when Iberville's fondness for the Jesuits waned. He "refused to return to the fort if only Jesuits there resided," and sought instead to establish Seminary missionaries at Mobile.[123] Iberville's and Bienville's opinions of the Jesuits greatly diminished once they realized that the Seminary missionaries were the ones actually working with the region's Native communities and not the Jesuits. Although du Ru had proven himself to be young and spirited, his own enthusiasm faltered, leading to outbursts and disdain for the Native peoples, calling them "lazy," with nothing but the desire to get out of him what they wanted. Dongé, who had arrived after du Ru, seemed more tolerant of conditions compared to the latter but also proved to have little patience with the Native communities.[124]

With Bienville's and Iberville's change in opinion, Saint-Vallier saw an opening. To remove the Jesuits from the Mississippi, he wielded his episcopal authority and canonically erected the Mobile Parish on July 20, 1703, in hopes that "by the King's piety and the zeal of those who are there in charge by his authority, a church will be built." In addition to the elevation of the parish, Saint-Vallier chose the first resident priest from the Séminaire des Missions Étrangères in Paris: Henri Roulleaux de la Vente, "who for a long time has already done praiseworthy work both in France and in the missions in the Indies, and who can and may perform all the functions of pastor among this Christian people." A younger, yet more feeble priest, Alexandre Huvé, was chosen to work with him.[125]

Tremblay's response to the selection of de la Vente for the Mobile Parish was moderate at best. He felt that he was "a good subject, but old, and does not know how to learn languages, but will be proper [to work with] the French since he has some talent for the word of God. He is wise, hard-working, and *fort detaché*."[126] Despite Tremblay's modest support, de la Vente did not have the vigor and zealous nature that Bienville longed for in a parish priest, nor did the two ever get along. But more important, and as Saint-Vallier had hoped, the Jesuits had no interest in working under the Seminary priests, "whose knowledge of the conditions of the mission field was, at best, often little more than theoretical, whose tendency was to settle all questions *a priori*, and who would not fail to make the Jesuit missionaries realize who held the whip." Thus, the Jesuits recalled du Ru, de Limoges, and Dongé back to Paris. By September 1704, Saint-Vallier and the Seminary finally saw their deepest desire come to fruition: From the Tamarois village to the Gulf of Mexico, the Seminary missionaries were Saint-Vallier's diocesan representatives. It was up to them alone to Christianize the Mississippi's Native peoples.[127]

The battle for the Tamarois did not simply go away when the decision arrived from Paris in 1702, nor did the work of the Seminary priests go uncontested once the Jesuits left the southern region. As late as 1719, the Jesuit Father Jean-Marie de Ville made his way to Mobile to briefly serve for six months, but did not stay long: "He had so well won over their spirits and won their hearts, everyone—officers, soldiers, *habitants*—wanted to keep him there. The fear of the interdiction on the part of the Missions Étrangères, who were *Grands Vicaires* in this location, kept him from acquiescing to their requests and [he] decided to leave." On June 6, 1720, Father de Ville died among the Natchez. Father Davion gave him his last rites.[128]

The initial warm collegiality experienced between the Jesuits and the Seminary missionaries in the late seventeenth century was severely tested, for once the two religious groups found themselves side-by-side in the Tamarois village, a long period of competition and strife ensued. No one went unscathed, not even the Tamarois, who clearly perceived the discord between the two groups. While relationships functioned more amicably to the south, a subtle tenseness filled the air nonetheless until the Jesuits were removed. Rumpuses of the *vigne contesté* aside, the Seminary missionaries variously served along the Mississippi between 1699 and 1725. Each had a mission to attend to, but each also suffered from the environment, lack of funds and goods, and communication woes. And yet, each found himself engaged in cultural interactions that had the potential to transform one's own beliefs and understandings, whether recognized or not.

CHAPTER 6

De Montigny, the Taensas, and the Natchez

D e Montigny had long desired to be a missionary and was the most likely one to have developed the idea for the Mississippi missions in the first place. But de Montigny's Mississippi story is more the tale of an administrator than that of a missionary, a man who strove to address cultures and peoples with rigid diocesan authority rather than through adjustments, much less a middle ground. As he himself soon found, missioning was never straightforward. He and his colleagues suffered from significant trials that none could resolve—poor funding and access to goods, communication and language barriers, cultural misunderstandings, lack of community, and the effects of the harsh climate and terrain on their health. It was a lonely endeavor being a Mississippi missionary, with experiences that went well beyond those of a small parish priest in Québec. No missionary went untested, not even Saint-Vallier's *Grand Vicaire*.

De Montigny's work began slowly. For at least four months after his midsummer trip to Fort Maurepas, he suffered from the effects of poor food, stagnant water, and fatigue. Nonetheless, as the missionary leader, de Montigny had administrative duties to attend to. The men who had traveled the Mississippi with him had to be paid. But de Montigny "could not get them to accept the payment in Canadian funds since some live among the Illinois, married to Illinois women, [and] some don't want to return to Québec." As for others, they "have such small wages that I couldn't let them leave without buying some clothing and other goods that they needed." De Montigny knew that if his workers were not adequately paid, harm could come to the missions either through loss of help or loss of alliance with Frenchmen in the region. Consequently, de Montigny requested understanding from Tremblay to accept 1,000 livres in receipts for goods purchased at the fort. As he so often did, Tremblay responded with frustration: "This will increase our debt even more, and it is up to you, Monseigneur [Laval], to see how we are going to recover from this . . . if I pay these debts, I won't be able to send you anything."[1]

The demand for dissimilar forms of payment was but one of several confrontations that occurred between de Montigny and his workers. During the summer of 1699, de Montigny, Davion, and sixteen other men literally dragged themselves through the gates of Fort Maurepas, terribly influenced by the dangerous effects of climate, terrain, and poor water that they had had to endure. Although the French soldiers and officers tried to help them recover from such physical strife, an extended stay was impossible since there were not enough foodstuffs even for the inhabitants of the fort. Thus, after nine days of rest, Commander Sauvolle "asked them to leave," an initiative on the officer's part that "pleased" de Montigny since it protected him from relaying the bad news to his men himself. Certainly de Montigny did not desire to leave, but extreme animosity had developed between the missionary and his Frenchmen. He "did not dare command his men that were with him [to leave]; they would have wanted to do him some harm if he spoke to them himself."[2]

Even de Montigny's personal servant proved troublesome. Initially, each missionary was to have been accompanied by a second priest so that they might work together, participate in prayer and liturgy, and help secure goods in one's cabin. However, de Montigny made no such assignments and each missionary, at best, had only a valet as an assistant. But valets "were [often] the largest crosses a missionary had to bear." Some were particularly intolerable when needed the most. "Iberville told me that when he was in the mission," wrote Tremblay, that de Montigny "had to threaten his valet [Charles Dumont] with a stick. He was more the master than de Montigny," witnessed Iberville.[3]

Frenchmen enjoyed the freedoms of the Mississippi. Often without any oversight, they could liberally travel about and do as they wished. Many of these men, in fact, were transforming into a lifeway that was "beyond the control of legitimate authority," a point they seemed to glory in. De Montigny certainly found this to be true, for although he had authority over Dumont, there seemed to be hesitation or even an inability to maintain influence over his own servant.[4] For this and other reasons, de Montigny requested release from his role as *Grand Vicaire*. He preferred that the Seminary leadership assign another missionary "to take care of the day to day activities of the missions because I am not proper for this." De Montigny had already developed "an extreme repugnance, not wanting to do anything more than to care for the mission I serve," and preferred to "distance myself from *les affaires* so as to advance my righteousness, one of the principle motives that brought me to these missions."[5]

Without any chance of a quick response from Québec, work had to move on. As de Montigny sought to ease the challenges before him, he proposed to "obtain some concessions within each mission, or two or three leagues of land" to help their work.[6] Several previous missionaries had received land from various Native communities. Saint-Cosme accepted an offer from the chief of the Cahokias to provide him land on which to build a house and a chapel. A reciprocal exchange was expected—land for teaching; a chapel and a place to learn more about the white man's *manitou*. Father du Ru negotiated for land behind his church. Once again, a reciprocal exchange occurred—land for a knife and other goods; again, a place behind the chapel to expand the mission and access to the white man's powers.

When Native peoples welcomed the stranger into their village, they sought to develop firm social accords that strengthened their community. To build and maintain these relationships, the Native communities embraced the institution of reciprocity that included the exchange of goods, even an offering of land in exchange for access to a missionary's *manitou*. Its introduction into their world was hoped to increase protection, prosperity in hunt, success in war, and defense from disease. No matter the exchange, a reciprocal response was key in building the newly established relationship.[7] But de Montigny made no mention of reciprocity in his proposal for concessions. He did not understand that any attempt to take land on his part could quickly threaten a Native community that relied on its terrain for farming, hunting, and sacred ceremonies. Ultimately, Native peoples "defended passionately the connections between land and identity that emerged through centuries of living with the land, an association that contained an essential spiritual element."[8]

One simply could not take acreage from a nation at his pleasure, a point made all too clear among the Natchez some twenty-nine years after de Montigny lived among them. At that time, a French colonial commandant named Sieur de Chépart spotted a prized patch of land in the center of the Natchez village that he wished to take for himself. The Natchez protested, telling Chépart that the "bones of their ancestors were held there in their temple." But Chépart made threats and promised "to set fire to the temple" if they did not give him this land. Finally, the Natchez seemingly conceded but needed "two moons longer . . . to prepare their new home." This time was granted but with further penalty that they "pay a large sum in poultry, grain, and pots of oil, as well as pelts to serve as interest for the delay that he was allowing them." The Natchez accepted his demands but quietly and carefully planned an assault on Chépart and the French for their disrespect. The morning of November 28, 1729, they began their attack. By the end of the day, some 230 French lives were lost and dozens more enslaved. The analysis of this event by Lieutenant Jean-François-Benjamin Dumont de Montigny (no relation to Father de Montigny) proved exact: "Never had the lands of Indians been so brazenly confiscated. Up until then, if one had built on the Indians' lands, either the Indians themselves had granted the land so as to gain the friendship and protection of the French for themselves and their habitations, or else those who had settled on the Indian lands had paid them in advance with trade goods."[9] The Natchez "were the dominant people casting out the disrespectful newcomers who would not play by Natchez rules."[10]

Aside from thoughts of taking land, Father de Montigny also considered gathering all Native communities into one area through enticements of gifts and well-ornamented churches that "caught their eye."[11] Saint-Cosme, who replaced de Montigny among the Natchez in July 1700, had thoughts of doing much the same. But the dispersal of Natchez homesteads over thirty square miles made either priest's work quite difficult, as it forced them to go it on foot and to rely on the generosity of the Natchez for sustenance. Saint-Cosme in particular found that at best he could baptize a few children, "the only profit one can make in these missions." Otherwise, he believed that the fruits of the Natchez would not be large "because during the four or five days it takes to make a tour of a village, children can die before a missionary knows it."[12] To counter the dispersal of his flock, Saint-Cosme proposed moving himself and a small group of Natchez to a more controlled village that was "advantageous for farming, hunting, and fishing." Saint-Cosme intended to establish himself to be the "*maître* [master] of this location," and in so doing to "bring along several cabins of individuals who have already promised to follow me so as to distance themselves from shameful nighttime assemblies that take place among these nations," gatherings that "cause all sorts of disorder and are in opposition to the Gospel."[13]

Like de Montigny, Saint-Cosme wanted to create his own community, but the use of the word *maître* suggested a vertical relationship, a hierarchy with

oppression, dominance, and force that could negatively impact one's relationship with the Natchez. While among the Tamarois, Saint-Cosme had used
this term when discussing with Binneteau just which religious group would
serve as "master" of the Tamarois mission. Saint-Cosme even advised against
establishing additional missions along the Mississippi, at least until the French
were better fortified in the region and could serve as "masters of the Indians."[14]
Aggressively approaching any Native community could compromise one's ability to negotiate relationship. Reacting with force could prevent some form of
consensus or even a middle ground.

Either priest's suggestion was rather short-sighted, given the well-known
failure of the Jesuit reservation of Sillery near Québec. Like many missionaries
before and after them, the Jesuits had grown weary of having to travel between
villages or with hunting parties. They longed to have greater and perhaps easier contact with and control over their flocks, certain that "European-styled
agricultural communities" could enhance their Christianization efforts. But
Sillery proved problematic. While some among the Montagnais nation felt
that the village was an answer to warfare and economic problems, others of
this Native community felt that gathering them together into one village and
then having Christianity imposed upon them was unacceptable. "All the elders
favored French aid but there was a nearly uniform rejection of any moves towards accepting Christianity." In the end, Sillery proved far too disruptive to
the lifeway patterns, the spirituality, and the society of the Native peoples and
subsequently failed. The Montagnais tenaciously held on to their traditions
and their world view.[15]

No matter the Native community, each chose their village center for good
reason—freedom from flooding, fertile soil, abundant sources of fresh water,
game and fish. The appeal of their land stemmed from its suitability for trade
and defense as well as important associations with their spirituality. Each village contained a central plaza whereby they engaged in traditional games and
carried out ceremonial activities. Within a sacred temple, some maintained a
perpetual flame and preserved the bones of deceased leaders. Out from this
central village were clusters of dwellings where the members of the community
lived and watched over their cultivated fields. These farmsteads, the ceremonial
center, the plaza, and the hunting grounds gave dispersed hamlets a sense of
unity.[16] Any attempt to move largely distributed Indian communities into one
gathered village was simply untenable.

Aside from geographical attentions, de Montigny also had great interest in reforming the Taensas' simple manner of dress. "The men here are all naked. Most girls as well, up until age seven or eight; some even to the age of ten or twelve," wrote the Seminary priest. "All the other girls, until they are married, only have a belt as wide as a half foot to a foot with a fringe that falls to their knees or their feet. Sometimes they wear a cloak but slip it off when they work." De Montigny was decidedly troubled but hopeful concerning their nakedness: "What with their mild composure, and their respect for the missionaries, I am persuaded that once I know the language a little, I will reform this abuse that otherwise does not seem to concern them, being accustomed to it since birth."[17]

De Montigny was correct—the Taensas were long accustomed to their cultural vestment. A Native community's clothing was designed based on the climate and the region's materials. But as co-leader of the Québec diocese for some three years, de Montigny was used to enforcing ordinances that sought to maintain high moral order among French men and women. Bishop and clergy alike believed that "the nakedness of their [the women's] necks and shoulders is scandalous. . . . They cannot, in conscious, and without rendering themselves guilty of sin, appear in this manner neither inside nor outside their houses." To de Montigny and fellow clergy, immoral dress "weakened the personal spiritual connection to God and threatened one's place in the transcendent [Christian] spiritual community." Consequently, priests could "not receive women in this state at communion, at marriage, or at baptism to hold children, or at the offertory. This [ordinance is] for all those who dress in this manner, either inside or outside their houses."[18] Only familiar with the authority of a priest and a diocesan leader, de Montigny preferred a higher moral standard along the Mississippi rather than an adjustment toward the Taensas culture. Women's necks and shoulders were a threat to the Catholic faith. De Montigny had to "reform this abuse" and make Taensas fashion more conducive to Christian carriage.

De Montigny also intended to transform the Taensas' adherence to particular practices that venerated their chief. Taensas leaders were to be honored, to be treated with great admiration and respect. Only specific elders or the most considered individuals of the Taensas were allowed to enter his cabin, never women and children. "One did not dare sit on his bed, drink from his goblet, nor pass between the chief and the evening flame" that one lit in his cabin. Even sowing and harvesting were in reverence to the chief, as the entire

Sauvagesse Femme du Chef, by Jean-François-Benjamin Dumont de Montigny. Courtesy of the Newberry Library, Edward E. Ayer Digital Collection, Ayer MS 257, no. 17.

village was expected to participate. After a great dance and meal to which all contributed, "the men and the women went to the Chief's land and within a half a day had either worked, sowed, or harvested the field." When repairs were needed for the chief's house or their sacred temple, many contributed to these activities as well.[19]

Such honor to a chief was well and good, much like many a European's respect for his or her sovereign. Nonetheless, some of the admiration given to a Taensas leader deeply troubled de Montigny, for whenever a Taensas chief died, numerous individuals who had served him in his earthly life were sacrificed to serve him in his afterlife. Consequently, upon the death of one Taensas chief, de Montigny put a stop to the sacrificial aspect of the funeral.[20] While he believed he saved the lives of those not sacrificed, de Montigny's disruption of their Native tradition impeded the society's reverence of their chief as well as balance within their spiritual world.

Soon after, Iberville arrived in the village and witnessed an event that placed the Taensas' spirituality and world view in direct opposition to de Montigny's audacious action just a few days prior. As Iberville described it, the night of March 16–17, 1700, "it rained and thundered a great deal . . . lightning struck the Taensas' temple, set it on fire, and burned it up. To appease the Spirit who they say is angry, these Indians threw five little infants-in-arms into the temple fire. They would have thrown several others into it had it not been for three Frenchmen who rushed up and prevented them from doing so." Iberville explained, "An old man, about sixty-five years old who played the role of a chief priest, took his stand close to the fire, shouting in a loud voice, 'Women, bring your children and offer them to the Spirit as a sacrifice to appease him.' Five of those women did so, bringing him their infants whom he seized and hurled into the middle of the flames. The act of those women was considered by the Indians as one of the noblest that could be performed." Within a matter of days, these women, "clothed in a white robe made from mulberry bark, and [with] a big white feather [that] was put on the head of each," seated themselves before the home of the soon to be chief of the Taensas. "All day they showed themselves at the door of the chief's hut, seated on cane mats, where many brought presents to them. Everybody in the village kept busy that day, surrounding the dead chief's hut with a palisade of cane mats, reserving the hut to be used as a temple. In it, the fire was lighted, in keeping with their custom."[21]

For both the Taensas and the neighboring Natchez, their spirituality was comprised of three important realms—the upper realm, the lower realm, and the present realm. The upper realm held the sky, the sun, the moon, the stars, lightning, and thunder. The lower realm held the reptiles, fishes, snakes, and legendary monsters. The present realm, the earthly realm, held animals, plants, and human beings. Within both traditions, only the Great Sun (the tribe's paramount chief) had the ability to transcend beyond the present realm into the others and to maintain unity and balance within the cosmos. As such, when a chief died, elaborate ceremonies took place to offer him food and gifts for the beyond. The sacrifice of his servants who had long performed duties on earth allowed them to follow their master into the afterlife and serve him there.[22] But when lightning destroyed their sacred temple, the Taensas believed that "the spirit was incensed because no one was put to death on the decease of the last Chief, and that it was necessary to appease him."[23] Thus, when the "five heroines" sacrificed their children to accompany the deceased chief into the afterworld, they returned order and unity to the Taensas' spiritual realm.

Death and convoy of Serpent Piqué, a Great Sun of the Natchez. Du Pratz, *Histoire de la Louisiane,* vol. 3 (Paris: De Bure, l'Aîné, 1758), 55.

Despite his own horror at the events that had transpired, de Montigny found a sense of order and unity through his own spirituality. While some Frenchmen had "prevented them from throwing more children into the fire," wrote de Montigny, "four [or five] children were thus burned, fortunately they had been recently baptized."[24] The Taensas' spirit was appeased through these sacrifices, but de Montigny also took comfort in knowing that through the sacrament of baptism, the sacrificed children had entered heaven. Like the Taensas, de Montigny felt a sense of balance had returned between this world and the beyond.

Some four days after lightning struck the temple, de Montigny packed up his belongings and, with the assistance of Iberville and six Taensas, left for the Natchez, who were more numerous and "much more disposed to accept a missionary's teaching," suggested du Ru.[25] Like the Taensas, they too had great reverence for their paramount leader. The Great Sun himself lived in a large house on top of a platform mound that served as the ceremonial center for the people of their nation. Opposite the Great Sun's mound was the temple mound. The Great Sun, his children (the Little Suns), along with his sister and her children formed the highest class in Natchez society known as the Suns. Below the Suns were the Nobles, followed by the Honored People, then the Stinkards, the lowest ranked members of the nation. Much like the Taensas, the Suns' subjects and village chiefs could never be in their presence "without saluting them thrice, and raising a cry, or rather a sort of howling." When walking along a path, Natchez villagers were "obliged to stop, range themselves in order on the road, and howl in the manner above mentioned till they are passed." Even during meals, "no one, not even their nearest relations, and those who compose their nobility, when they have the honour to eat with them, have a right to drink out of the same cup, or put their hands in the same dish."[26]

As he had experienced among the Taensas, de Montigny witnessed the beginnings of a sacrificial funeral upon the death of a Great Sun of the Natchez. As villagers prepared to sacrifice individuals, de Montigny attempted to prevent them from carrying out their tradition. He "made them promise to not put anyone to death." To appease de Montigny, the Natchez "gave him a little female slave whom they had resolved to put to death but for his prohibition." To further keep de Montigny from disrupting the funeral sacrifices, the chief's sister, Ouachil Tamail, persuaded him "to retire to a distant village so as not to have his head split with the noise they would make in a ceremony where they all were to take part." De Montigny, in turn, "believed her and withdrew, but in his absence, they put to death those whom they believed to be necessary to go to cook and to wait on the chief in the other world."[27]

The Taensas believed de Montigny's interference in the sacrifice of Taensas villagers angered spirits of the upper realm, leading to the lightning strike that destroyed their temple. To appease their gods, they countered by sacrificing children so as to return balance to their society. To work around de Montigny's unwelcomed demands, the Natchez provided him with a female slave and sent him away using as an excuse the noise that might disturb him. They found a way to ensure that order remained within their spiritual realm without his interference. But neither the Natchez nor the Taensas seemed to take any steps toward harming or killing de Montigny. Since neither had previous experience with a French missionary and his spiritual powers, they were likely unsure, if not fearful, of the power and reaction of de Montigny's *manitou* if the priest were put to death. They did not want to disrupt the balance they otherwise worked to maintain within their world view.

To achieve any sense of middle ground, de Montigny had to "find a means, other than force, to gain the cooperation or consent" of the Taensas and Natchez. He "had, of necessity, to attempt to understand the world and the reasoning of others and to assimilate enough of that reasoning to put it to their [his] own purposes."[28] But de Montigny did not appear to try and learn about the Taensas or the Natchez cultures, nor to find commonalities or congruences to help him introduce Christianity to them in a manner that could devise even a hint of middle ground. From the beginning of his contact with them, he intended to change their clothing, to move them or possibly take their land, even to end their sacrifices. He seemed unwilling to understand the people he chose to work with, to let go of his standards as a Québec priest or even as a diocesan leader. Against the advice of the Seminary leaders, de Montigny was unwilling to adjust to the cultures among which he lived.

By May of 1700, after less than ten months among the Taensas and the Natchez, de Montigny chose to leave the region. Fear and frustration, the lack of control over the Native communities, their insistence on maintaining cultural traditions, not to mention his inability to control his workers, ingest palatable food, or find a middle ground were all the impetus for his departure. In modern terms, de Montigny's repugnance was the result of pure culture shock, the "anxiety resulting from the disorientation encountered upon entering a new culture." As Leahey describes it, "in the case of someone who may have had a very responsible position in his home country but finds himself as a 'foreigner' in a much less prestigious occupation," he becomes unsure even of his own identity.[29] De Montigny had been a co-leader of the diocese, literally the head of the Québec church for three years with religious authority over the clergy and colonists in New France. He had enforced ordinances when needed throughout the diocese and expected them to be followed. But while serving as *Grand Vicaire* on the Mississippi was certainly prestigious enough, de Montigny could not use the authority he once held. For a man who had long desired to serve as a Mississippi missionary, who had had the energy to descend the Mississippi not once but twice in a nine-month span, and was convinced of the need to save the "thousands of souls" found along the river's banks and tributaries, all desires to fulfill his calling had vanished.

On May 19, 1700, after just a few weeks among the Natchez, and "not having been able to make any progress," de Montigny made his way to Fort Maurepas.[30] On May 25, Iberville announced that de Montigny was returning to France with him, and by May 28 the broken priest was on board a ship bound for Europe, vowing never to return to the Mississippi River. Once in France, de Montigny and his valet Charles recuperated at the Séminaire.[31] When de Montigny began to share his experiences, he overwhelmed many with his unanticipated words. "All that he told us greatly disgusted us with regard to these missions and made us fear that it was not at all what one had reported," wrote Tremblay.[32] De Montigny was deeply revolted by the Mississippi Valley and knew firsthand the grossly exaggerated error—there were not thousands, nor millions of Native peoples present. Instead, "there were many small nations divided one from the other by war, but that there were not five or six nations in that region that were known by the French that merited two missionaries and were capable of being occupied."[33] In his long list of frustrations, de Montigny expressed annoyance "that the Jesuits crossed them at every corner; the Indians pillaged them, short of stripping and robbing them, pushed by others [perhaps the English] to do this; travel was fatiguing, harsh, and expensive; it was difficult to carry on in faith for those there present."[34]

When de Montigny left the Mississippi River Valley, he abandoned all responsibilities entrusted to him, not to mention the morale and safety of his colleagues. For two and a half months the Parisian leadership pleaded with him "to go back to Québec, to serve as one of the directors of the Séminaire, to which de Montigny had nothing but complete opposition." The Parisian leadership even went so far as to tell him "that he was going to demoralize all those that he left there, that it wasn't good to start something and then leave it, that one would view that as uncommitted."[35] But nothing swayed de Montigny, who "brought back from the Mississippi such a pessimistic view of what one can do there that he is completely resolved never to return."[36] De Montigny preferred, instead, to either become a Trappist monk or to travel to China to satisfy his missionary desires. In the end, "feeling it would be unfortunate to lose a good subject to a monastery," the Seminary leadership gave in and sent de Montigny to East Asia. Although he did serve as a missionary for some ten years, by 1712 he was back in Paris as Tremblay's assistant with oversight of the missions in East Asia and along the Mississippi River.[37]

De Montigny was the early, firsthand witness to the plight of the Mississippi missionaries, the first to relay their hardships to Paris. Consequently, he penned a long list of issues he felt had to be addressed to support colleagues who remained along the river. He demanded assurances that the Mississippi region be fully colonized so that the missionaries could better plan their course of action. He further suggested that the missions not be set up so far from the sea, nor be so separated one from the other to ensure greater safety. While on the Mississippi, de Montigny himself certainly had had the power to make adjustments, especially as he learned of the difficult terrain, transportation woes, and the like. But his initial placement of missionaries in select villages led to the vast distance between the Tamarois and all other missions to the south. His own choices led to some of the challenges each faced and for which there were no easy answers.[38]

Communication woes concerned de Montigny. "The danger that they [letters] are taken and opened by passing through so many hands, and the long time it takes to get an answer" troubled him.[39] Living in de Montigny's long-desired Tamarois mission, Bergier went without word from Paris or Québec for months and years at a time.[40] The Jesuits controlled the more northern missions, and any letters sent south from Québec had to "to pass through the hands of those who regard us as their persecutors." Indeed, Fathers Mermet and Marest handed Bergier an opened letter that was sent to him by Saint-Vallier. "They believed that the letter was addressed to them as well as to our missionaries," wrote Tremblay.[41] Alternatively, the Jesuits' affairs and communication went better than they did for the Seminary priests. Often "the Jesuits received news of importance to them," such as the Chinese Rites controversy and strife with the Seminary in Paris. Consequently, Bergier implored the Seminary leadership to provide him with any news of East Asia "to serve as our fair defense when needed."[42] To try and maintain communication with Québec, Bergier even negotiated with Chief 8ananghissé of the Poux nation to transport his letters to and from Canada. Although willing to facilitate such delivery, 8ananghissé died shortly after their meeting. With that, Bergier's opportunity to secure more reliable communication ended.[43]

Originally, all communication was to have flowed to and from Québec.

But seasonal changes disrupted regular correspondence, seeded feelings of isolation, and kept the missionaries from knowing how they were each proceeding with their work, or even if they were alive. With a transition toward using the Gulf of Mexico as the portal for moving correspondence and supplies northward, de Montigny's long-desired Tamarois mission looked more and more obsolete since "the travelers were not wanting to bring our provisions up here from the sea." Consequently, Bergier had to "send a canoe down river each year to get our goods [and letters]." This entailed hiring on additional workers "if one wants to subsist and maintain correspondence."[44] And yet, receiving letters and supplies via the Gulf was never secure. Simply outfitting a boat to traverse the Atlantic was arduous at best. Depending on the ship's size, not to mention the weather and the weight of cargo, it could take weeks to complete a trip across the Atlantic, if the ship made it at all.[45] Consequently, missionaries often spent extended periods of time at the Gulf, away from their villages, awaiting the arrival of goods from France.

De Montigny himself began the precedent of making purchases at Fort Maurepas near modern-day Biloxi, Mississippi, an action that promoted nothing but cold, hardened feelings on both sides of the Atlantic. Although de Montigny put forth an effort to pay off one bill of 75 livres that he personally owed, and to provide money to Tremblay for a debt he owed to Davion, he otherwise left it to Tremblay to cover his expenses at Fort Maurepas. But because de Montigny had left behind "clothes and all of his equipment in the Natchez village," Tremblay had to pay "sixty livres for clothing for de Montigny's valet, Charles, sixty livres for his return to Canada, sixty livres for expenses at La Rochelle, and some fifty livres for expenses at the Séminaire in Paris." Additionally, Tremblay sent some 300 livres to Iberville for the funds he advanced to de Montigny for his departure from the Baie de Biloxi. All of this was wasted funds in the eyes of Tremblay.[46]

Even Saint-Cosme, Davion, and Boutteville followed de Montigny's example. They became regular customers at Fort Louis at Mobile, and often spent beyond their means, a process that continued "as long as one did not regulate their spending."[47] But expenses were not necessarily amassed willy-nilly. To move about, one had to hire canoes. To equip canoes, this too cost money. Some items were needed to help maintain calm within the region, "to make a small present to approach this or that village, to keep them at peace, to win over several chiefs for the good of his mission."[48] If and when supplies did arrive, they proved helpful for some, useless for others: "I have learned of the poor state of our missionaries on the Mississippi," wrote Tremblay. "They send me their requests and their bills. I have sent them five cassocks, six hats, twelve pairs of shoes, six pairs of stockings, twenty-eight or thirty shirts, three dozen collars, a missal, ten pounds of vermillion. . . . You will notice that these men do not agree. De Montigny remarked that I should send them flour, water, brandy, and oil, that these items are needed. . . . Saint-Cosme has since told me that these items are useless."[49]

Each missionary had specific needs and requests according to his own situation. De Montigny's "difficulty in adjusting to *sagamité* led to his request for flour." Alternatively, Saint-Cosme was acclimated to the Native corn stew and advised Tremblay "that one should not trouble oneself with sending flour," especially since "transporting barrels of flour in canoes is difficult," not to mention that oftentimes food shipped from France arrived spoiled.[50] But for Saint-Cosme, the commodity still had its purpose: "He easily trades away his flour . . . to obtain what he wants," wrote Tremblay.[51]

Despite his economic sensitivities, even Bergier had his limits: "I do not know what you are thinking about and which requests you are following to send us brandy, oil, and flour. Nothing is more useless than these items; this is wasted money. We need powder, vermillion, bells, small hatchets, knives, beads, rings . . . not so much for ourselves but for the payment of our workers." Clothing also had to be addressed: "I'm just as naked as Saint-Cosme and Boutteville; I am wearing my cassock from France in tatters, resewn with scraps tossed out by others."[52] While Bergier "did not wish to complain . . . as this does not please God," a good cassock was a small need that had to be met "to prevent unwanted whispers" regarding "his natural state, and the aftermath that could result."[53] Simply put, "if I don't receive some clothes [white collars and a cassock] . . . I will have to dress in skins."[54] Bergier intended to vest as a priest, to show himself to be a man of God, a Seminary missionary, not a Jesuit nor an Indian.

Colleagues also gave each other grief when attempting to acquire goods. Exasperated that needed supplies had not arrived, Bergier at first blamed Tremblay.[55] But after reviewing accounts of his colleagues, Bergier found that they, not Tremblay, were the problem. Davion had taken 300 livres that de Tonti had intended for Tremblay and "used these funds to pay his [Davion's] *engagé*." Rather than forwarding "150 livres worth of pelts" sent by Bergier for M. Grignon at La Rochelle to purchase goods, "Davion used them to trade for exorbitantly priced powder and vermillion at Mobile." Davion even took 100 ecus, owed to Bergier by de Tonti, and used them to pay off other debts at the mouth of the Mississippi. "I understand nothing within such conduct," wrote Bergier. "I never gave Davion nor Boutteville permission to make purchases at the store for us, nor to borrow anything. My intention has always been to content myself with goods sent from France."[56]

Tremblay constantly voiced his annoyance with the missionaries' spending activities. He threatened "to hide when bills came in [rather than] . . . to have to decide from where to pull funds." He further "demanded audits of his own work" to prove that he was doing all he could to appease the many requests received. So frustrated was Tremblay by the rising debt of the Mississippi missionaries that he "threatened to refuse payment" or even "to resign" if the missionaries continued to overspend.[57] But Tremblay's concerns were well-founded. Throughout the time frame of the missionaries on the Mississippi, France was struggling. The king's coffers were stretched thin with money spent to fight in Queen Anne's War, otherwise known as the War of Spanish Succession. The decentralization of the economy to port cities subsequently raised costs throughout Paris and made investments abroad nearly impossible to obtain. Even the Jesuits faced a decline in private donors willing to fund their missionary work, while the Catholic Church as a whole suffered from attacks by Huguenots on priests and churches alike in eastern France. With charitable giving nearly frozen, hunger proved the norm for many. And if wars, a poor economy, and the lack of donors were not enough, the Séminaire de Québec faced another debilitating event: a devastating fire that nearly cost Laval his life.[58] France was so miserable and funds so rare that no one was willing to lend money to a seemingly insignificant seminary in Canada. In the first year alone, the missionaries had already amassed so much debt for goods purchased that the king's 3,000 livres could not cover their needs on an annual basis. In 1703, some 2,700 livres in *lettres de change* were made just at the hands of Saint-Cosme and Boutteville, well before receiving the annual 3,000 livres.[59] Only Bergier, "a worthy worker," would ever please Tremblay. Eternally conscious of funding woes, Bergier humbly asked Tremblay "to fill only half of a list of goods and to wait until one had [additional] funds for the missions."[60] While Davion and Saint-Cosme demanded more and more funds and goods,

Bergier asked for less and less, preferring to live the impoverished life he was asked to maintain, longing to fulfill his call: "I will be happy [if God] makes me a missionary as his heart desires," wrote Bergier.[61]

Communication woes, lack of funds and supplies, and unanticipated transportation strategies all stemmed from de Montigny's hastily planned venture. His unwillingness to make adjustments while on the Mississippi meant that many of his complaints went unresolved. Consequently, a large row ensued between Tremblay and the fallen missionary: "I had a number of fights with him in the presence of our men," wrote Tremblay. "He wanted me to send more than 3,000 livres of goods to the Mississippi missionaries so as to pay their workers and put them into the position to subsist and build their establishments." To counter the high costs, Tremblay himself "prepared a list of things that I believed were needed by them [amounting to] six or seven hundred livres." But de Montigny was not content and looked at Tremblay "as a hard, uncompassionate man." Forced to provide his reasons before the Seminary leadership as to why he would not send the goods demanded, Tremblay exclaimed that they should have arrived through Québec and not through the mouth of the Mississippi since this route had not yet been fully established. Not one to back down, Tremblay was quick to remind de Montigny "that leaving the Mississippi, he compromised the missions that he had us undertake." But de Montigny fought back. He himself had paid "a third of the first expenses made in this enterprise and was not obligated to pay anything else . . . it was already a lot that he left his equipment behind . . . but there was nothing more he could do."[62]

All that Tremblay learned from de Montigny created within him a great distaste for the Mississippi missions. He found little faith in the missionaries assigned to the region and could "only count on Bergier, Davion, and Foucault," although the latter two had health issues that remained on Tremblay's mind. With de Montigny out of the picture, Tremblay was adamant that the missionaries "work closer together and not be so far apart because of the immense travel expenses." His argument was clear: "Neither subjects nor goods should come from Canada. Such travel is too expensive, tiring and dangerous." So dire was the situation between Québec and the Mississippi that de Montigny even suggested that "Canada can neither serve as our spiritual guide nor our temporal support."[63] In the end, neither route ever functioned well during the

Seminary priests' time on the Mississippi and none of the missionaries ever made any effort to move closer together. The missionaries endlessly struggled to receive correspondence, goods, and spiritual support.

De Montigny's early firsthand accounting of the region and its challenges certainly impacted the attitudes of many. Even Saint-Vallier came to believe that the missions were destined to fail. To a man, the southern terrain proved near impossible to reside in. The missionaries were often sick and otherwise had to suffer through a period of "southern seasoning" to harden themselves for the climate and the terrain.[64] When game or fish could be consumed, therein was a reward. When *sagamité* or corn stew was the only fare, therein emerged a sick stomach and little nourishment. At times, with poor knowledge of the region and lack of solid subsistence strategies, the missionaries found themselves relying on Native communities just to survive.[65]

Extreme enthusiasm to convert Native peoples to Christianity led de Montigny to found missions that were greatly separated one from the other. Within each location, only one of the two prescribed missionaries was ever assigned. Facing poor communication, lack of supplies, and language and cultural challenges, not to mention concerns for safety and security, de Montigny chose to abandon the Mississippi venture. He was unwilling to find a middle ground in his work with the Native communities. He was unwilling to transform from the rigid strictness of a Québec priest, even a diocesan leader, to the life of a missionary on the Mississippi. From all appearances, his efforts to Christianize Native men, women, and children was through force, through learned Québecois strategies and ordinances, not through understanding or adjustment to the region. De Montigny sought a perfect situation where he could fulfill his longing to be a missionary with little effort. What he found was distasteful and insurmountable.

CHAPTER 7

Foucault and the Quapaws

The Quapaw *Three Villages Robe*, a gift that made its way to Versailles in the mid-eighteenth century, portrays three of the traditional villages of the Quapaws—Osotouy, Tourima, and Kappa—along with core cultural traditions of the Arkansas nation itself. Painted in the middle of the robe are the Sky People (those responsible for the spiritual needs of the community) and the Earth People (those responsible for agriculture and warfare). Entrances to Quapaw long houses are portrayed along with the two calumets—one of war and one of peace. Their eastern enemy, the Chickasaws, kneel with arms drawn; some Chickasaws flee. The Quapaws, in turn, confront their enemy with traditional bows and arrows as well as with long guns. Alone in the far corner stand four French houses, one possibly a chapel. Two Frenchmen dressed in knickers and boots lazily lean against the walls of these structures and smoke from long clay pipes. Another Frenchman stands to the side, seeming to fiddle with a traditional bow. Drawn by an anonymous Quapaw, the robe gives prominence to Quapaw culture, tradition, and spirituality. An aside is given to the Quapaws' interpretation of the French.[1]

Marquette and Jolliet first interacted with the Quapaws in 1673. Theirs was a cautious encounter, for the Quapaws were new residents in the region, having arrived sometime in the mid-seventeenth century. Isolated, the Quapaws had to find a way to strengthen and stabilize themselves. They certainly understood that "interdependence was a form of power," but they also knew that "a people with no links of interdependence could be in trouble."[2] Thus, as Marquette and Jolliet approached their community, the Quapaws were reassured of the strangers' peaceful intent only by their initial presentation of the calumet. The Quapaws welcomed the Frenchmen into their village and a calumet celebration soon followed.

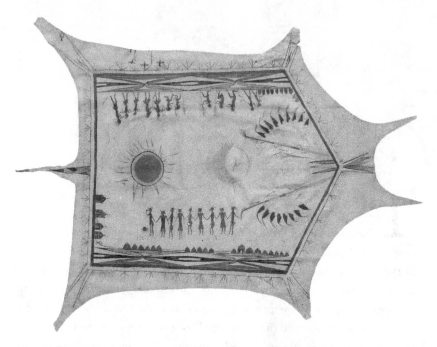

Three Villages Robe of the Quapaws. Inventory number 71.1934.33.7 D. Courtesy of the Musée du Quai Branly-Jacques Chirac, Dist.RMN-Grand Palais/Art Resource.

Nine years later, and again with caution, La Salle and de Tonti made their way to all four villages, the lost Quapaw village of Tongigua included. As La Salle and de Tonti approached, they heard what they thought were war chants coming from the village. Quickly, they moved to the opposite shore and felled trees to build a protective barricade along the river. The Quapaws themselves guardedly approached the Frenchmen. One warrior shot an arrow at de Tonti's feet to determine if he came in war or in peace. When de Tonti did not respond in kind, the Quapaws welcomed them into their village and celebrated the calumet once again.

After 1682, more frequent interactions between the French and the Quapaws occurred, particularly once de Tonti established Arkansas Post in 1686, making the French a more regular presence among this Native community. Subsequent visits took place throughout the 1690s, and then shortly after Christmas Day 1698 Fathers Saint-Cosme, de Montigny, and Davion encountered the Quapaws for their first time. Like others before them, the missionaries presented the calumet as they approached the Quapaws to demonstrate peaceful intentions. Once again, the calumet ceremony soon followed.

Both the Quapaws and the French understood that the presentation of the calumet could help delineate whether an unknown person came as friend or foe. But beyond this initial belief, their understanding of the sacred pipe's symbolism varied. For the French, the calumet was "a useful element of frontier diplomacy, based on principles of political and economic interaction held by Europeans during the colonial era." The French believed that the calumet ceremony created bonds of friendship that allowed for secure passage, trade relations, and defensive support between the two groups. For the Quapaws, the calumet ceremony helped them to maintain balance, order, and unity "according to a principle of complementary opposition in which separate but equal descent lines were linked by the rule of reciprocity." Consequently, the calumet ceremony "extend[ed] this principle to relations with outsiders through the creation of 'fictive' or ancillary kinship relations."[3]

Within Quapaw spirituality, the powers of their great spirit Wah-Kon-Dah, "the invisible and continuous life force," permeated all events that took place in life. It was "the primary force (derived from the conjunction of male/female life forces) that transcends and invests with purpose and meaning all human affairs and relations."[4] Since this life force was in every living and natural thing they encountered, the calumet ceremony obliged the "other" to engage in reciprocity with the entire nation, to participate in the sharing of the calumet, pole striking, and gift exchanges so as to develop an alliance, a kinship.[5] Consequently, Frenchmen who participated experienced "a kind of conversion towards Native tradition and spirituality."[6] They were deemed "father," a relationship that expected them to be "kind, generous, and protecting." Once French newcomers were accepted, "both the kinship relation and the tribe as a whole were renewed." But friendship was always more on Quapaw terms than European. If any Frenchman proved troublesome, the Quapaws had the right to divest themselves of him.[7]

The calumet ceremony was particularly important for the Quapaws, given their nonnative status in the Arkansas River Valley. This Dhegihan Sioux nation likely moved in from the Ohio Valley sometime after de Soto crossed the Mississippi into modern-day Arkansas in the 1540s. Groups such as the Chickasaws often "contested the Quapaws' right to be there."[8] Consequently, the Quapaws were cautious no matter who approached, for their presence along the Arkansas/Mississippi terrain "had its own social and environmental consequences. It disrupted older notions of territory." But like other refugee groups along the Mississippi, the Quapaws "sought ties with strangers precisely because they feared outsiders."[9] For both the French and the Quapaws, the calumet ceremony created a "framework for peace, alliance, exchange, and free movement" that served the region's diverse peoples. When peace was ratified and fictive kinships developed between the Quapaws and those honored by the calumet, they then became responsible for maintaining peace between their respective cultures.[10]

In addition to celebrating the calumet, La Salle and de Tonti erected a cross within the Quapaw village as well as a column with the coat of arms of Louis XIV painted on it. To the French, these symbols represented their alliance with the Quapaws as well as oversight of the region by God and king. While on some level the Quapaws believed that "His Majesty would fight those who attacked them," they also believed that the column and the cross contained spiritual powers. To honor these new spirits within their village, they built a palisade around them.[11] When Saint-Cosme and his colleagues planted a cross within the Quapaw village in 1698, weeks later they saw a new cross that the Quapaws had similarly erected along the banks of the Mississippi River. They used this Christian symbol to mark their terrain, highlight their relationship with the French, and display the presence of a new spiritual *manitou* in their midst.

Both the missionaries and the Quapaws understood that the cross had spiritual importance. For the missionaries, the cross symbolized God's presence and grace among them. Alternatively, the Quapaws believed that objects and animals possessed spiritual power that could bring forth protection, guidance, and good fortune when appropriately reciprocated. Thus, when crosses or a colorful column were planted in their midst, they treated such inanimate items as spirits themselves. Making sacrifices to the cross or building a symbolic, reverential palisade around it served as an offering to the spirit of the symbol. Assimilating new spiritual ideas and practices with those they already had increased diversity in their spirit world and "added a religious dimension to connections with other peoples." Thus, they expanded their spirituality but did not remove from it anything that was present otherwise. The Quapaws and the missionaries simply had "two distinct and different ideological interpretations of [the same] religious objects," differences that were subtle and could be "easily overlooked."[12]

Gravier was the last known Frenchman to visit the Quapaws prior to Father Foucault's arrival. When he encountered the Quapaws in late October 1700, he found them free of the devastating illness that had impacted them just prior to Saint-Cosme's visit two years earlier. Like others before him, Gravier was greeted with great respect and hospitality. This time, however, rather than being received immediately through the calumet ceremony, he was hosted with a fine feast that included "green Indian corn seasoned with a large quantity of dried peaches . . . a large dish of Ripe fruit of the Piakimina [persimmon], which is almost like the medlar of France." Gravier felt this to be "the most delicious fruit that the Native peoples have from the Illinois to the sea." As such, the chief "did not fail to begin his feast with it."[13]

As a reciprocal action to their hospitality, Gravier gave the Quapaws "a present of a little lead and powder, a box of vermillion wherewith to daub his young men, and some other trifles." Afterward, the chief invited Gravier to remain "because he wished with his young men to sing the Chief's calumet for me." But Gravier declined: "I thanked him for His good will, saying that I did not consider myself a Captain [a person of distinction], and that I was about to leave at Once." Gravier's response was pleasing to the French, some of whom may have previously gone through what they perceived was a long and involved ceremony during other visits to the village. However, for the Quapaws, it "was not very agreeable."[14]

Gravier, himself, certainly knew better the worth of the calumet, but on this day in 1700 he was in a hurry to meet with Iberville at the southern French fort and thus interpreted the offering of the ceremony as an attempt by the Quapaws "to gain presents from me."[15] Although a certain connection was made through the exchange of food and gifts during the feast, it was an exchange that likely left the Quapaws dissatisfied. As a newcomer, there was an expectation that Gravier share the calumet with their community so as to fit into the "system of real and fictive kinship," so that he might participate in shared, familial responsibilities. Consequently, Gravier's refusal affected his ability to enter more intimately into their society. As a stranger, it was risky to not participate in the calumet ceremony, as "enemies refused to exchange in mutually beneficial ways."[16]

No other encounters with the Quapaws are known to have taken place after Gravier's departure until Father Nicolas Foucault arrived in May 1701 and served as their first missionary until July 1702. Like his colleagues, Foucault hoped to convert the Quapaws to Christianity. But by most accounts his efforts appeared unsuccessful and he "was forced to leave the Arkansas because of the barbary of this nation by whom he was mistreated several times."[17] What this mistreatment was remains unclear as all letters by Foucault were lost either through fires at the Séminaire de Québec or through the haphazard handling of his personal effects when killed by the Koroas. Nonetheless, Father Bergier's words about Foucault's alleged mistreatment are quite disconcerting given that Gravier, de Montigny, and the Récollet Father Zénobe Membré all remarked of the Quapaws' mildness, warmth, cheerfulness, generosity, and politeness. Saint-Cosme described their extraordinary honesty and fidelity, that the Quapaws "had a good nature about them, and were extraordinarily loyal, having carried everything we had into a cabin where it remained for two days without anything taken or lost."[18] Saint-Cosme's companion, de la Source, was equally impressed: "They are the best made, frankest, and best tempered men that we have seen. . . . They await a missionary with great impatience."[19]

Any negative pictures of the Quapaws were simply misinterpretations that only masked their true intentions. Although the French explorer Jean-Baptiste Bénard de la Harpe described the Quapaws as "of ill will," in truth, their presumed mistreatment of him stemmed from their refusal to help him travel up the Arkansas River, where he could potentially provide guns to the Osages. Father Paul du Poisson, who served among the Quapaws twenty-five years after Foucault, described the Quapaws as greedy, certain that "gratitude is a virtue of which they have not the slightest idea."[20] But this attitude stemmed from a misunderstanding of their cultural institution of reciprocity, in which du Poisson refused to take part.

Foucault's last entry into his Batiscan church registry occurred on June 30, 1700. Soon after, he provided 1,350 livres in personal funds to support his trip from Québec to the Mississippi Valley. This was more than half of the total cost of 2,434 livres utilized to send him to the region. Likely, much of these funds went toward the purchase of liturgical items, such as confessional boxes and a cassock, trade items in the form of beads, signet rings, vermillion, tin plated mirrors, gardening tools and seeds, ammunition supplies, cooking utensils and spices such as pepper, nutmeg, cloves, cinnamon, a variety of grains and nuts, and finally miscellaneous items—a ream of paper, soap, oakgall, gum, maps of Paris and the world, and portraits of the king and queen of France.[21]

Many of these supplies were meant to support communication, construction, sustenance, and trade at the Arkansas mission. Further, they were to keep Foucault clothed and to help the missionary share a bit of his culture with the Quapaws. Some items were also meant to assist with food preparation and to add flavor to what might otherwise be a bland diet. But Foucault, like his colleagues, also brought along images of the Holy Mother, Joseph, Jesus Christ, St. Michael, the Resurrection, as well as small crucifixes, rosaries, and medals to teach Christianity to the Quapaws.[22]

Images were a vital resource for teaching Native peoples the mysteries and stories of Christianity—the annunciation and the crucified and risen Christ, among others. Marquette, for one, hung four large portraits of the Virgin Mary in an open prairie so as to teach the Illinois of the virgin birth.[23] Father Gravier used biblical images created through copper-plated engravings to teach the Illinois as well. Marie Rouensa took these same images and taught Christianity to the Kaskaskia community.[24] Some even utilized images that were more representative of the Native people among whom they worked. Such pictures contained clean-shaven individuals with straight hair, absent of halos or hats, oftentimes even a single individual in his or her last judgment.[25] But a more creative use of images came from Father Jean Pierron, who painted his own pictures so as to learn the language. As the Native people watched him draw or paint, he learned words and phrases from them as they identified particular objects or symbols he created. This activity not only enhanced his comprehension, it also allowed him to more accurately share his teachings to the Native community in which he lived.[26]

Catholic clergy and laypersons used imagery to develop their own spirituality. Pupils at the Petit Séminaire de Québec, a secondary school attached to the Seminary, often spent time in prayer before a painting of St. John the Evangelist, the Holy Mother, or the Apostles.[27] One also used images to increase his or her devotion. "Each holy day and Sunday, one exposed by dawn on one's door the image of his or her patron saint, to remember to honor him or her."[28] Laval used imagery to enhance Québec's dedication to the *Sainte Famille*. He "had printed in France an image of the Holy Family that he circulated . . . in great number in his diocese."[29] But a painting could even serve as a form of protection. During the 1690 siege of Québec by the English, the Québec villagers tied a painting of the *Saint Famille* to the cathedral's spire "to call down Heaven's protection." Cannonball after cannonball rained down in an effort to smash the image. Wasted gunpowder and an untouched painting were the end result. Ultimately, "the Protestants' failure to hit the painting or to take the city seemed predestined to the Canadians because it was unthinkable that the Almighty would permit heretics to triumph over those of the true faith."[30]

Creative or pre-made, missionaries used images to provide a sustaining, cognitive impression, a visual connection to the verbal lessons given so as to help the Native people remember and hopefully embrace the sacred mysteries "with a recognizable form of reality."[31] But the artistic style and symbolism of a European painting was not the same as that of a Native person's artwork, rendering questionable the extent to which the Native peoples understood the images and embraced what they truly symbolized. Indeed, "interest in them may have been related as much to perceptions of the images as powerful in themselves, as representations or objects of power, as to the more mundane pedagogical concerns." Some Indians might place food offerings at the image of Jesus during feasts, while others might destroy images out of fear of their power.[32]

While the European style of painting may have been foreign to Native groups, many, including the Quapaws and the Illinois, were quite familiar with expressing their own spirituality through visual messages. This chapter began with a discussion of the *Three Villages Robe* that visually shows segments of Quapaw spirituality and balance—the dual presentation of the calumet, the roles of the Sky People and the Earth People. But other robes from the seventeenth and eighteenth centuries survive that provide further evidence of Native spirituality. The *Thunderbird Robe,* housed at the Musée des Beaux-Arts et d'Archéologie de Besançon, appears to visually display a great spirit, "one who is preeminent above the others . . . because he is the maker of all things."[33] Although attributed to the Illinois, the symbolism of this robe shows remarkable similarity to Wah-Kon-Dah, the great spirit of the Quapaws. The Quapaw author, Velma Seamster Nieberding, describes how "everything they [the Quapaws] had came from Wah Kon Dah, the great over-all spirit. . . . Wah Kon Dah was of the sky-world from where they had fallen into the water in the creation time. He was remote, fearful and occasionally dangerous, but always the highest. His rays must warm mother earth before the seeds could grow in the spring and must ripen the corn before they could use it in summer. Their lives were regulated by the rising and setting of the sun. He was the master of all life."[34]

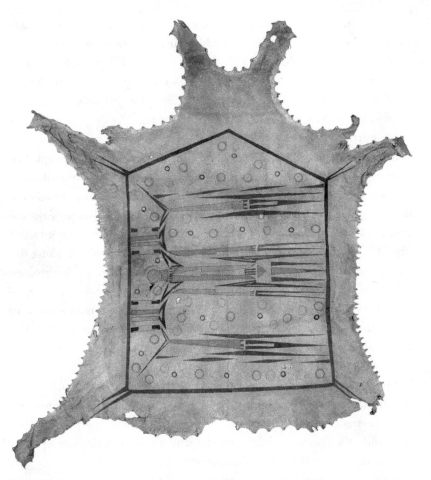

Thunderbird Robe, attributed to the Illinois. *Cape à l'Oiseau Tonnerre,* inv 853.50.2. Courtesy of the Musée des Beaux-Arts et d'Archéologie, Besançon.

The central figure of the *Thunderbird Robe* is a geometric bird that serves as the overarching spirit, with wings extended downward. Circles surround this bird—black, grey and red. Because everyone and everything helped to maintain equilibrium in the Quapaw world view and had a place in which to serve within their society, each circle on this robe could well represent the important, complimentary realms of their world view—the spiritual realm, the earth realm, and the aquatic realm. Circular shapes symbolize their unending presence; the randomization of placement symbolizes their manifestation throughout creation. The thunderbird—the Great Spirit—oversees these important elements. As master of all, the thunderbird can go no lower, no higher.

Beyond painted robes, the architectural layout of Dhegihan Sioux communities, to which the Quapaws belonged, also visually and spiritually helped to maintain order and unity within their society. The Quapaws lived in long houses, divided by a central road through the village. Sky People lived on the north side, Earth People on the south. It was this spatial arrangement that "sustained the entire web of relationships connecting human and spiritual communities." It demonstrated that the Quapaw nation was "a unified whole that was greater than the sum of its constituent parts."[35] Some 150 miles to the west of the eighteenth-century Quapaws, along the east-flowing Arkansas River, a distinct spatial pattern models this village architecture and spirituality. The Osages, the Quapaws' cultural kin, likely established villages along this part of the Arkansas River. Following the north/south division, archeological evidence highlights pictographs on the south side of the river that represent animals, plants, and anthropomorphic figures, drawings representative of the Earth People. Pictographs on the north side of the river represent mythic themes much more attuned with the Sky People. In between these two mountainous areas lived the Osages.[36]

All of these Native drawings showed "the fundamental interconnectedness of life," the importance of spirituality in the world view of Native communities.[37] Consequently, with their own experiences in visually expressing their spirituality, the Quapaws' ability to understand the spiritual elements of European works of art was possible. But even with the esteem and power they gave to such visualization, they likely interpreted European paintings as they best fit into their own world view. Much like other nations, the Quapaws likely saw images of Mary or Christ as representatives of additional spirits to assimilate into their own spirituality, not as their Christian saviors.

On April 28, 1701, Foucault arrived at the Tamarois village, where he served for a very brief time with Father Bergier. Still in the midst of the *vigne contesté,* and out of fear that the Jesuits might claim the Arkansas Valley ahead of the Seminary, Foucault soon after left for the Arkansas River to serve among the Quapaws.[38] By the time he arrived, de Tonti's Arkansas Post was probably inactive. Of the three Frenchmen known to have remained among the Quapaws in 1699, not one was present. Hunault, Charbonneau, and Perrot had already made their way back to Québec. Nonetheless, other Frenchmen and Englishmen still made their way to the Quapaws prior to Foucault's time among them. One Englishman had two concubines in the Kappa village. Others led by Jean Couture, an original occupant of Arkansas Post and now a French deserter, intermittently provided guns to the Quapaw community. Unfortunately for Foucault's strict Catholic standards, if any Europeans lived among the Quapaws when he arrived, they could well have been like others throughout the region—gamblers, immoral and debauched men, willing distributors of *eau de vie* to Native communities, men not at all favored by a priest longing to convince Native communities to embrace Christianity and Christian discipline.[39]

As a priest in Québec, Foucault expected colonists to adhere to the moral standards set by the church. Quite meticulous and inflexible, he was often at odds with officers and colonists along the St. Lawrence River. In the case of the affair between Madame Dizy and Captain Dejordy discussed in chapter 2, Foucault expected the couple to obey an excommunication imposed on them. When Dejordy disobeyed and showed up at church, Foucault stopped the ongoing funeral, removed everyone from the chapel, and then continued the service with only his assistant present. When not obeyed, Foucault responded harshly—a closed church, damning sermons from the pulpit, and ordinances.

Among the Quapaws, Foucault encountered a diversity of cultural characteristics that he had fought against among his countrymen in Québec. Foucault certainly encountered Quapaw women dressed in deerskin skirts that fell from the waist to the knees, or men with deerskin loin cloths and leggings. When cold temperatures abounded, more furs and pelts, particularly those made of otter skin, were worn to combat the freezing temperatures. In warmer seasons, partial nudity was the norm.[40] Like de Montigny, Foucault was used to modest standards for French fashion and likely felt compelled to address this among the Quapaws.

Dance was another cultural challenge in Québec that Foucault and Saint-Vallier addressed with an ordinance: "Because we have been informed that there have been, in various locations, dance gatherings and other sorts of activities on feast days and Sunday, and sometimes even during the divine service . . . we exhort and conjure, for the love of God, and for the honor of religion, all the faithful of our diocese to abstain in the future from these sorts of things." Dance gatherings as a whole engaged people of the opposite sex in "dangerous activities" with one another. "As experience shows, they lead next to a great number of considerable sins."[41]

It is true that Foucault was no longer dealing with unfaithful Québecois parishioners and colonials. It is also true that he knew of no other approach to Christianity than to stand by his moral order and Catholic principles. But daily and within the Quapaws' sacred ceremonies, Foucault witnessed partial or complete nudity that, in his world view, was harmful to the decorum of the Catholic faith. Bodily movements accompanied most if not all of the Quapaws' ceremonies, their "petitions to the spiritual world," for planting, harvesting, marriage, death, war, peace, and fertility. Ceremonial dance was simply a large part of their sacred, spiritual world view.

One Quapaw dance in particular occurred secretly at night around a large fire. In this deliberate ceremony, "both men and women danced completely nude, synchronizing their poses and gestures with songs that expressed their sexual desires." The ceremony itself was meant to achieve "a oneness with another facet of the Life Force of the universe."[42] Although recorded by Jean Bernard Bossu, whose writings can often be deemed sensationalist, his description nevertheless was quite similar to ceremonies that played a prominent role within other Native societies. The Wendat, for example, had a curing ritual called Endakwandet that included public sexual intercourse. Patients requested these ceremonies in hopes that the youthful vitality of those "enveloped in sex" might help cure those who suffered from illness. Consequently, those Jesuits who witnessed such ceremonies worked to suppress them.[43] If Foucault saw any of these types of sacred ceremonies, he likely considered them a threat to the "decorum and modesty" of the Christian faith and strove to suppress them as well.[44]

Superstitious practices, as missionaries described them, were also a part of Quapaw culture. Between the time de Tonti encountered them in 1682 and when Foucault arrived in 1701, the Quapaws' population had diminished by some 80 to 85 percent, mostly due to smallpox. While in 1682 de Tonti reported some six thousand Quapaws among the four villages, fourteen hundred of whom were warriors, by 1699 only one hundred to three hundred or so warriors remained.[45] Even during Foucault's time among them, further illness was reported. With such dramatic changes, devastating diseases assuredly frightened and confused the Quapaws, who called on whatever means necessary to overcome them. Diron d'Artaguiette described how Quapaw *jongleurs* (shamans) yelled at evil spirits to drive them out, threw water over those who suffered from illness, even visually acted out the capture of evil culprits, who were then tossed from the patient's abode. Assuredly Foucault, who suffered from his own illnesses, found no pleasure in water-throwing shamans or troublesome *jongleurs* who "employed slight-of-hand to mystify and impress spectators when they treated patients with herbal concoctions, drenching sweat baths, and invocations."[46]

The severity of any illnesses suffered and the fear and confusion that became inherent may have led some Quapaws more readily toward Foucault's god and Christian symbols. The Quapaws were certainly willing to welcome the stranger and to assimilate the powers of the cross and other symbols into their spirituality. They were not, however, willing to give up traditions or cultural norms that helped them to achieve a oneness with their life force, Wah-Kon-Dah. They chose what they believed were powerful spiritual sources to benefit their society or cure an illness. Otherwise, when any elements clashed with Quapaw culture and religion, resistance emerged. The Quapaws only meant to fit Catholicism into their world as it benefited them.[47]

Although Foucault's charge in Québec demanded separation of the impure (revealed necks, shoulders, and heads, dancing) from the pure (the church), among the Quapaws spiritual and secular events existed in a thin space. Nakedness, reciprocity, trade, ceremonial costumes, even sexual simulations served a distinct role in their spirituality and society and could not be separated.[48] When challenges to the church in Québec arose, Foucault always had a level of authority to turn to, namely Saint-Vallier. But if Foucault sought support from the village chief much as he had in New France with the bishop, not even the Quapaw leadership could support his efforts to change their world view since "the chief's authority rested on his power of persuasion not coercion."[49] Quapaw leadership abided by a system of balance and equality without force. Quapaw warriors could listen to the chief but could also do as they pleased and not embrace his requests. Chiefs were not rulers; they had no coercive powers. Instead, the *manitous* held power. Through visions, spiritual rituals, and reciprocal actions, these powerful spirits guided individuals throughout their lives. Thus, no mandates, ordinances, bishops, or chiefs could help Foucault draw the Quapaws away from their spiritual traditions.

All the while Foucault lived among the Quapaws, efforts continued to establish a Gulf Coast colony and to maintain some sense of peace with the region's Native communities. The Chickasaws were particularly important, as they lived near Fort Louis at Mobile, but they also had close ties to the English. Iberville had worked to develop goodwill with the Chickasaws and proposed establishing a trading post in their region if they maintained peace with the Choctaws. This trading post was also intended to alleviate the Chickasaws' need to interact with the Carolina English and to encourage trade with the French at "good prices." To further pull their favor toward the French, Iberville sought to place a missionary among them.

In March of 1702, two soldiers, François Danbourné and his companion, St. Laurent, were sent north by Iberville to settle a dispute between the Illinois and the Chickasaws. As one of the colony's most trusted lieutenants, Danbourné was to help secure Chickasaw prisoners from the Illinois while reassuring them that the Chickasaws aimed to discontinue aggression within the region.[50] Once their task was complete, the two soldiers traveled south from the Tamarois mission to the Quapaw village. They carried with them a letter that described Iberville's desire to have a missionary work among the Chickasaws, as well as Bergier's suggestion that Foucault leave the Quapaws, who were smaller in number, and establish a mission among the more southern nation. Foucault chose to seize this opportunity, but since Danbourné and St. Laurent were both ill, they hired two Koroa Indians to paddle the group down the Mississippi toward Mobile.[51]

Departing in late July 1702, the Frenchmen were no more than a day's journey below the Arkansas village when the two soldiers, Foucault, and his valet, Buison, were killed, "just before the fork of the river," a point where Big Island begins in the Mississippi.[52] The exact reason for their murders at first appeared unknown. Tremblay, for one, wondered whether the Quapaws had Foucault killed because he had abandoned them to go to another nation. Others questioned whether the English had had a hand in his death. Perhaps the strongest possible reason came from Charles Dumont, de Montigny's former valet who now worked with Father Davion. While in the Koroa village, he learned that two of their nation slaughtered the four Frenchmen, took much of their goods, but also hid even more for later retrieval.[53] The murders were a result of greed and nothing more.

Catholic tradition focused in part on the visual—chalices, cruets, patens, crucifixes, ornate vestments, and so on. To a Christian, their importance for the liturgy and worship of God was without question. But any such powerful objects that constantly remained in Foucault's possession may have perplexed the Quapaws, given what Kathleen Duval attests, that "many Native American Indians had come to disapprove of accumulating wealth and valued giving more than receiving."[54] Among the Quapaws, the reciprocal nature of the calumet ceremony reflected their system of mutual obligation. As a chief gained power and subsequently accumulated material goods, he became more responsible for sharing his goods with his people. A chief accrued respect by fulfilling community obligations. Quapaw chiefs had to be generous with their gifts.[55]

Neither Foucault nor the Quapaws seemed to understand the intentions of the other when it came to goods, but they both knew what they wanted—for Foucault, devotion to Christ without treasures or rewards; for the Quapaws, reciprocal offerings to serve their community, to enhance their power, and to solidify and enhance their on-going relationship with their French father. While Foucault lived among the Quapaws, they likely viewed him as a powerful spiritual leader who was obligated to share his potent spiritual goods with them as well. But when murdered, Foucault had more than 1,000 ecus (some 3,000–5,000 livres) of goods with him, an exorbitant amount for the wilds of the Mississippi. Since Foucault died with such a large amount of goods in his possession, it appears that he hoarded all that he owned for both personal and liturgical use, and exchanged very little with the Quapaws.

Foucault did not understand that the sharing of goods represented "generosity, cooperation, and concern for mutual welfare" between the Quapaws and their guests. Goods within a Native society were not owned by one single person but were meant to be shared with others. Kinship was supportive of the entire nation so that no one went unfed, unclothed, unattended. Cadillac himself noticed that bountiful hunters "profit the least from their hunting." Once returned from a rewarding hunting venture, they made feasts for family and friends, or distributed their bounty to others within the village. Indeed, those present were "permitted to appropriate all the meat in the canoe of the hunter who has killed it, and he merely laughs."[56] For the Quapaws, it simply was a joy to help all those in their society—"the widow, the orphan, the old, and the poor." The chief doled out any gifts received to support all members of the nation and otherwise received little as a result. Others' needs took precedence over profits. "They had an obligation to visitors, and the French had an obligation to them."[57] Ultimately, Foucault's unwillingness to share compromised his relationship with the Quapaws. His own "greediness" kept him from deeply entering their society and further kept the Quapaws from establishing a deeper connection with his god or his power.[58]

The death of the four Frenchmen shook the valley to its core. Bienville was deeply disturbed at the loss of a very valuable person in Danbourné, one of his most trusted and valued servants. Bienville had no men to spare, and Danbourné's death was of detriment to his colonial efforts. But Foucault's death also meant the loss of an opportunity to send a missionary to the Chickasaws. Foucault, perhaps Iberville's best candidate to serve among this Native community, was gone and there was no one to replace him or to help stabilize the Chickasaws in the region. What with Davion, Boutteville, Dongé, and de Limoges hunkered down at Mobile, only Saint-Cosme remained active as a missionary in the southern regions of the Mississippi.[59]

Sadness and disappointment aside, Bienville, hesitated in retaliating against the Koroas for the death of Foucault and the three Frenchmen. Davion urged, if not begged Bienville to send soldiers out to find the Koroa criminals and to bring them to Mobile for execution. The repercussions of Foucault's death stalled the work of the missionaries in the region and forced Davion to remain at Fort Louis out of fear for his own life. Bienville unremittingly dismissed him, arguing that he did not have the men to spare for retaliation.[60] But to Father Davion, it was simple: if Bienville wanted missionaries in the field, then he had to deal with the situation and bring the murderers to justice.

Eventually, the announcement came from Bienville in 1704—the Koroas had been almost entirely destroyed by the Quapaws with assistance from the Illinois, an effort that "merits a little present which I will give to them." Only the chief and a few others who were not in the village at the time were spared. Otherwise, revenge was made on the entire nation while the initial crime itself was nothing but a "non-political, spontaneous assault by a few greedy Koroas." In fact, the Koroas' chiefs had already executed the two murderers long before the Quapaws attacked.[61]

Unbeknownst to him, Foucault's interactions with the Quapaws transformed him into a second role of father through fictive kinship within Quapaw culture. Foucault, as spiritual father, was there to teach the Quapaws, to save their souls, to render them Christian. As their pastoral father, Foucault saw his role as patriarchal, "from God the Father, to the king (the father of his people), to the father in his home. Fathers commanded; sons obeyed." But the Quapaws saw his role differently. Foucault as a fictive father, albeit seemingly distant in engagement with their culture, became part of a social tie that strengthened the relationship of both cultures. To the Quapaws, fathers were

Arkansas Indian carving a declaration of war into a tree. A. Antoine de Saint Gervais, 1776–1836. *Nouvel album des peuples, ou, Collection de tableaux: représentant les usages et cérémonies les plus remarquables des diverses nations du monde, accompagnée d'un texte historique* (J. Langlumé et Peltier Paris, 1835), 98.

"kind, generous, and protecting." Children owed their fathers respect, but fathers "could not compel obedience."[62]

Although both interpretations of "father" differed, a congruence of the term led to a middle ground on the part of both cultures. Even if somewhat shaky in terms of how either side comprehended it, both cultures understood Foucault's role from their cultural perspective. As a priestly father, Foucault was there to share the spiritual gifts of Christianity. As a fictive father, Foucault served as a figure of alliance. When Foucault left and was murdered, his absence removed his spiritual power from their society; his departure removed a symbol of relationship between the French and the Quapaws. Nevertheless, he was still fictive kin, and as sons to the father, "the Quapaws understood full well what their obligation of defense and support were as sons."[63] The Quapaws, as children, had to avenge their father's death. Since other Frenchmen made up Foucault's doomed entourage, the Quapaws had their lives to avenge as well. Thus, out of loyalty to their French allies and to their French fictive kin, the Quapaws "took the opportunity to attack and win a victory over their old enemy."[64]

Even as fictive kin, Bergier claimed that Foucault "was forced to leave the Arkansas because of the barbary of this nation by whom he was mistreated several times."[65] More than likely, any mistreatment Foucault suffered was not holistic as implied. Mistreatment may have been as simple as poking fun at Foucault's language skills, as "those who had not yet mastered the local Amerindian language were mocked as having no sense. Faulty expression was taken as proof of deficient intellect."[66] While missionaries and Frenchmen thought they were properly learning a Native language, "others knew that the Indians would snicker among themselves at the Europeans for speaking the baby talk that the Indians had taught them."[67] Indeed, there were times when missionaries were taught obscenities rather than the actual translations of ordinary objects. Rather than learning and uttering words from the Gospel, some individuals were in fact uttering indecent phrases taught them by their Native language tutors.[68]

Foucault could have been the recipient of jokes and mistreatment for other reasons as well. Allouez, at one point, was abandoned by the Hurons once they determined that he "did not have the skill to paddle nor the strength to carry loads on a portage." Foucault was long known to be of ill health. Walking into a village and unable to fully support himself physically could have landed him in a quagmire of jokes and guffaws.[69] But mistreatment could also have been implied if the Quapaws ignored Foucault's teachings or simply did not listen to him. As Father Gravier quickly learned, the Quapaws were not always willing participants: "I was grieved because they would not listen to me when I wished to speak of God. I withdrew to pray for them while the kettles were boiling."[70] Gravier expected the reciprocal action of listening to his teachings, but experienced instead a community content to welcome the stranger into their world but determined "to maintain their own sovereign identities and make independent decisions regarding the ways they ran their societies," their spirituality and culture.[71]

Foucault's failure to share his goods or his exclusion of individuals from any Catholic services he held may have also led to ill-treatment. In veneration to the Catholic Church, those without proper clothing, or those who regularly engaged in ceremonial dance, may have been excluded from his spiritual activities. If denied access to Foucault's spiritual powers and goods, some may have verbally abused the Seminary priest. No matter the true circumstances of his alleged mistreatment, it is doubtful that the Quapaws were ever violent toward Foucault.

Upon announcement of his death, and despite their previous criticisms, Foucault's fellow missionaries were very supportive of his missionary efforts. Gravier, for one, believed that Foucault worked with great zeal among the Quapaws. To Bergier, "the loss of Foucault was irreparable," especially because of "his virtue and merit." He was "only consoled by the success Foucault had" while among the Quapaws.[72] After Foucault's death, no other Seminary missionary served along the Arkansas River.

We know very little about Foucault and the Quapaws in the early eighteenth century. We do not know if the Seminary priest operated through kindness or through force. We only know that a middle ground was forged when Foucault was adopted into Quapaw society as a fictive father, "transformed through ceremony from strangers to friends." By being brought into the culture, he sustained the role of spiritual father while the Quapaws embraced him as adopted father, a fictive position that was meant to include reciprocal actions between himself and the Quapaws. Although Foucault seems to have engaged in very little reciprocity, what with his vast collection of goods in his possession when killed, a common titular relationship had developed nonetheless— father. The Quapaws welcomed Foucault into their culture and society. They most likely celebrated the calumet ceremony with him, provided him a place to live as promised to de Montigny and Saint-Cosme, and established an irrevocable bond that lasted even through his subsequent departure and death.

CHAPTER 8

Saint-Cosme, the Tamarois, and the Natchez

Once the first three missionaries completed their initial exploration of the Mississippi, Saint-Cosme settled among the Tamarois and became deeply immersed in the early months of the Jesuit/Seminary mission dispute, or as Bergier called it, the *vigne contesté*. Immediately, Saint-Cosme had great disdain for the religious strife present, wanting "to exempt myself from this place until our differences were regulated," he wrote. But the Seminary missionaries needed to befriend the Jesuit Binneteau to gain access to the Illinois language. Consequently, Saint-Cosme invited him to use his home and chapel while they worked out their differences.[1] As a form of compromise, he boldly suggested that "if the mission was given to them, that he [Binneteau] would remain master of all, and that the language that I would learn would perhaps allow me to serve elsewhere." Otherwise, wrote Saint-Cosme, "if this mission remained as we believe, that he will have come here to instruct me and to introduce me, and that this would be a debt that the Seminary owed him." But Binneteau was not in agreement. Despite being shown Saint-Vallier's *lettres patentes*, he "all but shoved them back," wrote Saint-Cosme. Binneteau was convinced "that Saint-Vallier was out to destroy the Jesuits." Under no circumstances would he work with Saint-Cosme in instruction or prayer.[2]

Saint-Cosme did his best "to avoid scandal that these divisions could produce in these missions." He worked on his language skills and by March 1700, almost a year after his arrival in the village, was "ready to confess the women married to the French. They remained here, their husbands having gone to the sea."[3] Although learning as best he could, Saint-Cosme still needed help. Much to his relief, Bergier arrived from Québec to briefly assist him. Saint-Cosme could not have been any more pleased: "All the Mission[aries] are strongly thankful to your Holiness for having accorded to them a missionary as zealous and of such distinguished merit as Bergier."[4] Saint-Cosme also welcomed his younger brother Michel, whom the Seminary had sent to potentially accompany him westward to the Panis (Pawnees).[5]

By March 1700, and "with all the honesty and cordiality possible," the three Seminary representatives did their best to interact with Jesuit Fathers Pierre-François Pinet and Joseph de Limoges, the latter having replaced the deceased Binneteau. But mistrust filled the air. Saint-Cosme remained ever suspicious of the Jesuits' regional movements. Pinet had "abandoned" the Miami mission and replaced himself with Father Mermet, "who did not yet know the language," wrote Saint-Cosme. No one served among such neighboring groups as the Potawatomis, the Renards, the Lakis, the Folles Avoines, and the Kickapoos. "The Indians did not want to pray [in those locations]," exclaimed the Jesuits. But Saint-Cosme remained skeptical of any Jesuit undertaking among or near the Tamarois, certain that the Jesuits were content that the Seminary missionaries "make these Indians workable and then they would come in and drive the Seminary priests out."[6]

Ironically, Saint-Cosme's own wanderlust to move westward toward the Pawnees raised concerns among the Seminary leadership in Paris.[7] Saint-Cosme was certain that serving just on the Mississippi saddled them into that region alone, a limiting choice "because if one only occupies himself with the nations along the Mississippi, one will find himself soon without missions." French soldiers and *coureurs de bois* particularly concerned Saint-Cosme, who felt them a deterrent to missionary work, "something we already know by experience in Canada." In the west, a mission might be far enough away from the French, "unspoiled by their disorder," he believed.[8]

Saint-Cosme's search for a more perfect location was problematic if for no other reason than the French would find their way westward in due time, if they were not already there. In truth, the existence of Frenchmen and *coureurs de bois* within a village often meant that a trade alliance existed between themselves and a Native community. Trade better secured defense, access to French goods, and, at times, peace. Marriages between Frenchmen and Native women created a middle ground of cultural congruences that on certain levels benefited both Frenchmen and Native peoples. Ultimately, whether he recognized it or not, Saint-Cosme's safety was better secured with a French presence.[9]

Jesuits and rogue Frenchmen aside, Saint-Cosme had a relatively easy time of it among the Tamarois. He had a community of coworkers with him, served in a mission free of "debauched souls," as he saw it, and, although limited, had access to a few prayers and the catechism in the Illinois language. Slowly but surely, Saint-Cosme learned enough Illinois to confess women married to Frenchmen, and to baptize those that he could.[10] Saint-Cosme seemed to do his utmost to avoid scandal, to be charitable with the key players within the *vigne contesté*. More than anything, he prayed that the Tamarois might "soon escape from the blindness in which they lived," and thus "receive salvation and entry into heaven." But the Jesuits' different Christianization strategies and the astuteness of the Tamarois left Saint-Cosme fearful that he "will not bear much fruit based on the divisions that they have remarked between the missionaries."[11]

Both Saint-Cosme and Bergier noted procedural differences between themselves and the Jesuits in relation to baptism. As Bergier remembered from his seminary days, "professors had advised that one not baptize children if there was no hope in their maintaining their faith." Thus, Seminary priests were only to baptize infants when near death. In contrast, Jesuits were directed years before to "take care to baptize the newborn children . . . without fearing anyone. There is nothing more important than that. Do not wait for mothers and fathers to call on you . . . they easily neglect this. Go into the villages, go into the homes and baptize the infants."[12] Noting their differences in approach, Saint-Cosme wrote to the Seminary leadership in Paris for advice. He asked if one must "baptize all of the girls who attend prayer," remarking that some "attend for a while but then stop; others have some desire to pray but, being married to men who are not drawn to prayer, abandon it so as to comply with their husband's wishes." Saint-Cosme wondered if one should "wait to baptize the girls once they are married to be assured that they will continue to pray? Or, if baptizing them before marriage, must one require them to not marry infidels, something that they have a hard time observing since few young men pray?"[13]

Saint-Vallier along with *Docteurs* at the Sorbonne discussed these questions and came to determine that the Seminary missionaries should "baptize all of the children." Once the newly baptized had attained the ability to reason, the missionaries then had to choose Native Christians within the village to help them teach the children to live as Christians and to not embrace their parents' superstitions.[14] In truth, missionaries would find this task hard to pursue. Tamarois youth had responsibilities to their family and village. They supported the life of the community through hunting, warfare, agriculture, and spiritual and ritual obligations. Once young women married *à la façon du pays,* they had to obey husbands who were far less accustomed to—if not disinterested in—practicing any form of Christianity. Young men could not abandon such cultural activities as fishing, hunting, and warfare. They had to demonstrate maturity in these skills before they could marry. Even if these young people pursued Christianity and embraced elements of it, they could not ignore their *manitous,* their dreams and visions, particularly as they related to warfare. "It was simply too risky, unless there were obvious signs that Christianity could successfully augment or replace the power upon which they had been trained to rely."[15]

Saint-Cosme likely did not receive direction from Saint-Vallier in time to implement procedural changes within the village, for by the summer of 1700 de Montigny asked him to come to the Natchez village to discuss the addition of more missions in the lower region of the Mississippi and "to hold his place while he traveled to France." Saint-Cosme quickly expressed his extreme displeasure: "I assure you sir," he wrote, "that it is with all possible repugnance that I take on this voyage and that there is nothing except the interest of the Seminary that could oblige me to go there." As he had expressed so often before, Saint-Cosme had "no inclination or desire for the Native people along the lower Mississippi, where disorder is already so strong and will increase even more by the frequenting of the French."[16] Saint-Cosme was certain that "there is too much risk for a young man in these overwhelming places. Based on what I have seen and heard from Frenchmen traveling with de Montigny, areas are terribly debauched."[17]

Saint-Cosme and his contemporaries took particular note of the Natchez women. Diron d'Artaguiette, a French officer in the colonial army, remarked that they "generally like all the Frenchmen, to whom they refuse none of their favors, in return for a few glass beads or other trifles."[18] André Pénicaut, a carpenter and explorer, characterized the village women as "lustful and devoid of restraint."[19] As Saint-Cosme himself later described them, the Natchez were far from docile. "They practice polygamy, steal, and are very vicious, the girls and women more than the men and boys, among whom there is much to reform before anything can be expected of them."[20] Even the Jesuit Father Etienne de Carheil voiced concerns about the Mississippi region as a whole, that it only offered "a thousand dangers for both their Bodies and their souls . . . it takes them away from all the holy places; it separates them from all Ecclesiastical

and religious persons; it abandons them to a total deprivation of all Instruc-
tion, both public and private, of all devotional Exercises, and, finally, of all the
Spiritual aids to Christianity."[21] As a soon-to-be resident of the Natchez village,
Saint-Cosme could only pray that "God inspire in those to whom he gave his
sword to reprimand these wretches and to make an exemplary punishment.
After this, we can rest."[22]

For both the Tamarois and the southern Native nations, sexuality was deeply
woven into the life of the community and ensured the continuance of the
village and the culture as a whole. The loss of life in warfare led to a 3:1 or 4:1
ratio of women to men, but the practice of polygamy meant that the population was less affected by infants dying in childbirth or by war casualties among
the men. Males who survived warfare could still father children with their
other wives, and widowed wives could still marry remaining males and bear
more children.[23] But the French looked at sexual relations among Native communities as two polar opposites: "marriage at one extreme and prostitution
and adultery at the other." Women were often deemed "disorderly and lewd,"
unfortunate characterizations that compared their approach to sexuality to
the behavior of good, monogamist Catholic women. In truth, village women
"were subject to moral codes and societal expectations every bit as culturally
constrained as women in European societies," while enslaved women within
the same community were not. European terms such as marriage, prostitution,
and adultery simply could not embody all of the sexual relationships that existed within Native sexuality. Nevertheless, the French *coureurs de bois* regularly took advantage of the sexual freedom within a community and thus saw
women, likely those enslaved within a village, as willing to share their bodies,
willing to take what these men offered in return. While the missionaries referred to Native women as prostitutes, in truth they "did not solicit customers,
and they did not sell discrete sexual acts." There was simply no French category
that could apply to unmarried Native women enjoying their sexual rights.[24]

Native peoples likely looked at the French as polar opposites as well—
sexual freedom at one extreme and sexual abstinence at the other. Celibate
missionaries were initially regarded by Native peoples as a "combination of curiosity and revulsion." How unusual it was that a man did not engage in a sexual relationship. How ironic it was that "the supreme arbiters of sex among the
French [and attempted toward the Native peoples] were precisely those who,
theoretically, had the least practical experience."[25] Missionaries were, of course,

expected to maintain their celibacy and to ensure strong, moral Catholic standards of comportment from their flocks. They had particular clothing to wear that covered their entire body and rendered it neutral, absent of any hint of masculinity or sexuality. The color black signified mourning and poverty—the dying of self to serve God in all ways; the letting go of all things to focus solely on God. But with "inclinations" toward women witnessed by Tremblay and Glandelet during Saint-Cosme's priesthood in Acadie, and with the mention of "debauched souls" within many a letter he penned, Saint-Cosme seemed to foreshadow his own weakness. No longer in the Québec region, far from military and government officials, Saint-Cosme's self-carriage was in his own hands. There along the Mississippi, no one had easy oversight of his actions, particularly once he lived among the Natchez.

Saint-Cosme was correct to assume that the Tamarois differed from the Natchez. The greater Illinois nation itself included such communities as the Kaskaskias, the Peorias, the Tamarois, and the Cahokias. Each named village was egalitarian and served as its own "permanent political unit." Numerous households within its boundaries consisted of individual cabins that each contained an extended family.[26] A chief served as the leader of each household that maintained its individual identity within the village as a whole. Likely, prestige in war, trade, or spirituality played a part in how a chief was selected. Some may have even been shaman for the village since "confidence in the chief's relationship with the supernatural may have helped in maintaining [or securing] his [or her] position."[27] Regardless of how they were chosen, chiefs' authority over their people was slight and members could dismiss their advice when they disagreed with suggestions made.

Certain spiritual obligations both celebrated and united the different Illinois communities. Each village observed its own calumet ceremony, played lacrosse as a village celebration before leaving for the summer hunt, and made decisions independent of other villages. At times, individuals from different villages gathered together for these same ceremonies to celebrate the death of a chief or a great warrior.[28] Quite possibly, each village represented a particular clan, "an extension of real or defined kin ties" that held different ritual functions for the good of the entire nation. When a chief or a warrior died, relatives of the deceased gathered together and identified the villages they each represented. They then sent for the chiefs and dancers of these villages to join them in their celebration of the deceased soul. Bringing in other villages for particular celebrations renewed clan ties that formed the greater Illinois nation.[29]

The Natchez were quite different from the Tamarois. Their language was certainly dissimilar, as was their governmental structure. While the Tamarois were egalitarian, the Natchez had an elaborate social system made up of the Great Sun, Little Suns, and those who served beneath them. The Natchez abided by a societal classification whereby they married outside of their rank. That is, the upper class of their society chose a mate from among the lower class. Accordingly, the Great Sun was the offspring of a Sun mother and a Stinkard father. As such, children of lower-class fathers were born into a higher class.[30] To avert a paradox whereby the Natchez might run out of "eligible commoner mates," the Natchez absorbed foreigners through intermarriage, a practice that increased the number of lower-class individuals for the upper classes.[31]

How the Natchez and the Illinois celebrated the death of a chief also differed sharply. The Illinois venerated a deceased chief through ceremonies that included a funeral dance, paintings of his achievements on peeled trees, and burial with fresh clothes and items necessary for the afterlife—corn, a pot, tobacco, a calumet, and traditional arms.[32] Alternatively, as we saw in chapter 6, the Natchez sacrificed villagers to honorably accompany a deceased leader into the afterlife. Some volunteered, but when more sacrifices were needed, one offered presents to a family that then honorably selected a member to die with the chief.[33]

Called by de Montigny to come south, Saint-Cosme reluctantly left the Tamarois in July of 1700. During his first winter among the Natchez, Saint-Cosme learned enough of the language "to compose some catechism lessons and some prayers." He baptized infants and adults near death, visited the Taensas nearby, and thought it best "to combine the Taensas with the Natchez, the former so few in number, but who speak the same language [as the Natchez]." But when Boutteville and Saint-Cosme's brother, Michel, arrived among the Natchez in June 1701, they gave Saint-Cosme a letter with permission, from Québec, "to travel to the west and to make a mission among the Pawnees." With this long-desired opportunity before him, the excited Saint-Cosme went down to Mobile to relay the news to de Montigny, who, he presumed, was at Fort Louis. Although a year since de Montigny had actually left the region, Saint-Cosme finally learned, "with sadness, that de Montigny had deserted the Mississippi and had gone to China."[34]

The reality of de Montigny's permanent departure hit Saint-Cosme hard. Consequently, he resigned himself to stay among the Natchez. "I am beginning to find favor toward this region and southward toward the French," wrote Saint-Cosme. "It is true that there will be some disorder, but it won't be continual because the French will only pass through villages, not stopping in them since there is no profit to make. Instead, they will make their ordinary dwellings in the distant places where there is no commander. They are masters and do as they wish. The Indians from here south being near the French will always trade. This will make them more docile. Those further away are so proud that they are incapable of any instruction, which is what we see among the Illinois."[35]

Saint-Cosme had to muster some optimism to reassure Tremblay that their work on the Mississippi was of benefit to the king's subjects, the Native peoples. He asked Tremblay to "not believe all the bad impressions that de Montigny had expressed regarding the missions." He wanted Tremblay to trust that "there is much more profit to gain. . . . Even if not stellar, there is much to sanctify." Saint-Cosme needed Tremblay to believe that they could "help these poor people, French subjects rather than strangers . . . by giving them instruction for their salvation."[36] But Tremblay's cynicism remained: "As for the spiritual essence of the region, it appears that Fathers Saint-Cosme and Davion are doing nothing in the region. Saint-Cosme has a hard time staying put in the same location. If I'm not mistaken, he will abandon the Natchez the first moment he can to go with French explorers near the Pawnees."[37]

Despite Tremblay's negativity, Saint-Cosme remained. In time he developed his language skills, so much so that he could recognize differences in speech patterns—"to one, to two, to several, all is different." When the Natchez spoke to the sun, he observed that they "invoke it with a language that is not otherwise heard."[38] Saint-Cosme even recognized language differences as they related to their spirituality and their higher power. "When they speak of the Great Spirit, this is another way of speaking. For example, to say that I offended the Great Spirit, they say, 'I hurt myself,' rather than say, 'I hurt the spirit.'"[39] Such self-scolding was linked to their tradition of the stone idol maintained inside their temple. As Saint-Cosme described it:

It is a statue of rock that is locked up in a wooden chest. They say that it isn't actually the great spirit but one of his kin formerly sent to this region to be master. This chief, so terrible because of his regal zeal, caused men to die. . . . He had them build a cabin where upon he entered and changed himself into a stone statue. . . . He is the first of their chiefs from which all others descend. He is the one who sends illnesses, causes death when one displays a lack of respect for his descendants. He also sends generosity and health when his descendant chiefs are well served, thus the premise to display great esteem for their chiefs, and to not speak against them.[40]

Order and unity were crucial to the Natchez's spiritual realm. If one offended their greatest god, if one hurt the idol, it was of more harm toward him or herself than it was to the spirit in question.

Despite any progress made, Tremblay remained exacerbated by the expenses Saint-Cosme amassed while among the Natchez. Saint-Cosme's request for more money for his mission "that is larger and more populated than the three others" fell on deaf ears. His argument that he had far fewer food sources in his region as compared to others proved weak. Crops of "corn, beans, pumpkins and melons" were plentiful in the spring and summer, indicative of fertile soil that he himself could work. Deer and fish were ever present as well.[41] Abundance was all but certain except during harsher seasons of drought or inundation. Instead, what seemed to diminish Saint-Cosme's supplies and sustenance was the continual presence of unanticipated guests. Several times a year, younger brother Michel and Father Davion accustomed the impoverished Saint-Cosme to their *bonne compagnie* and costly needs. Davion and his helper often stayed with Saint-Cosme, especially when Davion's colic was at its "greatest point of inconvenience." Even Father Boutteville, along with his young Indian companion, lived with Saint-Cosme for a time because "he believed he needed to be among the Natchez to help deliver provisions."[42]

It was hard enough for Saint-Cosme to feed himself, much less three guests and any others who traveled with them. Often, they ate only "small fish cooked in the cinders along with a little *blé* [corn]," a sustenance strategy that could improve "if one had a man capable of hunting," Saint-Cosme quipped. Otherwise, with little meat, one had to live on the little things the Indians brought them, albeit costly in terms of beads, vermillion, and bells: "The Indians would not give *un épi de blé d'inde* [an ear of corn] without some form of payment," Saint-Cosme cried. Funds had to be relegated, he believed, for "how can a missionary build a chapel and supply the mission with other needs if he does not know how much money he has." Saint-Cosme was so adamant that one create a sound funding system that he asked to be recalled if it did not occur.[43]

Although quite aware that wages were his greatest expense, Saint-Cosme, "weary of having to live with a little Indian," continually asked for men to serve with him, even young boys "capable of tending a garden . . . serving at Mass and making sagamité."[44] Saint-Cosme urged Tremblay to send him a second missionary "because one is much more consoled when there are two priests together rather than one."[45] Alternatively, Tremblay suggested that Saint-Cosme make use of Indians in his daily needs. While Saint-Cosme "admired" Tremblay's frugal suggestion, he could not make his point any clearer—"You don't know the mentality of the Indians here. They are all thieves who don't yet know the missionaries. They consider them to be like the other French from whom they always try to snatch something." Indeed, his request for a New Testament and other books was a result of "rats who stole them during the night."[46]

Saint-Cosme often criticized the Natchez, certain that "one had to make these barbarians men before making them Christians."[47] To Saint-Cosme, "a missionary without good men cannot leave his house. Every day he is exposed to several insults and it is frustrating for a missionary to have to punch an Indian. . . . Two good men are needed . . . good, strong workers, without fear, capable of standing up to the meanest Indian."[48] As a livestock owner, Saint-Cosme "needed a man who could take care of his cows and pigs, shoot a gun, and beat an insolent Indian since it was rather untoward for a priest to hit him."[49] Unwilling to settle for just anyone, Saint-Cosme requested a strong and determined man, capable of "kicking an Indian out of his house if he became impertinent," as it was "not at all agreeable that a missionary chase an Indian out with punches."[50] Frustrations abounded, but when Tremblay attempted to appease Saint-Cosme and provided him with a thirteen- or fourteen-year-old lad, the Natchez missionary immediately refused him and instead left him with the Mobile curate, de la Vente, under the pretext that he was too young.[51]

Saint-Cosme's vexations with thievery and the need to fight back likely stemmed from some of his own actions and misunderstandings of the Natchez people. Like Foucault, Saint-Cosme probably hoarded goods within his hut to keep them safe, but also to keep them at hand for the various Christian services he officiated. For the Natchez, these goods were attractive—if not vital—

to expanding their spiritual world. Chalices, cruets, patens, crucifixes, rosaries, even a New Testament that Saint-Cosme held in his hands and that spoke to him, all were curious objects that they believed held spiritual power. All served as formidable spiritual treasures, and the Natchez wanted a part of that spirit. Entering into his hut was likely an attempt to reach these spiritual goods, to possess them and their powers in hopes of adding them to their own spirituality. Keeping such goods within his hut denied the Natchez access to the most visual elements of the Frenchman's spiritual world. Hoarding his goods kept Saint-Cosme from developing a stronger relationship with the Natchez.

Despite harsh criticism of the Natchez, Saint-Cosme decided "to remain here forever."[52] Saint-Cosme's positive views of the Tamarois seemed forgotten. He came to believe that they, the very ones so many labeled as the most "Christianable," lacked docility and a willingness to learn. He found the Tamarois so distasteful that "if the leadership asks me to move again I will, as long as it is not to the Tamarois. If so, I would prefer to return to Québec."[53] Saint-Cosme backtracked on all he fought against, but why? Theologically, he may have deemed the Natchez as the "more fallen," God's children who needed God the most since missionaries deemed them the more aggressive and debauched compared to other Native communities along the Mississippi. Personally, he was further away from the *vigne contesté* and no longer had to endure strife with the Jesuits. Culturally, the Natchez likely welcomed Frenchmen who could increase their access to French goods, or, as in the case of Saint-Cosme, their spiritual powers. They may have demonstrated greater willingness to embrace Saint-Cosme, unlike the Tamarois and the Illinois, who were somewhat "spoiled" by the decades-old presence of French and missionaries in their region.

Similarities between the Natchez religious tradition and Catholicism could have attracted Saint-Cosme as well. The Jesuit Father Petit remarked that the Natchez nation was "the only one on this continent that appears to have any regular worship."[54] The Natchez revered the sun, the supreme being, and believed in afterlives of good and evil much like the Christian heaven and hell.[55] The daily regimen of the Great Sun was much like a devout Catholic. Each morning he arose, he went to the door of his home, extended his arms, and turned to the east to greet the rising sun as if to give thanks for a new day, much like a priest who lifts upward his hands to give thanks for the blessed body and blood of Christ. The Great Sun and his wife also took part in daily and evening spiritual rituals within the temple, much like a Christian's morning and evening prayer. The Natchez's sacred structure held the bones of deceased Great Suns, the bones of those that traveled with them to their new land, as well as a perpetual fire maintained by elders. Catholic churches also held the bones of priests, saints, and others with a perpetual flame maintained at the aumbry, where blessed sacraments remained housed after Mass.[56] Whatever the reason—religious similarities, Christianization needs, easier trade, absence of Jesuits—Saint-Cosme remained among the Natchez until his death in 1706.

Saint-Cosme had found favor toward the Natchez. But as the years lingered, his health deteriorated. He felt, at times, that his "memory was failing," that he had a *teste dure* (was a bit thick-headed) and "no longer had the faculties for language." Consequently, further negativity and criticism crept in.[57] Only the presence of one French family and the scant promise that a French settlement might develop near the Natchez Grand Village made Saint-Cosme hold out, not to mention the occasional visit from his colleague Davion, who gave Saint-Cosme "the consolation of seeing [him] from time to time." But Saint-Cosme needed to see stronger resilience on the part of the French. They needed to be "masters of the Indians," a sign that he approached Christianization through oppression and force, not assimilation. From the Tamarois village, Bergier's frustrations with Saint-Cosme showed through. Quoting St. Gregoire: "*virtus boni operis perseverantia est* [perseverance is good work]." That is, "one should not be so quickly repulsed or alienated if one wants to succeed."[58] From afar, Tremblay was certain that Saint-Cosme had no talent as a missionary and "will never do any good."[59] Tremblay skeptically added: "If the trouble that these missions cause us at least produces some fruit, God knows what the fruit of Saint-Cosme" will be.[60]

Throughout the early eighteenth century, Natchez loyalties were divided. Some related villages worked in collaboration with the English, others with the French. Those loyal to the English were long caught up in the slave trade. Given presents by the English to entice them to obtain slaves, they and other Native groups, notably the Chickasaws, struck fear among the smaller regional nations. The Chitimacha community, hit hard by the slave trade, was particularly angered by such activities. Knowing the deep connection between the Natchez, one of their enemies, and the French, the Chitimachas felt certain that both had had a hand in the latest assaults against their village. Consequently, they took it upon themselves to react in kind. In November 1706, Saint-Cosme, who was suffering from a "cruel infirmity," left his Natchez mission with several Frenchmen to travel to Mobile.[61] While they slept along the banks of the Mississippi, the Chitimachas attacked them. A young Native slave managed to escape from the violent melée and recounted that the Chitimachas hacked the Frenchmen to death while Saint-Cosme received six arrows into his body.[62]

Once again, Bienville had deaths to avenge. But his responses to the murders of Foucault and Saint-Cosme were like night and day. When Foucault was killed in July of 1702, Bienville made no move toward the Koroas and allowed the Quapaws to avenge the deaths of Foucault and the other Frenchmen. Perhaps he felt the Koroas were too distant from Mobile, not much of a threat to the security of the settlement he was attempting to solidify. Perhaps he truly could not provide the manpower needed to avenge the deaths. But the Chitimachas were far closer to Mobile and were much more of a threat to regional peace. Through gifts sent to the Biloxis, Houmas, and Bayougoulas, Bienville recruited some eighty warriors who, together with his own men, attacked a Chitimacha village, killed a number of warriors, imprisoned several men, women, and children, and escorted their prizes back to Mobile for punishment. Among their captives was the Chitimacha who had killed Saint-Cosme. Rather than follow judicial procedure, French soldiers tied him to a stake and "I had him tomahawked in the square of the fort after having consulted all the officers of this garrison, who knew as I did the manner of the Indians," wrote Bienville. After he was killed, the Chitimacha was scalped and then thrown into the river.[63] Bienville explained such violence to the Comte de Pontchartrain: "It is the custom in all the nations not only of this continent but also of those of Canada, to kill as many of the men of their enemies as they have lost on their side. Otherwise it is disgraceful among them to speak of reconciliation if they have not got vengeance man for man."[64] Balance, order, and unity were crucial. The Chitimachas had lives to avenge, but so did the French.

Bienville "violently rejected the social and moral standards of France" when he had the Chitimacha killed *à la façon du pays*. He moved away from the French standard of judicial procedure toward acting in the manner of the region. And yet, he felt compelled to clarify his actions with Pontchartrain, "who was opposed to summary executions and incapable of conceiving that they might be the only means of saving the French from the charge of cowardice."[65] As Bienville exclaimed to Pontchartrain, "I did not do it, my lord, without knowing the good effect it would produce in the villages of other nations. . . . You blame me, my lord, for having done it. I promise you that in the future, I will not do this again."[66] Bienville wanted to send a message that the French were not weak but could manifest revenge without hesitation. But his promise was short lived. Some ten years later, as tensions increased with the Natchez, Bienville captured three of their minor chiefs and two of their warriors in response to the deaths of five Frenchmen at the hands of this Native community. Rather than pursuing judicial action at Fort Louis, "these people were tomahawked . . . on the trail to Mobile."[67]

Then in 1730, Marc Antoine Caillot, a clerk in New Orleans, was a witness to an execution similar to that of the Chitimacha warrior. A Natchez woman who had been captured after her community had killed over 230 French men, women, and children in November 1729 was escorted to New Orleans by the Tunicas. She was offered to the French but was refused. The French preferred that she suffer in much the same way as had French women during the Natchez attack of Fort Rosalie. While the Tunicas alone were to carry out the execution, the French "joined in, and [had] even outdone the Tunica methods of torture by fire." For Caillot, the treatment of the Natchez woman, even the eating of her flesh by the French, "perturbed him, for it raised questions about the risk of ostensibly civilized French colonists becoming *sauvage*."[68] In particular, "what I found odious and execrable," wrote Caillot, "was a soldier who, when she was dying, cut a piece of her . . . [Caillot's ellipses] and ate it; as punishment he was put in irons and made to run the gauntlet."[69]

The Natchez woman was left to the devices of the Tunicas, but the French, bitter at the loss of over 230 compatriots, played a distinct part in her torture and execution. The placement of the woman's execution near New Orleans was "within reach of French onlookers."[70] The French colonists could be satisfied in seeing revenge rendered in a manner similar to what their countrymen had suffered. Bienville similarly chose a location for the Chitimacha's execution, in the middle of the French fort, where all French men, women, and children could bear witness to his killing. Neighboring Native communities that threatened the French could easily learn about Bienville's undaunted task of rendering sentence without trial. But later, as he killed the Natchez along the trail, his reasoning seemed different, as if he preferred to hide his violent sentence of the Natchez captives from the eyes of other Native peoples. In either instance, Bienville understood that he had transformed from pursuing a disciplined French response to a Native strategy of revenge. By promising never to do it again, he was attempting to revert to "normative roles" so as to "reaffirm, restore, and strengthen the status quo." Nonetheless, his actions served as a stark reminder that "Frenchness was not permanent and stable and that the colonial environment could erode this identity."[71]

Unlike Foucault and later Bergier, who received numerous posthumous accolades from Seminary and Jesuit priests alike, praises and compliments for Saint-Cosme were not forthcoming. Difficult questions and unfortunate dialogue arose concerning "slander to the darkest degree, suspiciously instigated by authors that charity would not allow me to name," wrote de la Vente.[72] A rumor had emerged that Saint-Cosme had had a sexual relationship with the Great Sun's sister. Written under the assumption that Saint-Cosme was still alive, Tremblay discussed the matter secretly in Latin with his Québec confident, Glandelet, a fellow witness to Saint-Cosme's previous "inclinations."[73]

> I had instructed [the Jesuit] Father Lamberville about the secret of a scandal which was blamed on a brother and the society so that if the matter was a rumor, he might resolve it [among his brethren]. I don't know whether it was through accusation and jealousy, or through charity. . . . I prefer the Lord work within Saint-Cosme since the sexual activity has also been made known to those French seculars [Huvé and de la Vente]. You clearly know how important this is to know for certain, and if the matter continues as it is, [you] must recall such an indignant servant back to you 1) so that he may be healed; 2) so that he may be moved to penance; 3) so that the scandal stops.[74]

A follow-up statement, also in Latin, mentioned Frenchmen who knew that Saint-Cosme had "a venereal illness" and "suffered from continuous discharge," likely the "cruel infirmity" cited earlier. As before, Tremblay insisted that Saint-Cosme work through a process of healing, penance, and cessation of the scandal.[75]

While neither text served as a perfect accusation, both suggested that Saint-Cosme's most lingering Mississippi legacy was his relationship with the Great Sun's sister and a son named St. Cosme (spelling altered to help differentiate the two) who was conceived sometime in the early 1700s during Father Saint-Cosme's tenure among the Natchez. A manuscript housed at the Bibliothèque Nationale de France entitled *Grand Soleil, Fils d'un Français en 1728* describes this *Grand Soleil* as the bastard son of "Saint-Cosme, a well-made man, strong and vigorous, about 28 to 30 years of age," although in truth, he was perhaps thirty-five. Saint-Cosme, at some point, became "attached to the sister of the Great Sun" during his residency. She was about the same age as he, "with children of different husbands that she had taken." Among the Natchez, women chiefs as sisters of different Suns only took men "of nothingness" and only "to appease the needs of nature." This particular sister "had a lot of spirit, without much beauty, but hid her *commerce* with Saint-Cosme" until after his death. When Saint-Cosme's son was born, there were already "fifteen Suns before him." Each died one after the other until the priest's son became a *Grand Soleil* in 1728. He was an extraordinary force who "hated to a supreme degree the nation of his father." He never went before the French without his face and body painted in multiple colors.[76]

St. Cosme took part in the Natchez revolt that marked the death of over 230 French men, women, and children. Out of fear of French retaliation, St. Cosme and numerous Natchez villagers fled to the Natchitoches region along the Red River, where they were defeated by the French in the fall of 1731. St. Cosme, several other Suns, three dozen warriors, and over two hundred women and children were captured, herded onto the *Venus,* and subsequently sent to Cap Français on St. Domingue, where the French sold them as slaves to sugar plantations.[77] Some two years later, when Bienville was on the island en route from Louisiana to France, he wrote of a meeting he had with St. Cosme. "I have seen here . . . the chiefs of the Natchez who are slaves, among others the man named St. Cosme, who had been made to hope that they would be able to return with me. They assured me that it was only their nation that had entered into the revolt and that the harsh treatment that had been given them [at the hands of Chépart] had forced them to it, and that they had decided upon it without taking council of the other nations."[78] While St. Cosme admitted that only his nation took part in the attack against the French, Bienville made no gestures toward returning St. Cosme and his people to their lands.

The Jesuit explorer Pierre François Xavier de Charlevoix suggested that it was a case of kindness and respect on the part of the Great Sun's sister to name her child after Saint-Cosme. Knowing the difficult history between the Jesuits and the Seminary priests, Charlevoix certainly had an opportunity to continue the rumor. By not doing so, he seemed to suggest that the scandal itself was simply not true.[79] Nonetheless the rumor lingered for centuries. An 1860 satirical article in the French publication *Chroniques de l'Oeil-de-Boeuf* remarked:

> This clergyman, adventurer by character, was sent successively, as missionary, to Canada, to Louisiana, and to the Natchez. History does not say the exact number of conversions that he made during his first two missions. One knows only that at the third place, it was he who led himself not to convert but to be perverted by a beautiful queen of the Indians whose vigor seduced this priest. This princess, widow of a sovereign named Grand Soleil, offered her hand to Father Saint-Cosme who married her and became, himself, the Grand Soleil. The former missionary governed his people with much wisdom, they say. But, among the Natchez as elsewhere, despite the greatness of his adventures, either the queen did not find herself sufficiently warmed by the rays of this European Grand Soleil, or the Indians tired of his domination, or even his flowerful cheeks whet their appetite. Thus, they killed him one morning and made a dinner of his majesty.[80]

Father Saint-Cosme did not marry the Great Sun's sister, nor did he become a *Grand Soleil* or serve as sustenance for the Natchez community. Nonetheless, suspicions, rumors, innuendos, and guffaws continued for decades if not centuries.

Warning signs had been there for years. De Montigny informed Tremblay of "the extreme danger of exposing a young priest to such a corrupt nation [as the Natchez], if he does not have a co-worker to support him." As he saw things, "it is dangerous to abandon a man to his good faith all alone *in medio nationis prava et perversa*—in the midst of a crooked and perverse nation."[81] De la Vente recognized the difficulties and dangers of having one missionary in place among the Natchez as well. He poignantly remarked of Saint-Cosme that "to live alone in a mission, one must have maturity of age and of morals."[82] De la Vente was not fond of Saint-Cosme and had grave concerns for his moral and spiritual stamina. But Tremblay's concerns moved far beyond the banks of the Mississippi. "I believed I needed to tell him [de la Vente] . . . that if there was some evidence, he would use his authority to recall Saint-Cosme. But where would one send him? There is my trouble. In France, he would cause us scandal. One would learn of this on a boat, etc. In Canada, the path is quite long and quite uncomfortable. Nonetheless, I would prefer best this last suggestion over the other. You will do better to bring him back to you [Québec] than to us."[83]

Some modern historians have dismissed the allegations, particularly "if one bears in mind the intransigence which the missionary demonstrated to those about him as regards morals and the vigor with which he stigmatized throughout his correspondence the debauchery of the French and the depravity of the Indians."[84] Others have taken the side of Charlevoix's more benign explanation, that the name St. Cosme was utilized to memorialize the Seminary priest.[85] Still others highlight truisms with regard to Saint-Cosme and his time among the Natchez that may serve as the explanation for his actions:

> S[ain]t-Cosme's poor language skills and lack of social acumen required remediation if he and his people were to become members of the chiefdom. His grasp of the Natchez world and how to survive in it were weak. He lacked adequate means to feed himself. The priest did not comprehend the expectations of his hosts, that he distribute his 'prestige' goods in order to curry favor. . . . [He had] the despair of a stranger adrift in a land that he understood poorly and in which he knew he did not belong. From the indigenes' perspective, he was an important man in need of help.[86]

These comments are exacting. Saint-Cosme long knew that he was in trouble in the region. Desperate for men for protection, constantly referring to debauched souls, strongly voicing his desire to not work among them—all seemed to be Saint-Cosme's own cry for help. He did not want to be exposed to such risks, he feared for his own weakness, he passively begged for support to avoid the inclinations he felt. Saint-Cosme even requested prayers from Tremblay: "I have a great need to be lifted up by the prayers of God's workers, only capable of miscarriage of myself and losing others."[87] Ultimately, with no Frenchmen readily accessible to him, Saint-Cosme's best choice to help him was a prospective mate from among the Natchez, much like a *coureurs de bois* who sought to marry a Native woman so as to find sustenance, trade opportunities, and relationship with the community in which he lived. Thus, "if the Natchez were to inculcate S[ain]t-Cosme into the chiefdom, a high-ranking woman was a logical choice," indeed the only choice since Saint-Cosme was likely classified as a Stinkard. Saint-Cosme was alone, he was hard pressed to receive goods, and had little to no interaction with colleagues in his later years. He was lonely, hungry, and in need of security. Saint-Cosme no doubt "projected an image of an impoverished people who needed guidance and protection."[88] Without good language and coping skills, he likely had feelings, at times, of inadequacy, shame, perhaps even guilt.[89] Without colleagues and community, he likely sensed alienation, as if he belonged "neither to his native culture nor to the new culture."[90]

Tremblay had witnessed Saint-Cosme's weaknesses in Québec and had wanted him to muster strength from within, to call on God and to do the right thing—to relinquish his desires for women or to remove himself from the priesthood. But Saint-Cosme did not follow through. Upon hearing of the Mississippi scandal, Tremblay once again hoped that Saint-Cosme might call on God for strength. But Saint-Cosme himself moved away from serving as a dutiful soldier of God and toward being a man who chose, instead, to take control of his life. As he himself stated: "I don't believe we will speak any more about moving me, despite what repugnance I may have for this locale. So many things have happened that have led me to perceive that it is God's will that I live here, that God wants above all that I captivate my own inclinations."[91] Sometime before the fall of 1706, Saint-Cosme gave into his "inclinations" and thus lost his identity as a celibate Catholic priest, suggesting that his decision not to go to the Pawnees in 1702 may have been more related to his sexual relationship than for the theological, logistical, or cultural reasons discussed earlier.

While the personal challenges Saint-Cosme faced within the village were highly plausible reasons for engaging in a relationship with the Great Sun's sister, there is yet one other scenario that could paint Saint-Cosme in a much more favorable, albeit liberal Christian light. Two poignant conversations highlight attempts at negotiation, at least on the part of the Great Sun's sister, to end human sacrifices within the Natchez culture. Allegedly, Saint-Cosme asked her of her own beliefs with regard to the Suns' lineage, a Great Sun's death, and the sacrifice of followers.[92] The sister purportedly stated "that she did not believe that the Great Sun of their nation who gave himself the name *Grand Soleil* was the brother of the sun, nor that she was a part of the sun's family. Instead, their ancestors invented this idea to make themselves masters of the nation, and to make slaves [of its members]." By creating this tradition, "the Great Sun had total authority, which gave him and his family an easy life without anything to do." Thus, lower class individuals served the Great Sun through planting and harvesting, fishing and hunting. But as servants to a Sun, "all the slaves are strangled when a Sun to whom they belong dies." The Great Sun's sister allegedly told Saint-Cosme that she and her family "thought that members of their nation did not need to respect or venerate them, or go into this afterlife with a deceased chief, but that their particular interest or devotion obliged them to take on this *naiveté*."[93]

Antoine-Simone le Page du Pratz had a similar encounter with the Great Sun's sister, who further complained that it was inhumane to have the wives follow husbands upon their death. As she put it, the younger Suns "did not have enough sense to listen to reason on this important business." For that matter, the Natchez leadership could not count on "female Suns to oppose this [practice] to which they consent voluntarily." Thus, the sister of the Great Sun proposed to du Pratz that he marry her daughter. She believed that if he did so, then as the husband of the daughter of an important leader, the funeral sacrifices would end. "The People of the Sun would have to relent or face open war with the colonists," she reiterated, "because you would have the protection of the French, and you have enough sense not to execute this law." But du Pratz refused. He did not want to be deemed a Stinkard. "To the contrary," she exclaimed, "it was because they wanted to extinguish this practice that I [du Pratz] had been brought to their attention, that it was, in effect, to establish among them our [European] practice which was much better." Her offer, in effect, implied that she recognized a certain power among the French and was "willing for the Europeans to intervene in the Natchez order of things." If du Pratz married a Sun, it would place him in a beneficial and influential position among the leadership. But the Frenchman remained unconvinced and politely declined for religious reasons and personal safety.[94]

Father Gravier met the Great Sun's sister and described her as a woman who was "very intelligent and enjoys greater influence than one thinks."[95] She was not a passive individual but rather had her own sense of power and could negotiate with the French on her own. Her sexuality and hospitality, her ability to choose the individuals who surrounded her, allowed her to control politics and diplomacy within the village. She herself made decisions concerning her sexual partners and the future Suns in her lineage.[96] But in the conversations cited above, she made emboldened statements against her own family, had daring ideas about how to move beyond a cultural institution that she seemed to abhor, and sought to find a mate from the French culture who, she believed, could potentially change the sacrificial element within her society. Consequently, and perhaps from a humanitarian standpoint, Saint-Cosme may have believed that if he entered into a sexual relationship with the sister, he could help end the human sacrifices present within their culture. Geared toward saving souls and averting what he deemed were unnecessary deaths, such an action still allowed room for Saint-Cosme's comment "that God wants above all that I captivate my own inclinations."[97]

De Montigny himself had tried, in unknown ways, to end the human sacrifices. Unable to attain a middle ground, he could not end the cultural traditions of the Taensas nor the Natchez. Alternatively, Saint-Cosme may have felt that a relationship with the sister was a way to end the sacrificial component of a Sun's funeral. While it compromised his adherence to celibacy as demanded by the Catholic Church, it nevertheless provided a humane resolution, one that appeased the Christian commandment to not kill others. This approach could unite both himself and the sister into a middle ground to attain what they both wanted—an end to human sacrifices within the Natchez culture.

Unknown frontiers were often "messy, complicated, and informal." Within such places, "individuals used their social connections as a means to negotiate their ways at the frontiers."[98] Both Saint-Cosme and the Great Sun's sister had particular needs that could not be attained without the help of the other. But to achieve the middle ground, they had to create an infrastructure that was possible "only when there was both a rough balance of power and a mutual need between the parties involved."[99] Much like a French trader who needed relationship to secure trade with a community, Saint-Cosme needed relationship with someone to help lift up his Christian God, to find sustenance, to find safety in the village. He needed "to win over the chiefs" to have a chance to convert them to Christianity.[100] The sister needed a relationship outside of her culture to help dispel the senseless sacrifices, as she saw them. She needed the strength of a Frenchman behind her because his culture had "enough sense not to execute this law [of sacrificial deaths]."[101] And if Saint-Cosme was following his heart, longing to end the human sacrifices by sacrificing his own priesthood, both he and the sister again found a middle ground that had the potential to resolve the cultural challenge at hand. Thus, for these two individuals, a sexual relationship seemed the best way forward.

While both Saint-Cosme and the sister entered a middle ground, its benefits for either individual or culture did not endure. The offspring of Saint-

Cosme and the Great Sister, by order of the Natchez rules of succession, was born into a matrilineal society. St. Cosme belonged to his mother's people. As such, St. Cosme "had no formal kin ties" to his father, while Saint-Cosme "had no right to exercise any authority over" his son. Instead, the education of St. Cosme "fell to the mother's family, and the individual who performed many of the functions Europeans associated with fatherhood was the maternal uncle, the mother's brother."[102] Educating Saint-Cosme's son fell to a ranked Sun of the Natchez, preventing the missionary from raising his son as a Christian. As for the human sacrifices, they continued on into the eighteenth century.

Saint-Cosme's reputation as a missionary was quite poor in comparison to that of his Mississippi colleagues. No posthumous words of praise emerged to celebrate his interactions with the Tamarois or the Natchez. Instead, he remained known as the Seminary missionary who spent too much money and remained ever critical of all those who surrounded them. Those knowledgeable of his entire career forever questioned his actions and strongly suspected that the scandalous affair with the Great Sun's sister was true. But as advised, Saint-Cosme did adjust to what surrounded him. He transformed from serving as a priest in Acadie to serving as a missionary who worked as he thought best. Through his "own inclinations" and a relationship with the Great Sun's sister, he worked to protect himself and to assimilate his own understanding of Christianity among the Natchez. He and the sister touched the foundation of a middle ground out of "interests derived from their own culture[s]." Perhaps they both felt that this relationship was "fair and legitimate." But in the end, Saint-Cosme did not further Christianity among the Natchez, nor did he or the sister end the human sacrifices in honor of the Suns. Instead, a child was born who fully entered the Natchez society.[103]

CHAPTER 9

Bergier and the Tamarois

Marc Bergier was capable of succeeding at just about anything—as a lawyer, which he was, a Cathedral priest, or even a professor in theology, a position that the Séminaire de Québec considered offering him just months after he left for the Mississippi.[1] No one ever doubted his patience, wisdom, and devotion to his faith, his genuine understanding of self, and his full commitment to the expectations of those who governed him and his work. Saint-Vallier was so impressed with this young, devout priest that he named him *Grand Vicaire* of the Mississippi region alongside de Montigny. It was his responsibility to help communicate the needs and news of the Mississippi missionaries to the leadership in Québec and Paris. More importantly, all trusted Bergier, a man of justice and truth, to stand up to and "to not kowtow to the Jesuits, what they otherwise liked to see non-Jesuits do."[2] As one might expect, hardly before his foot hit Tamarois soil, the Jesuits labeled Bergier "Jansenist." Tremblay's retort: Categorizing others as Jansenists "is the fantasy the Jesuits create out of fear of those who do not blindly follow their views."[3]

After an arduous six-month wintertime trip down from Québec, Bergier arrived among the Tamarois in February 1700 and immediately set the tone concerning his own work. Initially unable to speak the language, he chose to model a Christ-like life toward the Tamarois people in hopes of curtailing the violence and cultural challenges he saw before him. Each day he intended to "do brief prayers at four o'clock, made up of the Our Father, Hail Mary, and Creed, the commandments, and an act of faith that Saint-Cosme gave me and that he had received from Father Binneteau." He further intended "to assemble all those who would like to come [and pray]."[4] Most strikingly, Bergier dedicated himself to what he called *sanctum canibus*. According to the Gospel story, when Jesus told the woman that it was not right to take the children's crumbs and throw them to the dogs, the woman's response reminded Jesus that "when it comes to God's love, there is always enough, even for the uninvited, the poor." Bergier believed himself in the same position of Jesus and the Canaanite woman and no doubt referenced this passage of "crumbs and dogs" as a reminder of her admonition, an oblique reprimand to Christ to keep himself in his proper place. Bergier had to get down to Christ's work, to have love and compassion for all—French, Jesuit, and Tamarois alike.[5]

Soon enough, Bergier met Fathers Pinet and de Limoges, who felt Bergier's presence among them to be a further injustice toward their Jesuit order.[6] Although he had arrived with his credentials as *Grand Vicaire*, Bergier knew that he was not fully prepared to take on the tasks of missionary or Seminary leader on the Mississippi. Thus, he chose to accept the Jesuits' assistance in the Tamarois mission rather than to fight it. He recognized that "they work in the mission with a tireless zeal, with no appearance that I can take it on as long as they are here. . . . I only think of obeying so as to avoid strife, advantageous or disadvantageous to the mission."[7] Ever an optimist, Bergier believed that their differences would "end with God's help," that both groups could find a collegial way to serve the Tamarois people. While Tremblay had hoped that Bergier might stand up to the Jesuits, Bergier instead chose a path of moderation and acceptance, quite literally a middle ground where both groups could cohabitate, serve within the mission, and potentially lessen the strife of the *vigne contesté*.[8]

Bergier and Saint-Cosme had both questioned whether one needed to baptize all children, a point discussed in the previous chapter, but Bergier also felt compelled to "re-baptize several children." Although against Christian principle—one need only to be baptized once to receive God's blessing—Bergier was concerned that "their parents often send them . . . [in order to] receive rewards." Searching for material gifts rather than the gift of baptism or Christian teaching troubled Bergier.[9] But such was the Jesuits' strategy. They regularly used specially requisitioned beads, rosaries, and other trinkets when they taught Illinois children. Once correct answers were given, a reward soon followed, and children "learn[ed] a great deal in a short time."[10] The Jesuits' "acceptance and transformation of another people's customs" led to this middle ground in their work. Through their own understanding of reciprocity, they provided rewards to children who demonstrated growth in their knowledge of the Christian faith. The Jesuits saw their pupils advance; the children and parents obtained new items they believed held spiritual powers.[11]

Bergier was unwilling to step into such a middle ground to entice learning. He believed instead: "*Non enim misit me christus baptisare, sed evangelisare* [For Christ did not send me to baptize, but to evangelize]." It was far more important to him to place all of his "foundation and confidence into Christ on the cross since it is in the teaching of the cross that blessed God is fortified." In this light, he strove to teach that "whoever does not believe in Christ crucified will burn eternally."[12] He hoped that the Tamarois would acknowledge the Christian God as the supreme authority of their universe, discontinue their "evil, superstitious ways," and learn the fundamental truths of the Catholic Church and Christianity as a whole. Bergier wanted the Tamarois to understand that a place in God's Kingdom was secured through the spiritual regeneration of one's soul made clean by washing away sins with holy water.[13] Baptism and membership in the Kingdom of God were the preferred rewards for good learning, not beads, trinkets, and the like. Learning came first, then the gift of baptism and a place in God's Kingdom.

As priests in Québec, the Seminary missionaries were quite familiar with an ardent Christianity, one with expectations of obedience and abstinence of activities considered disruptive to the church. But on the Mississippi the Seminary missionaries were advised to adjust so as to accommodate any unforeseen scenarios that could impact their work. While unwilling to reciprocate learning with gifts, several times during his tenure Bergier did make adjustments. After all, he was well educated in law, justice, and religion. With sound reflection, reason, and compassion, he too could work within certain Native cultural norms.

Concerning marriage, for example, the Jesuits believed that a Native couple could marry based on mutual consent, *à la façon du pays* (in the manner of the region). Alternatively, Seminary priests insisted that only Christian marriage with God's blessing strengthened one's resolve in such a holy institution. Tremblay was quite troubled that the Jesuits allowed Native men and women to "test their relationship before marrying [in the church] so as to permit them the experience of marriage before doing so."[14] Father Bergier was equally disturbed by the Jesuits' approach and wondered how one hoped "to reasonably determine if they will be devoted, not receiving the sacrament [of marriage], and the grace that would strengthen them?"[15]

Bergier's opinion was quickly tested. A young Peoria named Paraflèche married an Illinois Christian named Cécile *à la façon du pays*. Father Gravier "approved the marriage" and the two "lived together eight years and bore five children." With time, Paraflèche rejected Cécile so as to divorce her. Several months later, during their winter hunt, Paraflèche married Sabine, again *à la façon du pays*. Upon their return from the winter hunt, Sabine, as Paraflèche's second wife, was excluded from prayer. To address this indignity, Paraflèche advised Gravier that he had rejected Cécile, and that he wanted to pray and to marry Sabine in the church. Gravier separated the couple for nearly two weeks, instructed Paraflèche, baptized him, and then married the two in the Christian tradition.[16]

When the Kaskaskias moved down river in 1700, to a point across from the Tamarois village, Paraflèche, Sabine, and Cécile all moved down as well. Sabine attended prayers every day but not Cécile. Bergier asked the young Illinois woman why. "She responded to me publicly that we and the Robes Noires both were saying that only first wives were legitimate, and that we chased all others from the church. Thus, we received Sabine, her rival, second wife of her husband [because they were married in the Christian tradition]. I responded that her husband had tricked Father Gravier, telling him that he had rejected her forever and that for this reason he had married Sabine in the church." Cécile continued: "And that is what astounds me, that you took away my husband and you gave him to another, me, a Christian, and after having lived eight years together with five children, one still in my arms and at my breast."[17]

Cécile's response "deeply troubled" Bergier, who "did not know how to answer her." Nonetheless, he allowed Sabine to continue attending prayers "in good faith" until the issue was resolved. But those who attended prayers with Bergier and with the Jesuits further pressed the priests, asking: "Why do you allow this second wife to attend?" After a few months of reflection, investigation, and protests with the Jesuits, Bergier "solemnly declared the Christian marriage of Paraflèche and Sabine null and void and ordered the two to separate under threat of being chased from the church."[18]

The Illinois process for marriage began when the husband-to-be was absent from the village. "His father, or the father's brother, gathered a variety of goods together, according to their wealth, and had them taken by female relatives to the home of the desired bride. The boy's father asked that he might warm himself at the fire and that he might have moccasins, as it was the woman who built the cabins, supplied the firewood and dressed the skins. . . . If accepted, the girl's family then dressed her carefully and went with her to the man's home bearing gifts. This was done four times and the last time she stayed."[19] Gifts were exchanged, a reciprocal action of a warm fire and moccasins ensued. Several similar visits announced the man's intent, similar to European marriage banns. It was a balanced ceremonial process that engaged two families in preparation for uniting a couple.

Bergier thoroughly examined the traditional Illinois marriage from the Christian perspective, the Native perspective, and his own sense of compassion. After much reflection, he came to believe that the Illinois marriage was deeply sacred, much like that of two Christians. Consequently, the first marriage between Cécile and Paraflèche could not be dissolved. To Bergier, it was a matter of *triplici authoritate*—three authorities: "1) The Institution of Marriage in the Laws of Nature: And the two shall be one flesh so then they are no longer a separate flesh but one; 2) Laws of grace: Therefore what God has put together, let no one put asunder; he who puts away his wife and marries another commits adultery; 3) The sixteenth resolution of Rome that positively marks the inability to dissolve a marriage of a Christian with an infidel, even if the latter leaves her."[20] With these different sources of authority, Bergier declared Paraflèche and Cécile married, never divorced. The Jesuits consequently argued that "the first marriage with Cécile was made without dispensation from Rome," but Bergier held firm: "Since there was no law at the time, there was no need for a dispensation." As for Paraflèche, he "was ready to obey" Bergier and to reject his second wife, Sabine, but only if the Jesuits agreed with Bergier. Consequently, the Jesuits did all they could to keep Paraflèche and Sabine together.[21]

For both Cécile and Bergier, "Christianity was negotiated and transformed on a middle ground."[22] Both strove to observe Christian teaching but did so through two different cultural lenses. Although he had strong belief in the sanctity of Christian marriage, Bergier came to understand Native marriage as one equally embraced within the eyes of God. Two people were united as one and their union could not be broken. Cécile believed herself married and faithful. Her Christian teaching spoke to her of the sanctity of marriage, even, she believed, if *à la façon du pays*. Both Bergier and Cécile saw her union with Paraflèche as granted with God's blessing.

Women like Cécile had always had a certain amount of power within their culture. But with Christianity they embraced a new, special higher power that went beyond their cultural experience. They found "a comforting source of spiritual renewal and a viable outlet for their social energy."[23] As a Kaskaskian Christian, Cécile, like Marie Rouensa, developed "new and very powerful models of assertive behavior." She fought for her rights and access to the church.[24] As a baptized soul, she challenged Christian law, an assertion that put Bergier back on his heels and forced him to deeply reflect on his own spirituality, his Catholic teachings, the sanctity of marriage, even if in the Native tradition. Both negotiated a middle ground whereby the congruence of a blessed union was accepted. Consequently, just as a marriage in the Catholic tradition was to be honored, the first marriage, albeit à la façon du pays, was to be honored as well. Cécile could return to prayer and Bergier could better address the cultural needs of the region with his own sense of compassion and reason.[25]

Although the exact date of this marriage debate is unclear, by 1705 a new threat to regional marriages emerged when the Holy See demanded that one separate Christians and infidels who married à la façon du pays and thus without dispensation from Rome. Bergier "did not dare let the Indians know about this decision," for if it had been executed, it "would have meant chasing from the church those people who had acted in good faith, and who otherwise live with much restraint and piety." Bergier rejected the orders of the Holy See for, as he put it, the execution would have led some to "having their noses cut off, others scalped, and still more possibly killed." To prevent violence against Tamarois women, Bergier again detached himself from concerns of the Catholic Church and personally identified with Christ and his expression of love for all of God's children. He looked at the situation with compassion and took Tamarois tradition into consideration. For their part, Tamarois women found in Bergier an ally who was willing to adjust his own traditions to protect them. As for Gravier, Bergier wrote that he was "of the same mind," though his own thoughts and actions remain unknown to this point.[26]

Bergier was also troubled that "the older women scold, threaten, or beat their Christian girls when they do not want to work, as they do on Sundays." Bergier asked: "Must one, or can one, to avoid these inconveniences, permit or tolerate these young girls to obey their mothers or other relatives who demand that they work? . . . Can one, out of fear of repelling them or rendering the joy of God too heavy, tolerate work as a wood cutter or harvester, skin worker, or other occupations [on Sundays]? . . . Before one baptizes the catechumens, isn't one obligated to observe the Sabbath and other precepts of the ten commandments as a necessary starting point, and does it suffice that they promise to observe these when baptized?"[27] As he had done concerning marriage, Bergier straddled two world views—his Christian tradition and that of the Tamarois. Two demands tugged at him: keep the Sabbath or support the commandment of honoring the father and the mother? Maintain Catholic tradition or allow the Tamarois tradition to continue for the safety of the children and the sacredness of a mother and father? While no known answers were given to these specific questions, whether he realized it or not, Bergier was, again, adapting Christianity within the framework of the Tamarois culture while bringing elements of the Native culture into his decision making. Bergier and the Tamarois women were stepping into a new middle ground while resolving mutual concerns between Christianity and Native traditions. He could ensure the sanctity of the sacred commandment to "honor thy father and thy mother," while the men, women, and children could benefit as well—work accomplished without strife, parents honored, children unpunished, Christianity viewed as nonforced.

While willing, at times, to adjust to the Tamarois culture, Bergier was never open to changing his posture toward the *coureurs de bois,* whose regular activities of drinking, gambling, and debauchery frustrated Seminary and Jesuit missionaries alike. Bergier knew that many Frenchmen had evolved into a lifeway that was beyond his or any other's authority.[28] Among the three dozen or so present in the Tamarois village, many publicly dissented against Louis XIV's 1696 injunction that forbade them, under penalty of imprisonment, from trading furs or distributing goods with the region's Native peoples.[29] They elected their own leadership, a captain and a lieutenant, and defended themselves against those who tried to arrest them. Several went so far as to travel to the Carolinas to carry out commercial activity with the English.[30] Bergier tried to remind them "of the obligation they had to obey the order . . . to abandon the life of a *coureur de bois* so as to receive amnesty, and to leave the region based on the intentions of the king."[31] But the *coureurs de bois* had no desire to obey Bergier, much less a king who lived thousands of miles away.

Although regional Frenchmen raised many a priest's ire, not all were unruly rapscallions. In one known exception, Bergier traveled fifteen leagues to serve seventeen men who had come down from the Sioux territory for safety and had asked for an opportunity to celebrate Easter.[32] Otherwise, Bergier had no interest in hearing confessions of disruptive countrymen, nor of absolving them of their sins. To Bergier, "the looseness that held reign among these *coureurs de bois,* many of whom spent entire years without a missionary, and as a result, without sacraments, without Mass, without instruction, no longer following holy days, Sundays, Fridays, Saturdays, nor Lent, and living a beastly life, abandoning themselves to going about naked like the Indians, even to the point of publicly fornicating with Native females," proved intolerable.[33] Gravier certainly knew that disruptive behavior surfaced when they indulged in alcohol: "Drunkenness is nearly always followed by quarrels that arise among them. When these occur publicly before the eyes of the Indians, they give rise to three grave scandals: the first, at seeing them intoxicated; the second, at witnessing them fighting furiously with one another—sometimes to the point of seizing their guns in order to kill each other; the third, at observing that the missionaries cannot remedy these evils."[34] Nonetheless, the Jesuits proved unhelpful to Bergier. They simply remarked that these men "ought to obey" the resolution but otherwise allowed them to receive the sacraments. Bergier "loved nothing more than truth and justice," but the disobedience of these Frenchmen and the lack of support from the Jesuits was simply more than he could endure.[35] Even Gravier, who had complained about their "libertine" attitudes and their disruption of the religious work among the Native peoples, proved unsupportive. He and the Jesuits had a point to make—Bergier did not belong in the Tamarois mission. Under no circumstances were they willing to help him, even if they both had disgruntled feelings toward their mutually disorderly countrymen.[36]

Challenges abounded, be it from the *coureurs de bois,* the Jesuits, or the Tamarois, but the fall of 1700 only heightened the trials of the *vigne contesté* when the Jesuits abandoned their more northern Illinois village, "their most advanced mission," and moved several dozen cabins of Kaskaskias to within two leagues of the Tamarois mission, on the west side of the Mississippi. This move, supported by Chief Rouensa and his daughter, Marie, was meant in part to separate the Christian Kaskaskias from the non-Christian Peorias, who were such staunch traditionalists that nothing the Jesuits attempted led them to embrace any elements of Christianity.[37] This separation of the Kaskaskias from the Peorias was also made to move the former closer to the French colony under development in the south. Iberville had made plans for resettlement of various nations down the Mississippi and had encouraged them to participate. Consequently, the Christian Kaskaskias, under the watchful eye of Father Gabriel Marest, left the Illinois mission. Believing it "too precipitately made on vague news of the establishment on the Mississippi," Gravier proved unfavorable to the move but could not stop it.[38]

Once the Kaskaskias settled nearby, the Jesuits "used the name and the authority of Iberville" to threaten the loyalty of any Frenchmen who refused to cross over to the Kaskaskia village. Marest passively threatened them, saying, "'Iberville is our friend [and] we could easily put a little word in a letter,' by which the French conceived that they could be poorly received by Iberville if they refused to go to their mission," wrote Bergier. Frustrated, the Seminary missionary was certain that the Jesuits "destroy our work little by little . . . because the Indian, who loves to live with the French, either out of fear of the enemy or for trade, will soon leave, cabin by cabin, for the other side of the river to live with them, something that has already begun."[39]

One particularly trying day, Chief Rouensa sent some twenty-three pirogues across river "to take the Tamarois, a third of this village," to the Jesuit mission. Pinet "did nothing to stop this part of his flock," and instead chastised Bergier "for counseling the Tamarois to remain." Promises of presents from Rouensa pulled some twelve Tamarois cabins to the other side. Even Le Cou Long, chief of the Tamarois, harangued additional villagers to cross the river and to join the Kaskaskias. When the Tamarois began to move westward, Bergier witnessed that "most of them mourned the loss of their land, which is better than that on the other side, and that they went over only as a result of pleadings and presents."[40] Bergier's frustrations reached a boiling point:

> The advantages that they have over me for languages, the knowledge they
> have of the Indians, the authority that they take on in the manner of in-
> struction and baptisms, that which regards souls, remedies, and cures, that
> which regards the body, the protection, and the considerable presents that
> they promise them from Governors and other powers, or the bad treatment
> and punishment that they make them fear through their threats, that they
> extend even to the French who did not want to leave the Tamarois or the
> Cahokias to live on the other bank with the Kaskaskias. Father Marest has
> forgotten nothing to pull them over to the point of raising up the authority
> of Iberville. I see myself, as such, prohibited in my mission, with regard the
> French and the Indians, and reduced to saying Mass in my church with
> Frère Brébant and Pottier [a *hospitalier* and an *engagé*].[41]

Bergier longed to interact with the Tamarois as a prayerful Christian and not as a tradesman. Nonetheless, to entice the Tamarois to remain, he adjusted his tactics, engaged in the institution of reciprocity, as he interpreted it, and countered Chief Rouensa's gifts to the Tamarois with some five hundred *coups de poudre* (powder charges) and other goods. Having secured help from the Cahokias, he provided gifts for their support as well—a kettle, four additional pounds of powder, a pound of colored glass beads, vermillion, and a dozen knives. Angered by Bergier's action, Pinet dug into his conscience, accused him of "putting a plague into the mission . . . working contrary to God's glory and thus, responsible to God for the wrong he had done to the Tamarois, and for the lost converts who would not witness the good example of the Christianized Kaskaskias." Certain of his actions, Bergier had no remorse, particularly when told that the Tamarois had never wanted to leave and had only feigned this desire to get presents from him. "Thank God," wrote Bergier, "my conscience was relieved."[42]

Bergier had not wanted to give gifts, but to keep the Tamarois from moving to the Kaskaskia mission, he had to step into a middle ground and embrace the Native institution of reciprocity to interact with those who were leaving and those who compelled them to stay. While he went against his principles and likely saw his gifts as material enticements and nothing more, the Tamarois instead saw this as Bergier's willingness to strengthen their relationship, to develop deeper trust one for the other, to ensure their alliance. Regardless of interpretation, by entering this middle ground, both received what they desired the most—the Tamarois' continued presence within their own village.

For almost two years, Bergier alone dealt with the *vigne contesté*. Frustrated that "the Jesuits do not recognize the *Grand Vicaire* of the bishop and pretend to be *Grand Vicaire*" themselves, Bergier could only exclaim: "A missionary without a mission, a superior without a command, and a *Grand Vicaire* without authority . . . God is the Master, his will be done, but I avow that this state is not at all advantageous for me, for our missions, for the seminary, nor for the bishops. . . . I am only wasting my time and spending lots of money."[43] Endless challenges with the Tamarois language and the lack of assistance from the Jesuits deeply frustrated him. Bergier "pleaded with the Jesuits" to give him "the principles of the language . . . their dictionary or their *grammaire*, without ever obtaining this grace from them. They always referred to the decision for this mission," he wrote, "saying that if it remained with me, they would serve me." Even when Bergier protested that languages are not learned so quickly, the Jesuits refused to help, arguing instead that "it was against the glory of God to give me what I asked."[44]

Bergier's feelings of inadequacy tore at his conscience. "This delay," he exclaimed, "does not appear to me to be advantageous, neither for the edification of the church nor for the satisfaction of the missionaries. . . . What good is there in spending money and wasting our time. This is the fourth year that we are useless."[45] His continual good will toward the Jesuits was unlike that of Pinet, who followed the advice of the Jesuits' regional superior, Father Joseph Marest, brother to the Kaskaskia missionary, Gabriet Marest, to keep working, to stay put, to keep Bergier from fully serving the Tamarois. As Bergier described it, "it is trouble, scandal, and division in this village—altar against altar, missionary against missionary, Indian against Indian."[46] Little by little, Bergier's fortitude waned, and the strife of the *vigne contesté* spilled into the sharing of wine for Holy Mass that, for some eight months, Bergier had provided to the Jesuits out of generosity and kindness. One particular morning, Father Gabriel Marest came from his Kaskaskia village to fill his cruet with wine. Bergier hesitated: "If you need wine, I need Illinois; perhaps we could accommodate each other." Marest asked, "Which Illinois?" To which Bergier replied: "The Illinois that need a missionary." Marest offered none and took away his cruet, and returned to his mission across river. "*Voilà où nous en sommes* [Here's where we are]," exclaimed Bergier.[47]

In an impassioned letter to the Jesuit leader in Québec, Martin Bouvart, Bergier longed "to open up my heart to you on this subject." As he wrote, "wherein we are all brothers, we have the honor of belonging to Jesus Christ and to be his ministers . . . we all profess to search only for his greatest glory. Does it not seem that we search to supplant one or the other? If this is so, how could we ever hope to attain his Kingdom? Assuredly, we will not succeed as soon as we forget to be righteous and sincere."[48] Bergier wanted to get along with the Jesuits as brothers of Jesus Christ, as "seekers of God's glory." He simply could not see how the Jesuits could accuse him or the others "of being among their enemies or their persecutors." As he saw it, "we have only sought to defend the purity of our religion, to destroy superstitions and idolatry and not to persecute the Jesuits for whom we are not lacking in esteem nor veneration. I pray that God gives us peace."[49] But secrecy and power struggles continued to raise concerns with how either side could ever expect to "attain God's right hand" without goodness, sincerity, collegiality, a middle ground.[50]

Bergier's patience was waning. Even when Pinet needed Bergier's assistance, he quickly refused it when objectionable demands were made by Bergier, such as access to Pinet's book of prayers. While Bergier sought a middle ground where both experienced mutual benefit in serving the Tamarois, the Jesuit resisted. One September, "Pinet fell ill," wrote Bergier. "He asked me to say Mass in his chapel. I wanted very much to help out so as to not increase his suffering, but also hoped to gain access to Pinet's book of prayers to officiate at evening prayer. But, he kept it, preferring instead that an Indian woman lead prayer through memorization." During Lent of 1702, Pinet was to go across river to the Kaskaskia village to teach for Marest and asked Bergier to say Mass for him in his chapel. Bergier suggested that "it would do no harm for them to come to Mass in my church while Pinet was absent." But Pinet disagreed. Bergier relented and offered instead to go to Pinet's church to do the Mass but "wanted to know who would do prayer that evening. 'Domitille would do it,' said Pinet. I remarked—wouldn't it be more proper to have a priest rather than a woman do the evening prayer after having officiated at Mass in the morning?" Displeased with Bergier's challenges, Pinet stayed put "to ensure that the Indians did not hear Mass in my church nor that I said prayers in his church using his prayer book."[51]

As a general rule, women had far more exposure to Catholicism and were relied upon to participate in Christian endeavors more so than men, who were often away hunting, fishing, or participating in skirmishes. Since women more often remained in the village, it was through them that priests gained more immediate access to other women and children. Domitille's role as a prayer leader was not unusual. Among the Kaskaskias, the Jesuits "promoted a Christianity that publicly enhanced female power and authority."[52] As such, women often led prayers or summoned their people to daily worship, morning and evening, after bringing them together with rung bells. Pinet did much the same thing among the Tamarois. He relied on women, like Domitille, to serve and to teach Christianity to others. Encouraging Domitille's leadership in prayer with her own people made perfect sense to Pinet.

With all that had occurred over the course of the three years—the long delay without an answer to the dispute, the daily authority the Jesuits claimed they held, their refusal to assist Bergier with language and liturgy, Bergier's own criticism of his tireless patience and kindness, and his delay in exercising his functions as Saint-Vallier's *Grand Vicaire*—come May of 1702, Bergier's frustrations reached their limits. Without warning, at least in the eyes of Pinet,

Bergier suspended the Jesuit's efforts among the Tamarois: "The third of May, I informed Pinet that I was finally resolved to begin my functions. . . . I asked that he willingly abstain from continuing his and not cause me any trouble."[53] Pinet laughed at Bergier's newfound conduct, a reaction the Jesuit described as "simply the result of pure emotion," although Bergier preferred to call it "patience pushed to the limit." But as the seriousness of Bergier's action set in, the Jesuits cried "persecution," once again linking the quarrel over the Tamarois mission with the strife of the Chinese Rites controversy in East Asia.[54]

Bergier had weighed the consequences of his reaction for some time, but the day of the pronouncement, a rather benign event determined Bergier to demand that Pinet cease his work in the mission. "At Sunrise, Pinet sent out a boy with his church's bell [to call the Indians to Mass], all in conflict with our church that had begun to ring its own bell. . . . We asked the boy to stop ringing and he obeyed. Shortly thereafter, Pinet himself passed by with bell clanging, pulling Indians to his chapel rather than to ours." With that, Bergier ordered Pinet's church closed, but the Jesuit ignored him and continued to offer morning prayers and Mass.[55]

No matter how legitimate his actions, the Jesuits called Bergier a *brouillon* (muddle-head), an *envieux* (a jealous type), and suggested "that all they ever did that was perhaps inappropriate was to deny him access to their Illinois dictionary," nothing more.[56] Believing himself an excommunicate in his own mission, Pinet authored a scathing letter against Bergier, who viewed the penned proclamation as full of lies, with only one tiny exception that amounted to "not much of anything to even bring up." In this one normally insignificant event, Bergier had falsely stated that "Pinet had started his Mass before I [Bergier] had finished processing through the village. In truth, Pinet's Mass had not begun but candles were lit and the Tamarois were already singing in the church like the other days when they say Mass." Pinet said Mass three hours later. Bergier's slight miscalculation gave the Jesuits an opportunity to claim mistreatment on the part of the Seminary missionary. Once again, a sigh of frustration: "Here, sir, is where we find ourselves reduced in this mission. I pray that it will please God to put order into this place for his glory and for our rest."[57] But Bergier knew that any attempts to ameliorate the situation were destined to fail:

> The Jesuits consider me the lone author of these woes because I decided
> to begin my functions. I argue that they were the first and most truthful

authors by their continued efforts and open resistance to the orders of the church. God will judge and will have mercy on us if it pleases Him. However, the grace that I ask is to ensure that either the Jesuits leave this mission or that you send me somewhere else because nothing is more detrimental for the Glory of God, for the salvation of souls, or even for the satisfaction of the missionaries, that the Jesuits and the Seminary priests both remain here. Outside of a miracle of grace, it will only be a continuation of jealousy, suspicions, rumors, coldness, and arguments. To maintain peace, it would even be appropriate that the Jesuit Pinet, supposing he leaves this mission, not become a missionary among the Kaskaskia who are two leagues from here since he could pull a good number of those whom he baptized or taught over the last three years toward that mission and thus reduce my mission. Moreover, after all that has passed between him and me, and all that happens each day, there is no evidence that we will ever have a good relationship, nor great confidence in each other.[58]

The residual effects of Bergier's interdiction and the separation of the two bodies of Christ distressed him greatly. Bergier certainly had the right to carry out his functions as *Grand Vicaire*. But without communicating or sharing the holy sacraments with the Jesuits, whom he had all but excommunicated from the mission, the resulting division was all too painful. Bergier even reached the point of confessing to Gravier his anguish over the situation. Quite naturally, Gravier suggested Bergier annul Pinet's interdiction so as to clear his (Bergier's) conscience. But Bergier understood the political underpinnings therein. He had to get to work. The censure of the Jesuits was long overdue and came with Saint-Vallier's full support. To this end, Bergier had to move forward, stand firm, "not kowtow."[59]

Ironically, one month after Bergier's interdiction, the decision to maintain the Tamarois mission with the Séminaire finally reached him. Hand-delivered a packet of correspondence brought up from Mobile, Bergier discovered the year-old proclamation of oversight made by the archbishops of Chartres and Marseilles at the king's request: "The priests of the Foreign Missions are to remain alone in the place called Tamarois and are to receive fraternally the Reverend Jesuit Fathers when they pass through."[60] Bergier immediately informed Pinet, whose own actions were swift: "He conducted evening prayer, then Mass the next day." Per Pinet's wishes, Bergier helped him with a farewell feast during which the Jesuit "exhorted the Tamarois to persevere in prayer, to listen to Bergier, told them that it was the same prayer [as the Jesuits'], and consoled them that he would not be far away, that he was not abandoning them, that he loved them and would always consider them as his children." Pinet also gave Bergier the long-requested baptismal registry "so that I could know who had and had not been baptized." As for his house, Pinet left it to the Frenchman, Le Lorrain. Such a significant act, Bergier believed, only gave the Tamarois a sense that one day Pinet just might return. With that, Pinet left for the Kaskaskias, just two leagues away.[61]

The *vigne contesté* did not so easily dissipate. The Jesuits could still continue to interact with the Tamarois based on the official proclamation.[62] However, Pinet's unexpected death on August 1, 1702, brought calmer waters to the region. As Gabriel Marest described it, "Pinet fell ill while helping some other Frenchmen. After eighteen days of great suffering, he died very saintly in my arms."[63] Likely, it was his strong work ethic that led to his death. Gravier wrote: "Father Pinet and Father Marest are wearing out their strength. They are two saints who take pleasure in being deprived of everything—in order, they say, that they may soon be nearer paradise."[64]

Although Bergier had not hoped for Pinet's death, he could not help but "thank God for my deliverance," as this averted any "new troubles and scandals that would have arisen between this Father and I." Pinet, it seems, had already "arranged for the right to come from his village to visit those who were ill within mine," wrote Bergier, "that when they were ill, they could send for him. All of this [occurred] after the decision from France and without my participation, and even while censored on my part."[65] Despite Bergier's feelings toward Pinet, Marest asked the Seminary missionary to officiate at his funeral, "this for the edification of the people, and to let them know that we live in perfect union and communication." Bergier graciously obliged, sensing in the end that "Pinet, whose piety he well knew, had disobeyed the interdict only to obey his superiors."[66]

Finally, after three years of strife, the two religious bodies stepped into a semblance of middle ground and began to find ways to work within the region in peace. Gabriel Marest and Bergier developed "a great union and great communication on all things." Because the two had not been in direct conflict within the Tamarois village, their ability to work with one another was less compromised. Just after Pinet's death, the Kaskaskia missionary gave Bergier material in the Illinois language, likely helped Bergier with his own dictionary he was writing, and promised Bergier that he would act with him just as he would with a Jesuit. For his part, Bergier showed no lingering animosity toward his Jesuit brother.[67] Sometimes Bergier would go to the Kaskaskia village, twenty-five leagues to the south by 1703, to make his confession and to obtain a supply of holy oils. During visits, he would dine with the Jesuits, who characterized Bergier as "a worthy member of the Missions Étrangères."[68] Even when Bergier was left alone in his village during a summer hunt, "Father Marest offered me his house" in the Kaskaskia village.[69] Just a few days before a trip to the Ouabache Post, Marest "sent two canoes with eight Frenchmen to help bring my goods to his home." After Bergier visited the Ouabache fort and mission, he returned to the Kaskaskia village, "where I had left all of the goods from my mission and where I will stay until the return of the Cahokias and the Tamarois from their summer hunt."[70]

Bergier initially welcomed the departure of the Jesuits from the Tamarois village, but the long-anticipated decision led to unexpected disappointment. "The secrets of Providence are truly impenetrable," wrote Bergier. "God does not judge as men do since he took this mission from the Jesuits and gave it to me, which seems to go against all reason. And I fear that this is an effect of his justice toward me and on the Indians for having so poorly corresponded, each toward his grace. Here they are, reduced to *mamelles seches* [dried-up breasts]."[71] Bergier only made slow progress in the Tamarois mission. He was alone, albeit "by the grace of God, delivered from the trouble [of the *vigne contesté*]," but not in calm waters by any means. He recognized that "only knowing poorly the language, it is not possible for me to maintain this mission on the same footing as that of the Jesuits."[72]

Bergier certainly had the right to be frustrated, for as the Jesuit Le Jeune once wrote, "faith enters through the ear. How can a mute preach the Gospel?"[73] But with assistance from Gabriel Marest, who graciously provided him with the catechism in the Illinois language after Pinet's death, Bergier soon began to prepare young and old adults for baptism. In October 1702, Bergier had twelve adults prepared for the Easter 1703 baptism, "if they persevere" in learning of the Christian faith.[74] During the Easter service "five men, two women, one older girl, and three others around the age of twelve received the sacrament of Baptism."[75] In October 1703, Bergier had a number of catechists preparing for the 1704 celebration of Easter, but "there were hardly any male catechists. They were in position to be baptized but their war parties, from which I cannot get them to abstain, called them [to battle]."[76] Among those prepared for the Easter 1704 baptism, several "fasted during Lent," but the "*esprit immonde* [unclean spirit]" shattered his hopes. That Good Friday, most of his catechists and several Christians participated in "*danses impudiques*," indecent dances that went counter to Bergier's Christian teachings. In the end, Bergier baptized only a handful of his original eighteen catechists while several were "chased away" from the church. "Henry Chipe8kia, Henriette his wife, Anne Pina8a, daughter of la Biche, Catherine Tacahaganu8e, Agashi Tchicantec8a, Jeane Apiri8a, Er8chihec8e, Ematchihec8e, daughter of Merangha, Kinti8a, niece of l'Automne, were each denied baptism," wrote Bergier. Among these, "Ematchihec8e made a public penance, Anne continues this, and Henriette is disposed to do so. The others perhaps will follow their example with God's help."[77]

While Bergier, at times, stepped into a middle ground to support the needs of the Tamarois, when it came to catechism and baptism, he was less willing to accept cultural excuses. But Easter always took place during the spring. Any ceremonies or dances that occurred and that drew the Tamarois away from Christian tradition could have been in celebration of planting the fields, a good hunt, perhaps a deceased chief, even success in war. Although the Tamarois assimilated new Christian words and spirits into their culture, they were not so willing to allow catechism and the resulting baptism to alter their spiritual traditions that were in thanks to their *manitous* for good planting, success in hunting, and the like. As with other Native communities, the Tamarois were "practiced in the arts not just of accommodation but also of resistance."[78]

Bergier also sought to distance himself from the Tamarois practice of reciprocity through detachment from all goods since "*pondus est, non subsidium* [the weight does not help]."[79] He became particularly concerned that the Tamarois "view us as rich traders rather than as poor people [and] disciples of Christ," as merchants rather than as representatives of God:

Besides trading, the missionary who has goods is bothered by the continuous demands of those who pray as well as those who do not. In order to give, you have to have a beautiful store, and not giving, 'you are hard, mean, miserly, you . . . lie when you say that you are poor. We [the Tamarois] are the ones who are poor, you are rich, you have everything, you lack nothing, and you preach to us about poverty. You trick us, etc.' They have reproached me about it a hundred times, and I do not see how to overcome this other than through the approach I want to take, to give them generally all of my provisions, and then live off of their alms.[80]

Both cultures knew what they wanted most: Bergier—devotion to Christ without treasures or rewards; the Tamarois—reciprocal offerings to serve their community, spiritual items to support their expanding spirituality, and most importantly, a relationship strengthened through the reciprocal actions of giving and receiving. But Bergier found any form of trade most inconvenient, especially when bartering led to inflation of prices, disputes, and the like. He tried to rely on one of his catechists to oversee this activity, but she "tricked him," which forced him to remove his case of goods and "chase her from prayer."[81]

Bergier did not understand that reciprocal offerings spoke with power, so much so that the term "gift" was "called 'the word,'" wrote Father Le Jeune, "in order to make clear that it is the present which speaks more forcibly than the lips."[82] Gifts established and strengthened relationship and kinship with mutual obligation and reciprocity at their core. Gifts also created "'peace and a sort of conditional friendship . . . [that] to break off the gift giving [was] to break off the peaceful relationships.'"[83] Through reciprocity, Native peoples made "presents of all their possessions, stripping themselves of even necessary articles, in their eager desire to be accounted liberal." But such an action was always with reinforcement—more hunting, gathering, crafting, trading, and the like to acquire more goods and share them in community. In sharp contrast, Bergier gave away everything he owned as he did not want to continue such actions. Consequently, with the arrival of goods from France so tenuous, he had no material reinforcements. Circumventing reciprocity created a wall between Bergier and the Tamarois that weakened trust between the two cultures.[84]

Convinced that he had to sacrifice much in his life to carry out his work, Bergier became intent on living an impoverished life through an "annihilation of self and separation from the world."[85] Gravier admired Bergier's approach as it "could only come from the spirit of God," but cautioned him to wait for word from his superiors before executing his idea. Bergier was hopeful for the Seminary's support, exclaiming: "*duc in altum laxa retia tua in capturam* [put out into the deep water and let down your nets for a catch]. According to St. Matthew, my poor boat that still flounders will become *repleretur piscibus* [filled with fishes]."[86] Bergier sounded much like Marquette or Allouez, who had similarly denied self in their own attempts to convert the Illinois. Like these men, he was not going to have it any other way.

Bergier's colleagues soon witnessed the effects of his self-imposed poverty firsthand. In the fall of 1706, Bergier took some time to go to Mobile to retrieve needed supplies for his mission. Once in Mobile, Bienville welcomed the Mississippi's *Grand Vicaire,* but happy greetings soon faded away. Rather than seeing a strong, healthy man, they saw a missionary who was actively engaged in abandoning himself fully for the benefit of his flock. Bergier's gaunt and gangly appearance troubled many.[87] For some time, Bergier had "completely abstained from eating meat, fish and eggs . . . [and] allowed himself only one meal a day, which he ate at night. On the days of fasting, he ate a little ground corn, boiled in water or fried on the fire." Bergier's sleeping habits were trying as well, "only three or four hours of sleep each night, on the ground, with the remainder of his hours awake spent in prayer and work." De la Vente tried to persuade Bergier to not go to such extremes, that it was "simply unacceptable to allow oneself to die . . . that neither our life nor our body belonged to us but to Jesus Christ." But Bergier believed "such a life was necessary for him and for the Tamarois. They were possessed by a demon that Jesus Christ assured could only be chased away by fasting and prayer." Bergier's "soul was already in Heaven," wrote de la Vente. There was nothing he nor anyone else could say or do.[88]

Once back in the Tamarois village, Bergier found an epidemic spreading throughout the community. Day and night, the wearied missionary walked through the village and urged the Tamarois to abandon their *manitous,* their personal bundles consisting of objects that represented their original vision quests and that provided them with their life guidance. He wanted them to fully embrace the Christian God so as to dispel their rampant illness. When an individual's health did improve, Bergier attributed it to Christ and not to the sacred *manitous.* Bergier longed for them to accept the transformative powers of Christianity. He worked so tirelessly that "the oldest and most superstitious Tamarois brought him those things they had yet to detach from," their *manitous.*[89] But Bergier's own health deteriorated. Knowing his death was near, he called on Father Marest to come and give him his final rites. Although by this time Marest lived with the Kaskaskias some twenty-five leagues below the Tamarois village, he rushed to Bergier's bedside:

Having learned that he was dangerously sick, I immediately went to assist him. I remained eight entire days with this worthy Ecclesiastic; the care that I took of him and the remedies which I gave him seemed gradually to restore him, so that, believing himself better, and knowing, besides, how necessary my presence was to my own Mission, on account of the departure of the Indians, he urged me to return to it. Before leaving him, I administered to him, by way of precaution, the Holy Viaticum. He instructed me as to the condition of his Mission, recommending it to me in case that God should take him away. I charged the Frenchman who took care of the patient to inform us at once if he were in danger; and I retraced the way to my mission.[90]

Marest returned to the Kaskaskia village but could not spend one undisturbed moment without thinking of Bergier:

I wished to go to see Monsieur Bergier; but the people opposed this, alleging as a cause that, no one having brought news of him, as had been promised in case he were worse, they could not doubt that his health was reestablished. I yielded to this reasoning; but, a few days afterward, I felt genuine regret for not having followed my first plan. A young slave came, about two o'clock in the afternoon, to apprise us of his death, and beg us to go to perform the funeral rites. I set out forthwith. I had already gone six leagues when night overtook me; a heavy rain which had fallen did not permit my taking a few hours rest. Therefore, I walked until daybreak, when, the weather having cleared a little, I lighted a fire to dry myself, and then continued my way. I arrived at the village toward evening, God having given me strength to make these fifteen leagues in a day and a night. The next day at dawn I said Mass for the deceased and buried him.[91]

In his final days, Bergier remained in his hut with a crucifix in his hand day and night. The Canadian Michel Bizaillon remained at his bedside throughout his struggle. After days of suffering, Bergier "lovingly kissed the crucifix and expired." Bergier died on November 9, 1707, "conserved in his reason, word, and good sense." His colleagues' misgivings were justified—"His abdomen [was] filled with abscesses inside and out, without medicine, without surgeons other than God alone." A Canadian opened one abscess out of which came "the worst of substances."[92]

After Bergier's death, accolades poured in. Tremblay was well pleased with Bergier's assignment to the region, as he was "a man after his own heart," with "*bec et ongles* [tooth and claws]," certainly one to stand by his convictions and to carry out all duties the bishop asked of him.[93] To de la Vente, "Bergier had placed the mission on such good footing that none came to prayer for presents, something which is not common in other missions."[94] Even the Jesuit Father Marest described Bergier as "a missionary of true merit" who, despite having had to endure the difficulties he faced, eventually found success in the mission.[95] Tremblay, himself, was grateful that "the Jesuits, neighbors of his mission, have not refused him any praise that he earned for his Saintly life, and that he earned even more through his precious death before God."[96]

For their part, the Tamarois offered no such accolades for Bergier. When they welcomed the Seminary missionaries into their village, they hoped to develop a deep reciprocal relationship with them. They invited these spiritually powerful men to teach them, all the while expecting the priests "to form lasting social bonds through ritual and exchange."[97] But Bergier's refusal to engage in reciprocity prevented him from developing such a meaningful relationship. Bergier's complete abstinence of goods threw up an impenetrable wall that led to mistrust, a barrier to a lasting bond between the two cultures. Consequently, shamans and villagers alike were quite gleeful when Bergier died. As they saw it, Bergier's Christian *manitou* failed him. Their traditional spirits, they believed, defeated the spirit of the cross. Indeed, "his death was for them a cause of triumph. They gathered around the cross that he had erected, and there they invoked their *manitous*, each one dancing, and attributing to himself the glory of having killed the Missionary, after which they broke the cross into a thousand pieces."[98]

The Tamarois' response to Bergier's death deeply troubled Marest: "I thought that such an outrage ought not to go unpunished. Therefore, I entreated the French to no longer trade with them unless they should make reparation for the insult which they had offered to Religion." To Father Marest, "this punishment had all the effect that I could desire." With time, "the chiefs of the village came twice in succession to declare their keen regret for their fault. By this avowal, they induced me to visit them from time to time." But a piecemeal approach to working with the Tamarois would not make much gain, Marest believed. Instead, a missionary had to live with them and "continually watch their conduct. Without this, they very soon forget the instructions that he has given them, and, little by little, they return to their former licentiousness." Consequently, the Tamarois remained without a missionary for a number of years. Any progress made during Bergier's time among them was compromised.[99]

Bergier's devout life was a large part of his lingering legacy. He gained the respect and admiration of many with whom he interacted, Jesuits included. At times, Bergier himself transformed, particularly when he looked not through Catholic rules but through God's eyes and stepped into a middle ground with the Tamarois in support of their marriage and parental traditions. Otherwise, Bergier's resistance to reciprocity kept relationship with the Tamarois at arm's length and prevented the deeper trust needed to allow for fuller acceptance of one by the other. But the detachment from goods and his own individual needs in conjunction with his adherence to the message of Christ—to pray for and to serve others—was his eternal focus. Allouez's own comment could not reflect Bergier more clearly: "I am where God wants me . . . the more I suffer, the more I will be consoled . . . one never finds a cross, nails, and thorns where one does not also find Jesus."[100]

Bergier poured himself into his work. He suffered far more alive but without complaint or wanting sympathy than if he had been killed outright. It was a complete divergence of spirit from flesh: "The two inclinations were irreconcilable; the triumph of one required the defeat of the other. The way to elevate one's mind and heart to the spiritual world and to achieve mental union with God, then called 'perfection,' was to subdue one's body and all concerns for the material world."[101] Ultimately, de la Vente viewed Bergier's life and death as more heroic than that of Saint François Xavier since Bergier "had not found support during his solitary agony, and yet maintained an indefatigable patience. He worked for Jesus Christ, without gift of languages and without miracle other than to work purely by faith."[102]

The death of Bergier did not necessarily end certain squabbles between Jesuits and Seminary priests. From Mobile, de la Vente was quite suspicious of Father Marest. Months before Bergier's death, he wrote to the Jesuit and asked him to make an inventory of all of the Seminary priest's possessions, as well as those of the mission, should he pass away. When Bergier died, his French caretaker Bizaillon gave Bergier's affects to Marest.[103] Ultimately, these goods were transferred to Kaskaskia to avoid theft. Although more private goods were sent to the Séminaire de Québec, some items came into Davion's possession while others were sold at auction. A total of 500 écus (1,500–3,000 livres) were gained from the sale of Bergier's meager possessions, but de la Vente was certain that more should have been received. More importantly, de la Vente was convinced that the Jesuits were trying to destroy any attempt the Seminary might make to hold on to the Tamarois mission. For that matter, Tremblay was concerned that private, sensitive letters might fall into the wrong hands: "I don't know if the priest [Marest] found all the letters one wrote to Bergier and all his papers. It is very troubling that things one wrote to him in confidence fall into the hands of a Jesuit. This persuades me more and more that if we send missionaries to work among the Indians, that they are always sent two together, and that we never do [again] as we have done—individual by individual."[104] Thus, the *vigne contesté* continued despite the fact that all of its original primary players—Pinet, Binneteau, Gravier, Bergier, Saint-Cosme, de Limoges, and de Montigny—were now dead or out of the region altogether. More importantly, the tenure of the region's brightest and most devout priest was over. Only Davion remained on the Mississippi.

CHAPTER 10

Davion, the Tunicas,
and the French

D
avion's story is literally a tale of two cultural forays. Although expected to serve as a missionary among the Tunicas, Davion spent significant portions of his time working among the French at Mobile and later in New Orleans. No matter if he served as a missionary or as a priest, Davion pleased some individuals but caught the critical eye of others who thought he could do better. Useless, old, of ill health, fearful, wandering, kind, helpful, quiet, demanding, gracious—each was used to describe Davion, the longest serving of the five Seminary missionaries on the Mississippi. From his inaugural descent of the majestic river with his colleagues in 1698 to the arrival of the first women in the colony; from the failure of investors such as Antoine Crozat and John Law, who attempted to stabilize the colony's economic woes, to changes in religious oversight; from the movement of regional forts and Native villages to the establishment of New Orleans, Davion's twenty-seven years of multiple roles and experiences perfectly positioned him to witness a tremendous amount of history along the Mississippi River.

Davion penned his last entry into the St. Jean church registry on April 24, 1698. Three months later, he, along with de Montigny and Saint-Cosme, journeyed south from Québec toward the Mississippi River. Although Tremblay described him as "a very good priest," the Seminary leader was certain that Davion was "of such weak and delicate health that the hard life he must endure was not suitable for him by any means."[1] Just as Tremblay had predicted, hardly one year into his work, Father Gravier visited Davion's mission and found the Seminary priest quite ill, "in bed with the fever." Despite his illness, Davion arose the next day, shared communion with Gravier, and took him on a tour of the village. The Jesuit priest was pleased: "God blesses his zeal and the study that he made of the language which he is beginning to speak better than might usually be expected from a person of His age."[2]

Even with some linguistic success, the Tunicas were so unassuming and "so secret regarding all the mysteries of their religion," wrote Gravier, that the Seminary priest "can discover nothing about them." Nevertheless, Davion learned that the Tunicas reverenced spiritual forces within nature—plants, animals, the sky, and water—and acknowledged nine gods: "the sun, thunder, fire, the god of the east, south, north and west, of heaven and earth." Everything in their universe was held in proper balance between the sky world and the earth world. Prominent in the sky realm were the forces of the sun, thunder, lightning, and fire. Within the earth realm lived the plants, animals, and humans. The Tunicas' hallowed temple, raised on a mound of earth in the center of the village, held the sacred fire that preserved stability and balance within their culture and between the two worlds. To symbolize this balance, the temple housed two earthen statues—a female deity of the sun that represented the sky world and a frog that represented the earth world. The temple itself was never entered except when returning from or going to war. There was a time and purpose for entering the temple and for calling upon the *manitous* of the upper and the lower worlds. Balance was of utmost importance.[3]

As with other Native nations, Tunica shamans worked to dispel illnesses and demons, helped with council and tribal decisions, and addressed other needs within the village. Although of great service to the spirituality and welfare of the Tunica people, shamans were Davion's least favored members of the community, the least favorite of any missionary for that matter, for so often the two distinctly different spiritual leaders were at odds with one another. In one incident, Davion encountered an "unhappy shaman, to whom I had not wanted to give him what he asked." The shaman, out of anger, "raised a hatchet against us. It was of God's great grace that Charles Dumont pushed him away as best he could with a stick and only had a finger cut off. For in the manner that this unhappy man struck, he would have killed him if he had hit him on the head."[4]

Missionaries were direct threats to a shaman's spiritual power because of their efforts to transform Native spiritual traditions and their verbal assaults on their spiritual authority. Any introduction of Christianity to villagers quickly raised a shaman's suspicions, particularly when members of the nation seemed drawn toward missionaries whose gestures, touches, and words seemed to coincide with the arrival of illness and death. The shaman's violent action was likely a response to Davion's own assault against the Tunica spiritual world. Rather early in his work, Davion destroyed their temple, broke their sacred idols, and placed those that he could not break in his own hut. Well aware of the dangers of reacting so, and certain that the Tunicas "were coming the next day to kill him," Davion asked his young assistant Brunot—"a wise and good boy who has great fear of God"—to go and stay with the French. Soon enough, the Tunicas came to confront Davion. But despite their anger, their chief, "who loved that priest, made them go away and kept them from killing Davion or the little boy."[5]

The destruction of their sacred temple and idols certainly seemed worthy of a response by the Tunicas, but the chief saw Davion's disruption as "a part of order just as storms preceded great calms," simply a natural process in their world view.[6] Others, such as Charlevoix, saw the chief's passive reaction and the delay in rebuilding the temple as "certain proof of their little attachment to their false religion."[7] But such an opinion was unfounded. Even in the absence of a sacred temple, the Tunicas continued their spiritual traditions. Bénard de la Harpe visited the Tunica village in 1719 and still saw the sacred idols—frog and woman. In the 1720s, the Jesuit Father Paul du Poisson remarked that the Tunica temple fire was still burning, for if the Natchez fire went out, they could relight it from the fire of the Tunicas.[8] Even in the 1730s, Jean-François-Benjamin Dumont de Montigny drew a map of a Tunica village with the temple, the focal point of village life, situated on the north side of the village plaza surrounded by Tunica houses.[9]

Like other Native communities, the Tunicas guarded their traditions and only embraced elements of Christianity that fit into their world view. Tunica males were particularly resistant to Catholicism—"the rules were too hard," and thus they were not willing to give up one of their wives, wrote de la Harpe.[10] Nonetheless, the chief of the Tunicas, Cahura-Joligo, was drawn in by Davion's efforts. The chief's son, fifteen years of age, was the linchpin in their relationship. Davion taught the young fellow about Christianity and baptized him. Sometime later, the son fell ill. His recovery fell into the hands of a shaman, who was unable to save the child. According to de la Harpe, the shaman remarked: "had the [boy's] father given him a present, he would have saved the boy's life." Quite possibly the shaman had lingering anger toward Cahura-Joglio, who had not punished Davion after he destroyed their sacred

Tunica Village by Jean-François-Benjamin Dumont de Montigny, from *Poème en Vers Touchant l'Établissement de la Province de la Louisiane.* Courtesy of Bibliothèque de l'Arsenal de Paris, MS 3459.

Legend: A—Tunica village; B—Their temple; CC—Indian huts; D—French houses; E—Fort Flaubois (or Loubois); EE—Post planted in front of the temple.

temple. He thus sought reciprocity in a seemingly spiteful way. Upon learning of the shaman's words, Cahura-Joligo ordered the man's immediate execution. For his part, Davion had no expectations of gifts for the prayers and baptism he offered to the young son other than God's grace upon the baptized. Consequently, as a reciprocal gesture to Davion's work, the chief and his family came every day to participate in prayer and to listen to Davion's teachings, this despite Davion's opposition to their feasts and their polygamous traditions.[11]

Davion faced many challenges, just like his colleagues. Although he made early progress with the Tunica language, his skills remained anemic and he subsequently abandoned learning the language beyond a functional level.[12] Davion's health was perpetually precarious as well. He intermittently suffered from colic, with one episode so severe that he made his final confession to a *coureurs de bois*. Davion wrote of how this illness "normally arrives in fall or winter, especially when I have feet wettened by the frost, and winds out of the southwest or northwest. The suffering attacks the intestines and the belly, and eventually it attacks my knees, my legs, and arms, much like gout—In its final days, I cannot urinate most of the time . . . I cannot have a bowel movement."[13]

Illness and languages were common challenges for every missionary, particularly, it seemed, for Davion. But nothing impacted the Seminary missionary more than discovering the brutal death of Father Foucault. During the last days of July 1702, Davion, with an escort of twenty Tunicas, was headed to the Quapaw mission to interact with his colleague. He was no more than a day away from connecting with Foucault when he came upon "the debris of this massacre." Davion recognized Foucault's "hat, plates, a [portable] altar dressed for the Holy Eucharist, and papers written in Foucault's hand" and knew that something had gone terribly wrong.[14] The horrific scene of Foucault's death along the Mississippi's banks stunned Davion and immediately led to questions of trust between himself, his travel companions, and the Quapaws. "I told my Indians who were discussing this that it was not prudent for me to go into a region where one had dipped his hands into the blood of my colleague and our men. That they needed to determine if they were assured of their alliance with this nation . . . if we could continue on safely, as this would be the means to learn what happened in this fatal strike." Since none of the Tunicas expressed a willingness to continue toward the Arkansas River, Davion and his entourage retraced their steps and fled "night and day" from the murder scene. As they journeyed south, Davion retrieved the Jesuit Father de Limoges from the Houmas. Together they went to Mobile to alert Bienville.[15]

The impact of Foucault's death on Davion's own life and sense of safety was so profound that he did not return to the Tunicas for well over two years, not until Foucault's death was avenged, not until after the Tunicas came to Mobile to solicit his return in December of 1704. From afar, Bergier tried to encourage Davion to not be so quickly repulsed or alienated if he was to succeed, "for what good is there to begin these missions and then abandon them shortly thereafter?"[16] Despite Bergier's pointed encouragement, Davion's frustrations toward the missionary enterprise remained. "How can faith establish itself," he wondered, "if one kills each other, if one abandons others, or if one does not take the necessary measures needed within this colony, where every year, one lacks everything, or where there are always delays that destroy the ability to advance. In a word, if peace is not established, it is in vain that one hopes to do something here."[17]

Davion himself had served as a peacemaker three years earlier when, as the *esprit blanc,* he gained a period of calm between the Chickasaws and the Tunicas. But disruptions such as the strike against Foucault convinced him that the missionaries could "bear no fruit for the conversion of these poor Indians." He had little if any trust in the Native people along the Mississippi, nor for the French at Mobile, who refused to take action against the Koroa murderers. As he exclaimed to Saint-Vallier: "You be the judge, Monseigneur, that the news from the Mississippi is not that which can bring some softening to our sufferings."[18]

For two years, Davion begged Bienville to send soldiers to avenge the murders of Foucault and the Frenchmen, but Bienville relentlessly dismissed him, citing the inability of his army to retaliate with so few men. Instead, Bienville grumbled at how Saint-Cosme remained bravely in the field while Davion cowered in Mobile.[19] Davion snapped back: What with Bienville's slowness to act on Foucault's death, soon another missionary would lay bloodied in the field.[20] Davion was adamant—if Bienville wanted him among the Tunicas, then justice had to be served. Come December 21, 1704, Bienville saw his chance. When the Tunicas arrived at Fort Louis to plead with Davion to return to their village, Bienville, in support of their plea, and to rid Mobile of the recoiling missionary, struck a deal: If the Tunicas wanted Davion, then let them attack the Koroas and bring the heads of Foucault's murderers to him. As a part of this agreement, Bienville imprudently offered a group of Canadian soldiers under Louis Juchereau de Saint-Denis's leadership to assist them. However, Saint-Denis quickly balked at this proposition since it was, after all, a "non-political, spontaneous assault by a few greedy Koroa underlings . . . who seized an opportunity to gain coveted possessions." The Koroa chiefs themselves had already avenged the deaths long before any retaliation took place.[21] In the end, the Tunicas did not attack the Koroas, for the Quapaws had already avenged Foucault's death. Saint-Denis escorted Davion back to the Tunica village two months later.

During the time that Davion was absent from his mission, he settled into life at Fort Louis and remained there from August 1702 until the early spring of 1705. Initially, Davion, Boutteville, and Jesuits Dongé and de Limoges lived in perfect harmony, much unlike their contentious Seminary and Jesuit colleagues among the Tamarois.[22] But this collegiality ended when, from afar, Saint-Vallier erected the Mobile Parish on July 20, 1703, and forced the Jesuits to leave. Two priests from the Séminaire des Missions Étrangères succeeded them at Mobile: Henri Roulleaux de la Vente and Alexandre Huvé.[23]

Prior to the arrival of these new Parisian priests, Davion began construction of a house. Situated at the corner of Rue du Séminaire and Rue d'Iberville in Mobile, the structure measured "sixteen feet by forty-two feet and contained a salon, a living room, and two studies, hardly large enough for two priests along with their provisions." Only the walls and a thatched roof were completed—no door or windows—by the time de la Vente and Huvé arrived in the late summer of 1704. Fresh off of the boat from France, de la Vente quickly referred to Davion's precious, humble abode as "nothing short of a barn," and borrowed 700 livres from the still lingering Jesuit, Father Dongé, to enhance the quality of the home.[24] De la Vente additionally asked Tremblay to send a carpenter to Mobile to continue the work. Paying 700 livres plus the cost of a carpenter to refurbish a "carcass of a house" hardly pleased Tremblay.[25] But it was not just a completed house that was lacking. Davion "slept on the bare ground," sustained himself with salt pork, water, and "fruits of his mission," all of which amounted to little nutritional value. Although Davion seemed willing to suffer such conditions, de la Vente was far less inclined to do so and immediately complained of his lack of goods—flour, brandy, carpenters' tools, nails, and the like. He demanded that Tremblay send him barley for his cow, glasswares, hatchets, and gun flints. Most importantly, de la Vente's newly devised parish needed a church, for only a chapel was present in the fort, far too small for those willing to worship.[26] To counter his request, Saint-Vallier suggested that "where there was no church, missionaries select three of the most appropriate houses for mass."[27] Housing, religious structures, fetid conditions, personal items—such issues became the source of squabbles between Bienville, Tremblay, and de la Vente for years to come.

Huvé and de la Vente had traveled from France on board the *Pélican* and arrived at Mobile in August of 1704. Some two dozen or so single women, handpicked by Saint-Vallier to help populate the colony, accompanied the

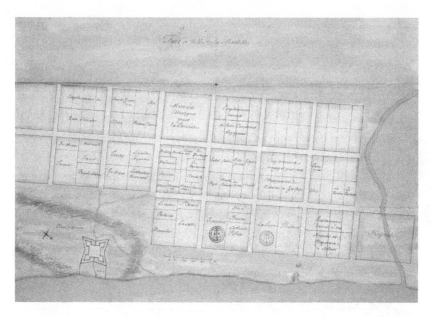

Mobile in 1702, where Davion lived until the early spring of 1705. *Ville de la Maubille 1702.* Courtesy of the Archives Nationales d'Outre-Mer (France), Dépôt des Fortifications des Colonies, Cote: FR ANOM 04DFC119A.

priests. Iberville had asked that one send "sturdy girls," women with a strong constitution who could not only withstand the wandering tendencies of the men there present, but also the difficulties of the Lower Mississippi Valley.[28] Within a matter of days of their arrival, agreements took place between several young ladies and their newfound beaus. Davion and de la Vente served as notaries to draw up contracts for the proposed marriages. By August 17, after hardly two weeks in Mobile, at least thirteen marriages had taken place, each consecrated by Davion and de la Vente. The other eight young women "did not wish to hurry."[29]

Yellow fever also arrived in Mobile at the same time as the *Pélican.* One young lady, Louise-François Lefevre, succumbed to the illness almost immediately. Davion officiated at her funeral. Many more suffered, and Davion's house became the hospital, with the cemetery close at hand.[30] The illness spared no one, not even the regional Apalaches, who had fled westward from Florida. Many had been introduced to Christianity by Spanish missionaries and were far more ardent in their faith compared to the region's Frenchmen. Longing to have their children baptized, Davion went to their village to assist, offering the holy sacrament to a young Apalache girl who died shortly after his blessing. Since the Mobile Parish had been installed by this time, hers became the first entry in the parish registry, penned by Davion.[31]

As yellow fever continued to spread throughout Mobile, all three priests contracted the dreaded sickness. De la Vente and Huvé remained bedridden in their quarters, souring Bienville's opinion of de la Vente's fortitude and willingness to work under duress. Far more accustomed to working under the harshness of illness, Davion continued to minister to those around him despite his own need to be tended to.[32] But sadly for many, Henri de Tonti contracted the disease toward the end of August. Weariness, fever, chills, and joint and muscle pain soon were joined by the black vomit. By September 4, 1704, de Tonti was dead.[33] The loss of the Mississippi explorer was a severe blow to many. He was engaged to be married and certainly left behind a deep knowledge of the Mississippi terrain and its Native peoples. After his death, "Iron Hand" was solemnly laid to rest in the cemetery across from the Seminary priests' home. Once again, Davion officiated.[34]

As summer 1704 turned to fall, yellow fever abated and life moved on within the struggling hamlet. Daily, the French clergymen carried out a full complement of religious services, including morning prayer, vespers, compline, evening prayer, and the *examen de conscience*.[35] But frustrations lingered. As far as Bienville was concerned, Davion was too old, too useless, and doing nothing short of endangering the colony's attempt to Christianize the Native peoples, if not "jeopardizing the entire colonial enterprise." Why, Bienville wondered, "when the Native communities needed missionaries so desperately," when the colony needed docile and friendly Native communities, was this "shrinking servant of God huddled in the town," ignoring God's work? From afar, Bergier felt Davion needed "renewed, God-given force" to continue as a missionary in the region. Tremblay's own opinion of Davion remained the same—Davion was a good priest but was not suited to serve in a mission. He was old, linguistically untalented, and of such poor and delicate health that rustic living was destined to do him in.[36]

Everyone criticized Davion. None celebrated the very fact that, despite his expressed anguish, that he "never again wanted to serve as a curate," he fully embraced this role while in Mobile. He devoted himself to "never cease to work hard, [despite my distaste], be they confessions or catechism, as long as my health permits it."[37] As the colony needed it, Davion served at baptisms, weddings, and funerals, even while dreadfully ill with yellow fever. He notarized wedding agreements for Frenchmen and Pelican Girls and worked with the Native communities nearby. He even presided over the installation of de la Vente as curate of the newly established Mobile Parish, a position the Parisian priest held for the next six years.[38] Davion may not have been in the Tunica mission, but he was addressing important matters for the Frenchmen with whom he resided. He was meeting the colony in a middle ground, serving the men and women there, fulfilling their needs, adhering to the requests of his leadership, the advice given him, and his own ordination vows, despite his wariness for being placed in such a position. And yet, all good efforts on his part seemed quickly forgotten. Instead, the never-ending saga of overspending and his growing reputation as an old and fearful man, unable to remain in his Tunica village, carried far greater weight in opinions of the Seminary missionary.[39]

Once Davion did return to the Tunicas, he lived steadily among them from 1705 to 1708. During this time, the Tunicas moved south from the Yazoo River to a Houma village near the Red River and modern-day Angola, Louisiana, this due to threats from the Chickasaws, the Natchez, and the English.[40] When the Tunicas moved into the village, they built their own round houses but also inhabited the squared Houma structures. Even more intriguing was Cahura-Joligo's house, which Charlevoix described as "quite ornamented for the house of an Indian, with figures in relief that are not as bad as you might expect." Quite possibly the chief was living in the former Houma temple, "in order to signify the Tunicas' domination in their new land."[41]

The Tunicas' decision to settle at Portage de la Croix was not made haphazardly. Unlike more northern Native communities, such as the Illinois, the Tunicas were never very active in the fur trade.[42] Instead, they purposefully settled near the confluences of major rivers, "important crossroads of communication," so as to regulate and engage in the salt and horse trade. The Red and Ouachita River valleys, in particular, were vital to their industries. Horses could be acquired, the result of contact with the Spanish territory in the southwest; salt could be expunged through travels into the Ouachita river system.[43] Such entrepreneurial skills heightened the Tunicas' importance to the French, particularly since the Gulf Coast colonizers were much less concerned with the fur trade and more focused on "the very survival of Louisiana itself." In their new location, the Tunicas could more easily help the French obtain "the basic needs of the colony remarkably well."[44]

As Charlevoix wrote, the Tunicas were "the ones that count the most."[45] Although not strong enough to fully support the French in battle, the Tunica nation, nonetheless, was "the only tribe the French could consistently count on for military aid."[46] This allied assistance was so important to the French that Cahura-Joligo was commissioned as Brigadier of the Red Armies by Louis XV, while the Tunicas as a whole regularly received annual gifts above the trade goods received.[47] Cahura-Joligo embraced the French title along with a French mode of dress. He was "not at all troubled by this style of clothing . . . for it had been a long time since he dressed as an Indian." He was "perfectly comfortable" with his "status and practices" as a Tunica but, regularly exposed to Frenchmen in his midst, "had to arrive at some common conception of suitable ways of acting."[48] As such, the chief's astuteness with economic affairs led Charlevoix to refer to him as a great negotiator who "understands his trade very well. He has learned how to hoard up money and he is reckoned very rich."[49]

The "Tunica Treasure," an extraordinary cache of European and Indian trade goods found in the late 1960s near Angola, Louisiana, is a strong indication of the riches Cahura-Joligo and the Tunicas accumulated in their interactions with the French during the early eighteenth century. European ceramics (Westerwald, Faience), 200,000 trade beads, bottles for brandy, wine, and gin, and metal goods (kettles, pots, and skillets) were placed within this impressive burial site, the contents of which are housed today at the Tunica-Biloxi Reservation in Marksville, Louisiana. What was not found, however, was a significant Christian presence. Only four crucifixes and just a handful of rosary beads were unearthed. Although Christianity was introduced to their culture by 1699, the lack of Christian goods, on the one hand, suggests that Christianity was not deeply embraced by the community.[50] But the lack of such goods could also indicate that Davion worked with the Tunicas in a manner much like Bergier—teaching and learning not through material rewards but through the gift of God's grace.

Cahura-Joligo excelled in his relationship with the French. No matter how they were interpreted, Christian activities seemed an important part of the Tunica chief's interactions with the numerous Frenchmen who visited his village from time to time. But such was not the case for Chief Rouensa of the Kaskaskias. While the marriage of his daughter Marie to Michel Accault and his own acceptance of Christianity were meant to strengthen the Illinois' relationship with the French, those "who had displayed the greatest friendship toward him would not even look at him since he was a Christian." Something had shifted, and though Chief Rouensa "had overcome all the obstacles to his baptism," the commandant now despised him. Astounded by such a reaction, Chief Rouensa "knew not what to think or say of such conduct, unless it were that the French preferred to see him lead the life of a savage rather than that of a Christian."[51]

Rouensa had worked for a middle ground for the benefit of his community. He had encouraged his Christian daughter to marry a Frenchman, and from this he anticipated strengthened trade agreements and alliances throughout the region. But Rouensa's Christianity seemed to suppress the French fondness he once enjoyed. Although marriage and entrance into Kaskaskian society helped one to better infiltrate the trade network, such marriage also came with societal demands within both cultures. Those who married into the Illinois community had systems of kinship and reciprocity to adhere to. Christianity had its own demands—monogamous, unadulterated relationships and permanent unions. For wandering *coureurs de bois,* tradesmen, or even French soldiers, such permanency potentially restricted feelings of freedom they embraced otherwise. Consequently, within the Kaskaskia village, any immoral antics on the part of Frenchmen likely became more and more distasteful for Rouensa and his growing Christian community. Any reactions on the part of Rouensa toward disorderly Frenchmen may have lessened his acceptance by the commandant and others.

Among the Tunicas, there were no strings attached, there was no need to marry. Christianity, at least as far as Bienville was concerned, was not disruptive to the Frenchman's plans to colonize the Lower Mississippi Valley. Christianity, in fact, was welcomed. But a threat to this Christian easiness emerged nonetheless. In 1704, the arrival of the Pelican Girls and many others had been meant to sustain the presence of women at the French fort, to expand the population, and to keep Frenchmen and soldiers from taking on sexual partners from the neighboring Native communities. But the number of French women dwindled, leading "officers as well as the *habitants* who are not married . . . [to] fish, as one says, in troubled waters." Father de la Vente was particularly displeased that "they have taken on the mindset to have domestique services through Indian women slaves."[52] Consequently, de la Vente saw French and Indian relationships out of wedlock as immoral and instead "praised intermarriage as a way to people the colony." But Bienville disapproved of such mixed marriages: "The intention of the king was that no Frenchman be married to a Native girl in the villages of this new colony," for if French soldiers married Native women, they ultimately became "dispersed among the Indian villages to live like libertines and under no authority, under the pretext that they have married among the Indians."[53]

Unwilling to obey Bienville, de la Vente "made the missionary to the Tunicas [Davion] perform a marriage of a Frenchman to a young female *sauvage* and three among those with the Natchez, where there is no Christian nor any adult who wants to become one and who have been little instructed during the seven years that the missionary has been among them." Pointing out the absurdity of such unions, Bienville criticized how "de la Vente had recently gotten it into his head to have a good carpenter marry an Indian woman, even after telling him [de la Vente] several times that you [Pontchartrain] were against these sorts of marriages. He married them before day break without publishing any banns out of fear that one of his brothers would put a stop to it, himself knowing the Indian woman."[54] Needless to say, Christian fervor had different results in the Illinois country and the Lower Mississippi Valley. The relationship between Rouensa and the French commandant was likely stressed due to the former's willingness to become a Christian and the likelihood that he and his daughter, Marie, took a strict approach to the Catholic faith as it fit into their world view. Alternatively, any stress felt in the Lower Mississippi Valley between Bienville, his soldiers, and Father de la Vente was due to the latter's insistence on enforcing moral Christian measures, forcing soldiers to marry. Ultimately, Rouensa's Christianity got in the way of French-Kaskaskian relations, while de la Vente created strife between the church, the military, and the government, but not the Tunicas. Cahura-Joligo played no part in this Christian strife. There was no need for intermarriage within his community. Frenchmen and Tunica people enjoyed the support of each other through trade, military support, and occasional Christian services with no need for matrimony.

Pontchartrain was so alarmed by the bickering between de la Vente and Bienville that he demanded the former's recall to France. Come June of 1710, a ship arrived and de la Vente boarded it, never to return.[55] With de la Vente's departure, expectations for Davion again fell into two places—as the Tunica missionary and as acting curate at Mobile, serving in the place that he least desired to be, carrying out duties that he least longed to pursue. But Mobile was suffering. Religion was ignored, if not lost altogether. The town itself had to be moved to safer ground, with the remaining priests distributed into three separate places: Huvé, to the port at Massacre Island; François Le Maire, from the Séminaire des Missions Étrangères de Paris, to Old Mobile; and Davion, to "New Mobile" to serve those there present.[56] This dispersal of the priests to three locations only increased the amount of funds necessary for sustenance, houses, chapels, and religious supplies.

Davion was miserable. Only from his amicable old friend Charles Rochon did he find some semblance of comfort. Rochon had built his own house "twenty-seven feet long, twenty feet wide," and lived there with his brother-in-law, Louis Marchand. When the latter decided to leave the region, half of Rochon's home became available for purchase. Davion paid 240 livres, "credited to Tremblay's coffer," and moved in next to his old friend so as to not sleep "*à la belle étoile* [out in the open]."[57] But as the years passed, Davion's sense of community floundered. In 1711, "even though I have written several letters to France and Canada, I only received one from Saint-Vallier and one from you [de la Vente]," exclaimed Davion.[58] When his letters did reach Paris, Tremblay found Davion making the usual demands—more helpers needed (especially linguistically talented folks) and more items desired. In an all too common response, Tremblay threatened to not pay for Davion's purchases at Mobile.[59] Even Davion's poor handwriting was all that Tremblay could bear: "The letter from Davion . . . is a little too long, but so poorly written and of such a high style that I would leave my post as overseer of these missions if I had to continue to receive such letters."[60]

Tremblay was certain that Davion had no talent as a missionary and should never have been sent to the Mississippi. As far as his spirituality was concerned, Tremblay was certain that Davion did little in the region. "Davion is so ill that we have left it to him to return to France and then return to Canada, or to go straight to Canada," wrote Tremblay. "He appears to be so broken to us that the life of a missionary is not sustainable for him."[61] Even Bienville's mind was made up. Davion "bears no fruit here and does not yet know their [the Tunicas'] language." As far as Bienville was concerned, "he doesn't connect with them at all. If, in the eleven years that this country was colonized, the Jesuits had been here, we would by now see flourishing missions."[62]

Despite Tremblay's and Bienville's dispirited feelings toward Davion, many came to recognize the integrity and benevolence that the Seminary missionary provided in that wild and unhospitable place. Pénicaut spoke of Davion's kindness and their sharing of mass together with Cahura-Joligo in the Tunica village.[63] Diron d'Artaguiette wrote of Davion's "mildness, his pleasant conversation, and his apostolic discourse," that such actions "brought many strayed sheep back to their duty." D'Artaguiette was certain that Davion was a "holy man," so willing to listen to others, while others, even the most fallen, listened to him, "so strongly imbued . . . with what he preaches to others, that the lowest criminals cannot but believe in the eternal truth he espouses."[64] Charles Levasseur *dit* Ruessavel, an officer who died of yellow fever, willed, among other things, 150 livres worth of nails to be used to finish the Seminary missionary's house and to also help build a church.[65] Davion was even given funds by a privateer to build a church on Massacre Island (also known as Ile Dauphine), surely of benefit to the region's efforts to strengthen itself religiously.[66]

Although frustrated as a curate in Acadie and hesitant to serve similarly in Mobile, Davion served well. But at this time and in this place, Davion struggled. Call it an absence of belief in his work or a loss of internal strength, but the aging missionary could only grieve at his inability to leave as de la Vente had done. Indeed, once in Paris, the seemingly insensitive de la Vente wrote to Davion and gleefully told him of the joyous reception he had received at the Seminary and that all had a new optimism for the Louisiana region. No doubt, de la Vente had grossly embellished the truth, for despite appearances, de la Vente "was moribund, beaten to the point of dying" when he left for Paris. His unanticipated departure was so quick that he abandoned more than 12,000 livres worth of goods accumulated during his six years in Louisiana.[67] Davion confessed to his former colleague: "I am completely resolved to leave here as soon as possible, unable as I am to resign myself to stay in a colony where there is so much licentiousness, which we have not been able to correct, and which is going from bad to worse every day. . . . I look at you, Monsieur, as being very fortunate to have been able to return to France, and I beg you by the bowels of compassion of our Lord Jesus Christ to work at procuring me some good fortune, seeing how useless I am in this colony."[68] Davion, who had only come to the region "not to serve the French but to serve the Indians," thought only of leaving. His optimism was depleted, he felt himself "useless in this colony, too morally severe to serve the French, too simple, unable to confess hardly anyone," and "too old to perfect the Tunica languages." What the colony needed, he believed, were "missionaries who are assertive, have talents, and everything else to change the face of this horrid colony."[69]

In 1711, Davion was offered a chance to return to Canada. Although "unable to continue living in a colony with so many disruptions and without remedies, where religion was completely lost," he did not go. Perhaps he felt the voyage up the Mississippi would prove far too grueling, or that the cold "would be horrendous" for him. Maybe he recognized something good that was happening by his continuous service in the region. More than likely, Davion could not amass the resources needed to make the trip. He simply wanted to return directly to France, but the lack of personal funds and ships sailing into and out of the Gulf prevented him from leaving. Despite his aching to go home, Davion had to remain in the region for another fourteen years.[70]

By 1712, management of the Louisiana colony passed into the hands of the financier Antoine Crozat, whose strategy it was to establish trade and to tap into the mines that he hoped existed within the region. For Crozat, "Louisiana was not so much either a mission to convert savages or a bulwark against the English inroads on the North American continent as it was above all a business venture."[71] But troubles abounded. Cadillac had replaced Bienville as governor of Louisiana, and his interests pulled him more toward mines than toward trade or diplomacy. Seminary officials in Paris were "not certain that Louisiana would survive," and in fact understood that if it failed, they "would no longer send ships there." Under Crozat's leadership, Davion, they believed, "was destined to die without the goods needed to survive."[72] Just as they had anticipated, Crozat failed miserably and the colony continued to struggle. The inability to sustain oneself led colonists, soldiers, families, and clergy alike to depend on assistance from the Native communities that surrounded them just to stave off hunger.[73]

John Law, an aggressive Scotsman, banker, risk-taker, and gambler next worked with the colonial finances. He persuaded young Louis XV's regent, Philippe, Duc d'Orléans, to take on his financial schemes relevant to the Mississippi Valley. In so doing, Law revived the Compagnie des Indes to take control of the fledgling colony. Shares upon shares of ownership in the Compagnie were sold, all with grandiose promises of regional success. Luring, conniving advertisements spoke of fertile land, natural resources, an idyllic world, with mountains filled with gold, silver, copper, and the like, houses a plenty, and a port ready to accept all ships that sailed. The Compagnie proposed to bring in thousands of settlers, and to enhance religion in the region by teaching the catechism, building churches, and increasing the presence of clergy. But significant obstacles quickly emerged. Very few stable individuals were willing to leave France for the Mississippi. To obtain the number of people needed to solidify and eventually expand the colony, the French government and the Compagnie rounded up France's riff-raff—prostitutes, the destitute, prisoners, the homeless, good-for-nothings, undesirables, the mentally ill—and sent them to the Gulf Coast.[74] But the Compagnie did very little to support these men and women. Those chosen to come to the Mississippi colony suffered mightily if they survived the crossing. Even religion suffered, as it "was not realistic to expect a great deal of financial support for maintaining and increasing the missions unless they could prove themselves of economic and political value, which they had not."[75] Consequently, neither population nor religious support improved. Bienville's new hamlet called *Nouvelle Orléans* was little more than "a partly cleared mud pit, home to a few dozen hastily built shacks and only primitive port facilities." The colony's future showed no signs of development and could not shake its long-held reputation as "an inhospitable and even deadly place."[76]

It was during the Crozat phase that Davion again found himself in the position of peacemaker, as he had been in 1699 with the Chickasaws. As it unfolded, Natchez anger toward the French reached a new pinnacle. Mistrust had developed. Bienville and Iberville, as citizens to New France, had long "accepted and participated in Native customs." They were always willing to share the calumet, to strengthen alliances, to negotiate with Native communities. Governor Cadillac, on the other hand, had passed through the Natchez village and had "haughtily refused to smoke the calumet, thinking himself above such messy and undignified affairs."[77] Gifts were given to the French, but none were offered in return. Reassurance of their alliance failed. The Natchez came to believe that Cadillac had bad designs toward their nation. In response, they robbed and killed four Frenchmen who were headed to the Illinois. Other deaths at the hands of the Natchez occurred and mistrust only grew.[78]

One day, the adventurer André Pénicaut arrived in the Tunica village after he and others had traveled through the Natchez region. Upon their arrival, Davion "embraced us all," wrote Pénicaut. "He told us that he had believed that we were dead. Then he said Mass for us, to thank God for the mercy He had done to us. After Mass, we told him how everything had happened, for which he thanked God a hundred times."[79] Shortly thereafter, a delegation of Natchez came to the village to ask the Tunicas to rise up against all Frenchmen,

Pénicaut and Davion included. One Tunica, "an honest man, who was sincerely a friend of the French and outraged by this request," wanted to "break open the heads" of the Natchez there present, but Davion stood in opposition and no violence occurred.[80] Recognizing regional dangers, and the increasing violence of the Natchez toward the French, Davion quickly penned a letter of warning for Governor Cadillac, which Pénicaut took to Mobile. Surprised by the Natchez aggression, Cadillac ordered Bienville to select fifty to one hundred soldiers so that they might at once go and confront the angered nation. But further strife quickly ensued. Knowing that Cadillac, Bienville, and others were soon to pass by the village, Davion quickly penned an additional letter of warning entitled "To the First Frenchman who Passes By." Once completed, he placed his letter in a sack, scrambled up a tree by the Baye des Tunicas, and there hung his all-important correspondence. As the Frenchmen passed by in their canoes, they saw the sack hanging from a branch along the water's bank and retrieved Davion's letter. The Seminary missionary advised the entourage that a Frenchman named Richard, returning from the Illinois country, was taken by the Natchez. They confiscated his goods and took him to their village. They cut off his hands and feet and threw him into a slough. With this horrifying news, Cadillac, Bienville, and their soldiers stopped in their tracks, built a makeshift fort, and carefully planned their next moves.[81]

Davion had again helped to avert violence along the Mississippi. More importantly, a level of trust was present between Davion and the Tunicas. The fact that he could convince the eager Tunicas not to hurt the Natchez was a powerful testament to a relationship in place between himself and this Native community. There was a deep sense of commitment and kinship present. Davion had developed a profound sense of compassion for these people, so much so that when le Page du Pratz passed by the village at Christmas in 1718, he asked Davion of the progress made within. "He answered, with tears in his eyes, that he had great respect for these people but could only baptize a few children before their death," wrote the French explorer. "Otherwise, those old enough to reason simply excused themselves from embracing our religion. Those too old to accustom themselves to it would not suffer themselves to follow its rules." Nonetheless, the chief was not lacking in prayer and participated in Davion's services, morning and evening. Some women and girls attended as well, while the men preferred to ring the bell.[82]

There Davion had been, on and off for some nineteen years, in an attempt to convert the Tunicas to Christianity. Davion never wavered in his belief that the Tunicas were fully capable of achieving all the benefits of salvation. Unable to attain his ultimate goal, he had resigned himself to remain in prayer with his flock and subsequently developed a deep sense of commitment between himself and the Tunicas, albeit with a sense of resignation that he could do little else except to be there to pray as God's representative. His own understanding of self, the Tunica culture, and the reality he faced seemed to lead to a relationship that all could embrace, a relationship that welcomed his presence and his teachings, but without embracing Christianity any more than simply accepting its powers as they saw fit. Even with little progress made, Davion and Cahura-Joligo found a middle ground. Davion recognized in the Tunicas "the image of a God who had Created them, who had died for them, and who destined them to the same happiness as the Europeans."[83] Cahura-Joligo embraced Christianity through participation in prayer and Davion's teaching, but with his culture's traditions intact.

Why such success in their relationship? Certainly the usual reason could apply—Davion possessed new spiritual powers previously unseen or unheard of among them, and the Tunicas sought to assimilate these new powers into their own spirituality. But the fondness and attachment went further, so much so that whenever Davion fled from the village, they always beckoned him to return, for as Charlevoix exclaimed, Davion was so well-liked by the Tunicas that they "wanted to make him their Chief." As one might expect, the Tunicas could not persuade Davion to serve as a village leader, just as he could not influence them to fully embrace Christianity. No matter how much Davion tried to teach them, they only participated with an "indolence that he could never overcome," and yet a fondness and connection lingered for many years.[84]

Davion was known to have a gentle voice and a calm demeanor. From the very beginning, he always sought peace and presumed a "mildness [and] strongly imbued himself with what he preaches to others."[85] His willingness to listen may have satisfied the Tunicas' senses for oratory and decorum. Davion had in fact been named the "White Spirit" after he traveled to the Chickasaws in 1699 to encourage peace with the Tunicas. Living among them, this *esprit blanc* could bring them safety and security. And although Davion had destroyed their temple and their idols, no harm came to him. No further disruptive behavior toward their spirituality is known to have taken place either. Instead, Davion resigned himself to allow a certain level of syncretism to hold reign within the village rather than holistic transformation to Christianity. As de la Harpe wrote in 1719, Davion "had to 'surrender' to these peoples the greatest part of their idolatry, their household gods," including the frog and the woman that figured prominently in their spirituality and within their great temple.[86]

Health could also have boosted the fondness between Davion and the Tunicas. The Seminary priests were the first Frenchmen to significantly interact with the Tunicas in 1699, this at a time when a devastating illness was taking its toll on their people. Unlike other nations, where a stark connection was made between disease, baptism, and death, the Tunicas may not have made such a profound connection since their illness began before the missionaries' arrival. And although in 1702 the Tunicas were "reduced to a small number due to illness," Davion ministered to the suffering and proved helpful during such a frightening time. As a residual effect to this loss of life, a smaller village allowed for closer contact between Davion and the Tunicas, resulting in a stronger, more intimate relationship of benefit to both cultures.[87] But more than anything, the Tunicas may have greatly valued Davion because he was a direct link to the French community and "provided a continuing opportunity for the Tunicas to bargain and trade for coveted European goods."[88] The Tunicas amassed many European items during Davion's time among them. Their sustained connection with the French and their ability to provide the soldiers and colonists with basic needs strengthened their fondness for Davion and the French. It was a mutual benefit—trade goods, protection, alliance, Christian *manitous*—but never complete acceptance of Christianity.[89]

The year 1719 saw Davion still lingering in the Tunica village, still welcoming visitors, including one Monsieur Pellerin, his family, and Madame de Bellecourt, who were touring the region so as to select a concession in which to establish themselves. During their six-day *séjour* (stay), they "were well received." They "marveled" at what Davion had within his abode and the ample amounts of food they enjoyed. Likely, they saw the effects of living within a village where agriculture and poultry abounded. Tunica societal structures were such that "the men do here what peasants do in France; they cultivate and dig the earth, plant and harvest the crops, cut the wood and bring it to the cabin, dress the deer and buffalo skins when they have any. The women do only indoor work, make the earthen pots and their clothes." Within the village, the Tunicas raised domesticated chickens and harvested corn, pumpkins, squash, fruits, nuts, and other wild edibles.[90] With so much food at hand, Davion gave the Pellerin family some of his own chickens and vegetables so that they might sell them and gain access to any goods needed along their journey.[91] Most importantly, these visitors were a sign of things to come as more and more French began to establish homesteads near the Tunica village. By 1722, twenty-one French men, women, and children had settled nearby. The following year, fifteen French places were charted in the Tunicas' homeland. And by 1727, a population of some forty-eight people was confirmed by Father du Poisson in and around the Tunica village. As the decades continued, more and more French abodes emerged. Though the French settlements were never as large as those that surrounded other nations, such as the Natchez, these French places "were large enough to keep the Tunicas firmly committed to the French cause."[92] The Tunicas maintained a strong alliance with the French and continued to benefit from trade with their European neighbors.

Davion was most certainly in New Orleans by 1722, having finally left the Tunicas for good, and having finally left the "uncivilized terrains" of Mobile and Biloxi. But life within the burgeoning town of New Orleans was not any easier. He continued to struggle with lingering financial woes. While the annual subsidy provided by Louis XIV had continued faithfully until 1717, all sources of funding came to an end when the court handed oversight of the colony to the Compagnie des Indes. Davion confronted Compagnie officers in search of what was owed to him. Pushing him off on the Compagnie's store, Davion inquired as to the support promised, but the surly attendants quipped that they had nothing for him. Tremblay further tried to help Davion and others. He requested payment in the range of 13,000 livres in back funds for all those still serving under the Séminaire's wing, but no payments came. No resolution was to be found, and what supplies or funds Davion eventually received were only out of the generous graces of Tremblay and others who felt his enormous plight.[93]

Davion did not just find financial woes in the capital city. A new wave of Frenchmen had arrived. They were not any more appealing than those he had lived among during his previous twenty years in the region. Many were degenerate, corrupt, fraudulent, disorderly, incorrigible, lazy. Those that could work were mediocre at best, often underqualified for the needs of the colony, always demanding in pay. Church time activities took place more at the local billiards hall than in any makeshift churches that one could produce. New Orleans was aching for good people, desperate for proper supplies, and in need of religious reform.[94]

While in New Orleans, Davion continued to carry out the duties of a *Vicaire Général*, including granting dispensations and faculties as documented in the registers of St. Louis Cathedral. However, Davion's usefulness and/or acceptance in the village unraveled. From 1721 to 1722, the Carmelites proved a thorn to Davion's position and Saint-Vallier's diocese. Invited to the region by an engineer named Adrien Pauger, this Catholic order believed that they could come and work under their own devices. Displeased that they were not under his authority, nor that of the bishop, Davion confronted the Carmelite leaders. Since they had entered the region without proper credentials, and overtly usurped the power of Saint-Vallier, they were promptly removed.[95]

Further changes in the air eventually diminished Davion's standing in the region altogether. The French court longed to see colonization fortified in and around New Orleans, and this included strengthening the religious standing in the otherwise debauched hamlet. To appease the king and his government, Capuchins were sent to New Orleans to oversee the Lower Mississippi Valley up to the Ohio River Valley, while the Jesuits maintained control of the Upper Mississippi Valley.[96] Saint-Vallier approved this assignment and subsequently granted the Capuchins exclusive oversight of Lower Louisiana with the title of *Vicaire Général*. Whether he recognized it or not, with this single decision Saint-Vallier and the diocese removed Davion and the Séminaire de Québec from virtually any role in Louisiana.[97]

Unaware that his oversight had been removed, the Seminary priest continued to work in the town. After all, he was the longest serving clergyman in the region, and for that alone he demanded respect. But once the Capuchins arrived, Davion soon had run-ins with Father Raphael, Saint-Vallier's new *Vicaire Général*. In one instance, Sieur de la Chaise, a special commissioner sent to Louisiana in 1722, was gathering information on criminal activity in the colony. To move forward, he needed a *promulgation* signed either by the bishop or by his *Vicaire Général*. Father Davion, who regarded himself as the latter, expected to sign the order, but de la Chaise asked Father Raphael for his signature instead. Davion immediately objected, but when he could not produce his titular credentials (he had lost them), de la Chaise turned to Father Raphael, who immediately provided his documentation as *Vicaire Général*. Naturally exasperated, Davion filed a petition with the Superior Council to block the Capuchins from exercising any powers. De la Chaise countered with a

petition that Davion was "annoying the Capuchins in performing their functions." There was nothing the Council could do. It was an ecclesiastical issue,
not one they intended to entertain.[98]

No doubt dismayed and demoralized, Davion and his *Procureur,* Tremblay,
sought answers and solutions. Thoughts turned toward sending Davion to the
Tamarois mission if he did not return to France. Assigning him to this post
would "not disturb the Capuchins." For their part, the Compagnie suggested
that Davion simply return to France since he was not getting along with the
Capuchins and no longer served as *Vicaire Général.*[99] Not willing to stand idly
by, Davion took action. Beginning in 1722, the fallen Seminary priest began
sending all of his goods to the Tamarois mission, where Fathers Jean-Paul
Mercier and Dominique Antoine-René Thaumur de la Source were serving,
having been assigned by the Séminaire in Paris to attempt to run the Tamarois
mission in 1719.[100] Twenty-four years of life on the Mississippi had led Davion
to accumulate a large amount of goods, including religious objects, carpen-
try tools, dining utensils and cookware, foodstuffs, as well as various arms
and supplies, including paper, a fishing guide, bed veils to combat mosquitos,
and a clock with its weights and counterweights.[101] Davion also had amassed
the largest library to date within the region, with some three hundred books
catalogued in May of 1724. Likely some had been brought with him during
his 1698 descent of the Mississippi. Others had been obtained over the years,
perhaps even after the deaths of Bergier, Foucault, and Saint-Cosme. Knowing the impossibility of handling these books if he returned to France, Davion
made the conscious decision to offer them to the Tamarois mission.[102] But
such a huge collection that contained books on theology, saints, the catechism,
piety, sermons, sacred history, philosophy, science and agriculture, literature,
languages, and medicine could only lead one to surmise that Davion's ultimate
goal was to establish a seminary. He had obtained, after all, a piece of property
on the east bank below New Orleans on behalf of himself and the Séminaire,
a sign that permanency was on his mind. Nonetheless, such an institution was
never built.[103] Other than for his own enjoyment or reference, these books
likely served no one. Many books were ravaged by mice and insects, molded
by weather and mud, unbound by the heat and humidity. And yet, they survived. Davion remained ever hopeful for their use.[104]

With most of his goods sent to where he believed they could best be utilized, Davion sought other venues away from New Orleans in which to work.
He soon found one where the Capuchins were unwilling to serve, as it was "too

difficult a task," La Balize. Engineers had established this point of reference for ships entering the Mississippi. There, Davion could have a chapel with a tall steeple that could serve as a lighthouse along the coast. Consequently, the long-term Mississippi priest left the mainland aboard *La Galathée* and arrived at this tiny speck of land just near the mouth of the Mississippi to serve soldiers and workers. Perhaps pleased to be away from the strife of New Orleans, Davion nonetheless found La Balize to be an inhospitable place. It was at water level, easily flooded, and possessed a constant array of mud all around. Low on food, and with workers almost constantly ill, Davion had his hands full. As he ministered to those who suffered, the near-sixty-year-old Davion's own health continued to decline, so much so that the Compagnie des Indes insisted that he return to France. Traveling aboard the *Chameau,* he arrived in France sometime in 1725.[105]

Once Davion was back at the Séminaire in Paris, de Montigny was happy to reconnect with "this good missionary, my old traveling companion." But Davion did not tarry long, as he wanted to go see his parents, for they had "not seen each other for some forty years." Sadly, once with his parents, Davion was soon "struck by a bout of gout" and died April 8, 1726. As de Montigny wrote of his death to the Séminaire de Québec, he fondly described his old friend as "a Saint missionary."[106] More importantly, with Davion's departure and subsequent passing, the Séminaire de Québec's work with Native communities along the Mississippi was over.

Davion's legacy, as far as the leadership in Paris and Québec was concerned, paled in comparison to the good he actually accomplished in the region. Lags in communication between the mouth of the Mississippi and Tremblay in Paris likely prevented Tremblay from knowing the many things Davion did to the benefit of the colony itself. Among the early forts at Mobile and Biloxi, those who noticed his helpfulness expressed appreciation. Those who did not felt he was a waste of funds for the entire colonial endeavor. How odd it is that although he was considered the least healthy of all the missionaries, he remained in the region the longest.[107] How ironic it is that Davion, who desired to never again work among the French while in Acadie, became the very one who oversaw many a baptism, wedding, and funeral and who faithfully served the men and women in some of their most difficult times. Fear got the best of him after Foucault's death, but even during his self-imposed exile to Mobile he was of benefit to those in need.

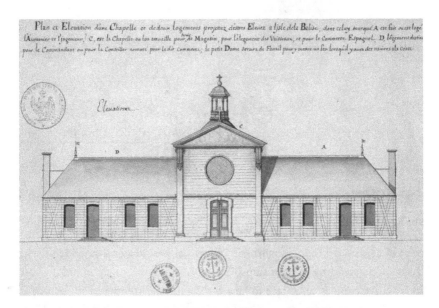

La Balize Church, the last place Davion served before his return to France. *Plan et Elevation d'une Chapelle et de Deux Logements Projetez d'Estres Elevez à l'Isle de la Balise.* Courtesy of the Archives Nationales d'Outre-Mer (France), September 23, 1723, Dépôt des Fortifications des Colonies, Depauger, Cote: FR ANOM 04DFC107C.

As for his ultimate assignment, a missionary along the Mississippi, Davion served among the Tunicas on and off for some twenty years. He never outright abandoned them until the very end. While he is presumed to have made little progress among the Tunicas, tears flowed when he spoke of his flock and the care that he had for them. A deep connection had been made between himself and the Tunicas. And while the Native community itself hardly embraced Christianity, the chief and his family often attended prayer sessions with Davion after their son's death. Thus, a certain amount of respect between Davion and the Tunicas emerged. A certain middle ground of kindness and generosity, one toward the other, came into being. Some seven years after Davion left the region, the Tunicas fondly asked of him, only to be saddened by news that he had passed away.[108] Even ten years after his departure, Father Anselm de Langres, a Capuchin assigned to Pointe Coupée, visited Davion's former flock. The Tunicas "who had been baptized by Davion" specifically asked him to baptize their children.[109]

Conclusion

We know very little about the interactions that took place between Seminary missionaries and Native peoples along the Mississippi during the early part of the eighteenth century. And yet, small bits of evidence within the historic record have survived to provide us with some understanding of what transpired when these missionaries and the various Native peoples came face to face with cultural systems and spirituality in tow. What has emerged in an overall accounting of their work is that the Catholic faith had little to do with change within these early eighteenth-century cultures along the Mississippi. Instead, while Native peoples opened their communities to the Seminary priests and variously adapted elements and symbols of Christianity that fit into their world view, it was the traditions of the Native communities therein and the missionaries' adherence to Christ-like compassion that drove any level of syncretism between the two cultures.

Most conscious of the need to make self-adjustments were Bergier and Saint-Cosme. Bergier's deep sense of compassion and his adherence to Christ's teachings led him to abandon strict Catholic canons and instead open his heart, soul, and mind to the presence and significance of a blessed union between a Native couple, even if *à la façon du pays*. So too did he choose to ignore Catholic rule and instead allow Christians and non-Christians to remain married, even to consider allowing children to work on the Sabbath, this to maintain safety and peace and render Christianity nonforced. Bergier's alterations and adjustments were made not from Catholic law but from a Christ-like stance that led to a middle ground whereby both cultures could attain a common goal—the safety and security of the women and children.

Saint-Cosme's own transformation emerged when he abandoned a part of his priestly vows so as to end human sacrifices among the Natchez. Both he and the Great Sun's sister had a common purpose, and in attempting to meet that goal, Saint-Cosme, like Bergier, dismissed Catholic rule and pursued his own "inclinations," his own sense of compassion. By stepping into that middle ground, he and the sister both embraced the Natchez institution of relationship and the openness of Native sexuality in hopes that the French culture might override Natchez tradition and end human sacrifices.

Other missionaries transformed little if at all. De Montigny's enthusiasm for serving in the missions floundered. He abandoned the entire venture altogether after less than one year with the Taensas and the Natchez. Having long served as a diocesan leader in Québec, he found no authority on the Mississippi, refused to adjust to all that he encountered, and left before he could hardly begin to serve. Davion's own transformation among the Tunicas was one of acquiescence. Unable to move forward with pure Christianization, he resigned himself to live sporadically among them, to pray for them, and to allow elements of their culture's spirituality to continue. He developed a compassionate attitude toward the Tunicas, tearful when he spoke of them, saddened that he could not convert them to Christianity. This compassion was apparent to the Tunicas, who showed great fondness for Davion, considered making him a chief, and even mourned his death years after he left them for good.

The missionaries' willingness to adjust emerged particularly in those moments where they could prevent harm within particular Native traditions. But never did they develop a disposition toward accepting and participating in the cultural institution of reciprocity. Foucault dismissed this cultural tradition and likely received mistreatment for his inflexibility toward it. Bergier also refused to engage in any form of a reciprocal relationship except when his hand was forced as the Tamarois began to move across the river and join the Kaskaskia mission. Even then, his understanding of the institution was short-sighted— a material gesture, he believed, and nothing more. But the Tamarois saw Bergier's willingness to respond to their departure with gifts as a symbol of alliance that temporarily led to a new sense of trust in the Seminary missionary. Consequently, a middle ground was forged—the Tamarois remained within their own village as both they and Bergier desired. Within little time, however, Bergier dismissed any further participation in a reciprocal relationship and unknowingly reduced himself to something other than friend or ally. The end result was a gleeful community and a shattered cross upon his death.

When adjustments were made and middle grounds forged, the Native communities were often the greater beneficiaries. Cécile felt heard and affirmed in her growth toward Christianity by having her marriage *à la façon de pays* respected by Bergier. Women and children felt their cultural traditions confirmed and supported as well when Christianity was not forced upon them and they could safely exist without fear of reprimand. Chief Cahura-Joligo's willingness to share Christian services with Davion and other Frenchmen who visited his village strengthened his own reputation among the foreign culture and increased his opportunities for trade and acceptance by the French nearby. And yes, when gifts were offered, albeit a materialistic gesture from the perspective of Bergier, the Tamarois benefited as well—continued existence on their sacred land.

Despite the deep strife of the *vigne contesté*, Jesuits and Seminary missionaries alike found points in their tenuous relationship where they too could step into a middle ground. Through the baptism of a condemned Sioux and the baptism of a dying Cahokia chief, both experienced an opportunity to serve together for the salvation of an expiring soul. Bergier's willingness to share wine or to argue in favor of his Jesuit brothers who faced their own struggles on the Mississippi proved favorable to a middle ground as well. For his part, Father Gabriel Marest provided Bergier with linguistic support after Pinet's death and offered his abode and assistance to secure Bergier's goods when, as *Grand Vicaire*, he traveled to visit other missions. Marest also caringly supported Bergier in his illness and death.

In the most unlikely of circumstances, adjustments and transformations even arose between the Seminary priests and roaming French Canadians. Indeed, new ways of proceeding developed when interactions between these loosely affiliated Frenchmen and the Seminary missionaries changed their understanding of the other in times of need. Feeling his death was near, Davion relied on a *coureur de bois* for his final rites. And though he had never again wanted to serve in a church, Davion found himself doing so by adhering to his vows and officiating at many a funeral, baptism, confession, wedding, and Mass along the Gulf Coast, much to the benefit of many French men and women. For that matter, while de Tonti was never deemed a French rapscallion, a reputation of allowing unsavory behavior within missions and/or forts had preceded him. Time and interaction with Saint-Cosme led to a strengthening of both men's acceptance of the other and an understanding of the good services both could provide on the Mississippi.

Ultimately, when logistical support remained unchanged, the missionaries suffered the most. Throughout their varied times on the Mississippi, funding never improved, the Seminary men incessantly lacked colleagues and workers within their missions, the arrival of goods and letters remained perpetually unpredictable, with communication being absent for months and years at a time. The seminary missionaries could never forge a solid foundation, nor experience a firm sense of commitment from those who controlled the purse strings from so very far away. They were quite literally alone on the Mississippi with only faith in God and the willingness of the Native peoples to support them. With all of these overwhelming and irresolvable trials, their hopes to Christianize the Native peoples were shattered.

By 1725, all Seminary missionaries from Québec were gone from the Mississippi River. For a time, the Native communities continued on. Each likely remembered their assigned missionary, lingered in their understanding and perhaps even appreciation of some of the patches of middle ground forged, and continued to include elements of Christian spirituality within their world view. Some even went on to receive new missionaries—Jesuits or priests from the Séminaire des Missions Étrangères in Paris. And yet, for all intents and purposes, each Native community maintained its spirituality, its way of life, its traditions. Unfortunately, by the nineteenth century many of their customs vanished as Americans moved westward and pushed surviving Native communities from their lands. These new white men dictated, demanded, and forced their way westward, with no interest in creating middle grounds. They only sought to plow through border lands, grossly impact cultures and traditions, and make their way to new grounds they could claim as their own.

NOTES

Abbreviations

AA	Greffe d'Antoine Adhémar
AAQ	Archives de l'Archdiocèse de Québec
AAUM	Archives Acadiennes, Université de Moncton (Canada)
AC	Archives Coloniales
ADD	Archives Départementales de Drôme (France)
ADI	Archives Départmentales Isère (France)
ADM	Archives of the Diocese of Mobile
AETR	Archives de l'Évêché de Trois-Rivières
AJM	Archives Judiciaires de Montréal
AJQ	Archives Judiciaires de Québec
AMV	Archives Munincipales de Vienne (France)
ANF	Archives Nationales de France
ANOM	Archives Nationales d'Outre Mer (France)
APL	Archives du Port de Lorient (France)
APNDQ	Archives de la Paroisse de Notre Dame de Québec
ASG	Archives des Soeurs Grises (Canada)
ASPF	Archivio Storico di Propaganda Fide (Italy)
ASQ	Archives du Séminaire de Québec
AV	Archives Vaticanes (Italy)
BANQ-Q	Bibliothèque et Archives Nationales de Québec à Québec
BANQ-TR	Bibliothèque et Archives Nationales de Québec à Trois-Rivières
BNF	Bibliothèque Nationale de France
CHA	Chicago Historical Association
JAM	Jesuit Archives of Montréal
JRAD	*Jesuit Relations and Allied Documents*
LAC	Library and Archives Canada
RAC	Rapport sur les Archives du Canada
RAPQ	*Rapport de l'Archiviste de la Province de Québec*
RAQ	Rapport des Archives du Québec
SMEP	Archives du Séminaire des Missions Étrangères de Paris
SSS	Archives du Séminaire de Saint Sulpice à Paris
WHSDLA	Wisconsin Historical Society Digital Library and Archives

Introduction

1. Linda C. Jones, "Nicolas Foucault and the Quapaws," *Arkansas Historical Quarterly* 75 (spring 2016): 4.

2. "Marc Bergier to Jacques de Brisacier," March 10, 1703, ASQ, Lettres R, no. 60, p. 2.

3. "François de Montigny to Ma Révérende Mère," January 2, 1699, ANF, Série K 1374, no. 84, p. 1; Marion A. Habig, *The Franciscan Père Marquette: A Critical Biography of Father Zénobe Membré, O.F.M.* (New York: Joseph F. Wagner, 1934), 210; John Gilmary Shea, *Discovery and Exploration of the Mississippi Valley* (New York: Redfield, 1852), 169; "Jean-François Buisson de Saint-Cosme to Mgr de Laval," January 2, 1699, ASQ, Lettres R, no. 26, p. 16.

4. "Mémoire de la Mothe de Cadillac," September 28, 1694, ANOM, AC, C11A, vol. 13, folios 178–191v; "Lettre de M. de Lamothe Cadillac," *RAPQ,* 1923–1924 (Québec: Louis-A, Proulx, Imprimeur de Sa Majesté le Roi, 1924), 80–93.

5. Richard White, *The Middle Ground: Indians, Empires, and Republics in the Great Lakes Region, 1650–1815* (New York: Cambridge University Press, 2011).

1. Prelude to the Mississippi

1. Barbara Widenor Maggs, "Science, Mathematics, and Reason: The Missionary Methods of the Jesuit Alexandre de Rhodes in Seventeenth-Century Vietnam," *Catholic Historical Review* 86, no. 3 (July 2000): 444.

2. Raymond Rossignol, "The Society of Foreign Missions of Paris," trans. George Christian and Richard Christian (Paris, France, 2007), 2.

3. Carole Blackburn, *Harvest of Souls: The Jesuit Missions and Colonialism in North America, 1632–1650* (Montréal: McGill-Queen's Univ. Press, 2000), 23; Joseph Bergin, *Church, Society, and Religious Change in France, 1580–1730* (New Haven, Conn.: Yale Univ. Press, 2009), 119, 194.

4. Georges-Edouard Demers, "Nomination et Sacre de Mgr de Laval," *Rapport-Société Canadienne d'Histoire de l'Église Catholique* 25 (1957–1958): 15; Ferdinand Cavallera, "Aux Origines de la Société des Missions Étrangères, L'AA de Paris," *Bulletin de Littérature Ecclésiastique* 34 (1933): 173–176; Georges Goyau, *Les Prêtres des Missions Étrangères* (Collection "Les Grandes Ordres Monastiques et Instituts Religieux," dirigée par Edouard Schneider) (Paris: Editions Bernard Grasset, 1932), 13–18; Catherine Marin, ed., *La Société des Missions Étrangères de Paris: 350 Ans à la Rencontre de l'Asie: 1658–2008: Colloque à l'Institut Catholique de Paris (4 et 5 avril 2008)* (Paris: Karthala, 2011), 72.

5. Gilbert J. Garraghan, "The Ecclesiastical Rule of Old Québec in Mid-America," *Catholic Historical Review* 19, no. 1 (April 1933): 19; Robert Choquette, *Canada's Religions* (Ottawa: Univ. of Ottawa Press, 2004), 105; John W. O'Malley, *The First Jesuits* (Cambridge, Mass.: Harvard Univ. Press. 1993), 296.

6. Henry Horace Walsh, *The Church in the French Era: From Colonization to the British Conquest* (Toronto: Ryerson Press, 1966), 104–105; Demers, "Nomination"; Henri Têtu, *Biographies de Mgr de Laval et de Mgr Plessis, Évêques de Québec* (Montréal: Librairie Beauchemin, 1913), 13; ASPF, Series 3, Scritture Originali riferite nelle Congregazioni Generali (1657), vol. 317, folios

107rv, 110rv, 117rv, and 128rv; see also ASPF, Series 2, Acta (June 14, 1657), vol. 26, folios 142–145; Series 2, Acta (February 21, 1658), vol. 27, folio 50rv; Reuben Gold Thwaites, *JRAD*, vol. 45 (Cleveland, Ohio: Burrows Brothers, 1899), 35.

7. Lawrence Wroth, "The Jesuit Relations from New France," *Papers of the Bibliographic Society of America* 30 (1936): 132–133; Demers, "Nomination," 13–14; "Mémoire Touchant M. de Laval," 1708, SSS, Documents pour Servir à l'Histoire de l'Eglise du Canada, vol. 1, Liasse de Papiers sur Mgr de Laval, folio 3.

8. André Vachon, "François de Laval," *Dictionary of Canadian Biography*, vol. 2 (Toronto: University of Toronto/Université Laval, 1969), 360; Demers, "Nomination," 17–18; Adrien Leblond de Brumath, *Bishop Laval* (Toronto: Morang, 1906), 23.

9. Vachon, "Laval," 359.

10. Guy-Marie Oury, "Le Sentiment Religieux en Nouvelle-France au XVIIe siècle," *Sessions d'Etude-Société Canadienne d'Histoire de l'Église Catholique* 50, no. 1 (1983): 277; Demers, "Nomination," 21, 27–30; AV, Lettere di principi, vol. 81, folio 4; Camille de Rochemonteix, *Les Jésuites et la Nouvelle-France au XVIIe Siècle*, Tome 2 (Paris: Letouzey et Ane, 1895–1896), 498–499; "Bulles de Nomination de Mgr de Laval," AAQ; "Nomination de François de Montmorency Laval de Montigny au poste de vicaire apostolique de la Nouvelle-France, Copie d'un document royal du 27 mars 1659,"ASQ, Chapître, no. 263; "La Reine-Mère Anne d'Autriche au Gouverneur de la Nouvelle France Pierre Voyer d'Argenson," March 31, 1659, ASQ, Lettres N, no. 1.

11. Adrien Launay, *Histoire Générale de la Société des Missions Étrangères*, vol. 1 (Paris: Téqui, 1894), 39–40, 156–157; Adrien Launay and François Pallu, *Lettres de Monseigneur Pallu, Vicaire Apostolique du Tonkin . . . de 1658 à 1680, Vicaire Apostolique du Fo-kien . . . de 1680 à 1684, Principal Fondateur de la Société des Missions Étrangères, Annotées par A. Launay*, vol. 1 (Paris: Société des Missions Étrangères, 1905), 1–2; "Postulation addressée à la Sacrée Congrégation de la Propagande pour Obtenir la Fondation d'un Séminaire des Missions-Étrangères," July 1, 1658, SMEP, vol. 27, p. 265; Noel Baillargeon, "La Vocation et les Réalisations Missionnaires du Séminaire des Missions Étrangères de Québec au XVIIe and XVIIIe Siècles," *Rapport Société Canadienne d'Histoire de l'Eglise Catholique* 30 (1963): 35–52.

12. Adrien Launay, *Nos Missionnaires Précédés d'une Etude Historique sur la Société des Missions Étrangères* (Paris: Rétaux-Bray, Librarie-Éditeur, 1886), 27; Goyau, *Prêtres*, 55; Bergin, *Church*, 291; Jean-Baptiste Etcharren, "Les Grandes Dates de l'Histoire des MEP depuis le XVIIe Siècle jusqu'à Nos Jours," in *La Société des Missions Étrangères de Paris: 350 Ans à la Rencontre de l'Asie: 1658–2008: Colloque à l'Institut Catholique de Paris (4 et 5 avril 2008)*, ed. Catherine Marin (Paris: Karthala, 2011), 20; Bérnard Pitaud, "Influence de l'École Française sur la Spiritualité des Premiers Vicaires Apostoliques," in *La Société des Missions Étrangères de Paris: 350 Ans à la Rencontre de l'Asie: 1658–2008: Colloque à l'Institut Catholique de Paris (4 et 5 avril 2008)*, ed. Catherine Marin (Paris: Karthala, 2011), 45.

13. Noël Baillargeon, "Le Séminaire de Québec et la Fondation des Missions de la Louisiane, 1698–1699" (BA thesis, Université Laval, Québec, 1964), 42; "Règlements absolument nécessaires pour le soutien et la conservation du Séminaire et Ceux qui ont seulement Rapport au Bon Ordre qui doit être gardé et ce qu'on appellee les Usages du Séminaire," ASQ, Séminaire 95, no. 14, p. 1; Noël Baillargeon, "325 Ans d'Histoire. Le Séminaire de Québec (1663–1988)," *Caps-aux-Diamants: La Revue d'Histoire du Québec* 4, no. 1 (1998): 13–16; Honorius Provost, *Le Séminaire*

de Québec: Documents et Biographies (Québec: Publications des Archives du Séminaire de Québec, 1964), 1; "Donation par les Marguilliers de Québec d'un Emplacement pour le Séminaire," December 30, 1663, ASQ, Paroisse de Québec, no. 127, p. 2; Sforza Pallavicino, *Histoire du Concile de Trente I* (Montrouge: Imprimerie Catholique de Migne, 1844), 107–110; Oury, "Sentiment Religieux," 278; "Établissement du Séminaire de Québec par Mgr de Laval," March 26, 1663, ASQ, Polygraphie 9, no. 1; "Acte de Fondation du Séminaire de Québec par Mgr de Laval," March 26, 1663, ASQ, Séminaire 2, no. 36; Baillargeon, "Fondation," 47.

14. "Mgr de Laval aux Directeurs du Séminaire des Missions-Étrangères de Paris," August 20, 1664, ASQ, Séminaire 5, no. 2; "Laval to Séminaire des Missions-Étrangères de Paris," August 20, 1664, ASQ, Séminaire 2, no. 51; Launay, *Histoire Générale*, 1:159; "Permission au Séminaire des Missions Étrangères de S'Établir à Québec," August 22, 1664, ASQ, Séminaire 2, no. 28b; "Première Union du Séminaire de Québec avec le Séminaire des Missions-Étrangères de Paris," January 29, 1665, ASQ, Séminaire 2, no. 28a; "Nouvelle Permission au Séminaire des Missions Étrangères de Paris de S'Établir à Québec," October 6, 1665, ASQ, Séminaire 1, no. 12; André Vachon, "Séminaire de Québec et Séminaire des Missions Étrangères de Paris," *Les Cahiers des Dix* 44 (1989): 17; Mgr H. Têtu and l'Abbé C.-O Gagnon, *Mandements, Lettres Pastorales et Circulaires des Evêques de Québec*, vol. 1 (Québec: Imprimerie Générale A. Coté et Cie, 1887), 95–97; "Union du Séminaire des Missions Étrangères de Paris avec le Séminaire et la Curé de Québec," January 29, 1665, ASQ, Polygraphie 17, no. 7.

15. Vachon, "Laval," 371; "Acte de Fondation," ASQ, Séminaire 2, no. 36; "Mémoire sur l'etat de l'Eglise de Canada sous l'Ancien Evêque et sous le Nouvel Evêque," ASQ, Polygraphie 3, no. 87; "Mgr de Laval to the Directors of the Séminaire de Québec, Paris," 1685, ASQ, Séminaire 5, no. 10, pp. 6–7; Baillargeon, "Vocation," 43; "Mgr de Saint-Vallier Nomme l'Abbé Louis-Pierre Thury Grand Vicaire pour l'Acadie," May 4, 1698, ASQ, Polygraphie 9, no. 21; "Louis Ango de Maizerets nomme Louis-Pierre Thury Supérieur Général pour les Missions de l'Acadie," May 12, 1698, ASQ, Polygraphie 9, no. 23; Provost, *Séminaire*, 423–424.

16. Oury, "Sentiment Religieux," 278; Launay, *Histoire Générale*, 1:157.

17. Noël Baillargeon, *Le Séminaire de Québec de 1685 à 1760* (Québec: Presses de l'Université Laval, 1977), 4–6; Walsh, *Church*, 151–152.

18. Amédée Gosselin, *Mgr de Saint-Vallier et Son Temps* (Évreux: Imprimerie de l'Eure, 1989), 5–6; Marion Marcel, *Dictionnaire des Institutions de la France au XVIIe et XVIIIe Siècles* (Paris: A. Picard, 1923), 346–347; Baillargeon, *Séminaire*, 6; "Jean Dudouyt to Bishop Laval," March 28, 1684, ASQ, Lettres N, no. 79, p. 6; Henri Têtu, *Notices Bibliographiques: Les Évêques de Québec* (Québec: Narciss S. Hardy, 1889), 50, 81–82; "Tronson to Dollier," February 15, 1685, ASQ, Manuscrit no. 414, p. 119; "Jean Dudouyt, Director of the Seminary of Paris, to the Leadership of the Seminary in Québec," April 26, 1685, ASQ, Lettres M, no. 1, pp. 10–11.

19. Gosselin, *Saint-Vallier*, 12; "Dudouyt," ASQ, Lettres M, no. 1; "Jean Dudouyt, Director of the Seminary of Paris, to the Leadership of the Seminary in Québec," March 1687, ASQ, Lettres M, no. 2.

20. "Saint-Vallier to Père de la Chaise," November 13, 1685, ASQ, Lettres P, no. 46, pp. 1–2; Jean Baptiste de la Croix Chevrières de Saint-Vallier, *Estat Présent de l'Eglise et de la Colonie Françoise dans la Nouvelle France, par M. l'Évêque de Québec* (Paris: Chez Robert Pepie, 1688), 16–17; Baillargeon, *Séminaire*, 17–18; "De l'Église de Canada Depuis l'Arrivée du Nouvel Évêque,"

ASQ, Lettres O, no. 58, p. 14; "Mgr de Laval to Saint-Vallier," February 15, 1686, ASQ, Séminaire 1, no. 47, p. 4; Gosselin, *Saint-Vallier*, 17; Baillargeon, *Séminaire*, 114; "Copie des demandes faites au Roy contre le Séminaire en 1692, par Mgr et Observations du Séminaire," ASQ, Séminaire 95, no. 46, p. 5; Roger Magnuson, *Education in New France* (Montreal: McGill-Queen's Univ. Press, 1992), 182–183.

21. "Dudouyt," ASQ, Lettres N, no. 79, pp. 6–7; "Eglise," ASQ, Lettres O, no. 58, p. 15; "Différends entre Mgr de Laval et Mgr de St. Vallier," 1687, SMEP, vol. 345, folio 91; Alfred Rambaud, "La Croix de Chevrières de Saint-Vallier, Jean-Baptiste de," in *Dictionary of Canadian Biography*, vol. 2 (Toronto: University of Toronto/Université Laval, 1969), 328–334; Pierre-Lionel Laberge, *Messire Gaspard Dufournel et l'Histoire de l'Ange-Gardien, de Ses Curés, de Ses Églises, de Son Trésor 1664–1760* (L'Ange-Gardien: Éditions Bois-Lotinville, 1992), 122; Baillargeon, *Séminaire*, 57–64; "Laval," ASQ, Séminaire 1, 47, pp. 3–4; Gosselin, *Saint-Vallier*, 4, 9–13; "Dudouyt," ASQ, Lettres M, no. 2, p. 3; "Tronson," ASQ, Manuscrit no. 414, p. 121s; "Mémoire du Roi à MM de Denonville et de Champigny," March 30, 1687, ANOM, AC, Série B, vol. 13, folio 163.

22. "Tronson," ASQ, Manuscrit no. 414, 121s; "Bishop Laval to the Leadership of the Seminary of Québec," June 9, 1687, ASQ, Lettres N, no. 87, p. 1; Edmond Charles Hippolyte Langevin and François de Laval, *Notice Biographique sur François de Laval de Montmorency, 1er Évêque de Québec, Suivie de Quarante-Une Lettres et de Notes Historiques sur le Chapitre de la Cathédrale* (Montréal: La Compagnie d'Impression et de Publication de Lovell, 1874), 138–139.

23. Langevin and Laval, *Notice Biographique*, 142–144; "Saint-Vallier to Laval," April 12, 1688, AAQ, Copies des Lettres, II, 81; "Etablissement de la Petite Communauté des Jeunes Seminaristes," SMEP, vol. 535; "Lettre de Denonville au Ministre," October 31, 1687, ANOM, AC, C11A, vol. 10, folios 94–95; "Champigny au Ministre," August 8, 1688, ANOM, AC, C11A, vol. 10, folios 119–126; Baillargeon, *Séminaire*, 63; Noël Baillargeon and Danielle Aubin, *Les Missions du Séminaire de Québec dans la Vallée du Mississippi, 1698–1699* (Québec: Service des Archives et de la Documentation, Musée de la Civilisation, 2002).

24. Mother Saint-Thomas and Mother Sainte-Marie, *Les Ursulines de Québec depuis leur Établissement jusqu'à Nos Jours I* (Québec: Des Presses de C. Darveau, 1863–1866), 454–455; Guy-Marie Oury, *Monseigneur de Saint-Vallier et Ses Pauvres* (Québec: Les Editions de la Liberté, 1993), 53–54.

25. "Établissement," ASQ, Polygraphie 9, no. 1; Vachon, "Séminaire," 15; "Ordre qu'il faut Garder pour le Temporel du Séminaire," March 29, 1686, ASQ, Séminaire 1, no. 61; "Pour éviter les Brouilleries entre Mgr de Québec et son Séminaire," November 1688, ASQ, Chapître, no. 30; "Memoire sur les Prétentions des Jésuites à la Mission des Tamarois," ASQ, Missions, no. 82, pp. 19–20; "Henri-Jean Tremblay to Mgr Laval," May 10, 1695, ASQ, Lettres N, no. 101, p. 34; "Henri-Jean Tremblay to Mgr Laval," May 12, 1695, ASQ, Lettres N, no. 102, p. 8; "Bishop Laval to l'Abbé Jacques-Charles de Brisacier," 1688, ASQ, Lettres N, no. 90, p. 5; Baillargeon, *Séminaire*, 23–32, 59, 79.

26. "Jacques de Brisacier to the Leadership of the Seminary of Québec," June 19, 1689, ASQ, Lettres M, no. 8, p. 4; "Jacques de Brisacier to the Leadership of the Seminary of Québec," June 19, 1689, ASQ, Lettres M, no. 7, pp. 3–4.

27. Baillargeon, *Séminaire*, 67; "Laval," ASQ, Lettres N, no. 90, p. 1.

28. Baillargeon, *Séminaire*, 68, 73; "Église," ASQ, Lettres O, no. 58, p. 16; "Mgr de Laval to

Mgr de Saint-Vallier," April 17, 1691, ASQ, Lettres N, no. 97, p. 1; "L'Abbé Charles Glandelet du Séminaire de Québec to l'abbé Jacques-Charles de Brisacier," September 3, 1691, ASQ, Lettres M, no. 11; "Response à la Plainte sans Fondement que fait Mgr de Québec d'Avoir Trouvé son Clergé Revolté," ASQ, Chapitre 30b, p. 1; Gosselin, *Saint-Vallier,* 17–18, 26; "de Brisacier," ASQ, Lettres M, no. 8, p. 5; René-E. Casgrain, *Histoire de la Paroisse de l'Ange-Gardien* (Québec: Dussault and Proulx, Imprimeurs, 1902), 80, 84; Baillargeon, *Séminaire,* 93–98; "l'Abbé Jacques-Charles de Brisacier to Leadership of the Seminary of Québec," July 19, 1690, ASQ, Lettres M, no. 9, and Lettres M, no. 10, pp. 1–3; Laberge, *Ange-Gardien,* 127–129; Oury, *Saint-Vallier,* 58.

29. Gosselin, *Saint-Vallier,* 21–30; "Laval," ASQ, Lettres N, no. 97, p. 2; "Louis Ango de Maizerets to Denonville," October 12, 1691, ASQ, Lettres P, no. 110a; Jean-Baptiste de la Croix Chevrières de Saint-Vallier, *Statuts, Ordonnances, et Lettres Pastorales de Monseigneur de Saint-Vallier, Évêque de Québec* (Paris: Chez Simon Langlois, 1703), 12; Jean-Baptiste de la Croix de Chevrières de Saint-Vallier, *Ordonnance de Monseigneur l'Evesque de Québec Touchant l'Ivrognerie & l'Impureté* (Paris: Chez Urbain Coustelier, Marchand Libraire, Rue St. Jacques, October 31, 1690); Têtu and Gagnon, *Mandements,* 1:267–270; Jones, "Foucault," 9; Guy Plante, *Le Rigorisme au XVIIe siècle, Mgr de Saint-Vallier et le Sacrement de Pénitence* (Montréal: Editions J. Duculot, S.A., Gembloux, 1970), 35.

30. "L'Affaire du Prie-Dieu, À Montréal, 1694," *RAPQ,* 1923–1924, 71–74; "Lettre de Cadillac," *RAPQ,* 1923–1924, 91; "Sentence d'Interdit de Mgr de Saint-Vallier Contre les Récollets de Montréal, May 13, 1694," *RAPQ,* 1923–1924, 74–75; "Première Monition de Mgr de Saint-Vallier aux Révérends Pères Récollets, July 19, 1694," *RAPQ,* 1923–1924, 75–76; Gosselin, *Saint-Vallier,* 42; "Ordonnance de Mgr de Saint-Vallier qui Lève l'Interdit contre les Récollets de Montréal (15 Juillet 1695)," *RAPQ,* 1923–1924, 80.

31. Vachon, "Laval," 364.

32. "Henri-Jean Tremblay to Leadership at the Seminary in Québec," May 15, 1695, ASQ, Lettres M, no. 20, pp. 69–73; Baillargeon, *Séminaire,* 152; "Archbishop of Paris to Saint-Vallier," April 15, 1694, ASQ, Chapitre, no. 4; "Henri-Jean Tremblay to Charles Glandelet," March 4, 1684, ASQ, Lettres O, no. 5, pp. 9, 16.

33. Casgrain, *Ange-Gardien,* 85; "Mgr de Laval to Saint-Vallier," April 1696, ASQ, Lettres N, no. 0, p. 3; "Jacques-René de Brisay Marquis de Denonville to Mgr de Laval," March 23, 1696, ASQ, Lettres N, no. 103, p. 2.

34. "Tremblay," ASQ, Lettres M, no. 20, p. 68; "Laval," ASQ, Lettres N, no. 0, p. 3; "Henri-Jean Tremblay to Seminary Leadership," June 3, 1696, ASQ, Lettres M, no. 22, p. 47.

35. "Tremblay," ASQ, Lettres M, no. 20, p. 68.

36. "Henri-Jean Tremblay to Mgr Laval," June 8, 1696, ASQ, Lettres N, no. 106, pp. 14–16; "Henri-Jean Tremblay to Henri de Bernières," June 3, 1696, ASQ, Lettres O, no. 18, p. 4; "Tremblay," ASQ, Lettres M, no. 22, pp. 49–51, 55.

37. "Bishop Saint-Vallier to Mgr de Laval," March 25, 1696, ASQ, Lettres N, no. 104, pp. 3–4; "Mgr de Laval to the Archbishop of Paris Concerning the Saint-Vallier Affair," ASQ, Lettres N, no. 107, pp. 2–3.

38. "Laval," ASQ, Lettres N, no. 0, pp. 1–4; Gosselin, *Saint-Vallier,* 11.

39. "Henri-Jean Tremblay to Québec Seminary Leadership," 1697, ASQ, Lettres M, no. 23, pp. 33–35.

40. "Tremblay," ASQ, Lettres M, no. 23, pp. 48, 53.

41. "Mgr de Saint-Vallier au Cardinal de Noailles," April 26, 1707, AAQ, II, 176; "Henri-Jean Tremblay to Louis Ango de Maizerets," May 4, 1698, ASQ, Lettres O, no. 21; "Henri-Jean Tremblay to Louis Ango de Maizerets," May 4, 1698, ASQ, Lettres O, no. 22, p. 2; "Henri-Jean Tremblay to Charles de Glandelet," May 3, 2698, ASQ, Lettres O, no. 23, p. 3; "Louis Tiberge & Henri-Jean Tremblay to the Québec Seminary Leadership," June 6, 1698, ASQ, Lettres M, no. 25, p. 1.

42. Baillargeon, *Séminaire,* 165.

43. "Lettres Patentes de Mgr de Saint-Vallier au Séminaire de Québec pour l'Établissement des Missions du Mississippi," May 1, 1698, ASQ, Polygraphie 9, no. 2; "Lettres Patentes de Mgr de Saint-Vallier au Séminaire de Québec pour l'Établissement des Missions du Mississippi," April 30, 1698, ASQ, Polygraphie 9, no. 3; "Lettres Patentes pour les Tamarois en Faveur du Séminaire de Québec," July 14, 1698, ASQ, Polygraphie 9, no. 4; "Mémoire," ASQ, Missions, no. 82, p. 1; "Permission d'Établir une Mission Chez les Tamarois," July 14, 1698, ASQ, Missions, nos. 54 and 54b; "Henri-Jean Tremblay to Charles Glandelet," May 7, 1700, ASQ, Lettres O, no. 28; "Henri-Jean Tremblay to Louis Ango de Maizerets," April 2, 1701, ASQ, Lettres O, no. 31, pp. 17–18.

44. Rough drafts of the *Lettres Patentes* granting permission from Saint-Vallier to establish missions along the Mississippi, April 30, 1698, and May 1, 1698, ASQ, Missions, no. 53, A–E; Baillargeon, *Séminaire,* 378–379.

45. "Marc Bergier to the Venerable Mother Burdier," September 24, 1698, AMV, E334, p. 3.

46. "Marc Bergier to Saint-Vallier," August 18, 1704, ASQ, Lettres R, no. 68, p. 4; "Henri-Jean Tremblay to Charles Glandelet," May 1, 1699, ASQ, Lettres O, no. 55, p. 25.

2. The Seminary, the Church, and Its Priests

1. "l'Eglise," ASQ, Lettres O, no. 58, p. 12.

2. Raymond Douville and Jacques Casanova, *Daily Life in Early Canada, from Champlain to Montcalm* (London: George Allen and Unwin, 1968), 120–122.

3. Colin MacMillan Coates, "The Boundaries of Rural Society in Early Quebec: Batiscan and Sainte-Anne de la Pérade to 1825" (Ph.D. diss., York University, Ontario, 1992); Carl J. Ekberg, *French Roots in the Illinois Country: The Mississippi Frontier in Colonial Times* (Chicago: Univ. of Illinois Press, 1998), 9, 11; Richard C. Harris, *Seigneurial System in Early Canada: A Geographical Study* (Madison: Univ. of Wisconsin Press, 1966), 120–121; J. C. Farlardeau, "The Seventeenth-Century Parish in French Canada," in *French-Canadian Society: Volume 1,* ed. M. Rioux and Y. Martin (Toronto: McClelland and Steward, 1964), 23; Peter N. Moogk, *La Nouvelle France: The Making of French Canada—A Cultural History* (East Lansing: Michigan State Univ. Press, 2000), 210; Farlardeau, "French Canada," 23–25.

4. Cavallera, "Origines," 173–176; Noël Baillargeon, *Le Séminaire de Québec sous l'Episcopat de Mgr de Laval* (Québec: Presses de l'Université Laval, 1972), 5–6.

5. Baillargeon, "Fondation," 11; Bertrand de la Tour, *Mémoires sur la Vie de M. de Laval, Premier Evêque de Québec* (Cologne: Chez Jean-Frederic Motiens, 1761), 7; Rossignol, "Society," 33–35.

6. Rossignol, "Society," 34.

7. Baillargeon, "Fondation," 31.

8. Dennis Martin, "Les Collections de Gravures du Séminaire de Québec" (Master's thesis, Université Laval, 1980), 10; Mgr Amedee Gosselin, "Les Grandes Devotions au Canada 92eme cahier," ASQ, Manuscrit no. 367, pp. 13–14; Oury, "Sentiment Religieux," 278.

9. Bergin, *Church,* 66; Baillargeon, *Laval,* 96, 101; "Règles des Ecclesiastiques Associés au Corps du Séminaire des Missions Étrangères de Québec sous le Titre de la Sainte Famille de Jésus, Marie, Joseph et des Saints Anges," June 7, 1686, ASQ, Seminaire 95, no. 21.

10. Launay, *Histoire Générale,* 1:431; Baillargeon, *Laval,* 105; Provost, *Le Séminaire,* 2; Têtu, *Biographies,* 34; Henri Sy, *La Société des Missions Étrangères: la Fondation du Séminaire, 1663–1700* (Paris: Églises d'Asie, Série Histoire, 2000), 192–200.

11. Bergin, *Church,* 61–62; Launay, *Histoire Générale,* 1:415–417.

12. "Catalogue des noms des missionnaires (1660–1855)," SMEP, vol. 95, p. 148; Registres du Fonds Drouin, *Le Site de Généalogie sur l'Amérique Française,* https://www.genealogiequebec.com/en/, Registres Paroissiaux de St. Jean, Ile d'Orléans, 1621–1876 (accessed March 3, 2017); Registres Paroissiaux de St. François, Ile d'Orléans, 1621–1876; Registres Paroissiaux de Sainte Famille, Ile d'Orléans, 1621–1876; Registres Paroissiaux de St. Laurent, Ile d'Orléans, 1621–1876; Registres Paroissiaux de St.-Michel-de-la-Durantaye, 1621–1876.

13. De la Tour, *Mémoires,* 53.

14. Ibid., 25.

15. Jean-Paul Foley, *Batiscan S'Érige: Prémices Paroissiales 1670–1708* (Trois-Rivières: Editions du Bien Public, 1981), 71; "Mémoire sur l'Établissement de la Mission des Tamarois de 1699 à 1724," ASQ, Polygraphie 9, no. 26, p. 1; "Journal des Affaires Avant 1700," SMEP, vol. 2, p. 535; Langevin and Laval, *Notice Biographique,* 142–143; "Saint-Vallier to Laval," April 12, 1688, AAQ, Copies des Lettres, II, 81; "Petite Communauté," SMEP, vol. 535; "Denonville," ANOM, AC, CIIA, vol. 10, folios 94–95; "Champigny," ANOM, AC, CIIA, vol. 10, folios 119–126.

16. "Acte de Prêtrise de MM. Thédore-Godefroy d'Herbery et Nicolas Foucault (dans la Cathédrale de Québec, 3 décembre 1689)," *RAPQ,* 1939–1940 (Québec: Redempti Paradis, Imprimeur de sa Majesté le Roi, 1940), 292; See also AAQ, Registre A, 281–282; "M. Foucault, Crediteur, 1692–1698," ASQ, Manuscrit C-4, pp. 167–168, 416.

17. "Bergier," AMV, E334, pp. 2–3.

18. "Erection en Cure de la Paroisse Saint-Jean de l'Ile d'Orléans avec Lettre de Provisions, Prise de Possession," September 26, 1694, ASQ, Paroisses Divers, no. 47, pp. 1–4; "Collation et Provision de la Cure de Saint-Jean, Ile d'Orléans, Addressée à l'Abbé Albert Davion," September 18, 1694, ASQ, Paroisses Divers, no. 48, pp. 1–4; Raymond Letourneau, *Un Visage de L'Ile d'Orléans: St. Jean* (Beauceville [Quebec]: Presses de l'Eclaireur, 1979), 30.

19. Douville and Casanova, *Daily Life,* 123; Farlardeau, "French Canada," 28; Foley, *Batiscan,* 73; "Registre Contenant les Affaires de l'Eglise Paroissiale de St. François-Xavier Située en la Seigneurie de Batiscan depuis l'Année 1670," AETR; "Registre des Deliberations des Marguilliers de la Paroisse de Saint-François-Xavier de Batiscan, 1670–1735," AETR.

20. One must distinguish this particular priest from another who had the same name during this time frame. The subject of this book signed his name as *Saint-Cosme,* while the other, who served at the Seminary, signed his name as *Buisson.*

21. "Recensement de 1681," LAC, Series G-1, vol. 460; Joseph Emond Roy, *Histoire de la Seigneurie de Lauzon,* vol. 1 (Levis: Mercier et Cie, Libraires, Imprimeurs, et Relieurs, 1897), 354; Raymond Letourneau, *Sainte Famille: l'Aînée de l'Ile d'Orléans* (Québec: Bibliothèque Nationale, 1984), 407; Amédée Gosselin, *l'Instruction au Canada Sous le Régime Français (1635–1760)* (Québec: Typ. LaFlamme et Roulx, 1911), 210–216; "Livres de Compte," ASQ, 1698; Baillargeon and Aubin, *Les Missions,* 37; Stéphan Bujold, "l'Acadie vers 1750. Essai de Chronologie des Paroisses Acadiennes du Basin des Mines (Minas Basin, NS) Avant le *Grand* Dérangement," *Société Canadienne d'Histoire de l'Église Catholique, Études d'Histoire Religieuse* 70 (2004): 66; "Mémoire Concernant la Conduite de Messieurs les Missionaires," AAUM, 1-50-7, p. 7; John Clarence Webster, *Acadia at the End of the Seventeenth Century: Letters, Journals and Memoirs of Joseph Robineau de Villebon, Commandant in Acadia, 1690–1700, and Other Contemporary Documents,* Monographic Services No. 1 (Saint John, New Brunswick: New Brunswick Museum, 1934), 52; "Quelques Explications sur la Monnaie," Centre d'Archives de Vaudreuil-Soulanges, http://www.chlapresquile. qc.ca/histo/lettres-fc/monnaie.html (accessed November 24, 2018).

22. Moogk, *Nouvelle France,* 238; Peter Kalm, *The America of 1750: Peter Kalm's Travels in North America,* vol. 2, trans. A. B. Benson, 2 vols. (New York: Dover, 1966), 416.

23. "Henri-Jean Tremblay to Charles Glandelet," April 8, 1696, ASQ, Lettres O, no. 12, pp. 8–9.

24. "Davion to Saint-Vallier," September 23, 1703, SMEP, Amérique-Canada, no. 344, p. 71.

25. Allan Greer, *The People of New France* (Toronto: Univ. of Toronto Press, 2012), 36; Daniel A. Scalberg, "Hijacking the Host: Lay Religion and Tridentine Reform in New France" (Presented at the Northwest Regional Meeting of the Evangelical Theological Society, April 4, 1992, Portland, Oregon), 5–6; "de l'Intention avec laquelle On Doit Demeurer dans le Séminaire," 1679, ASQ, Manuscrit no. 284; "Petite Note sur le Spirituel de Certains Paroissiens de St. Michel," ASQ, "Eveques de Québec," no. 207; Reuben Gold Thwaites, ed., *New Voyages to North America by the Baron de Lahontan,* vol. 2 (New York: Burt Franklin, 1905), 538.

26. Moogk, *Nouvelle France,* 236; Kalm, *America,* 2:422.

27. Moogk, *Nouvelle France,* 258n63, 259.

28. Anne-Marie Rivard, *Histoire de la Paroisse Saint-François-Xavier de Batiscan, 1684–1984* (Trois-Rivières: Éditions du Bien Public, 1984), 44–45; Janine Trépanier-Massicotte, *Chez-Nous en Nouvelle-France, 1608–1787: Origine des Familles, Arrivée des Ancêtres, Débuts de la Colonie et de la Région: Fondation de Saint-Stanislas* (Trois-Rivières: Éditions du Bien Public, 1978), 48; Coates, "Boundaries," 39.

29. Robert-Lionel Séguin, "Les Divertissements au Québec aux XVIIe et au XVIIIe Siècles," *Revue Française d'Histoire d'Outre-Mer* 61, no. 222 (1er trimestre 1974): 15.

30. Trépanier-Massicotte, *Chez-Nous,* 48; Moogk, *Nouvelle France,* 128.

31. Coates, "Boundaries," 340; Saint-Vallier, *Statuts,* 34–35; Têtu and Gagnon, *Mandements,* 1:347–350.

32. "Lettre du Gouverneur de Frontenac au Ministre (November 4, 1695)," *RAPQ,* 1928–1929 (Québec: Rédempti Paradis, Imprimeur de Sa Majesté le Roi, 1929), 281; Raymond Douville, "Deux Officiers, Indésirables des Troupes de la Marine," *Les Cahiers de Dix* 19 (1954): 67–98.

33. "Mémoire," ANOM, AC, C11A, vol. 13, folios 178–191v.

34. "Paroisse Saint-François-Xavier-de-Batiscan, Registres d'état Civil," 1689–1799,

BANQ-TR, Fonds Famille Mailhot, 121–123; "Lettre de Champigny au Ministre," October 27, 1694, ANOM, CA, C11A, vol. 13, folios 95–98v.

35. "Mémoire," ANOM, CA, C11A, vol. 13, folios 178–191v; "Lettre de Cadillac," *RAPQ*, 1923–1924, 82–83; Jones, "Foucault," 12–13.

36. "Remontrance de Monsieur le Gouverneur," March 23, 1694, BANQ-Q, Fonds Conseil Souverain, Jugements et Délibérations, Registre no. 10 des arrêts, jugements et délibérations du Conseil souverain de la Nouvelle-France (11 janvier 1694 au 30 mai 1702), folio 22; Douville and Casanova, *Daily Life,* 126–127; De LaHontan, *Voyages du Baron de LaHontan dans l'Amérique Septentrionale, Tome Premier* (Amsterdam: Chez François L'Honoré, Vis-à-Vis de la Bourse, 1728), 70–75; "Présentation d'une requête du sieur François de Jordy (Desjordy)," March 8, 1694, BANQ-Q, Fonds Conseil Souverain, Jugements et Délibérations, Registre no. 10 des arrêts, jugements et délibérations du Conseil souverain de la Nouvelle-France (11 janvier 1694 au 30 mai 1702), folio 13v; Coates, "Boundaries," 336–337; "Lettre de Cadillac," *RAPQ*, 1923–1924, 80–83; "Requête de François de Jordy (Desjordy) . . . ," March 23, 1694, BANQ-Q, Fonds Conseil Souverain; Jugements et Délibérations, Registre no. 10 des arrêts, jugements et délibérations du Conseil souverain de la Nouvelle-France (11 janvier 1694 au 30 mai 1702), folios 21–21v; "Arrêt ordonnant aux parties," October 18, 1694, BANQ-Q, Fonds Conseil Souverain, Jugements et Délibérations, Registre no. 10 des arrêts, jugements et délibérations du Conseil souverain de la Nouvelle-France (11 janvier 1694 au 30 mai 1702), folios 56–58v; Douville, "Deux Officiers," 80; Foley, *Batiscan,* 72.

37. Webster, *Acadia,* 35; Geneviève Massignon, *Les Parlers Français d'Acadie: Enquête Linguistique,* 2 vols. (Paris: Klinksieck, 1962); Moogk, *Nouvelle France,* 7, 73.

38. "Mémoire," AAUM, 1-50-7, p. 16.

39. "Mémoire," AAUM, 1-50-7, p. 11; "Degoutin to the Minister," September 9, 1694, AAUM, 1-3-10, p. 5

40. "Mémoire," AAUM, 1-50-7, p. 2.

41. Webster, *Acadia,* 47; "Degoutin au Ministre, Extrait de la Journal de l'Acadie," September 9, 1694, ANOM, AC, C11D, vol. 2, folios 232–234; Ekberg, *French Roots,* 141.

42. "Degoutin au Ministre," ANOM, AC, C11D, vol. 2, folios 232–234; "Degoutin," AAUM, 1-3-10, pp. 1, 2.

43. Webster, *Acadia,* 56.

44. "Mémoire," AAUM, 1-50-7, p. 19.

45. "Missionnaires des Mines," AAUM, 1-56-27, p. 1.

46. "Degoutin," AAUM, 1-3-10, pp. 2–5.

47. Ibid., p. 4.

48. "Henri-Jean Tremblay to Charles de Glandelet," May 21, 1695, ASQ, Lettres O, no. 7, p. 25.

49. "Tremblay," ASQ, Lettres O, no. 12, p. 8.

50. "Tremblay," ASQ, Lettres O, no. 7, p. 25.

51. "le Ministre à l'Évêque de Québec," April 16, 1695, ANOM, AC, Série B, vol. 17, 142v–143v; "le ministre," ANOM, AC, Série B, vol. 17, folios 123–134; "Tremblay," ASQ, Lettres O, no. 7, p. 25; "Tremblay," ASQ, Lettres O, no. 12, p. 8.

52. Bergin, *Church,* 61–62; Launay, *Histoire Générale,* 1:415–417.

53. "Mémoire," AAUM 1-50-7, pp. 12–13; "Observations sur L'Acadie," February, 1695, ANOM, AC, C11A, vol. 13, folios 280–281.

54. "Mémoire," AAUM, 1-50-7, p. 13.

55. "Érection de la Curé des Mines en Acadie et Union au Séminaire de Québec par Mgr de Saint-Vallier," August 8, 1698, ASQ, Polygraphie 9, no. 22; Webster, *Acadia,* 122.

56. "Registres de Déliberations des Universités de Valence," 1684–1695, D9, ADD, Valence, France; Joseph Cyprien Nadal, *Histoire de l'Université de Valence* (Valence: L'imprimerie E. Marc Aurel, Editeur, 1861), 206–211.

57. Provost, *Séminaire,* 435.

58. "Bergier," AMV, E334, p. 1.

59. "Tremblay," ASQ, Lettres M, no. 23, p. 58.

60. "Bergier," AMV, E334, p. 1.

61. Ibid.

62. Ibid., pp. 2–3.

63. Ibid.

64. Ibid., p. 4–5.

65. Ibid.

66. Ibid., pp. 4–6.

67. "Entrées, Séminaire, Paris," 1687, SSS, p. III.

68. Casgrain, *Ange-Gardien,* 87.

69. "Denonville," ASQ, Lettres N, no. 103, p. 2; "Laval," ASQ, Lettres N, no. 0, p. 3; Casgrain, *Ange-Gardien,* 85; AAQ, Registre A, p. 593; AAQ, Registre B, folio 169v.

70. "P. de Lamberville to Mgr de Laval," April 1, 1700, ASQ, Missions, no. 88, p. 3.

71. "Bergier," AMV, E334, p. 4–5.

72. Ibid.

73. François Xavier Cloutier, *Histoire de la Paroisse de Champlain,* vol. 1 (Trois-Rivières: Le Bien Public, 1915), 457; "Notre-Dame-de-la-Visitation, 1679–1913," BANQ-TR, Fonds Cour Supérieure, District Judiciaire de Trois-Rivières, État Civil; Sainte-Anne-de-la-Pérade, Registre 1, 1690–1700, BANQ-TR, Fonds Cour Supérieure, District Judiciaire de Trois-Rivières, État Civil; "Tremblay," ASQ, Lettres O, no. 28, p. 22.

74. "Bergier," AMV, E334, pp. 5–6.

75. "Mgr de Saint-Vallier nomme l'abbé Marc Bergier Grand Vicaire," July 31, 1699, ASQ, Polygraphie 9, no. 11.

76. "Marc Bergier to Louis Tiberge," August 15, 1699, ASQ, Lettres R, no. 41, pp. 1–3.

77. "Mgr. Saint-Vallier révoque les pouvoirs de grand vicaire des Jésuites au Mississippi et y nom les abbés. D.-G Séré de la Colombière, François-J de Montigny, et Marc Bergier," July 6, 1700, ASQ, Polygraphie 9, nos. 10, 10A, and 10B.

3. Preparation for the Mississippi

1. Tracy Neal Leavelle, *The Catholic Calumet: Colonial Conversions in French and Indian North America* (Philadelphia: Univ. of Pennsylvania Press, 2012), 33.

2. Ibid., 134.

3. "Colbert to Mgr de Laval," March 7, 1668, ASQ, Lettres N, no. 27; Robert M. Morrissey,

"The Terms of Encounter: Language and Contested Visions of French Colonization in the Illinois Country, 1673–1702," in *French and Indians in the Heart of North America, 1630–1815*, ed. Robert Englebert and Guillaume Teasdale (East Lansing: Michigan State Univ. Press, 2013), 46.

4. Morris S. Arnold, *Colonial Arkansas, 1686–1804: A Social and Cultural History* (Fayetteville: Univ. of Arkansas Press, 1991), 5.

5. Thwaites, *JRAD*, vol. 59 (Cleveland, Ohio: Burrows Brothers, 1900), 119–127.

6. O'Malley, *First Jesuits*, 255–256, 371.

7. Ibid., 8, 370.

8. Leavelle, *Catholic Calumet*, 39; George E. Ganss, ed., *Ignatius of Loyola: The Spiritual Exercises and Selected Work* (New York: Paulist Press, 1991), 283–284.

9. Leavelle, *Catholic Calumet*, 40; François Xavier, *The Letters and Instructions of Francis Xavier*, trans. M. Joseph Costelloe (St. Louis, Mo.: Institute of Jesuit Sources, 1992), 51.

10. Thwaites, *JRAD*, vol. 46 (Cleveland, Ohio: Burrows Brothers, 1898), 79–80.

11. Leavelle, *Catholic Calumet*, 38; Ganss, *Spiritual Exercises*, 104; O'Malley, *First Jesuits*, 23–26.

12. Moogk, *Nouvelle France*, 240–241.

13. Katherine Ibbett, "Reconfiguring Martyrdom in the Colonial Context," in *Empires of God: Religious Encounters in the Early Modern Atlantic*, ed. Linda Gregerson and Susan Juster (Philadelphia: Univ. of Pennsylvania Press, 2011), 179; Frank Lestringant, *Lumière des Martyrs: Essai sur le Martyre au Siècles des Réformes* (Paris: Honoré Champion, 2004); Thwaites, *JRAD*, vol. 59, 91; Auguste Carayon, ed., *Le Père Chaumonot de la Compagnie de Jésus: Autobiographie et Piès Inédites* (Poitiers: Henri Oudin, 1869), xi–xvi; Leavelle, *Catholic Calumet*, 4, 126–127.

14. Leavelle, *Catholic Calumet*, 130–131.

15. O'Malley, *First Jesuits*, 371–372.

16. Blackburn, *Harvest*, 24; O'Malley, *First Jesuits*, 249.

17. Thwaites, *JRAD*, vol. 10 (Cleveland, Ohio: Burrows Brothers, 1897), 119–121; Sarah Rivett, *Unscripted America: Indigenous Languages and the Origins of a Literary Nation* (New York: Oxford Univ. Press, 2017).

18. Thwaites, *JRAD*, vol. 31 (Cleveland, Ohio: Burrows Brothers, 1898), 231.

19. Thwaites, *JRAD*, vol. 64 (Cleveland, Ohio: Burrows Brothers, 1900), 231.

20. Thwaites, *JRAD*, vol. 56 (Cleveland, Ohio: Burrows Brothers, 1899), 133; Thwaites, *JRAD*, vol. 66 (Cleveland, Ohio: Burrows Brothers, 1900), 243.

21. Robert S. Weddle, "Tarnished Hero: A La Salle Overview," *Southwestern Historical Quarterly* 113, no. 2 (October 2009): 161–163.

22. Garraghan, "Ecclesiastical Rule," 17.

23. Marin, *Société*, 86.

24. "Dudouyt," ASQ, Lettres M, no. 1, p. 8.

25. Garraghan, "Ecclesiastical Rule," 26.

26. George R. Healy, "The French Jesuits and the Idea of the Noble Savage," *William and Mary Quarterly*, 3rd Series, 15 (April 1958): 145–146; Morrissey, "Terms," 54–55; Louis Hennepin, *A New Discovery of a Vast Country in America*, ed. Reuben Gold Thwaites, vol. 1 (Chicago: A. C. McClurg, 1903), 168–169.

27. Christian Le Clercq, *First Establishment of the Faith in New France*, vol. 2, trans. John Gilmary Shea (New York: John G. Shea, 1881), 137–138; John S. C. Abbott, *The Adventures of the Chevalier de la Salle and His Companions* (New York: Dodd, Mead, 1903), 192.

28. Thwaites, *New Voyages*, 2:413.

29. Blackburn, *Harvest*, 30–31.

30. Arnold, *Colonial Arkansas*, 88.

31. George Sabo, "Inconsistent Kin: French-Quapaw Relations at Arkansas Post," in *Arkansas Before the Americans* (Arkansas Archeological Survey Research Series No. 40), ed. Hester Davis (Fayetteville: Arkansas Archeological Survey, 1991), 108.

32. "Henri de Tonti to Claude Dablon," November 1689, ASQ, Polygraphie 13, no. 33.

33. Gilbert J. Garraghan, "New Light in Old Cahokia," *Illinois Catholic Historical Review* 11, no. 2 (October, 1928): 116.

34. "Jacques Gravier to Mgr de Laval," September 17, 1697, ASQ, Lettres N, no. 131, pp. 2–3; Thwaites, *JRAD*, vol. 65 (Cleveland, Ohio: Burrows Brothers, 1899), 53–57.

35. "Gravier," ASQ, Lettres N, no. 131, pp. 2–3; Thwaites, *JRAD*, vol. 65, 53–57.

36. "Glandelet," October 11, 1697, ASQ, Seminaire 6, no. 73u, p. 2.

37. "Mgr de Saint-Vallier au Cardinal de Noailles, April 26, 1707, Mémoire de Ce Qui C'est Passé Entre l'Évêque de Québec et Messieurs des Missions-Étrangères de Paris depuis le Dernier Voyage que J'ai Fais dans mon Diocèse," AAQ, II, 176; "Tremblay," ASQ, Lettres O, no. 21, pp. 2–3; "Tremblay," ASQ, Lettres O, no. 22, p. 2; "Tremblay," ASQ, Lettres O, no. 23, p. 3; "Tiberge," ASQ, Lettres M, no. 25, p. 1.

38. "Tremblay," ASQ, Lettres M, no. 23, p. 58.

39. "Liste," ASQ, Chapitre, no. 164; "Mémoire," ASQ, Chapitre, no. 165; Baillargeon, *Séminaire*, 165.

40. Thwaites, *JRAD*, vol. 51 (Cleveland, Ohio: Burrows Brothers, 1899), 48–49; Thwaites, *JRAD*, vol. 47 (Cleveland, Ohio: Burrows Brothers, 1899), 114–115; "Lamberville," ASQ, Missions, no. 88, p. 3.

41. "Lettres Patentes," ASQ, Polygraphie 9, no. 2.

42. "Mémoire," ASQ, Polygraphie 9, no. 26, p. 1.

43. "Lamberville," ASQ, Missions, no. 88, p. 3.

44. "Mémoire sur la Jurisdiction pour les Missions du Mississippi," ASQ, Missions, no. 79, p. 1; "Mgr de Laval to Henri-Jean Tremblay," 1699, ASQ, Lettres N, no. 129, p. 1.

45. "Exposé des Jésuites du Canada sur leur Différend avec Mgr de Laval et son Séminaire au Sujet de la Mission des Tamarois," 1699, ASQ, Polygraphie 9, no. 25, p. 1; "Laval," ASQ, Lettres N, no. 129, p. 1; Launay, *Histoire Générale*, 1:446–447; "Lettres patentes," ASQ, Polygraphie 9, no. 4; "Érection," ASQ, Polygraphie 9, no. 22; "Lettres Patentes de Mgr de Saint-Vallier en Faveur du Séminaire de Québec pour les Missions de l'Acadie," May 4, 1698, ASQ, Polygraphie 9, no. 20.

46. "Nomination of Francois de Montigny as Superior of the Mississippi Missions," May 12, 1698, ASQ, Missions, no. 61.

47. "Mémoire des Effets à Envoyer aux Tamarois et Commentaire de l'Abbé Amédée Gosselin," ASQ, Missions, no. 107; RAQ, 1965, vol. 43 (Québec: Roch Lefebvre, Imprimeur de Sa Majesté la Reine, 1966), 28–32; "Ce que le Séminaire doit faire avec les Engagés," ASQ, Séminaire 5, no. 19; "Regles Communes pour les Domestiques et Engagés du Séminaire," June 7, 1686, ASQ, Séminaire 95, no. 31; Moogk, *Nouvelle France*, 29–30, 131–134.

48. Baillargeon and Aubin, *Les Missions*, 33; "Marché entre M. de Montigny et Claude Rivard Loranger et Jacques Rouillard," May 30, 1698, AJM, AA, no. 4115.

49. Registres du Fonds Drouin, *Le Site de Généalogie sur l'Amérique Française*, https://www
.genealogiequebec.com/en/ (accessed March 3, 2017); Baillargeon and Aubin, *Les Missions*, 33;
"Engagement de Fezeret à Mgr de Montigny," July 22, 1698, AJM, AA, no. 4181; Peter J. Gagné,
King's Daughters and Founding Mothers: The Filles du Roi, 1663–1673 (Pawtucket, R.I.: Quintin,
2001), 124–125; René Jetté, *Dictionnaire Généalogique des Familles du Québec des Origines à 1730*
(Montréal: Les Presses de l'Université de Montréal, 1983), 419.

50. "Engagement de Charbonneau à M. de Montigny," July 22, 1698, AJM, AA, no. 4177;
"Engagement d'André Heneaux à M. de Montigny," May 30, 1698, AJM, AA, no. 4118; "Obliga-
tion de Joseph Charbonneau à Pierre You de la Découverte," July 23, 1698, CHA; Cyprien Tan-
guay, *Dictionnaire Généalogique des Familles Canadiennes depuis la Fondation de la Colonie Jusqu'à
Nos Jours*, vol. 1 (Quebec: E. Senécal, 1871), 312; Pierre Margry, *Découvertes et Etablissements des
Français dans l'Ouest et le Sud de l'Amérique Septentrionale (1614–1754), Mémoires et Documents
Originaux*, vol. 1, *1614–1684* (Paris: Imprimerie de Jouaust, 1875), 297, 594; Theodore Pease and
Raymond C. Werner, *The French Foundations, 1680–1693*, vol. 1 (Springfield, Ill.: Trustees of the
Illinois State Historical Library, 1934), 24–25; Pierre Margry, *Découvertes et Etablissements des
Français dans l'Ouest et le Sud de l'Amérique Septentrionale (1614–1754), Mémoires et Documents
Originaux*, vol. 3, *1669–1698* (Paris: Imprimerie de Jouaust, 1878), 555.

51. "Requête de Marie-Madeleine Raclot," May 14, 1704, "Registres des Procès-Verbaux d'Au-
diences, Fonds Juridiction Royale des Trois-Rivières," BANQ-TR.

52. Tanguay, *Dictionnaire*, 1:475; Antoine Roy, *Inventaire des Greffes des Notaires du Régime
Française*, vol. 5 (Québec: Archives de la Province de Québec, 1944), 294.

53. APNDQ, Registre des Baptêmes; Nöel Baillargeon, "Un testament et une donation
à cause de mort au XVIIe siècle," *La Revue de l'Université Laval*, *XVIII* (March 1964): 655–
656; "Marc Bergier, Missionnaire aux Tamarois," June 14, 1700, ASQ, Lettres R, no. 44, p. 2;
"Mémoire," ASQ, Missions, no. 107; Baillargeon and Aubin, *Les Missions*, 46.

54. Grand Livre, 1688–1700, ASQ, Manuscrit C-4, p. 672; Jeffrey P. Brain, *Tunica Archaeology* (Cambridge, Mass.: Peabody Museum of Archaeology and Ethnology, Harvard University,
1988), 17; "Henri-Jean Tremblay to Mgr de Laval," June 19, 1705, ASQ, Lettres N, no. 123, p. 10;
"Henri-Jean Tremblay to Charles Glandelet," May 28, 1701, ASQ, Lettres O, no. 34, p. 10.

55. "Laval," ASQ, Lettres N, no. 129, p. 5; "François de Montigny to Saint-Vallier," August
25, 1699 ASQ, Missions, no. 41, p. 12; Baillargeon, "Testament," 650; Baillargeon and Aubin, *Les
Missions*, 34; Registre des Vêtures, Profession, Sépultres, etc. (1701–1748), des Frères Hospitaliers
de Saint-Joseph-de-la-Croix, ASG, Documents 1–3.

56. E.-Z. Massicotte, "Les Frères Charon ou Frères Hospitaliers de Saint-Joseph-de-la-Crois,"
Bulletin de Recherches Historiques 22 (December 1916): 365; Baillargeon, "Testament," 650.

57. "Testament de Sieur Alexandre Turpin, fils," July 22, 1698, AJM, AA, no. 4182.

58. "Passeport par M. de Frontenac pour les Missionnaires du Mississippi," July 17, 1698,
ASQ, Missions, no. 60; Launay, *Histoire Générale*, 1:375; "Mémoire," ASQ, Missions, no. 82, pp.
1–2, 5–7; "Louis XIV to Frontenac," April 15, 1676, in *RAPQ*, 1926–1927 (Québec: L.-Amable
Proulx, Imprimeur de Sa Majesté le Roi, 1927), 88; "Le Roi au Gouverneur Frontenac et à l'in-
tendant Champigny," April 27, 1697, *RAPQ*, 1928–1929, 332, 357.

59. James Joseph O'Brien, *The Louisiana and Mississippi Martyrs* (New York: Paulist Press,
1928), 5.

60. Leavelle, *Catholic Calumet*, 36; Thwaites, *JRAD*, vol. 46, 77–81.

61. Launay, *Histoire Générale*, 1:436. Monita ad Missionnarios, Paris, SMEP, vol. 1044 and 1045; François Bosquet, "L'esprit de famille des missions étrangères de Paris: Les Monita ad Missionarios de 1665," in *La Société des Missions Étrangères de Paris: 350 ans à la rencontre de l'Asie: 1658–2008: colloque à l'Institut Catholique de Paris (4 et 5 avril 2008)*, ed. Catherine Marin (Paris: Karthala, 2011), 173–182.

62. Sy, *La Société*, 192; SMEP, vol. 101, p. 372; Pitaud, "Influence," 50; Launay, *Histoire Générale*, 1:431; Baillargeon, *Laval*, 105; Provost, *Le Séminaire*, 2; Têtu, *Biographies*, 34.

63. "Quelques avis pour servir de règles aux missionnaires du Mississippi, puis envoyés à ceux de l'Acadie," ASQ, Polygraphie 9, no. 28, pp. 1–5; "Louis Tiberge and Jacques de Brisacier to Leaders of the Séminaire de Québec," June 8, 1700, ASQ, Lettres M, no. 27, 1–3.

64. "Quelques avis," July 1699, ASQ, Polygraphie 9, no. 28, pp. 3–4.

65. Ibid., pp. 3–5.

66. Ibid., pp. 3–4.

67. Ibid., p. 4.

68. Linda C. Jones, "Mississippi Missionaries' Workplace Spirituality and Organizational Commitment (1698–1725): A Case Study," *Journal of Management, Spirituality, and Religion* 13, no. 4 (2017): 324–344.

69. Rossignol, "Society," 25, 45.

70. "Mgr de Laval et Mgr de Saint-Vallier s'adressent à Louis Pontchartrain pour obtenir une rente annuelle pour la mission des Tamarois," September 25, 1698, ASQ, Polygraphie 9, no. 8, pp. 1–2; "Mgr de Laval et Mgr de Saint-Vallier s'adressent à Madame de Maintenon pour obtenir une rente annuelle pour la mission des Tamarois," September 25, 1698, ASQ, Polygraphie 9, no. 6; "Mgr de Laval et Mgr de Saint-Vallier s'adressent à M. de Maurepas pour obtenir une rente annuelle for the Tamarois Mission," September 25, 1698, ASQ, Polygraphie 9, no. 7; "Mgr de Laval et Mgr de Saint-Vallier s'adressent à Mgr de Paris pour obtenir une rente annuelle pour la mission des Tamarois," September 25, 1698, ASQ, Polygraphie 9, no. 9; "Mémoire," ASQ, Missions, no. 82, pp. 2–3.

71. "Tremblay," ASQ, Lettres N, no. 102, p. 4.

72. "Tremblay," ASQ, Lettres O, no. 21, p. 7; "Tremblay," ASQ, Lettres O, no. 22, p. 5.

73. "Tremblay," ASQ, Lettres O, no. 5, p. 11.

74. "Tremblay," ASQ, Lettres N, no. 106, p. 4.

75. "Louis Ango de Maizerets to Mgr de Laval," April 9, 1699, ASQ, Lettres N, no. 125, pp. 1–2.

76. "Mémoire," ASQ, Polygraphie 9, no. 26, pp. 1–2; "Louis Tiberge and Jacques-Charles de Brisacier to Mgr de Laval," June 10, 1699, ASQ, Lettres N, no. 127, pp. 1–2.

77. "Henri-Jean Tremblay to Louis Ango de Maizerets," June 1, 1699, ASQ, Lettres O, no. 56, p. 6; "Tremblay," ASQ, Lettres O, no. 55, p. 14.

78. "Henri-Jean Tremblay to Mrg de Laval," 1702, ASQ, Lettres N, no. 119a, p. 16.

79. "Henri-Jean Tremblay to Charles de Glandelet," June 5, 1712, ASQ, Lettres O, no. 53, pp. 18–19.

80. "Le Ministre to Mgr de Laval," May 27, 1999, ASQ, Lettres O, no. 63, p. 1.

81. "Mémoire," ASQ, Polygraphie 9, no. 26, p. 1.

82. Baillargeon, *Séminaire*, 386n30; "Compte des Missions," ASQ, Missions, no. 101, p. 1.

83. "Jean-François Buisson de Saint Cosme to Mgr de Laval," August 30, 1698, ASQ, Lettres R, no. 27, p. 1.

4. First Encounters and Final Choices

1. "Saint-Cosme," ASQ, Lettres R, no. 27, p. 1; "Mémoire," ASQ, Missions, no. 107; White, *Middle Ground,* xxiv; "Lettre de M. de Montigny, Missionaire et Grand Vicaire de M. l'Evêque de Québec, de la Louisiane," May 3, 1699, AAQ, W1, Eglise du Canada, vol. 4 (Document de Paris), p. 26; "Jean-François Buisson de Saint-Cosme to Mgr de Laval," September 13, 1698, ASQ, Lettres R, no. 28; "Jean-François Buisson de Saint-Cosme to Mgr de Laval," September 13, 1698, ASQ, Lettres R, no. 28a; "Saint-Cosme," ASQ, Lettres R, no. 26; "Lettre de Jean-François Buisson de Saint-Cosme," ANF, Série K 1374, no. 81; "Lettre de Thaumur de la Source à Ma Révérende Mère," April 19, 1699, ANF, Série K 1374, no. 85; "de Montigny," ANF, Série K 1374, no. 84; "Henri-Jean Tremblay to Mgr. de Laval," June 12, 1700, ASQ, Lettres N, no. 113, p. 3; "Henri-Jean Tremblay to Mgr de Saint-Vallier," June 12, 1700, ASQ, Lettres P, no. 6, p. 1.

2. "Marché entre Monsieur de Montigny et Claude Rivard et Jacques Roulliard," May 30, 1698, AJM, Greffe d'Antoine Adhémar, no. 4115; "Grand Livre," 1688–1700, ASQ, Manuscrit C-4, p. 244; "Saint-Cosme," ASQ, Lettres R, no. 27, p. 1.

3. "Saint-Cosme," ASQ, Lettres R, no. 27, pp. 2–3; Eric W. Morse, "Voyageurs Highway," *Canadian Geographical Journal* (May–July–August 1961): 7; RAQ, vol. 43, 34; Eric W. Morse, *Canoe Routes of the Voyageurs: The Geography and Logistics of the Canadian Fur Trade* (St. Paul: Minnesota Historical Society and The Quetico Foundation of Ontario, 1962).

4. Michilimackinac is a French corruption of an Anishinabe (Odawa) term that was used at the end of the seventeenth century with reference to the entire Straits area, including Mackinac Island.

5. "Saint-Cosme," ASQ, Lettres R, no. 28a, p. 1; "Jacques Gravier to François de Laval," September 20, 1698, ASQ, Lettres N, no. 132, p. 1; Thwaites, *JRAD,* vol. 65, 59.

6. "Tremblay," ASQ, Lettres O, no. 28, p. 21; "Gravier," ASQ, Lettres N, no. 132, pp. 1–2.

7. Baillargeon and Aubin, *Les Missions,* 43; "Henri de Tonti to Mgr de Saint-Vallier," September 13, 1698, ASQ, Missions, no. 50, pp. 1–2.

8. Baillargeon and Aubin, *Les Missions,* 46; Jean Delanglez, "Tonti Letters," *Mid-America* 21 (July 1939): 217–218n12; "Saint-Cosme," ASQ, Lettres R. no. 28a, p. 2; "Gravier," ASQ, Lettres N, no. 132, p. 2.

9. "Saint-Cosme," ASQ, Lettres R, no. 27, p. 3; "Saint-Cosme," ASQ, Lettres R, no. 26, p. 6; Baillargeon and Aubin, *Les Missions,* 40; "Saint-Cosme," ASQ, Lettres R, no. 28a, p. 2.

10. Moogk, *Nouvelle France,* 129–130; Thwaites, *JRAD,* vol. 65, 194–199.

11. White, *Middle Ground,* 64–65; Kathleen Duval, "Indian Intermarriage and Métissage in Colonial Louisiana," *William and Mary Quarterly* 65 (April 2008): 273.

12. "Saint-Cosme," ASQ, Lettres R, no. 28a, p. 3.

13. Ibid.; "Saint-Cosme," ASQ, Lettres R, no. 28, p. 1; Greffe de François Genaple, July 24, 1699, AJQ; Baillargeon and Aubin, *Les Missions,* 46.

14. "Saint-Cosme," ASQ, Lettres R, no. 26, p. 1; "Mémoire," ASQ, Missions, no. 107; "Saint-Cosme," ASQ, Lettres R, no. 28, p. 1.

15. "Saint-Cosme," ASQ, Lettres R, no. 26, p. 2.

16. Ibid., pp. 2–4.

17. Ibid., p. 4; "de Montigny to Monsieur . . . ," May 6, 1699, ANF, Série no. 3JJ, vol. 387, C3–52.

18. "Saint-Cosme," ASQ, Lettres R, no. 26, p. 4; "de Montigny," ANF, Série no. 3JJ, vol. 387, C3–52.

19. "Saint-Cosme," ASQ, Lettres R, no. 26, p. 5.

20. Ibid., p. 6.

21. Ibid., pp. 6–7.

22. Pierre Margry, *Découvertes et Etablissements des Français dans l'Ouest et le Sud de l'Amérique Septentrionale (1614–1754), Lettres de Cavelier de La Salle et correspondance relative à ses entreprises (1678–1685),* vol. 2 (Paris: Imprimerie de Jouaust, 1877), 175; Mary Borgias Palm, "Kaskaskia, Indian Mission Village, 1703–1718," *Mid America* 16, no. 1 (1933): 14; "Saint-Cosme," ASQ, Lettres R, no. 26, p. 7.

23. Thwaites, *JRAD,* vol. 65, 85.

24. "De Montigny," ANF, Série no. 3JJ, vol. 387, C3–52; "Saint-Cosme," ASQ, Lettres R, no. 26, pp. 7–8.

25. Sylvia Van Kirk, *Many Tender Ties: Women in Fur-Trade Society, 1670–1870* (Winnipeg, Canada: Watson and Dwyer, 2011), 4; Theda Perdue, "A Sprightly Lover Is the Most Prevailing Missionary, Intermarriage between Europeans and Indians in the Eighteenth-Century South," in *Light on the Path: The Anthropology and History of the Southeastern Indians,* ed. Thomas J. Pluckhahn and Robbie Ethridge (Tuscaloosa: Univ. of Alabama Press, 2006), 168.

26. Perdue, "Sprightly Lover," 169–171; White, *Middle Ground,* 57.

27. Thwaites, *JRAD,* vol. 64, 195, 205–213.

28. Ibid., 211; "Jean-François Buisson de Saint-Cosme to Mgr de Laval," March 1700, ASQ, Lettres R, no. 29, p. 12; "Marc Bergier to unknown," June 15, 1702, ASQ, Lettres R, no. 55, p. 4.

29. White, *Middle Ground,* 62.

30. Susan Sleeper-Smith, *Indian Women and French Men: Rethinking Cultural Encounter in the Western Great Lakes* (Amherst: Univ. of Massachusetts Press, 2001), 21–26; White, *Middle Ground,* 68.

31. Sleeper-Smith, *Indian Women,* 21–26; White, *Middle Ground,* 52, 72–73.

32. Thwaites, *JRAD,* vol. 51, 47–51.

33. Christopher Bilodeau, "'They Honor Our Lord among Themselves in Their Own Way': Colonial Christianity and the Illinois Indians," *American Indian Quarterly* vol. 25, no. 3 (summer 2001): 356–357; A. Irving Hallowell, "Ojibwa Ontology, Behavior, and World View," in *Teachings from the American Earth,* ed. Barbara Tedlock and Dennis Tedlock (New York: Liveright, 1975), 141–178.

34. Leavelle, *Catholic Calumet,* 23; Thwaites, *JRAD,* vol. 55 (Cleveland, Ohio: Burrows Brothers, 1899), 215; Bilodeau, "They Honor," 353, 356–358; Jordan Paper, *Offering Smoke: The Sacred Pipe and Native American Religion* (Moscow: Univ. of Idaho Press, 1988), 36.

35. Thwaites, *JRAD,* vol. 58 (Cleveland, Ohio: Burrows Brothers, 1899), 265; H. W. Beckwith, ed., *Collections of the Illinois State Historical Library,* vol. 1 (Springfield, Ill.: H. W. Rokker, 1903–1948), 15–16; Bilodeau, "They Honor," 366; Thwaites, *JRAD,* vol. 64, 219–221.

36. Leavelle, *Catholic Calumet,* 189–190.

37. Bilodeau, "They Honor," 369; Sleeper-Smith, *Indian Women,* 25–26.

38. RAQ, vol. 43, 32n31; "Mémoire," ASQ, Missions, no. 107; Maria Borgias Palm, A.M., "The Jesuit Missions of the Illinois Country 1673–1763" (Ph.D. diss., Saint Louis University, 1931), 38; "Saint-Cosme," ASQ, Lettres R, no. 26, pp. 7–8; RAQ, vol. 43, 30; "Mémoire," ASQ, Missions, no. 107, pp. 1, 3; "Repertoire des Engagements pour l'Ouest Conservés dans les Archives Judiciaires de Montréal (1670–1778)," *RAPQ,* 1929–1930 (Québec: Rédempti Paridis, Imprimeur de Sa Majesté le Roi, 1930), 195; "Pièces Justicatives," SMEP, vol. 345, Pièce G, Cahier B, Ferland, p. 912; "Justification de Michel Bisaillon, 1715," ANOM, AC, C11A, vol. 35, folios 99–100v.

39. "Saint-Cosme," ASQ, Lettres R, no. 26, p. 8.

40. Kathleen Duval, *The Native Ground* (Philadelphia: Univ. of Pennsylvania Press, 2006), 3, 92.

41. "Saint-Cosme," ASQ, Lettres R, no. 26, pp. 8–9.

42. Leavelle, *Catholic Calumet,* 94.

43. "Saint-Cosme," ASQ, Lettres R, no. 26, pp. 10–11.

44. "de la Source," ANF, Série K 1374, no. 85, p. 1; "Saint-Cosme," ASQ, Lettres R, no. 26, p. 11.

45. "Mémoire de l'Abbé Joseph de la Colombière sur l'établissement des Tamarois," 1700, ASQ, Polygraphie 9, no. 17, pp. 1–2; "Saint-Cosme," ASQ, Lettres R, no. 26, p. 12.

46. "de Montigny," ANF, Série no. 3JJ, vol. 387, C3–52; "de la Source," ANF, Série K 1374, no. 85, p. 4; "Saint-Cosme," ASQ, Lettres R, no. 26, pp. 12–13.

47. "de Montigny," ANF, Série no. 3JJ, vol. 387, C3–52; "de la Source," ANF, Série K 1374, no. 85, p. 4; "Saint-Cosme," ASQ, Lettres R, no. 26, pp. 12–13.

48. "Saint-Cosme," ASQ, Lettres R, no. 26, p. 13.

49. White, *Middle Ground,* 52–53.

50. "Saint-Cosme," ASQ, Lettres R, no. 26, pp. 13–14.

51. Ibid., pp. 14–15.

52. Thwaites, *JRAD,* vol. 65, 117; "Saint-Cosme," ASQ, Lettres R, no. 26, p. 15.

53. "Saint-Cosme," ASQ, Lettres R, no. 26, pp. 15–16.

54. Duval, *Native Ground,* 89.

55. Morris S. Arnold, *The Rumble of a Distant Drum: The Quapaw and the Old World Newcomers, 1673–1804* (Fayetteville: Univ. of Arkansas Press, 2000), 16–18.

56. George Sabo III, *Paths of Our Children: Historic Indians of Arkansas* (Fayetteville: Arkansas Archeological Survey, Popular Series No. 3. 2009), 32–34.

57. Sabo, *Paths,* 32–40; Jean Delanglez, ed., "Journal of Father Vitry of the Society of Jesus, Army Chaplain during the War Against the Chickasaw," *Mid-America* 28 (1941): 35.

58. "Saint-Cosme," ASQ, Lettres R, no. 26, p. 17.

59. "de la Source," ANF, Série K 1374, no. 85, p. 1; John Gilmary Shea, *Early Voyages Up and Down the Mississippi* (Albany, N.Y.: Joel Munsell, 1861), 79; Arnold, *Rumble,* 140.

60. "Saint-Cosme," ASQ, Lettres R, no. 26, p. 16; "De Montigny," ANF, Série no. 3JJ, vol. 387, C3–52; Baillargeon, *Séminaire,* 381–382.

61. Marvin Jeter, John Mintz, and Kathleen Cande, *Goldsmith Oliver 2 (3PU306): A Protohistoric Archeological Site Near Little Rock, Arkansas* (Fayetteville: Arkansas Archeological Series

Project, 1990), nos. 651 and 656, p. 56; J. Phillips, J. Ford, and J. B. Griffin, *Archeological Survey in the Lower Mississippi Alluvial Valley, 1940–1947,* 25 (Cambridge, Mass.: Papers of the Peabody Museum of Archaeology and Ethnology, 1951), 410.

62. "Saint-Cosme," ASQ, Lettres R, no. 26, pp. 15–17.

63. Jacques Marquette, "The Mississipi Voyage of Jolliet and Marquette, 1673," American Journeys Collection, AJ-051, WHSDLA, p. 244.

64. Duane Brayboy, "Two Spirits, One Heart, Five Genders," IndianCountryToday.com, September 7, 2017, https://indiancountrytoday.com/archive/two-spirits-one-heart-five-genders -9UH_xnbfVEWQHWkjNnorQQ.

65. Jean Bernard Bossu and Johann Reinhold Forster, *Travels through that part of North America formerly called Louisiana,* vol. 1 (London: T. Davies, 1771), 139.

66. Nancy Oestreich Lurie, "Winnebago Berdache," *American Anthropologist,* New Series 55, no. 5, part 1 (December 1953): 708–712.

67. "Saint-Cosme," ASQ, Lettres R, no. 26, pp. 16–17.

68. "de la Source," ANF, Série K 1374, no. 85, p. 1; Shea, *Early Voyages,* 79.

69. "Saint-Cosme," ASQ, Lettres R, no. 26, pp. 1, 11.

70. "de Montigny on the Missions of the Mississippi," January 27, 1700, ASQ, Missions, no. 41a, p. 6; "Jacques de Brisacier and Louis Tiberge to Mgr. de Laval," June 9, 1700, ASQ, Lettres N, no. 112, p. 4; RAQ, vol. 43, 55n114; "Tremblay," ASQ, Lettres O, no. 55, pp. 16, 43; "Tremblay," ASQ, Lettres O, no. 56, p. 7.

71. "de Montigny," ANF, Série no. 3JJ, vol. 387, C3–52; "Saint-Cosme," ASQ, Lettres R, no. 26, p. 18; "de Montigny," ANF, Série K 1374, no. 84, p. 1; Shea, *Early Voyages,* 76.

72. "Saint-Cosme," ASQ, Lettres R, no. 26, p. 18; "Mémoire," ASQ, Missions, no. 107; Tanguay, *Dictionnaire,* 1:94; "Engagement du Boeuf à Mr de Tonti, le 10 mai 1690," AJM, Greffe d'Antoine Adhémar; Baillargeon and Aubin, *Les Missions,* 34; "Pièces Justicatives," SMEP, vol. 345, Pièce E, p. 911; "de la Source," ANF, Série K 1374, no. 85, p. 1; Shea, *Early Voyages,* 80.

73. "de la Source," ANF, Série K 1374, no. 85, p. 1; Shea, *Early Voyages,* 80; Jeffrey P. Brain, *The Tunica-Biloxi* (New York: Chelsea House, 2014), 42; Sabo, *Paths,* 56–58.

74. "de Montigny," AAQ, W1, Eglise du Canada, vol. IV, 29; "de Montigny," ANF, Série K 1374, no. 84, pp. 2–3; "de la Source," ANF, Série K 1374, no. 85, p. 2.

75. "Saint-Cosme," ASQ, Lettres R, no. 26, pp. 7–9.

76. Leavelle, *Catholic Calumet,* 141.

77. Shea, *Early Voyages,* 78.

78. "Pièces Justicatives," SMEP, vol. 345, Pièce E, p. 911; Shea, *Early Voyages,* 81; "de Montigny," ANF, Série K 1374, no. 84, p. 1; "de la Source," ANF, Série K 1374, no. 85, pp. 2–3; Shea, *Early Voyages,* 82; "de Montigny," ASQ, Missions, no. 41, p 15.

79. "de Montigny," ASQ, Missions, no. 41, p 15.

80. White, *Middle Ground,* 102.

81. Moogk, *Nouvelle France,* 238.

82. Leavelle, *Catholic Calumet,* 15.

83. "de la Source," ANF, Série K 1374, no. 85, p. 3; Shea, *Early Voyages,* 82–83.

84. "de la Source," ANF, Série K 1374, no. 85, p. 3; "De Montigny," ASQ, Missions, no. 41, pp. 15–16.

85. Rossignol, "The Society," 24; Leavelle, *Catholic Calumet,* 70–71, 92; R. M. Morrissey, "'I Speak It Well': Language, Cultural Understanding, and the End of a Missionary Middle Ground in Illinois Country, 1673–1712," *Early American Studies* 9, no. 3 (fall 2011); James F. Barnett, *The Natchez Indians: A History to 1735* (Jackson: Univ. Press of Mississippi, 2007), 21; Francis Parkman, *La Salle and the Discovery of the Great West: France and England in North America* (Williamston, Mass.: Corner House Publishers, 1980), 122–123.

86. "de Montigny," ASQ, Missions, no. 41, p. 6.

87. Pierre le Moyne d'Iberville, *Iberville's Gulf Journals,* ed. and trans. Richebourg Gaillard McWilliams (Tuscaloosa: Univ. of Alabama Press, 1981), 125; "de Montigny," ASQ, Missions, no. 41, p. 13; Paraphrased from the website *Indians of Arkansas,* created by George Sabo: http://archeology .uark.edu/indiansofarkansas/index.html?pageName=The%20Natchez%20Indians (accessed June 24, 2018); "de Montigny," ASQ, Missions, no. 41, pp. 15–16; "de la Source," ANF, Série K 1374, no. 85, pp. 3–4.

88. "de Montigny," AAQ, W1, Eglise du Canada, vol. IV, p. 28; "de la Source," ANF, Série K 1374, no. 85, pp. 3–4; Shea, *Early Voyages,* 78, 83; "de Montigny," ANF, Série K 1374, no. 84, pp. 2–3.

89. "de la Source," ANF, Série K 1374, no. 85, pp. 3–4; "de Montigny," ANF, Série K 1374, no. 84, p. 1; "Mémoire," ASQ, Missions, no. 107; RAQ, vol. 43, 31n29.

90. "Pièces Justicatives," SMEP, vol. 345, Pièce E, p. 911; "de la Source," ANF, Série K 1374, no. 85, p. 4; Baillargeon, "Vocation," 47; Jean Delanglez, *French Jesuits in Lower Louisiana (1700–1763)* (Washington, D. C.: Catholic Univ. of America, 1935), 4–5; "Henri-Jean Tremblay to Mgr de Laval," May 10, 1701, ASQ, Lettres N, no. 114, pp. 11–12; "de Montigny," ASQ, Missions, no. 41, p. 1.

91. d'Iberville, *Gulf Journals,* 109, 125; Pierre Margry, *Découvertes et Établissements des Français dans l'Ouest et dans le Sud de l'Amérique Septentrionale (1614–1754): Mémoires et Documents Originaux,* vol. 4 (Paris: Imprimeur D. Jouaust, 1876–1886), 73; Baillargeon and Aubin, *Les Missions,* 90, FN 3; "de Montigny," AAQ, W1, Eglise du Canada, vol. 4, p. 29; "Pièces Justicatives," SMEP, vol. 345, Pièce E, p. 911; "de Montigny," ASQ, Missions, no. 41, p. 1; "de la Source," ANF, Série K 1374, no. 85, p. 4.

92. "de Montigny," ASQ, Missions, no. 41, p. 2; "Saint-Cosme," ASQ, Lettres R, no. 29, p. 1.

93. "De Montigny," ASQ, Missions, no. 41, p. 4.

94. Shea, *Early Voyages,* 126.

95. Margry, *Découvertes,* 4:430; *RAQ 1965,* 43, 59n131; Duval, *Native Ground,* 77.

96. "de Montigny," ASQ, Missions, no. 41, pp. 4–5.

97. Patricia Galloway, "Talking with Indians: Interpreters and Diplomacy in French Louisiana," in *Race and Family in the Colonial South,* ed. Winthrop D. Jordan and Sheila L. Skemp (Jackson: Univ. Press of Mississippi, 1987), 112.

98. "de Montigny," ASQ, Missions, no. 41, p. 5.

99. "de Tonti to Iberville," March 14, 1702, ANF, Série no. 2JJ, vol. 56, p. 20.

100. "de Montigny," ASQ, Missions, no. 41, pp. 5–7.

101. Galloway, "Talking," 114; "de Montigny," ASQ, Missions, no. 41, p. 7; Baillargeon and Aubin, *Les Missions,* 91n19.

102. "Au Nouvel Établissement de Biloxi," August 1, 1719, NF Z 43-120-14, BNF, p. 53; "de Montigny," ASQ, Missions, no. 41, pp. 8–9; "Tremblay," ASQ, Lettres N, no. 113, p. 3.

103. "de Montigny," ASQ, Missions, no. 41, pp. 9–10.

104. Margry, *Découvertes*, 4:452; "de Montigny," ASQ, Missions, no. 41, pp. 9–11.

105. Margry, *Découvertes*, 4:452; "de Montigny," ASQ, Missions, no. 41, pp. 9–12.

106. "de Montigny," ASQ, Missions, no. 41, pp. 12–13.

107. Margry, *Découvertes*, 4:452; "de Montigny," ASQ, Missions, no. 41, p. 9–13.

108. "de Montigny," ASQ, Missions, no. 41, p. 14.

109. Bilodeau, "They Honor," 353.

110. Leavelle, *Catholic Calumet*, 70–71, 92; Morrissey, "Speak It"; Barnett, *Natchez*, 21; Parkman, *La Salle*, 122–123; "de la Source," ANF, Série K 1374, no. 85, p. 3.

5. Les Vignes Contestés

1. Delanglez, *French Jesuits*, 38.

2. Marin, *Société*, 21; "Tremblay," ASQ, Lettres N, no. 106, pp. 6–7.

3. "La Chine," https://missionsetrangeres.com/eglises-asie/2001-09-16-la-catechese-du-pretre-chinois-andre-li-1692-1775/ (accessed March 16, 2020).

4. "Tremblay," ASQ, Lettres M, no. 23, pp. 25–26; "Tremblay," ASQ, Lettres O, no. 31, pp. 4–5; "Tiberge," ASQ, Lettres M, no. 25, p. 8.

5. "Tremblay," ASQ, Lettres N, no. 114, pp. 7–8; "Tremblay," ASQ, Lettres O, no. 31, pp. 7–9.

6. "Saint-Cosme," ASQ, Lettres R, no. 26, p. 11; "Saint-Cosme," ASQ, Lettres R, no. 29, p. 6.

7. "Saint-Cosme," ASQ, Lettres R, no. 26, pp. 12–13; Shea, *Early Voyages*, 84; "de la Source," ANF, Série K 1374, no. 85, p. 4; "Saint-Cosme," ASQ, Lettres R, no. 29, p. 6.

8. "Saint-Cosme," ASQ, Lettres R, no. 29, p. 7.

9. "de Tonti to Monseigneur," July 14, 1699, ASQ, Missions, no. 49, pp. 5–6.

10. "Jean-François Buisson de Saint-Cosme to Bishop Saint-Vallier," March 7, 1700, ASQ, Lettres R, no. 30, p. 3.

11. "Colombière," ASQ, Polygraphie 9, no. 17, p. 4.

12. "Jacques Gravier to Mgr de Québec," April 1, 1700, ASQ, Missions, no. 80, p. 2.

13. "Gravier," ASQ, Missions, no. 80, p. 1.

14. "Marc Bergier to Mgr Saint-Vallier," February 29, 1700, ASQ, Lettres R, no. 42, p. 4.

15. "Marc Bergier to unknown," June 10, 1702, ASQ, Lettres R, no. 54, p. 4.

16. "Saint-Cosme," ASQ, Lettres R, no. 29, pp. 6–7; Duval, *Native Ground*, 9.

17. White, *Middle Ground*, 16–17.

18. Margaret Kimball Brown, *Cultural Transformation among the Illinois. An Application of a Systems Model*, Anthropological Series, vol. 1, no. 3 (East Lansing: Publications of the Museum, Michigan State University, 1979), 234–235.

19. "Bergier," ASQ, Lettres R, no. 42, p. 6; Brown, *Cultural Transformation*, 234–235.

20. Leavelle, *Catholic Calumet*, 34.

21. "Gravier," ASQ, Missions, no. 80, p. 6.

22. Isabelle Bouchard, "Conflit de Juridictions des Tamarois, Ambiguïté du Territoire de la Mission Illinoise," in *Sociétés, populations et territorialité: actes des 15e et 16e colloques étudiants du*

CIEQ, ed. Rachel Caux, François Antaya, and Dorothée Kaupp (Québec: Centre interuniversi-taire d'études québécoises, 2012), 17; "Gravier," ASQ, Missions, no. 80, pp. 4–6.

23. "Saint-Cosme," ASQ, Lettres R, no. 29, p. 5.

24. "de Tonti," ASQ, Missions, no. 49, p. 4; "Saint-Cosme," ASQ, Lettres R, no. 29, pp. 5–6; Baillargeon, *Séminaire*, 389.

25. "Saint-Cosme," ASQ, Lettres R, no. 29, p. 5; "de Tonti," ASQ, Missions, no. 49, p. 4; "Bergier," ASQ, Lettres R, no. 42, p. 7.

26. "de Brisacier," ASQ, Lettres N, no. 112, pp. 3–4.

27. "Tremblay," ASQ, Lettres O, no. 28, p. 27; "Lamberville," ASQ, Missions, no. 88, p. 3.

28. "Tremblay," ASQ, Lettres O, no. 28, p. 28.

29. "Lamberville," ASQ, Missions, no. 88, p. 3.

30. "Tremblay," ASQ, Lettres O, no. 28, pp. 27–28.

31. "Jacques-René de Brisay Marquis de Denonville to Mgr de Laval," April 28, 1700, ASQ, Lettres N, no. 110, pp. 3–4; "Henri-Jean Tremblay to Louis Ango de Maizerets," June 15, 1703, ASQ, Lettres O, no. 39, p. 15.

32. "Louis Ango de Maizerets to Jacques Gravier," June 28, 1700, ASQ, Missions, no. 42, p. 1.

33. "Tremblay," ASQ, Lettres O, no. 28, pp. 9–10; "Henri-Jean Tremblay to Louis Ango de Maizerets," April 27, 1700, ASQ, Lettres O, no. 26, pp. 12–13; "Marc Bergier to Mgr de Saint-Vallier," March 13, 1702, ASQ, Lettres R, no. 50, p. 3.

34. "Tremblay," ASQ, Lettres N, no. 113, pp. 5–6; "Saint-Cosme," ASQ, Lettres R, no. 30, p. 1.

35. "Henri-Jean Tremblay to Mgr de Laval," March 12, 1700, ASQ, Lettres N, no. 109, p. 9; "Saint-Cosme," ASQ, Lettres R, no. 29, p. 8.

36. "Jean-Francois Buisson de Saint-Cosme, at Pimitéoui, to Mgr de Saint Vallier," March 27, 1700, ASQ, Lettres R, no. 31, p. 2; "Saint-Cosme," ASQ, Lettre R, no. 29, p. 7; "Saint-Cosme," ASQ, Lettres R, no. 30, p. 3.

37. Thwaites, *JRAD*, vol. 66, 117; Thwaites, *JRAD*, vol. 65, 71.

38. "Mgr de Saint-Vallier to Jacques Gravier," July 1699, ASQ, Missions, no. 56, p. 3.

39. "Saint-Cosme," ASQ, Lettres R, no. 29, p. 4; "Bergier," ASQ, Lettres R, no. 42, p. 10; Thwaites, *JRAD*, vol. 66, 253; "Journal de Levasseur," 1700, ANF, Série no. 2JJ, vol. 56, 16; Garraghan, "New Light," 113.

40. "Saint-Cosme," ASQ, Lettres R, no. 29, p. 10; "Saint-Vallier and the Rights of the Jesuits," 1700, ASQ, Missions, no. 58, p. 2; "Marc Bergier to Mgr de Saint-Vallier," March 7, 1700, ASQ, Lettres R, no. 43, p. 2.

41. "Saint-Cosme," ASQ, Lettres R, no. 29, p. 10.

42. "Saint-Cosme," ASQ, Lettres R, no. 31, p. 1.

43. "Bergier," ASQ, Lettres R, no. 43, pp. 1–3; "Bergier," ASQ, Lettres R, no. 42, pp. 5–6; "Marc Bergier to Louis Ango de Maizerets," March 19, 1702, ASQ, Lettres R, no. 51; "Bergier," ASQ, Lettres R, no. 44, pp. 2–3.

44. White, *Middle Ground*, 52.

45. Thwaites, *JRAD*, vol. 65, 103.

46. "Saint-Cosme," ASQ, Lettres R, no. 29, p. 3; "Saint-Cosme," ASQ, Lettres R, no. 30, p. 1.

47. White, *Middle Ground*, 52.

48. Ibid., 25; Thwaites, *JRAD*, vol. 65, 119–121; "Marc Bergier to Louis Tiberge," April 15,

1701, ASQ, Lettres R, no. 45, p. 8; "Marc Bergier to unknown," April 15, 1701, ASQ, Lettres R, no. 46, p. 3.

49. "Jacques-René Brisay de Denonville to Louis Ango de Maizerets," May 2, 1700, ASQ, Lettres O, no. 27, p. 2; Victor Egon Hanzeli, *Missionary Linguistics in New France: A Study of Seventeenth- and Eighteenth-Century Descriptions of American Indian Languages* (The Hague: Mouton, 1979); François-Xavier de Charlevoix, *Journal d'un Voyage Fait par Ordre du Roi dans l'Amérique Septentrionale*, ed. Pierre Berthiaume (Montréal: Les Presses de l'Université de Montréal, 1994), 448–50; Leavelle, *Catholic Calumet*, 101, 109; "Gravier," ASQ, Missions, no. 80, p. 6.

50. "Lamberville," ASQ, Missions, no. 88, p. 4.

51. "Saint-Cosme," ASQ, Lettres R, no. 29, p. 2.

52. Ibid., pp. 2–3.

53. "Bergier," ASQ, Lettres R, no. 42, pp. 8–10.

54. "Saint-Cosme," ASQ, Lettres R, no. 31, pp. 1–2.

55. "Extraits de la Lettre de M. de Montigny, datée de la Menace, au sujet de la mission des Tamarois et réponses qu'on y fait," July 17, 1700, ASQ, Polygraphie 9, no. 24, pp. 6–7.

56. "Saint-Cosme," ASQ, Lettres R, no. 29, pp. 4, 10–11; "Bergier," ASQ, Lettres R, no. 44, p. 2; "Bergier," ASQ, Lettres R, no. 42, pp. 8, 11–12.

57. Bernard C. Perley, "Zombie Linguistics: Experts, Endangered Languages, and the Curse of Undead Voices," *Anthropological Forum* 22, no. 2 (July 2012): 134.

58. "Bergier," ASQ, Lettres R, no. 50, p. 3.

59. Leavelle, *Catholic Calumet*, 15.

60. "Saint-Cosme," ASQ, Lettres R, no. 29, p. 4.

61. "Saint-Cosme," ASQ, Lettres R, no. 30, p. 3.

62. "Bergier," ASQ, Lettres R, no. 50, p. 13.

63. "Bergier," ASQ, Lettres R, no. 54 p. 1.

64. "Bergier," ASQ, Lettres R, no. 50, p. 4.

65. Ibid., p. 13.

66. White, *Middle Ground*, 143.

67. Conversation with George Sabo, Fayetteville, Arkansas, July 9, 2018.

68. Duval, *Native Ground*, 73.

69. "Bergier," ASQ, Lettres R, no. 42, p. 12.

70. "Marc Bergier to Bishop Saint-Vallier," October 13, 1704, ASQ, Lettres R, no. 69, p. 2.

71. "Marc Bergier to Martin Bouvart," March 21, 1702, ASQ, Lettres R, no. 52, pp. 4–6.

72. "Lettre du Pere Jesuite Missionnaire des Kaskaskias aux Jesuites de Canada," 1706, JAM, Q-0001, no. 4020, p. 213; Thwaites, *JRAD*, vol. 66, 57.

73. "Bergier," ASQ, Lettres R, no. 52, p. 1.

74. "Bergier," ASQ, Lettres R, no. 52, p. 1.

75. "Marc Bergier to Jacques de Brisacier," October 26, 1704, ASQ, Lettres R, no. 71, pp. 2–3.

76. "Tremblay," ASQ, Lettres N, no. 109, p. 11; "Tremblay," ASQ, Lettres O, no. 28, pp. 12–13.

77. "Bergier," ASQ, Lettres R, no. 42, p. 5; "Bergier," ASQ, Lettres R, no. 50, p. 4.

78. "Bergier," ASQ, Lettres R, no. 44, pp. 3–4.

79. Christina Snyder, *Slavery in Indian Country, The Changing Face of Captivity in Early America* (Cambridge, Mass.: Harvard Univ. Press, 2010), 82.

80. James Adair, *The History of the American Indians* (London: E. and C. Dilly, 1775), 151.

81. Joel W. Martin and Mark A. Nicholas, *Native Americans, Christianity, and the Reshaping of the American Religious Landscape* (Chapel Hill: Univ. of North Carolina Press, 2010), Kindle location 3194.

82. Snyder, *Slavery,* 84.

83. Juha Hiltunen, "Spiritual and Religious Aspects of Torture and Scalping among the Indian Cultures in Eastern North America, from Ancient to Colonial Times," *Scripta Instituti Donneriani Aboensis* (2011): 121.

84. Sophie White, "Massacre, Mardi Gras, and Torture in Early New Orleans," *William and Mary Quarterly* 70, no. 3 (July 2013): 531; Snyder, *Slavery,* 96.

85. Thwaites, *JRAD,* vol. 55, 209, 215; Thwaites, *JRAD,* vol. 58, 265.

86. Leavelle, *Catholic Calumet,* 84–85; Thwaites, *JRAD,* vol. 55, 209–215.

87. Morrissey, "Speak It," 619, 625.

88. Margaret J. Leahey, "'Comment peut un muet prescher l'évangile?' Jesuit Missionaries and the Native Languages of New France," *French Historical Studies* 19, no. 1 (spring 1995): 107.

89. Morrissey, "Speak It," 640.

90. Ibid., 641.

91. Ibid., 619.

92. "Bergier," ASQ, Lettres R, no. 69, p. 3; "Marc Bergier to de Brisacier," March 6, 1705, ASQ, Lettres R, no. 72, p. 2.

93. "Saint-Cosme," ASQ, Lettres R, no. 30, p. 2; "Tremblay," ASQ, Lettres O, no. 34, pp. 21–22.

94. "Tremblay," ASQ, Lettres O, no. 28, p. 11; "Tremblay," ASQ, Lettres N, no. 109, pp. 9, 12.

95. "Tremblay," ASQ, Lettres N, no. 109, p. 7; "Denonville," ASQ, Lettres N, no. 110, p. 4.

96. "Exposé," ASQ, Polygraphie 9, no. 25, p. 15.

97. "Mgr de Laval to Père de la Chaise," November 9, 1700, ASQ, Missions, no. 87, p. 1.

98. "Père de la Chaise to Mgr de Laval," June 1, 1700, ASQ, Missions, no. 86, pp. 1–2; "Père de la Chaise to Charles Glandelet," June 6, 1700, ASQ, Lettres O, no. 30, p. 1.

99. "Exposé," ASQ, Polygraphie 9, no. 25, pp. 1, 7, 9.

100. "Tremblay," ASQ, Lettres N, no. 114, pp. 3–5.

101. "Tremblay," ASQ, Lettres N, no. 119a, pp. 14–15.

102. Morrissey, "Terms," 46.

103. "Saint-Vallier," ASQ, Missions, no. 58, p. 1.

104. "Tremblay," ASQ, Lettres N, no. 113, p. 6; Delanglez, *French Jesuits,* 38; "Saint-Vallier," ASQ, Missions, no. 56, pp. 2–3; "Tremblay," ASQ, Lettres O, no. 31, p. 15; "Saint-Vallier," ASQ, Missions, no. 58, p. 2.

105. "Tremblay," ASQ, Lettres O, no. 34, p. 16.

106. "Jacques de Brisacier to Mgr de Laval," June 17, 1701, ASQ, Lettres N, no. 115, p. 4; "Tremblay," ASQ, Lettres N, no. 114, p. 11.

107. SMEP, vol. 345, Pièces Justicatives, Pièce M, Cahier B, Ferland, pp. 913–914; "de Brisacier," ASQ, Lettres N, no. 115, p. 4; "Accord Ménagé par Mgr l'Archevêque au sujet de la Mission des Tamarois," June 7, 1701, ASQ, Polygraphie 9, no. 5; Delanglez, *French Jesuits,* 21.

108. "Bergier," ASQ, Lettres R, no. 50, p. 19; "Bergier," ASQ, Lettres R, no. 55, p. 1; "Marc Bergier to unknown," June 25, 1702, ASQ, Lettres R, no. 56, p. 1.

109. ANF, Série B2, vol. 133, 80–80v; ASPF, *Atti 1699*, 169a; Delanglez, *French Jesuits*, 5–7; Margry, *Découvertes*, 4:196.

110. "Tremblay," ASQ, Lettres N, no. 109, pp. 3–6; "Tremblay," ASQ, Lettres O, no. 28, pp. 10–11, 21; "Tremblay," ASQ, Lettres O, no. 55, pp. 16–17; "Tremblay," ASQ, Lettres N, no. 114, pp. 11–12, 18.

111. Ruth Lapham Butler, *Journal of Paul du Ru [February 1 to May 8, 1700]. Missionary Priest to Louisiana* (Chicago: Printed for the Caxton Club, 1934), 11; Delanglez, *French Jesuits*, 8–11.

112. Delanglez, *French Jesuits*, 11; Butler, *Journal*, 8–9.

113. Butler, *Journal*, 47.

114. Delanglez, *French Jesuits*, 17; Butler, *Journal*, 51–54.

115. Butler, *Journal*, 36–37, 41.

116. "Extraits," ASQ, Polygraphie 9, no. 24, pp. 5–6; "Bergier," ASQ, Lettres R, no. 50, p. 7; Butler, *Journal*, 41–44.

117. Butler, *Journal*, 71; d'Iberville, *Gulf Journals*, 144–146; Delanglez, *French Jesuits*, 24.

118. Shea, *Early Voyages*, 136; "Henri-Jean Tremblay to Charles Glandelet," May 28, 1702, ASQ, Lettres O, no. 36, p. 13; Delanglez, *French Jesuits*, 28–29; "Davion to Saint-Vallier," December 12, 1702, SMEP, vol. 344, folio 57.

119. "Davion to Saint-Vallier," 1703, SMEP, vol. 344, folios 65, 69; Delanglez, *French Jesuits*, 35; "Jacques Gravier to Louis Ango de Maizerets," July 10, 1702, ASQ, Lettres N, no. 133, pp. 1–2.

120. "Marc Bergier to Henri-Jean Tremblay," October 12, 1704, ASQ, Lettres R, no. 70, p. 3.

121. "Extraits," ASQ, Polygraphie 9, no. 24, pp. 5–6; "Bergier," ASQ, Lettres R, no. 50, p. 7; Butler, *Journal*, 41–44.

122. Delanglez, *French Jesuits*, 44.

123. "Henri-Jean Tremblay to Mgr de Laval," June 15, 1703, ASQ, Lettres N, no. 121, p. 6.

124. Jay Higginbotham, *Old Mobile: Fort Louis de la Louisiane, 1702–1711* (Tuscaloosa: Univ. of Alabama Press, 1991), 98–101; "Journal d'Iberville," ANF, Série B4, vol. 23; "Père Saint-Gilles to Ministre," July 11, 1701, ANOM, AC, C13A, vol. 1, folios 313–314; BNF, FF, NA, 9295, folios 224–225; "Ministre to Père Saint-Gilles," July 27, 1701, ANF, AM, B2, 155, folio 186.

125. "Union de la Cure de la Mobile," July 20, 1703, ASQ, Missions, no. 65; Higginbotham, *Old Mobile*, 106–107; "Mémoire," ASQ, Missions, no. 82, p. 3; "Tremblay," ASQ, Lettres N, no. 121, p. 5.

126. "Henri-Jean Tremblay to Charles Glandelet," June 15, 1703, ASQ, Lettres O, no. 40, p. 64.

127. "Bienville to Ministre," October 10, 1706, ANOM, AC, C13B, vol. 1, no. 6, folios 3–8b; "de La Vente to Ministre," March 2, 1708, ANOM, AC, C13A, vol. 2, folios 160–164; Delanglez, *French Jesuits*, 33, 37n36, 40–42; "Lettre de Davion," September 23, 1703, SMEP, 344.

128. "Death of Father Jean-Maries de Villes," June 15, 1720, JAM, Q-0001, no. 748, pp. 23–25.

6. De Montigny, the Taensas, and the Natchez

1. "Letter," ASQ, Missions, no. 41a, pp. 1–3; "Tremblay," ASQ, Lettres N, no. 113, pp. 3–5.

2. Margry, *Découvertes*, 4:452.

3. "Tremblay," ASQ, Lettres O, no. 34, p. 4.

4. White, *Middle Ground*, 58.

5. "Letter," ASQ, Missions, no. 41a, pp. 3–4.

6. "Letter," ASQ, Missions, no. 41a, p. 3.

7. Duval, *Native Ground*, 7.

8. Leavelle, *Catholic Calumet*, 49.

9. Jean-François-Benjamin Dumont de Montigny, *The Memoir of Lieutenant Dumont, 1715–1747*, ed. Gordon M. Sayre and Carla Zecher (Chapel Hill: Univ. of North Carolina Press, 2012), 227–228.

10. Duval, *Native Ground*, 95.

11. "Extraits," ASQ, Polygraphie 9, no. 24, pp. 1, 7–10.

12. "Jean-François Buisson de Saint-Cosme to Louis Ango des Maizerets," April 19, 1702, ASQ, Lettres R, no. 35, p. 1; "Jean-François Buisson de Saint-Cosme to Henri-Jean Tremblay," May 4, 1704, ASQ, Lettres R, no. 37, p. 2; "Jean-François Buisson de Saint-Cosme to Henri-Jean Tremblay," January 8, 1706, ASQ, Lettres R, no. 40, pp. 1–2.

13. "Jean-François Buisson de Saint-Cosme to Henri-Jean Tremblay," October 21, 1702, ASQ, Lettres R, no. 36, p. 3.

14. "Saint-Cosme," ASQ, Lettres R, no. 37, p. 2; "Henri-Jean Tremblay to Mgr de Laval," April 4, 1705, ASQ, Lettres N, no. 122, p. 11; "Saint-Cosme," ASQ, Lettres R, no. 29, p. 2; "Saint-Cosme," ASQ, Lettres R, no. 30, pp. 1–2.

15. James P. Ronda, "The Sillery Experiment: A Jesuit-Indian Village in New France, 1637–1663," *American Indian Culture and Research Journal* 3, no. 1 (1979): 2–4, 10.

16. George Edward Milne, *Natchez Country: Indians, Colonists, and the Landscapes of Race in French Louisiana* (Athens: Univ. of Georgia Press, 2015), 6; Fred B. Kniffen, Hiram F. Gregory, and George A. Stokes, *The Historic Indian Tribes of Louisiana: From 1542 to the Present* (Baton Rouge: Louisiana State Univ. Press, 1987), 106–108; "Saint-Cosme," ASQ, Lettres R, no. 40, pp. 1–2; Leavelle, *Catholic Calumet*, 48–49.

17. "de Montigny," ANF, Série K 1374, no. 84, p. 2; Shea, *Early Voyages*, 77; "de Montigny," AAQ, W1, Eglise du Canada, vol. 4, 27–28.

18. Leavelle, *Catholic Calumet*, 142; Saint-Vallier, *Statuts*, 11, 15, 22.

19. "de Montigny," ASQ, Missions, no. 41, pp. 16–17.

20. Baillargeon and Aubin, *Les Missions*, 92n36; Margry, *Découvertes*, 4:415.

21. D'Iberville, *Gulf Journals*, 129–130.

22. Snyder, *Slavery*, 4.

23. Shea, *Early Voyages*, 137.

24. Ibid.; Delanglez, *French Jesuits*, 15n99.

25. Butler, *Journal*, 41–44.

26. Snyder, *Slavery*, 23–24; P.F.X Charlevoix, December 25, 1721, *Journal of a Voyage to North America*, trans. Louise Phelps Kellogg (London: Dodsley, 1761), 261.

27. Shea, *Early Voyages*, 140–141.

28. White, *Middle Ground*, 52.

29. Leahey, "Un muet," 114; John H. Schumann, "Affective Factors and the Problem of Age in Second Language Acquisition," *Language Learning* 25 (1975): 209–212.

30. Pierre Margry, *Découvertes et Établissements des Français dans l'Ouest et dans le Sud de l'Amérique Septentrionale (1614–1754), Mémoire et Documents Originaux Recueillis et Publiés*, vol. 5, *Première Formation d'Une Chaine de Postes Entre le Fleuve Saint-Laurent et le Golfe du Mexique (1683–1724)* (Paris: Maisonneuve Frères et Ch. LeClerc, 1887), 444.

31. "Tremblay," ASQ, Lettres O, no. 34, p. 2; "Henri-Jean Tremblay to Henri de Bernières," May 28, 1701, ASQ, Lettres O, no. 33, p. 10.

32. "Tremblay," ASQ, Lettres O, no. 31, p. 18.

33. "Laval," ASQ, Polygraphie 9, no. 8, p. 2; "Laval," ASQ, Polygraphie 9, no. 9, p. 2; "Tremblay," ASQ, Lettres O, no. 31, p. 18; "Tremblay," ASQ, Lettres O, no. 34, pp. 7–8.

34. "Tremblay," ASQ, Lettres O, no. 34, p. 3.

35. "Tremblay," ASQ, Lettres O, no. 31, p. 19; "Tremblay," ASQ, Lettres O, no. 34, p. 8.

36. "Tremblay," ASQ, Lettres O, no. 28, p. 20; "Tremblay," ASQ, Lettres N, no. 114, p. 23; "de Brisacier," ASQ, Lettres N, no. 115, p. 2.

37. "De Brisacier," ASQ, Lettres N, no. 115, p. 2; "Tremblay," ASQ, Lettres O, no. 34, p. 8.

38. "Tremblay," ASQ, Lettres O, no. 34, p. 4.

39. Ibid., p. 3.

40. "Marc Bergier to unknown," July 14, 1704, ASQ, Lettres R, no. 67, p. 1; "Tremblay," ASQ, Lettres O, no. 36, p. 13; "Henri-Jean Tremblay to Louis Ango des Maizerets," May 10, 1702, ASQ, Lettres O, no. 37, pp. 7–8.

41. "Tremblay to Saint-Vallier," ASQ, Lettres P, no. 8, p. 11; "Bergier," ASQ, Lettres R, no. 54, pp. 2–3.

42. "Bergier," ASQ, Lettres R, no. 51, p. 4; "Marc Bergier to Charles Glandelet," 1704, ASQ, Lettres R, no. 66, pp. 3–4.

43. "Bergier," ASQ, Lettres R, no. 50, p. 6.

44. "Bergier," ASQ, Lettres R, no. 55, p. 3.

45. Greenwald, *Caillot*, 69.

46. "Tremblay," ASQ, Lettres O, no. 34, pp. 9–10; "Tremblay," ASQ, Lettres N, no. 114, pp. 12–13.

47. "Jean-François Buisson de Saint-Cosme to Henri-Jean Tremblay," August 1, 1701, ASQ, Lettres R, no. 32, pp. 4, 6–7; "Jean-François Buisson de Saint-Cosme to Henri-Jean Tremblay," December 7, 1701, ASQ, Lettres R, no. 33, pp. 1, 4; "Saint-Cosme," ASQ, Lettres R, no. 35, p. 2.

48. "Saint-Cosme," ASQ, Lettres R, no. 32, pp. 2, 5.

49. "Tremblay," ASQ, Lettres O, no. 39, pp. 5–7.

50. "Henri-Jean Tremblay to Mgr de Laval," March 31, 1702, ASQ, Lettres N, no. 117, p. 17; "Saint-Cosme," ASQ, Lettres R, no. 32, p. 6.

51. "Tremblay," ASQ, Lettres N, no. 117, p. 17.

52. "Bergier," ASQ, Lettres R, no. 51, p. 2.

53. "Bergier," ASQ, Lettres R, no. 44, p. 4; "Bergier," ASQ, Lettres R, no. 51, p. 2.

54. "Bergier," ASQ, Lettres R, no. 67, p. 2; "Bergier," ASQ, Lettres R, no. 54, pp. 3–4.

55. Tremblay to Saint-Vallier, August 11, 1707, ASQ, Lettres P, no. 12, p. 6; "Bergier," ASQ, Lettres R, no. 67, pp. 1–3.

56. "Bergier," ASQ, Lettres R, no. 70, p. 4; "Bergier," ASQ, Lettres R, no. 67, p. 1.

57. "Tremblay," ASQ, Lettres N, no. 114, p. 13–17, 34; "Tremblay," ASQ, Lettres O, no. 31, p. 29–31.

58. Erin M. Greenwald, *Marc-Antoine Caillot and the Company of the Indies in Louisiana: Trade in the French Atlantic World* (Baton Rouge: Louisiana State Univ. Press, 2016), 16; Moogk, *Nouvelle France,* 36; "Tremblay," ASQ, Lettres O, no. 40, p. 38; "Tremblay," ASQ, Lettres O, no. 37, pp. 2–4; "Henri-Jean Tremblay to Louis Ango de Maizerets," June 7, 1702, ASQ, Lettres O, no. 38, p. 1; "Jacques de Brisacier to Mgr de Laval," May 20, 1702, ASQ, Lettres N, no. 120, pp. 1–4.

59. "Tremblay," ASQ, Lettres N, no. 121, p. 1; "Tremblay," ASQ, Lettres O, no. 39, p. 5.

60. "Marc Bergier to Henri-Jean Tremblay," May 26, 1701, ASQ, Lettres R, no. 48, p. 2.

61. "Tremblay," ASQ, Lettres N, no. 123, p. 8; "Henri-Jean Tremblay to Mgr de Laval," March 12, 1704, ASQ, Lettres M, no. 30, p. 13; "Bergier," ASQ, Lettres R, no. 68, p. 2.

62. "Tremblay," ASQ, Lettres O, no. 31, pp. 20–21.

63. Ibid., pp. 23–24; "Tremblay," ASQ, Lettres O, no. 34, pp. 13–14.

64. "Henri-Jean Tremblay to Louis Ango de Maizerets," July 9, 1703, ASQ, Lettres O, no. 41, p. 2; Greenwald, *Caillot,* 86–87.

65. Allan Greer, "A Wandering Jesuit in Europe and America: Father Chaumonot Finds a Home," in *Empires of God: Religious Encounters in the Early Modern Atlantic,* ed. Linda Gregerson and Susan Juster, 106–122 (Philadelphia: Univ. of Pennsylvania Press, 2011), 114; Thwaites, *JRAD,* vol. 18 (Cleveland, Ohio: Burrows Brothers, 1898), 14–35; Greenwald, *Caillot,* 22–23; "Bienville to Pontchartrain," August 12 and September 1, 1709, October 27, 1711, ANOM, AC, C13A, vol. 2, folios 415, 567; Daniel Usner, *Indians, Settlers, and Slaves in a Frontier Exchange Economy: The Lower Mississippi Valley before 1783* (Chapel Hill: Univ. of North Carolina Press, 1992), 17–18, 24–26; Barnett, *Natchez,* 51–54, 56–57.

7. Foucault and the Quapaws

1. Morris Arnold, "Eighteenth-Century Arkansas Illustrated," *Arkansas Historical Quarterly* 53, no. 2 (1994): 119–136.

2. Duval, *Native Ground,* 8.

3. George Sabo III, "Rituals of Encounter: Interpreting Native American Views of European Explorers," in *Cultural Encounters in the Early South: Indians and Europeans in Arkansas,* ed. Jeannie Whayne (Fayetteville: Univ. of Arkansas Press, 1995), 78–79.

4. Sabo, "Inconsistent Kin," 115; Joseph Patrick Key, "The Calumet and the Cross: Religious Encounters in the Lower Mississippi Valley," *Arkansas Historical Quarterly* 61 (summer 2002): 158.

5. Sabo, "Rituals," 79.

6. White, *Middle Ground,* 84; Leavelle, *Catholic Calumet,* 7.

7. Sabo, *Paths,* 40; Duval, *Native Ground,* 24–26, 70–76

8. Duval, *Native Ground,* 3.

9. White, *Middle Ground,* 11.

10. Ibid., 21.

11. W. David Baird, *The Quapaw Indians: A History of the Downstream People* (Norman: Univ. of Oklahoma Press, 1980), 23; Margry, *Découvertes,* 2:190–193, 207, 212.

12. Baird, *The Quapaw Indians,* 17; Duval, *Native Ground,* 24–26; Willard Hughes Rollings, *Unaffected by the Gospel: Osage Resistance to the Christian Invasion, 1673–1906: A Cultural Victory* (Albuquerque: Univ. of New Mexico Press, 2004), 16.

13. Thwaites, *JRAD*, vol. 65, 119.

14. Ibid., 121–123.

15. Ibid.

16. Ibid.; Duval, *Native Ground*, 9, 15.

17. "Bergier," ASQ, Lettres R, no. 60, p. 2.

18. "de Montigny," ANF, Série K 1374, no. 84, p. 1; Habig, *Marquette*, 210; "Saint-Cosme," ASQ, Lettres R, no. 26, p. 16.

19. "de la Source," ANF, Série K 1374, no. 85, p. 1; Shea, *Early Voyages*, 79; "De Tonti," ASQ, Polygraphie 13, no. 33.

20. Arnold, *Rumble*, 4; Thwaites, *JRAD*, vol. 67 (Cleveland, Ohio: Burrows Brothers, 1900), 255.

21. "Compte," ASQ, Missions, no. 101, p. 1; "Mémoire," ASQ, Missions, no. 107.

22. "Mémoire," ASQ, Missions, no. 107.

23. Thwaites, *JRAD*, vol. 59, 189; Thwaites, *JRAD*, vol. 56, 135; François Marc Gagnon, *La Conversion Par l'Image: Un Aspect de la Mission des Jésuites Auprès des Indiens du Canada au XVIIe Siècle* (Montréal: Bellarmin, 1975).

24. Leavelle, *Catholic Calumet*, 122, 159.

25. Edward G. Gray and Norman Fiering, eds., *The Language Encounter in the Americas, 1492–1800* (New York: Berghahn Books, 2008), 106.

26. Leahey, "un Muet," 123; Thwaites, *JRAD*, vol. 52 (Cleveland, Ohio: Burrows Brothers, 1899), 118–119.

27. "Très Ancien Règlement du Petit Séminaire de Québec," ASQ, Manuscrit 239, no. 7.

28. "Coutumier du Séminaire, Article Second," ASQ, Manuscrit no. 239, pp. 112–113.

29. Martin, "Gravures," 10; Gosselin, "Grandes Devotions," ASQ, Manuscrit no. 367, pp. 13–14; Oury, "Le Sentiment Religieux," 278.

30. Moogk, *Nouvelle France*, 239.

31. Tracy Neal Leavelle, "Religion, Encounter, and Community in French and Indian North America" (Ph.D. diss., Arizona State University, 2001), 119; Thwaites, *JRAD*, vol. 64, 225–237; Gagnon, *Conversion*, 81–108; Gray and Fiering, *Language Encounter*, 103.

32. Leavelle, "Religion," 120–122; Thwaites, *JRAD*, vol. 64, 231; "Mémoire," ASQ, Missions, no. 107.

33. Thwaites, *JRAD*, vol. 51, 47–51.

34. Velma Seamster Nieberding, *The Quapaws: Those Who Went Downstream* (Quapaw, Oklahoma: Quapaw Tribal Council, 1976), 3.

35. Sabo, "Rituals," 76.

36. Sabo, *Paths*, 36; George Sabo III, Jerry E. Hilliard, and Leslie C. Walker, "Cosmological Landscapes and Exotic Gods: American Indian Rock Art in Arkansas," *Cambridge Archaeological Journal* 25, no. 1 (February 2015): 261–273.

37. Leavelle, *Catholic Calumet*, 22.

38. "Marc Bergier to Nicolas Foucault," April 27, 1701, ASQ, Lettres R, no. 47, p. 1; "Bergier," ASQ, Lettres R, no. 52, p. 1; "Davion," December 12, 1702, SMEP, vol. 344, p. 61; "Bergier," ASQ, Lettres R, no. 50, pp. 1, 7.

39. Tanguay, *Dictionnaire*, 1:115, 312; "Saint-Cosme," ASQ, Lettres R, no. 32, p. 4; Stanley Faye, "The Arkansas Post of Louisiana: French Domination," *Louisiana Historical Quarterly*

(1943): 638–640, 646; Shea, *Early Voyages*, 127; Arnold, *Rumble*, 10, 15; Alan Gallay, *The Indian Slave Trade: The Rise of the English Empire in the American South, 1670–1717* (New Haven, Conn.: Yale Univ. Press, 2002), 102–105.

40. Sabo, *Paths*, 38.

41. Saint-Vallier, *Statuts*, 24–25.

42. Baird, *The Quapaw Indians*, 20; Bossu and Forster, *Travels*, 97–98.

43. Georges F. Sioui, *Huron-Wendat: The Heritage of the Circle* (Vancouver: University of British Colombia, 2000).

44. Saint-Vallier, *Statuts*, 11, 15, 22.

45. "Saint-Cosme," ASQ, Lettres R, no. 26, p. 16; Faye, "Arkansas Post," 636; "Bergier," ASQ, Lettres R, no. 50, p. 20; "Mémoire Pour Tremblay sur les Tamarois," 1699, ASQ, Polygraphie 9, no. 27, pp. 3–5; Arnold, *Rumble*, 157–160.

46. "Bergier," ASQ, Lettres R, no. 50, p. 10; Newton D. Mereness, *Travels in the American Colonies* (New York: Antiquarian Press, 1916), 57; Arnold, *Rumble*, 6; Samuel D. Dickinson, "Religion at Arkansas Post," in *Arkansas before the Americans*, ed. Hester A. Davis (Fayetteville: Arkansas Archeological Survey, 1991), 97.

47. Key, "The Calumet and the Cross," 153, 160; Duval, *Native Ground*, 65–70.

48. Sabo, "Inconsistent Kin," 123; Key, "The Calumet and the Cross," 159.

49. Key, "The Calumet and the Cross," 162.

50. "Relation de la Rivière de la Mobile," ANF, Série 3JJ, vol. 277, no. 8.

51. "Bergier," ASQ, Lettres R, no. 50, p. 20; Philomena Hauck, *Bienville: Father of Louisiana*, Louisiana Life Series no. 10 (Lafayette: Center for Louisiana Studies, University of Southwestern Louisiana, 2006), 23; "Davion," December 12, 1702, SMEP, vol. 344, 57–58.

52. "Davion," December 12, 1702, SMEP, vol. 344, 58; "Tremblay," ASQ, Lettres O, no. 39, p. 19; conversation with Morris "Buzz" Arnold, August 3, 2018, Little Rock, Arkansas.

53. "Tremblay," ASQ, Lettres O, no. 40, p. 61; "Tremblay," ASQ, Lettres N, no. 121, p. 6; Arnold, *Rumble*, 15; "Davion," December 12, 1702, SMEP, vol. 344, p. 58.

54. Duval, *Native Ground*, 70.

55. Key, "The Calumet and the Cross," 162; Duval, *Native Ground*, 70.

56. White, *Middle Ground*, 99; Milo Quaife, ed., *The Western Country in the Seventeenth Century: The Memoirs of Lamothe Cadillac and Pierre Liette* (Chicago: Lakeside Press, 1917), 21.

57. White, *Middle Ground*, 131.

58. Sabo, "Rituals," 80; Duval, *Native Ground*, 70, 85–86; "Compte," ASQ, Missions, no. 101, p. 1; "Tremblay," ASQ, Lettres N, no. 122, p. 9; Key, "The Calumet and the Cross," 164.

59. Higginbotham, *Old Mobile*, 102; "Memoire d'Iberville," 1704, ANOM, AC, C13C, vol. 2, folios 42–43; "Mémoire sur les establissements à faire à l'embouchure du Misisipi et à la Mobile," ANF, Série 3JJ, vol. 277, no. 4.

60. "Davion," December 12, 1702, and September 23, 1703, SMEP, vol. 344, pp. 57–71; "Bienville to Ministre," September 6, 1704, ANOM, AC, C13A, vol. 1, folios 45–51; "Bienville to Ministre," Feb. 20, 1707, ANOM, AC, C13A, vol. 2, folios 11–12.

61. "Bienville," ANOM, AC, C13A, vol. 1, folio 456; "Henri Roulleaux de la Vente and Alexandre Huvé to the Séminaire de Paris," September 20, 1705, ASQ, Lettres R, no. 77, p. 15; Dunbar Rowland and A.G. Sanders, eds., *Mississippi Provincial Archives: French Dominion*, vol.

3 (Mississippi: Department of Archives and History, 1973), 23; Higginbotham, *Old Mobile*, 208; "Davion," December 12, 1702, SMEP 344, pp. 57–65.

62. White, *Middle Ground*, 52, 84.

63. Duval, *Native Ground*, 86; Arnold, *Rumble*, 18.

64. Duval, *Native Ground*, 91.

65. "Bergier," ASQ, Lettres R, no. 60, p. 2.

66. Thwaites, *JRAD*, vol. 7 (Cleveland, Ohio: Burrows Brothers, 1897), 29; Moogk, *Nouvelle France*, 26, 29.

67. Ives Goddard, "Endangered Knowledge: What We Can Learn from Native American Languages," *Anthronotes: Museum of Natural History Publication for Educators* 25, no. 2 (2004): 2.

68. Moogk, *Nouvelle France*, 26, 29.

69. White, *Middle Ground*, 8; Rowland and Sanders, *Mississippi Provincial Archives*, 3:40.

70. Thwaites, *JRAD*, vol. 65, 117.

71. Duval, *Native Ground*, 5.

72. "Gravier," ASQ, Lettres N, no. 133, p. 2; "Tremblay," ASQ, Lettres O, no. 39, pp. 18–19; "Tremblay," ASQ, Lettres O, no. 40, pp. 61–62; "Marc Bergier to Henri-Jean Tremblay," July 3, 1703, ASQ, Lettres R, no. 62, p. 4; "Marc Bergier to Mgr X," April 16,1703, ASQ, Lettres R, no. 61, p. 2; E. A. Taschereau, *Histoire du Séminaire de Québec* (Paris: Manuscript Edition, Missions Étrangères, 1849), 1036.

8. Saint-Cosme, the Tamarois, and the Natchez

1. "Saint-Cosme," ASQ, Lettres R, no. 29, p. 2.

2. Ibid.; "Saint-Cosme," ASQ, Lettres R, no. 30, pp. 1–2.

3. "Saint-Cosme," ASQ, Lettres R, no. 30, p. 1; "Saint-Cosme," ASQ, Lettres R, no. 29, pp. 3–4.

4. "Saint-Cosme," ASQ, Lettres R, no. 30, p. 1.

5. "Saint-Cosme," ASQ, Lettres R, no. 29, p. 10.

6. Ibid., pp. 7–8; "Saint-Cosme," ASQ, Lettres R, no. 30, p. 3.

7. "Saint-Cosme," ASQ, Lettres R, no. 29, p. 11.

8. "Jean-François Buisson de Saint-Cosme to Henri-Jean Tremblay," June 27, 1700, ASQ, Lettres R, no. 34, p. 2.

9. "Tremblay," ASQ, Lettres O, no. 34, pp. 5–6.

10. "Saint-Cosme," ASQ, Lettres R, no. 29, pp. 4, 11–12.

11. "Saint-Cosme," ASQ, Lettres R, no. 30, p. 3; "Saint-Cosme," ASQ, Lettres R, no. 29, p. 12.

12. "Rules of Saint François Xavier," 1682, ASQ, Polygraphie 1, no. 79; "Bergier," ASQ, Lettres R, no. 42, p. 9.

13. "Saint-Cosme," ASQ, Lettres R, no. 30, pp. 3–4.

14. Saint-Vallier, *Statuts*, 131–132.

15. Leavelle, *Catholic Calumet*, 178.

16. "Saint-Cosme," ASQ, Lettres R, no. 34, p. 1.

17. "Saint-Cosme," ASQ, Lettres R, no. 29, p. 10.

18. Sonia Toudji, "'The Happiest Consequences': Sexual Unions and Frontier Survival at Arkansas Post," *Arkansas Historical Quarterly* 70, no. 1 (spring 2011): 48; Arnold, *Rumble*, 10.

19. André Pénicaut, *Fleur de Lys and Calumet: Being the Pénicaut Narrative of French Adventure in Louisiana*, ed. and trans. Richebourg Gaillard McWilliams (Tuscaloosa: Univ. of Alabama Press, 1988), 87.

20. Shea, *Early Voyages*, 136.

21. Thwaites, *JRAD*, vol. 65, 219–221.

22. "Saint-Cosme," ASQ, Lettres R, no. 36, p. 4.

23. Sleeper-Smith, *Indian Women*, 24–33.

24. White, *Middle Ground*, 61–65; Duval, "Indian Intermarriage," 273.

25. White, *Middle Ground*, 60.

26. Brown, *Cultural Transformation*, 31.

27. Ibid., 36–37.

28. Ibid., 28–29.

29. Ibid., 32–33.

30. Milne, *Natchez Country*, 36–37; paraphrased from the website *Indians of Arkansas*, created by George Sabo: http://archeology.uark.edu/indiansofarkansas/index.html?pageName=The%20Natchez%20Indians (accessed July 1, 2018).

31. Milne, *Natchez Country*, 37,

32. Brown, *Cultural Transformation*, 60–62.

33. "de Montigny," ASQ, Missions, no. 41, pp. 15–16; "de la Source," ANF, Série K 1374, no. 85, pp. 3–4.

34. "Saint-Cosme," ASQ, Lettres R, no. 32, p. 3.

35. Ibid., pp. 3–4.

36. Ibid., p. 6.

37. "Tremblay," ASQ, Lettres N, no. 114, p. 19; "Henri-Jean Tremblay to Mgr de Laval," March 12, 1704, ASQ, Lettres M, no. 30, p. 13.

38. "Saint-Cosme," ASQ, Lettres R, no. 35, pp. 3–4; "Saint-Cosme," ASQ, Lettres R, no. 36, p. 3.

39. "Saint-Cosme," ASQ, Lettres R, no. 35, p. 3.

40. "Saint-Cosme," ASQ, Lettres R, no. 40, pp. 2–3.

41. "Saint-Cosme," ASQ, Lettres R, no. 33, p. 3; Thwaites, *JRAD*, vol. 68 (Cleveland, Ohio: Burrows Brothers, 1900), 137; Barnett, *Natchez*, 19, 35.

42. "Saint-Cosme," ASQ, Lettres R, no. 32, p. 7; "Saint-Cosme," ASQ, Lettres R, no. 35, p. 2; "Saint-Cosme," ASQ, Lettres R, no. 37, p. 3; "Bergier," ASQ, Lettres R, no. 51, pp. 1–2; "Bergier," ASQ, Lettres R, no. 53, p. 1.

43. "Saint-Cosme," ASQ, Lettres R, no. 35, p. 2; "Saint-Cosme," ASQ, Lettres R, no. 33, p. 1; "Saint-Cosme," ASQ, Lettres R, no. 32, pp. 2–3.

44. "Saint-Cosme," ASQ, Lettres R, no. 37, p. 2; "Saint-Cosme," ASQ, Lettres R, no. 32, pp. 4–5.

45. "Saint-Cosme," ASQ, Lettres R, no. 35, pp. 2–3.

46. "Saint-Cosme," ASQ, Lettres R, no. 33, pp. 2–4.

47. "Saint-Cosme," ASQ, Lettres R, no. 37, p. 2;

48. "Saint-Cosme," ASQ, Lettres R, no. 36, p. 1–2.

49. "Saint-Cosme," ASQ, Lettres R, no. 35, p. 2.

50. "Saint-Cosme," ASQ, Lettres R, no. 33, p. 3.

51. "Tremblay," ASQ, Lettres N, no. 123, pp. 9–10. "Tremblay," ASQ, Lettres N, no. 122, p. 16.

52. "Saint-Cosme," ASQ, Lettres R, no. 32, p. 5.

53. Ibid., pp. 3–4. "Saint-Cosme," ASQ, Lettres R, no. 36, p. 4; "Saint-Cosme," ASQ, Lettres R, no. 35, p. 3; Greenwald, *Caillot*, 25.

54. Thwaites, *JRAD*, vol. 68, 123.

55. Milne, *Natchez Country*, 38; Thwaites, *JRAD*, vol. 68, 129–130.

56. Milne, *Natchez Country*, 39–40; Thwaites, *JRAD*, vol. 68, 127.

57. "Saint-Cosme," ASQ, Lettres R, no. 35, p. 3; "Saint-Cosme," ASQ, Lettres R, no. 32, p. 5; "Saint-Cosme," ASQ, Lettres R, no. 39, pp. 1–2.

58. "Saint-Cosme," ASQ, Lettres R, no. 38, p. 2; "Saint-Cosme," ASQ, Lettres R, no. 37, p. 2; "Tremblay," ASQ, Lettres N, no. 122, p. 11; "Bergier," ASQ, Lettres R, no. 61, p. 4.

59. "Tremblay," ASQ, Lettres N, no. 122, p. 9; "Tremblay," ASQ, Lettres M, no. 30, p. 13.

60. "Henri-Jean Tremblay to Seminary Leadership in Québec," June 18, 1707, ASQ, Lettres M, no. 38, p. 20.

61. Garraghan, "New Light," 117.

62. Baillargeon, *Séminaire*, 395n62.

63. "Bienville," ANOM, AC, C13A, vol. 2, folios 9–10; "Bienville to Ministre," February 25, 1708, ANOM, AC, C13A, vol. 2, folios 101–102; "La Salle to Ministre," July 25, 1707, ANOM, AC, C13B, vol. 1, no. 7, folio 7v.

64. "Bienville to Ministre," February 25, 1708, ANOM, C13A, vol. 2, folio 101; Margry, *Découvertes*, 5:434–435.

65. Marcel Giraud, *A History of French Louisiana*, vol. 1, *The Reign of Louis XIV, 1698–1715*, trans. Joseph C. Lambert (Baton Rouge: Louisiana State Univ. Press, 1990), 207.

66. "Bienville to Ministre," February 25, 1708, ANOM, C13A, vol. 2, folio 101.

67. Patricia D. Woods, "The French and the Natchez Indians in Louisiana: 1700–1731," *Louisiana History* 19, no. 4 (autumn 1978): 421; "Mémoire de M. de Richebourg sur la première guerre des Nathcez," in *Historical Collections of Louisiana*, ed. Benjamin French, 5 vols. (New York, 1846–1853), 3:250.

68. White, "Mardi Gras," 498.

69. Ibid., 529.

70. Ibid., 521.

71. Ibid., 500, 533.

72. Baillargeon, *Séminaire*, 395; "Henri Roulleaux de la Vente to unknown," June 27, 1708, ASQ, Lettres R, no. 82, p. 2.

73. "Tremblay to the Directors of the Seminary of Québec," May 8, 1707, ASQ, Lettres M, no. 37, p. 4.

74. "Tremblay," ASQ, Lettres M, no. 37, p. 4; translation by Joshua Byron Smith, Department of English, University of Arkansas.

75. "Tremblay," ASQ, Lettres M, no. 38, p. 19.

76. "Grand Soleil, Fils d'un Français en 1728," BNF, FF, NA, 2550, folios 115–118.

77. James Mooney, "The End of the Natchez," *American Anthropologist* 1, no. 3 (1899): 513–515.

78. Rowland and Sanders, *Mississippi Provincial Archives,* 3:581.

79. Pierre F. X. Charlevoix, *Charlevoix's Louisiana: Selections from the History and the Journal, Pierre F. X. de Charlevoix,* ed. Charles E. O'Neill, trans. John Gilmary Shea (Baton Rouge: Louisiana State Univ. Press, 1977), xviii, 258.

80. G. Touchard-LaFosse, *Chroniques de l'Oeil-de-Boeuf, des petits appartments de la cour et des salons de Paris, sous Louis XIV, la Régence, Louis XV et Louis XVI* (Paris: Gustave Barba, Libraire-Editeur, 1860), 97.

81. "Tremblay," ASQ, Lettres O, no. 31, p. 18; "Tremblay," ASQ, Lettres O, no. 34, p. 4.

82. "Henri Roulleaux de la Vente to Henri-Jean Tremblay," March 4, 1708, ASQ, Lettres R, no. 79, p. 9.

83. "Tremblay," ASQ, Lettres M, no. 38, p. 19.

84. Céline Dupré, "Buisson de Saint-Cosme, François," in *Dictionnaire Biographique du Canada,* vol. 2 (Toronto and Québec: University of Toronto Press, Les Presses de l'université Laval, 1982), 114–115.

85. Barnett, *Natchez Indians,* 55–56.

86. Milne, *Natchez Country,* 50.

87. "Saint-Cosme," ASQ, Lettres R, no. 34, pp. 1–2.

88. Milne, *Natchez Country,* 50–51.

89. Leahey, "Un Muet," 111–112.

90. Wallace Lambert, "A Social Psychology of Bilingualism," *Journal of Social Issues* 23 (1967): 91–109; Leahey, "Un Muet," 114n50.

91. "Saint-Cosme," ASQ, Lettres R, no. 35, p. 3.

92. "Grand Soleil," BNF, FF, NA, 2550, folios 115–118.

93. Ibid.

94. Antoine Simon le Page du Pratz, *Histoire de la Louisiane,* vol. 2 (Paris: Chez de Bure, l'Aîné, la Veuve Delaguette, Lambert, 1758), 401–403; Milne, *Natchez Country,* 132–133.

95. Thwaites, *JRAD,* vol. 65, 143–145.

96. Sonia Toudji, "Frontières Intimes: Indiens, Français, et Africains dans la Vallée du Mississippi" (Ph.D. diss., Univ. of Arkansas, 2011), 23–24.

97. "Saint-Cosme," ASQ, Lettres R, no. 35, p. 3.

98. Toudji, "Frontières Intimes," 9.

99. White, *Middle Ground,* xiii

100. "Saint-Cosme," ASQ, Lettres R, no. 40, p. 3.

101. du Pratz, *Histoire,* 2:401–403; Milne, *Natchez Country,* 132–133.

102. Perdue, "Sprightly Lover," 175.

103. White, *Middle Ground,* 52.

9. Bergier and the Tamarois

1. Provost, *Séminaire,* 435; "Tremblay," ASQ, Lettres M, no. 30, p. 42; "Henri-Jean Tremblay to Louis Ango de Maizerets," July 6, 1710, ASQ, Lettres O, no. 48, p. 4.

2. "Saint-Vallier," ASQ, Polygraphie 9, no. 11; "Tremblay," ASQ, Lettres O, no. 26, p. 20.

3. "Tremblay," ASQ, Lettres O, no. 28, p. 15.

4. "Bergier," ASQ, Lettres R, no. 42, p. 8.

5. Conversations with Evan D. Garner and Elliott West, Fayetteville, Arkansas; "Bergier," ASQ, Lettres R, no. 42, p. 9.

6. "Bergier," ASQ, Lettres R, no. 50, p. 6.

7. "Bergier," ASQ, Lettres R, no. 44, p. 2.

8. "Bergier," ASQ, Lettres R, no. 42, p. 10.

9. Ibid., pp. 8–10.

10. Thwaites, *JRAD*, vol. 65, 77.

11. Thwaites, *JRAD*, vol. 64, 231; White, *Middle Ground*, 114.

12. "Bergier," ASQ, Lettres R, no. 42, pp. 8–10.

13. Gray and Fiering, *Language Encounter*, 241, 245.

14. "Tremblay," ASQ, Lettres O, no. 34, p. 90.

15. "Bergier," ASQ, Lettres R, no. 47, p. 2.

16. "Cas sur le Marriage," ASQ, Missions, no. 78, pp. 1–2.

17. Ibid.

18. Ibid.

19. Brown, *Cultural Transformation*, 59.

20. "Cas sur le Marriage," ASQ, Missions, no. 78, pp. 1–2.

21. Ibid.

22. Sleeper-Smith, *Indian Women*, 35.

23. Leavelle, *Catholic Calumet*, 158.

24. Sleeper-Smith, *Indian Women*, 26.

25. White, *Middle Ground*, 52.

26. "Marc Bergier to Mgr de Saint-Vallier," April 15, 1705, ASQ, Lettres R, no. 73, p. 3.

27. "Bergier," ASQ, Lettres R, no. 66, pp. 1–3.

28. White, *Middle Ground*, 58.

29. Royal Proclamation, Versailles, May 21, 1696, ANF, Colonies, Series B, 19-1, 129–130; See also Royal Proclamation, May 23, 1696, ANF, Colonies, Series B, 19-1, 156–169; Sleeper-Smith, *Indian Women*, p. 42.

30. "Bergier," ASQ, Lettres R, no. 45, pp. 5–6; "Bergier," ASQ, Lettres R, no. 48, p. 3.

31. "Bergier," ASQ, Lettres R, no. 45, pp. 6–7.

32. "Marc Bergier to unknown," November 17, 1702, ASQ, Lettres R, no. 58, p. 1.

33. "Bergier," ASQ, Lettres R, no. 45, p. 7.

34. Thwaites, *JRAD*, vol. 65, 199.

35. "Bergier," ASQ, Lettres R, no. 45, pp. 7–8.

36. Thwaites, *JRAD*, vol. 64, 161, 197–211.

37. "Bergier," ASQ, Lettres R, no. 45, p. 2; "Bergier," ASQ, Lettres R, no. 46, p. 1.

38. Brown, *Cultural Transformation*, 18; Shea, *Early Voyages*, 116.

39. "Bergier," ASQ, Lettres R, no. 45, pp. 2–3.

40. Ibid., pp. 2–4; "Bergier," ASQ, Lettres R, no. 50, p. 15.

41. "Bergier," ASQ, Lettres R, no. 50, p. 12.

42. Ibid., pp. 15–17.

43. "Bergier," ASQ, Lettres R, no. 42, p. 5; "Bergier," ASQ, Lettres R, no. 51, p. 1.

44. "Bergier," ASQ, Lettres R, no. 45, pp. 4–5.

45. "Bergier," ASQ, Lettres R, no. 50, p. 2.

46. "Bergier," ASQ, Lettres R, no. 54, p. 2.

47. "Bergier," ASQ, Lettres R, no. 50, p. 11.

48. "Bergier," ASQ, Lettres R, no. 52, p. 2.

49. "Bergier," ASQ, Lettres R, no. 71, p. 4.

50. "Bergier," ASQ, Lettres R, no. 52, p. 2.

51. "Bergier," ASQ, Lettres R, no. 50, pp. 13–14.

52. Sleeper-Smith, *Indian Women*, 33.

53. "Bergier," ASQ, Lettres R, no. 54, p. 1.

54. "Bergier," ASQ, Lettres R, no. 50, pp. 13, 17–18; "Mémoire Touchant la Mission des Tamarois et la Juridiction dudit Pays," May 5, 1702, ASQ, Missions, no. 69, pp. 1–2.

55. "Mémoire," ASQ, Missions, no. 69, pp. 2–3.

56. "Tremblay," ASQ, Lettres O, no. 39, p. 11.

57. "Bergier," ASQ, Lettres R, no. 50, pp. 18–19.

58. "Bergier," ASQ, Lettres R, no. 54, p. 2.

59. "Bergier," ASQ, Lettres R, no. 55, pp. 2–3; "Bergier," ASQ, Lettres R, no. 50, pp. 19–20; "Marc Bergier to Mgr de Saint-Vallier," March 1, 1703, ASQ, Lettres R, no. 59, p. 2.

60. "Bergier," ASQ, Lettres R, no. 55, p. 1; "Accord," ASQ, Polygraphie 9, no. 5.

61. "Bergier," ASQ, Lettres R, no. 54, p. 3; "Bergier," ASQ, Lettres R, no. 55, p. 1; Thwaites, *JRAD*, vol. 66, 37.

62. "Pièces Justicatives," Pièce M, Cahier B, Ferland, SMEP, vol. 345, pp. 913–914; "Accord," ASQ, Polygraphie 9, no. 5.

63. "Gabriel Marest to a Jesuit Priest, aux Illinois sur le Mississippi, November 18, 1702," ASQ, Viger-Verreau, 13, no. 31.

64. Thwaites, *JRAD*, vol. 66, 25.

65. "Bergier," ASQ, Lettres R, no. 70, p. 2.

66. "Bergier," ASQ, Lettres R, no. 59, p. 4.

67. "Marest," ASQ, Viger-Verreau, 13, no. 31.

68. Thwaites, *JRAD*, vol. 66, 37.

69. "Bergier," ASQ, Lettres R, no. 62, p. 1.

70. "Bergier," ASQ, Lettres R, no. 67, p. 3.

71. "Bergier," ASQ, Lettres R, no. 55, p. 2.

72. Ibid.

73. Thwaites, *JRAD*, vol. 5 (Cleveland, Ohio: Burrows Brothers, 1897), 191–192.

74. "Bergier," ASQ, Lettres R, no. 58, p. 3.

75. "Bergier," ASQ, Lettres R, no. 61, p. 2.

76. "Marc Bergier to Henri-Jean Tremblay," October 18, 1703, ASQ, Lettres R, no. 63, pp. 1–2.

77. "Marc Bergier to Jacques Gravier," March 30, 1704, ASQ, Lettres R, no. 64, pp. 2–3.

78. Sleeper-Smith, *Indian Women*, 3.

79. "Bergier," ASQ, Lettres R, no. 44, p. 1.

80. "Marc Bergier to unknown," June 12, 1704, ASQ, Lettres R, no. 65, pp. 2–4.

81. "Bergier," ASQ, Lettres R, no. 65, pp. 2–4.

82. Thwaites, *JRAD*, vol. 21 (Cleveland, Ohio: Burrows Brothers, 1898), 47.

83. White, *Middle Ground,* 36, 98; George Dalton, "The Impact of Colonization on Aboriginal Economies in Stateless Societies," *Research in Economic Anthropology* 1 (1978): 138.

84. White, *Middle Ground,* 101; Emma Helen Blair, ed., *The Indian Tribes of the Upper Mississippi and Region of the Great Lakes,* vol. 1 (Cleveland, Ohio: Arthur H. Clark, 1911–1912), 302–303.

85. Leavelle, *Catholic Calumet,* 130.

86. "Bergier," ASQ, Lettres R, no. 65, p. 4.

87. "Henri Roulleaux De La Vente to unknown," February 5, 1709, ASQ, Lettres R, no. 86; "Bienville," ANOM, AC, C13A, vol. 2, folios 11–12, 24–25, 109–110; "Mémoire general des marchandises. . . . ," 1707, ASQ, Lettres R, no. 78; "Tremblay," ASQ, Lettres M, no. 38; "Henri-Jean Tremblay to Louis Ango des Maizerets," January 14, 1708, ASQ, Lettres O, no. 49.

88. "de la Vente," ASQ, Lettres R, no. 86, pp. 2–3.

89. Ibid., p. 3.

90. Thwaites, *JRAD,* vol. 66, 257.

91. Ibid., 261–263. Bergier cited the distance between his village and that of the Kaskaskias as twenty-five leagues. While not quoted here, Marest also cited twenty-five leagues travel earlier in his letter. The fifteen leagues may represent the remainder of his journey. Thwaites, *JRAD,* vol. 66, 257.

92. "de la Vente," ASQ, Lettres R, no. 86, pp. 3–4; Thwaites, *JRAD,* vol. 66, 262.

93. Provost, *Séminaire,* 434.

94. "de la Vente," ASQ, Lettres R, no. 86, p. 6.

95. Thwaites, *JRAD,* vol. 66, 263–265.

96. "Lettre de Tremblay," November 18, 1709, Seminaire de Vienne, 9G6, 1704–1738, ADI.

97. Leavelle, *Catholic Calumet,* 75.

98. Thwaites, *JRAD,* vol. 66, 263–265.

99. Ibid., 265.

100. Leavelle, *Catholic Calumet,* 130–131, 153.

101. Moogk, *Nouvelle France,* 253.

102. "de la Vente," ASQ, Lettres R, no. 86, p. 4.

103. Ibid., p. 6.

104. "Henri-Jean Tremblay to Louis Ango de Maizerets," May 22, 1710, ASQ, Lettres O, no. 50, p. 17; "Henri Roulleaux de la Vente to Jacques de Brisacier," August 10, 1708, ASQ, Lettres R, no. 84; AAQ, Registres d'insinuation, B 244; "Lettre du R. P. Marest aux Illinois to M. de la Vente," April 25, 1709, ASQ, Missions, no. 48.

10. Davion, the Tunicas, and the French

1. "Tremblay," ASQ, Lettres N, no. 123, p. 10.

2. Thwaites, *JRAD,* vol. 65, 129.

3. Ibid., 131; Sabo, *Paths,* 56–64.

4. "Davion," SMEP, vol. 344, p. 58.

5. Pénicaut, *Fleur de Lys,* 77; "Saint-Cosme," ASQ, Lettres R, no. 35, p. 2.

6. Kniffen et al., *Historic Indian,* 253.

7. Pierre François Xavier de Charlevoix, *Histoire et description générale de la Nouvelle France: avec le journal historique d'un voyage fait par ordre du Roi dans l'amerique septentrionale,* vol. 3 (Paris: Nyon, 1744), 433.

8. Brain, *Tunica-Biloxi,* 49.

9. *Journal de la Société des Américanistes,* vol. 3 (Paris: Au Siège de la Société, 1931): 321.

10. Brain, *Tunica-Biloxi,* 55.

11. Kniffen et al., *Historic Indian,* 252–253, 262.

12. "Davion," SMEP, vol. 344, p. 59

13. Ibid., p. 61.

14. Ibid., pp. 67–68.

15. Ibid.

16. "Bergier," ASQ, Lettres R, no. 61, p. 4.

17. "Davion," SMEP, vol. 344, p. 66.

18. Ibid.

19. Higginbotham, *Old Mobile,* 104; "Ministre to Bienville," January 30, 1704, ANOM, AC, B25, folio 4; "Bienville to Ministre," September 6, 1704, ANOM, AC, C13A, vol. 1, folios 450–51.

20. Higginbotham, *Old Mobile,* 107; "Davion," September 23, 1703, SMEP, vol. 344.

21. Higginbotham, *Old Mobile,* 207–208.

22. "Davion," SMEP, vol. 344, pp. 65–69.

23. Higginbotham, *Old Mobile,* 105, 161; "Union," ASQ, Missions, no. 65; "Tremblay," ASQ, Lettres O, no. 41, pp. 2–3.

24. Higginbotham, *Old Mobile,* 188; "Henri Roulleaux de La Vente to Henri-Jean Tremblay," September 10, 1704, ASQ, Lettres R, no. 75, p. 2; "de la Vente," ASQ, Lettres R, no. 77, p. 6.

25. "Tremblay," ASQ, Lettres N, no. 122, p. 13; "Tremblay," ASQ, Lettres N, no. 123, pp. 10–11.

26. "de la Vente," ASQ, Lettres R, no. 77, p. 6; Higginbotham, *Old Mobile,* 188; "Tremblay," ASQ, Lettres N, no. 122, p. 14.

27. Têtu and Gagnon, *Mandements,* 1:271.

28. See Iberville as quoted in Mathé Allain, "Manon Lescaut et ses Consoeurs: Women in the Early French Period, 1700–1731," in *Proceedings of the Fifth Meeting of the French Colonial Historical Society,* ed. James J. Cook (Lanham, Md.: French Colonial Historical Society, 1980): 18; Vaughn Baker, "Cherchez les Femmes: Some Glimpses of Women in Early Eighteenth-Century Louisiana," *Louisiana History* 31 (1990): 25–27; "Liste des Filles et des Deux Familles qui Doivent Passer en Louisiane," October 3, 1704, ANOM, AC, Series B (Royal Instructions), vol. 25, pp. 9–10.

29. "de la Vente," ASQ, Lettres R, no. 77, p. 7.

30. Higginbotham, *Old Mobile,* 178; "de la Vente," ASQ, Lettres R, no. 77, p. 7.

31. ADM, A, September 6, 1704.

32. Higginbotham, *Old Mobile,* 247; "de la Vente," ASQ, Lettres R, no. 77, p. 7.

33. Higginbotham, *Old Mobile,* 186; "Bienville," ANOM, AC, C13A, vol. 1, folios 458–465.

34. ANOM, AC, F1A, vol. 10, folios 282, 289; "Bienville," ANOM, AC, C13A, vol. 1, folio 465; Higginbotham, *Old Mobile,* 196, FN 49.

35. "Henri Roulleaux de la Vente to Jacques de Brisacier," July 4, 1708, ASQ, Lettres R, no. 83, pp. 16–17.

36. Higginbotham, *Old Mobile,* 103, 159; "Bienville," ANOM, AC, C13A, vol. 1, folio 460; "Bergier," ASQ, Lettres R, no. 64, p. 1.

37. "Davion," SMEP, vol. 344, p. 71.

38. "Induction de Roulleaux de la Vente," September 28, 1704, ADM, Miscellaneous French papers, 1704–1764.

39. "Comte," ASQ, Missions, no. 101, pp. 1–4.

40. "De la Vente," ASQ, Lettres R, no. 83, p. 9; "de la Vente," ASQ, Lettres R, no. 82, p. 1.

41. Brain, *Tunica-Biloxi,* 48–49.

42. Ibid., 44.

43. Jeffrey P. Brain, *The Tunica Treasure* (Cambridge, Mass: Peabody Museum, Harvard Univ. Press, 1970) 280; Sabo, *Paths,* 60.

44. Brain, *Tunica-Biloxi,* 45, 51.

45. Charlevoix, *Nouvelle France,* 3:433.

46. Brain, *Tunica Treasure,* 260.

47. Brain, *Tunica-Biloxi,* 51–52; Walter L. Williams, *Southeastern Indians since the Removal Era* (Athens: Univ. of Georgia Press, 2009), 73.

48. White, *Middle Ground,* xxi.

49. Charlevoix, *Nouvelle France,* 3:433.

50. Brain, *Tunica-Biloxi,* 60.

51. Leavelle, *Catholic Calumet,* 174; Thwaites, *JRAD,* vol. 64, 221–223.

52. "La Salle to Pontchartrain," May 12, 1709, ANOM, C13A, vol. 2, folio 400; "de la Vente," ASQ, Lettres R, no. 83, p. 17.

53. Higginbotham, *Old Mobile,* 282–283; White, *Middle Ground,* 70.

54. "Bienville to Pontchartrain," August 20, 1709, ANOM, C13A, vol. 2, folio 413.

55. "Bienville to Ministre," June 21, 1710, ANOM, AC, C13A, vol. 2, folios 553–554; "Mémoire de l'état present de la colonie de la Louisiane, suivant ce que jai appris par M. de la Vente," September 1710, ANOM, AC, C13A, vol. 2, folios 563–564; "Ministre to Brisacier," October 15, 1710, ANOM, AC, B, vol. 32, folio 214; "Mémoire sur la conduit des Français en Louisiane," 1714, ANOM, AC, C13A, vol. 3, folios 389–395.

56. "Bienville," ANOM, AC, C13A, vol. 2, folios 553–554; "Dartaguiette to ministre," January 10, 1711, ANOM, AC, C13A, vol. 2, folio 639; "Le Maire à Son Oncle," October 10, 1711, ANF, AM, Série 2JJ, vol. 56, 20; Baillargeon, *Séminaire,* 393.

57. "Bienville to Ministre," June 20, 1711, ANOM, AC, C13B, vol. 1, no. 11, folios 1–3; "Antoine Davion sur les Missions de l'île Dauphine," October 20, 1711, ASQ, Missions, no. 46; "Lettre d'Antoine Davion sur les Missions de l'île Dauphine," October 20, 1711, ASQ, Missions, no. 46a, p. 7.

58. "Davion," ASQ, Missions, no. 46a, pp. 3, 9.

59. "Tremblay," ASQ, Lettres N, no. 122, p. 13.

60. Ibid., p. 12.

61. "Tremblay," ASQ, Lettres M, no. 30, p. 13.

62. "Bienville to Pontchartrain," ANOM, C13A, 2ème série, Carton 1, p. 3.

63. Pénicaut, *Fleur de Lys,* 34.

64. "D'Artaguiette to Pontchartrain," January 10, 1711, ANOM, C13A, vol. 2, folios 633, 639.

65. "Extrait de Testament de Charles Levasseur," September 28, 1717, ANF, Fonds particuliers, Minutier Central: Étude pages XX–455.

66. "Davion," ASQ, Missions, no. 46; "Davion," ASQ, Missions, no. 46a, p. 5.

67. "Henri-Jean Tremblay to Charles de Glandelet," 1711, ASQ, Lettres O, no. 52, p. 16; "Henri-Jean Tremblay to Louis Ango des Maizerets," June 5, 1712, ASQ, Lettres O, no, 54, p. 15.

68. "Ministre," ANOM, AC, B, vol. 32, folios 385–85v; "Davion," ASQ, Missions, no. 46, pp. 2, 5; "Davion," ASQ, Missions, no. 46a, p. 10.

69. "Davion," ASQ, Missions, no. 46a, pp. 2–3, 10.

70. Ibid., pp. 2, 10; Baillargeon, *Séminaire*, 397.

71. Brain, *Tunica Treasure*, 262.

72. "M. de Brisacier on la Louisiane," October 31, 1716, ASQ, Missions, no. 45, p. 1.

73. Greenwald, *Caillot*, 25.

74. Ibid., 83.

75. Brain, *Tunica Treasure*, 261.

76. Greenwald, *Caillot*, 33, 48.

77. Brain, *Tunica Treasure*, 262.

78. Ibid., 262.

79. Pénicaut, *Fleur de Lys*, 174.

80. Pierre-François–avier de Charlevoix, *Histoire et Description Générale de la Nouvelle France, avec le Journal Historique d'un Voyage Fait par Ordre du Roi dans l'Amérique Septentrionnale. Par le P. De Charlevoix, de la Compagnie de Jesus. Tome second* (1744), 423–425.

81. Pénicaut, *Fleur de Lys*, 174–176.

82. du Pratz, *Histoire*, 1:122–124; White, *Middle Ground*, xxi.

83. Thwaites, *JRAD*, vol. 62 (Cleveland, Ohio: Burrows Brothers, 1900), 209–211.

84. Charlevoix, *Nouvelle France*, 3:433–434, 512.

85. "Dartaguiette," ANOM, AC, C13A, vol. 2, folio 639.

86. Kniffen et al., *Historic Indian*, 252.

87. "Marc Bergier to unknown," May 4, 1702, ASQ, Lettres R, no. 53, p. 1; "Bergier," ASQ, Lettres R, no. 50, p. 10.

88. Brain, *Tunica Treasure*, 260.

89. Brain, *Tunica-Biloxi*, 50–51.

90. Shea, *Early Voyages*, 134–135.

91. Roger Baudier, *The Catholic Church in Louisiana* (Baton Rouge: Provincial Press, Claitor's Pub. Division, 2013), 21–22.

92. Brain, *Tunica-Biloxi*, 50–51.

93. "Memoire," ASQ, Polygraphie 9, no. 26, pp. 5–6; "Deux requêtes du Séminaire à MM. de la Compagnie des Indes Occidentales," 1716, ASQ, Missions, no. 73c.

94. Greenwald, *Caillot*, 64–67.

95. Charles E. O'Neill, *Church and State in French Colonial Louisiana: Policy and Politics to 1732* (New Haven, Conn.: Yale Univ. Press, 1966), 123, 135; Marcel Giraud, *Histoire de la Louisiane Française: La Louisiane après le Système de Law (1721–1723) Tome IV* (Paris: Presses Universitaires de France, 1974), 372–377; "Lettre de Pauger," September 23, 1723, ANOM, AC, C13A, vol. 7, folio 264v; "Lettre de l'Évêque Coadjuteur to Raguet," December 8, 1726, ANOM, C13A, vol. 10, folio 35v.

96. ASPF, Series 2, Acta, vol. 92 (1722), folios 138rv–139r, April 13, 1722.

97. Baillargeon, *Séminaire*, 397n69; "Ordonnance servant de règlement pour l'établissement

des Capucins à la Louisiane, 16 mai, 1722," ANOM, AC, B, vol. 43, folios 108–111; O'Neill, *Church*, 130, 133.

98. Giraud, *Histoire*, 4:375; Baudier, *Catholic Church*, 94; Rowland and Sanders, *Mississippi Provincial Archives*, 2:346–347.

99. "Deux Requêtes," ASQ, Missions, no. 73c, p. 4.

100. "Memoire," ASQ, Polygraphie 9, no. 26, pp. 5–6.

101. "Mémoire de ce que la missions des Tamarois a reçu de MM. Varlet et Antoine Davion," 1718–1725, ASQ, Missions, no. 105b, pp. 4–8.

102. "Catalogue de la Bibliothèque d'Antoine Davion," ASQ, Missions, no. 104b; "Mémoire," ASQ, Missions, no. 105b; Antonio Drolet, *Les Bibliothèques Canadiens, 1604–1960* (Ottawa: Le Cercle du Livre de France, 1965).

103. Baudier, *Catholic Church*, 22.

104. Arthur Maheux, "La Bibliothèque du Missionnaire Davion au Dix-Huitième Siècle," *Le Canada Français* 27 (March: 1940): 650–661. Davion sent his book collection and goods to the Tamarois mission in the early 1720s before returning to France. A Seminary priest by the name of Jacques-François Forget Duverger served at the Tamarois mission from 1754 until 1763. Panic stricken that the British were on their way to the region after the cessation of Canada, he sold all of the goods and property of the mission to two traders—Jean-Baptiste Lagrange and Pierre-Étienne Marafret Layssard. Attempts were made by the Seminary to track down the goods and the money accumulated from the sales, but by 1772 all hopes were abandoned when nothing could be learned of their whereabouts. "l'abbé François Sorbier de Villars to l'abbé Henri-François Gravé de La Rive, supérieur du Séminaire de Québec," January 24, 1772, ASQ, Lettres M, no. 139.

105. O'Neill, *Church*, 151; Marcel Giraud, *A History of French Louisiana*, vol. 5, *The Company of the Indies, 1723–1731*, trans. Brian Pierce (Baton Rouge: Louisiana State Univ. Press, 1991), 79, 330; "Mémoire by Pauger to the Conseil de Régie," September 3, 1723, ANOM, AC, C13A, vol. 7, folio 254v; Giraud, *Histoire*, 4:377, 381–382; "Rôle des Passagers de *la Galatée* de Louisiane en France," APL, I, P 122, no. 9, pieces 7 and 22; "Deux Requêtes," ASQ, Missions, no. 73c, p. 3; "La Chaise to Commissaires Députés," September 6, 1723, ANOM, AC, C13A, vol. 7, folio 42v; "Passengers on the storeship *Chameau*," APL, 2 P 21-I, no. 19.

106. "de Montigny," ASQ, Lettres M, no. 48, p. 4.

107. Provost, *Séminaire*, 431.

108. Delanglez, *French Jesuits*, 431.

109. Baudier, *Catholic Church*, 143.

INDEX

CPSIA information can be obtained
at www.ICGtesting.com
Printed in the USA
LVHW092128060121
675780LV00020B/13